CAREER OPPORTUNITIES IN THEATER AND THE PERFORMING ARTS

Second Edition

CAREER OPPORTUNITIES IN THEATER AND THE PERFORMING ARTS

Second Edition

SHELLY FIELD

Checkmark Books™
An imprint of Facts On File, Inc.

This book is dedicated to the loving memory of my grandparents
Pauline and Samuel Kreisberg
& Frances and Richard Field

CAREER OPPORTUNITIES IN THEATER AND THE PERFORMING ARTS,
Second Edition

Copyright © 1992, 1999 by Shelly Field

Checkmark Books™
An imprint of Facts On File, Inc.
11 Penn Plaza
New York NY 10001

Library of Congress Cataloging-in-Publication Data

Field, Shelly.
    Career opportunities in theater and the performing arts / Shelly
Field.—2nd ed.
        p.   cm.
    Includes bibliographical references and index.
    ISBN 0-8160-3798-1 (hc.).—ISBN 0-8160-3799-X (pbk.)
    1. Performing arts—Vocational guidance. I. Title.
PN1580.F5   1999
791′.023—dc21   98-48728

Checkmark Books are available at special discounts when purchased in bulk quantities for businesses, associations, institutions or sales promotions. Please call our Special Sales Department in New York at (212) 967-8800 or (800) 322-8755.

You can find Facts On File on the World Wide Web at http://www.factsonfile.com

Cover design by Nora Wertz

Printed in the United States of America

VB FOF 10 9 8 7 6 5 4 3 2 1
   (pbk) 10 9 8 7 6 5 4 3 2 1

This book is printed on acid-free paper.

CONTENTS

PREFACE
How To Use This Book

Purpose

Since 1992, when this book was originally published, the theater and performing arts industries have exploded and expanded. In addition to being able to experience theater and other performing arts live, there are more opportunities than ever to view them on public, cable and network television. Blockbuster films, such as *The Lion King,* are inspiring very successful Broadway productions. And the proliferation of venues for the performing arts has created a multitude of career opportunities. The future looks bright in this field.

This book is written for the many thousands of people who aspire to work in theater and the other performing arts but do not know what the career opportunities are, where to locate them, or what training is required to be successful in the quest. The 70 jobs discussed in this book encompass careers not only for performing talent but also for those in the business end of the industry, as well as behind-the-scenes workers.

The performing arts industry requires a great variety of people with many different talents. It needs actors, writers, singers, dancers, costume designers, secretaries, receptionists, publicists, managers, teachers, production personnel, designers, electricians and more. The trick in locating a job is to develop your skills and use them to get a foot in the door. Once you're there, you have a good chance of climbing the career ladder up to other positions.

Read through the book and determine what you are qualified for or how you can obtain training in the field you want to enter. You can then work toward getting into an interesting, exciting and financially rewarding career in theater and the performing arts.

Sources of Information

Information for this updated and revised edition was obtained through interviews, questionnaires and a broad survey of books, magazines, newsletters, television and radio programs, college catalogs and other related publications. Some information came from personal experience working in the industry. Other data were obtained from friends and business associates who work in various phases of the theater and other performing arts.

Men and women in all aspects of the performing arts contributed their expertise. These people included individuals working in the business and administration end of the industry; theaters; operas; ballets and orchestra companies; arenas, halls and other venues; organizations; production companies; public relations and publicity firms; newspapers; magazines; radio and television stations; placement companies; arts councils and more. Also interviewed were agents, managers, publicists, theater owners and employees, music therapists, dance therapists, educators, and amateur and professional actors, dancers, singers and administrators. Information was also obtained from schools, colleges, universities, personnel offices, unions and trade associations.

Organization of Material

Career Opportunities in Theater and The Performing Arts is divided into 11 general employment sections. These sections are Career Opportunities for Performing Artists; Career Opportunities in Writing and Composing for the Performing Arts; Career Opportunities in Production, Directing and Design; Career Opportunities in Theatrical Administration and Business; Career Opportunities in Orchestra, Opera and Ballet Company Administration; Career Opportunities Behind the Scenes; Career Opportunities in Support Services for Performing Artists; Career Opportunities in Halls, Arenas and Other Venues; Career Opportunities in Performing Arts Education; Career Opportunities in Performing Arts Journalism and Miscellaneous Careers in Theater and the Performing Arts. Within each of these sections are descriptions of individual careers.

There are two parts to each job classification. The first part offers job information in a chart form. The second part presents information in a narrative text. In addition to the basic career description there is information on unions and associations as well as tips for entry.

Eighteen appendixes are offered to help you locate information useful for finding a job in your field of interest, general research about job possibilities, internships, educational opportunities and more.

These appendixes include practical, general information about college and university degree and nondegree programs in drama and theater arts, theater arts management and administration, dance, music therapy and dance therapy; workshops, seminars and symposiums; internships; trade associations and unions; Broadway theaters; off Broadway theaters; off-off Broadway theaters; dinner theaters; resident theaters; stock theaters; U.S. and Canadian orchestras; ballet companies; U.S. and Canadian opera companies; and arts councils and agencies. A bibliography of theater- and performing arts–related books and periodicals and a glossary are also included.

Whether you choose to be an actor, musician, dancer, composer, playwright, singer, arts council director, costume designer, wardrobe dresser, teacher, coach or usher, your job can be both exciting and fulfilling. Your career in theater and the performing arts is out there waiting for you. You just have to go after it. Persevere! The person who doesn't make it is usually the one who gave up a day too early.

Shelly Field

ACKNOWLEDGMENTS

I thank every individual, theater, opera company, orchestra, ballet company, agency, association and union who provided information, assistance and encouragement for this book and its previous edition.

I acknowledge with appreciation my editor, Jim Chambers, for his help and encouragement. I also must thank Neal Mailet, who as my initial editor, provided the original impetus for this book. I could not have successfully completed this project without the continuing assistance of Ed and Selma Field. Others whose help was invaluable include Actors' Equity Association; Alliance of Resident Theaters of New York; American Association for Music Therapy; American Dance Therapy Association; American Federation of Musicians; American Guild of Musical Artists; American Guild of Variety Artists; American Society of Composers and Publishers; American Society of Music Copyists; American Symphony Orchestra League; Barbara Ashworth, Beauty School of Middletown; Association of Theatrical Press Agents and Managers; John Balme, director, Lake George Opera Festival; Dan Barrett; Ryan Barrett; Allan Barrish; Jan Behr; Eugene Blabey, WVOS Radio; Fredda Briant; Broadcast Music, Inc.; Broadway Unit of Makeup Artists and Hairstylists; Katrina Bull; Theresa Bull; Eileen Casey; Anthony Cellini; Lilyan Chauvin, Organization of Professional Acting Coaches and Teachers; Sandra Clark; Karen Cobham; Dr. Jessica L. Cohen; Lorraine Cohen; Norman Cohen; Kathleen Conry, director/actress; Community General Hospital, Harris, New York; Jan Cornelius; Crawford Memorial Library Staff; Meike Cryan; Daniel Dayton; W. Lynne Dayton; The Dramatists Guild; Alex Dube, American Guild Musical Artists; Michelle Edwards; Scott Edwards; Louis Ephan; Lisa Estrada, coordinator/director, Los Angeles Laker Girls; Ernest Evans; Pat Farell, Argosy Gaming; Field Associates, Ltd.; Deborah K. Field, Esq.; Finkelstein Memorial Library staff; Forestburg Playhouse; Louise Fousy, Actors' Equity Association; John Gatto; Shelia Gatto; Gina Giambattista, administrator, University Resident Theatre Association, Inc.; Sally Gifft; Tina Gilbert, Apollo Plaza; George Glantzis; Kaytee Glantzis; Sam Goldych; Gail Haberle; Pat Heavey, American Federation of Musicians; Hermann Memorial Library staff; Paul Holmes, stage manager; Joan Howard; International Alliance of Theatrical Stage Employees; International Association of Auditorium Managers; International Brotherhood of Electrical Workers; Tom Jamerson, American Guild of Musical Artists; Jimmy "Handyman" Jones; Dr. John C. Koch; League of Resident Theaters; Ann J. Ledley, business representative, Actors' Equity Association; Local 162 IATSE; Bob Leone; Los Angeles Laker Girls; Ginger Maher; Phillip Mestman; Rima Mestman; Metropolitan Opera; Beverly Michaels, Esq.; Martin Michaels, Esq.; Jason Milligan; Monticello Central High School Guidance Department; Monticello Central School High School Library staff; Monticello Central School Middle School Library staff; Werner Mendel, New Age Health Spa; Sharon Morris; Music Business Institute; Music Educators National Conference; Florence Naistadt; National Association for Music Therapy; National Association of Broadcast Employees and Technicians; National Association of Broadcasters; National Association of Schools of Dance; National Association of Schools of Music; National Association of Schools of Theatre; National Dance Association; Chris Nelson; Earl Nesmith; New Dramatists; Jim Newton, New York State Employment Service; Nikkodo, U.S.A., Inc.; Organization of Professional Acting Coaches and Teachers; Don Paget, United Scenic Artists; Karen Pizzuto, communications director, IATSE; Ray Polgar; Anita Portas, IATSE; Public Relations Society of America; Ramapo Catskill Library System; Doug Richards; Jim Ryan, business representative, United Scenic Artists; Craig Sandquist, producer; Richard Schaefer, lighting designer; Nelson Sheeley, freelance director; Beverly Sloan, Equity; Society of Stage Directors and Choreographers; Laura Solomon; The Songwriters Guild; Matthew E. Strong; Sullivan County Performing Arts Council; Thrall Library staff; Theatrical Wardrobe Union; Marie Tremper; Leo Ullman; University Resident Theatre Association, Inc.; United Scenic Artists; Brenda Walker; Tonaya Watts, Association of Theatrical Press Agents and Managers; Lisa Weiss, dancer; Carol Williams; John Williams; Dr. Diana Worby and conductor Rachael Worby.

My thanks also to the many people, associations, companies and organizations who provided material for this book and wish to remain anonymous.

INTRODUCTION

Most people who hold theater and performing arts jobs are in the industry because they love it—there's no business like show business. You can be one of these people too. Almost any talent you have can be applied to obtaining a job in what is currently a multibillion dollar business. The possibilities are endless.

The performing arts industry offers variety. You can be anything from an actor, singer or dancer to the producer of a major theatrical production. If you prefer to work backstage, your job can be stage manager, lighting designer, sound designer, director, makeup artist, hairdresser, wardrobe dresser or costume designer. You might aspire to be the general manager of a theater, a conductor, arranger, composer, orchestrator or librettist. Perhaps you want to use your skills as a secretary, receptionist, fund-raiser or personnel manager, working on the administrative side of an orchestra, opera or ballet company. The performing arts need critics, journalists and press agents to communicate with the public, and booking agents, managers and literary agents to distribute the wealth. Those who want to incorporate education and the performing arts can teach drama, dance or music.

As you read the various sections in this book, searching for your dream job, keep in mind that there are many ways to get a foot in the door of the performing arts industry. Here are the guidelines, but the rest is up to you. Each section of this book has all the information necessary to acquaint you with most of the important jobs in theater and the performing arts. A key to the organization of each entry follows.

Career Profile

At a glance, the career profile offers a brief description, in chart form, of job responsibilities and duties, possible alternate job titles, employment prospects, best geographical location and any prerequisites necessary for the job.

Career Ladder

The career ladder illustrates job advancement potential. Remember that in theater and any of the other performing arts industries there are no hard-and-fast rules. Advancement can occur in any number of ways.

Position Description

Every effort has been made to give well-rounded job descriptions. Keep in mind that no two jobs in this industry are structured in exactly the same way. Job definitions, areas of responsibility and job hierarchies vary from one organization to the next.

Salaries

Salary ranges given for the 70 job titles in the book are as accurate as possible. Salary determinations for jobs in the performing arts are based on many variables. These include job type, level of experience and degree of responsibility. Earnings also depend on the type of theater that is hiring, as well as its size, location, prestige and geographic location.

Employment Prospects

If you choose a job that has an EXCELLENT, GOOD or FAIR rating, you should have an easier time finding a job. If, however, you find yourself interested in a job that has a POOR rating, don't despair. The rating only means that it is difficult to obtain a job—not totally impossible.

Advancement Prospects

Try to be as cooperative and helpful as possible in the workplace. Be enthusiastic, energetic and outgoing. Make an extra effort in your work. Learn as much as you can. When a job advancement possibility opens up make sure that you're prepared for it.

Education and Training

Although this book gives the minimum training and educational requirements for each job, you should try to get the best training and education possible. A college degree does not guarantee a job in any aspect of theater or the performing arts, but it does help prepare you for life in the workplace. Education and training also encompass theater-related courses, seminars, apprenticeships, programs, on-the-job training and internships.

Experience/Skills/Personality Traits

Experience, skills and personality traits required will differ from job to job. You will need a lot of perseverance and energy for any job in the theater—it's hard work. You will also have to be articulate and pleasantly aggressive. Being outgoing also helps. Contacts are important facets of the business—make as many as you can. Good contacts will help advance your career and expand your opportunities. Don't burn any bridges. The theater and performing arts world is small. You will encounter the same people over and over again throughout your career—stay on good terms with everyone.

Best Geographic Location

New York City is the theatrical capital of the country. This does not mean it is the only place to look for employment. Jobs in theater and the performing arts may be found throughout the country. Culturally active cities with theaters, orchestras, opera or ballet companies, halls, arenas and other venues also offer good opportunities. Smaller or less prestigious theaters or companies can be an excellent place to begin a career.

Unions/Associations

Unions and trade associations offer valuable help in getting access to many jobs in theater and the performing arts, as well as in making contacts. They may also offer scholarships, fellowships, seminars and other beneficial programs that you should investigate.

Tips for Entry

Use this section for ideas on how to gain entry to the areas that interest you and how to get a job in that area. When applying for any job always be professional. Dress neatly and conservatively. Don't wear sneakers. Don't chew gum. Don't smoke. Don't wear heavy perfume or cologne. Always have a few copies of your resume with you. These, too, should look neat and professional. Resumes should be typed and checked and rechecked for grammar, spelling and content.

If you are applying for a job as an actor, singer or dancer, dress properly for the audition. Bring your resume and professional photographs. Be thoroughly prepared for your audition.

Use every contact you have. Don't get hung up on the idea that you want to get a job without help. Ask for help. Find a mentor. People are usually flattered. If you are lucky enough to know someone who can help you get a job you want, accept their generosity. You alone will have to prove yourself at the interview or audition—and on the job. Nobody else can do that for you.

The last piece of advice in this section is never be late. Be on-time for job interviews, auditions, appointments and work. People remember when you're habitually late and frequent tardiness will slow your career advancement.

Have fun reading this book. Use it as intended, and it will help you find a career you will truly love. The world of theater and the performing arts can be both glamorous and exciting.

Don't get discouraged. Don't give up. Dealing well with rejection is part of the business. Not everyone gets the first job he or she applies for. Few become stars overnight. You may have to knock on a lot of doors, send out a lot of resumes, apply for a lot of positions and attend a great many auditions before you find the job of your dreams. Have faith and confidence in yourself. You *will* make it in the performing arts if you persevere. When you do get the job you have been dreaming about, share your knowledge and help others fulfill their dreams too. There really is no business like show business. Good luck!

CAREER OPPORTUNITIES
FOR
PERFORMING ARTISTS

ACTOR/ACTRESS—THEATRICAL

CAREER PROFILE

Duties: Performing in theatrical productions; learning lines; attending rehearsals.

Alternate Title(s): None.

Salary Range: Impossible to determine earnings due to nature of business.

Employment Prospects: Fair.

Best Geographical Location(s) for Position: Culturally active cities offer more opportunities.

Prerequisites:

Education or Training: No formal educational requirement; courses or workshops in acting and theater arts may be useful.

Experience: Experience acting in community and school productions helpful.

Special Skills and Personality Traits: Excellent acting skills; ability to deal with rejection; good memory; articulateness; poise; good stage presence; dependability.

CAREER LADDER

```
┌─────────────────────────┐
│    Successful Actor/     │
│   Actress Starring in    │
│   Broadway Production    │
└─────────────────────────┘

┌─────────────────────────┐
│      Actor/Actress       │
└─────────────────────────┘

┌─────────────────────────┐
│ Aspiring Amateur Actor/Actress │
└─────────────────────────┘
```

Position Description

Actors or Actresses working in theater are the people who interpret dramatic roles in plays and other theatrical productions. Individuals may perform in acting roles only, or may also sing and/or dance.

Actors and Actresses working in theater usually start out working in community and/or school productions. Some, who have decided that this is the vocation they want to pursue, attend either a college with a theater arts major or dramatic schools, classes and workshops.

Individuals then try to obtain experience in stock productions, touring or repertory companies, and dinner theater productions. The dream of most Actors and Actresses working in theater is to land a starring role in a Broadway play.

Actors and Actresses must audition for parts in plays. Individuals find out about auditions in a number of ways. They may have agents who set up auditions, or they may hear of open auditions through contacts or by reading the "trades." The trades are magazines and newspapers that report events in the entertainment industry.

Individuals may audition for many parts before they land a role. At an audition, the Actor or Actress may be asked to read a part of a script so that the director and producers can see if they are "right" for the role. Individuals may also be asked to leave a resume of acting experience and an 8 x 10 glossy photograph of themselves.

In some situations, the Actor or Actress may be called back to read a part a second or even third time. Sometimes they get the part, often they don't. Individuals must be thick skinned and have the ability to deal with rejection in this profession.

If they do get a part, the Actor or Actress will be required to learn their lines and attend rehearsals. In some situations, the individual will be hired as an understudy. An understudy must learn all his or her lines and movements just as the Actor or Actress who will be playing the part does. In the event that the Actor or Actress playing the part gets sick or is not able to play the role, the understudy will go on stage in his or her place.

While being an Actor or Actress in the theater is hard work, most individuals live for the day that they can see their name on the marquee of a Broadway theater.

Salaries

It is impossible to determine the salaries for Actors and Actresses who work in the theater. Earnings vary greatly depending on a number of factors, including the type of production that the individual is working in, his or her talent, experience, prestige and drawing power. Earnings will also depend on the amount of work the individual has done. There are some actors who never get a paying job. Others may have annual earnings of $500,000 plus, but this is rare.

In June 1998, Actors and Actresses working in a Broadway production earned a minimum of $1,135 per week, according to Actors' Equity Association. Those working in national tours or bus and truck tours earn a per diem.

Minimum weekly salaries for individuals working in off Broadway productions are set according to the seating capacity. For example, according to Equity, in June 1998 the minimum weekly salary of an Actor or Actress in an off Broadway production in a theater seating 100 to 199 people was $396; in a theater holding 200 to 250 seats the minimum weekly salary was $460; theaters seating 251 to 299 paid Actors and Actresses a minimum of $526 weekly; theaters seating 300 to 350 people paid a weekly minimum of $606; and theaters holding 351 to 499 seats had a weekly minimum salary of $678.

In order to be financially solvent, a great many Actors and Actresses are forced to work other jobs such as waiting on tables, teaching or freelance assignments.

Employment Prospects

Employment prospects are determined by a number of factors including the talent of the individual as well as connections, luck and being in the right place at the right time. Actors and Actresses, who are talented may locate positions in summer stock, touring companies, off Broadway and off-off Broadway productions, etc.

Those aspiring to work in Broadway productions have very limited prospects. That is not to say that individuals cannot get a job on Broadway, but it is extremely difficult. There are only a limited number of Broadway plays and competition for the positions is fierce.

Advancement Prospects

Advancement prospects for Actors and Actresses are dependent on the same types of factors that help the individuals get jobs in the first place. These factors include talent, luck, being in the right place at the right time and good contacts and connections.

The next rung up the career ladder might be obtaining a role in a more prestigious play, a larger role or different type of theater. An Actor or Actress working in a touring company may advance his or her career by signing a contract for a Broadway production.

For some individuals, advancement might be landing a role in a major movie; for others it would be a starring role in a television series. There is no one career path to success as an Actor or Actress. A number of individuals start in the theater and move on to television or the movies and others go from TV or motion pictures to the theater to attain super-stardom.

Education and Training

There is no formal educational requirement to become a theatrical Actor or Actress. Many individuals however, do have a college degree in theater arts or attend dramatic arts schools. Others take private acting lessons, participate in workshops or attend seminars. Many Actors and Actresses continue taking lessons and workshops throughout their careers.

Experience/Skills/Personality Traits

Most successful Actors and Actresses starring in Broadway productions have paid their dues by performing in a variety of situations including local, community and school productions, summer stock, touring companies, etc. Others have worked in television, motion pictures, or other fields in the entertainment industry.

Actors and Actresses working in the theater should be articulate with clear, pleasant speaking voices. They should be poised and have the ability to perform in front of groups of people.

While the physical "look" of Actors and Actresses is important, there is no one appearance that can guarantee success. There are many good-looking men and beautiful women who do not make it as Actors and Actresses. What is important however, is that individuals are talented in their craft and have the creative ability to portray different parts effectively.

It is worth repeating that individuals working in any field of entertainment need a thick skin. They should be able to deal with rejection that all Actors and Actresses run in to at one time or another in their career.

It is helpful in building a successful career for the individual to be personable and easy to get along with. He or she should also be dependable and on time for appointments, rehearsals and all performances.

Unions/Associations

The major union for theatrical Actors and Actresses is the Actors' Equity Association (AEA) also known as Equity. This organization sets minimum salaries and work conditions for its members. It also offers professional guidance and support. Individuals who work in unionized theaters must be members of this union.

Actors and Actresses who work in other fields may belong to other unions including Screen Actors Guild (SAG), the American Federation of Television and Radio Artists (AFTRA) or the American Federation of Musicians (AFM).

Tips for Entry

1. Get as much acting experience as possible. Perform in your school productions, community theater, summer stock, etc. The more you hone your skills, the better you will be.

2. Look for acting workshops, courses and seminars. These, too, will help you improve your craft, give you valuable advice, experience and offer you the opportunity to make important contacts.

3. Learn as much as you can about the entertainment industry. Take courses and seminars on business, law, management, etc. These courses will help prepare you for future success.

4. Prepare a professional resume listing your acting experience. A resume is often requested at casting calls and auditions. You may also be asked to leave an 8 inch x 10 inch glossy photograph of yourself. Many people have two different poses prepared, a head shot and a full body shot.

BALLET DANCER

Duties: Performing in ballets and recitals; attending rehearsals.

Alternate Title(s): Dancer; Prima Ballerina.

Salary Range: Minimum weekly earnings in unionized situation: $570.

Employment Prospects: Poor.

Best Geographical Location(s) for Position: Culturally active cities hosting a number of ballet companies will offer more opportunities.

Prerequisites:

Education or Training: Extensive training and lessons through ballet company training programs and ballet schools.

Experience: Experience in ballet is necessary.

Special Skills and Personality Traits: Dedication; creativity; gracefulness; determination; physical fitness.

```
┌─────────────────────────────────┐
│     Principal Dancer in More     │
│  Prestigious Production or Company │
└─────────────────────────────────┘

┌─────────────────────────────────┐
│          Ballet Dancer,          │
│      Member of the Corps         │
└─────────────────────────────────┘

┌─────────────────────────────────┐
│          Dance Student           │
└─────────────────────────────────┘
```

Position Description

Ballets are theatrical productions centered around dance. The story of a ballet is told through dance movement and music. Those who perform in ballets are called Dancers, or principals, and are very highly trained.

Ballets, like most other theatrical productions, are elaborate, using scenery and lighting to help create the mood of the story. Dancers wear specially designed costumes which allow them freedom of movement when performing. They may wear regular ballet slippers or toe shoes depending on the type of dancing required.

The music in a ballet may be performed by a live orchestra or may be recorded. To a great extent, the music used determines the type of steps the Dancers will perform. The Dancers use combinations of basic movements to interpret the story. These combinations are developed and put together by the choreographer.

Individuals go through many years of training to become Ballet Dancers. Many go through apprenticeship and other training programs with regional or national ballet companies.

Ballet companies usually hold auditions for new Dancers. Individuals may find out about these in a number of ways. Some Ballet Dancers have agents or managers who obtain auditions for them. Others find out about openings through word of mouth or reading about them in the trade papers such as *Backstage, Variety,* or in local entertainment publications. Many individuals contact various ballet companies on their own to determine when auditions will be held.

A Dancer's training does not stop when he or she becomes part of a company or production. The Ballet Dancer continues taking classes through his or her career.

The Dancer must attend all rehearsals set by the company. At the beginning of a production, the Dancer will find out what his or her part will be and learn the combinations and movements involved in that part. After the individual Dancers have learned their parts, they will practice putting them together with the other Dancers in the company.

At some time during the rehearsal period, the Dancers will be fitted for costumes. Ballet Dancers do not speak or sing during the performance. Costuming, therefore, is important to the story of the ballet. The costumes of the Dancers help the audience relate to what is happening on stage. Special hair styling and makeup are also used to create the aura.

The lifestyle of a Ballet Dancer takes a great deal of self-discipline. Individuals must keep themselves physically fit and in good health at all times. They must also take extra precautions to avoid injuries. A sprained ankle before a performance could jeopardize an entire production. Ballet Dancers must eat well, choosing their foods wisely. They can not afford to gain any extra weight.

Ballet Dancers are required to perform their parts at each production. Work hours may vary depending on the schedule of performances. Individuals may work in the afternoon, evening and/or on weekends.

Salaries

Earnings vary greatly for Ballet Dancers. Individuals may be paid by the performance or on a weekly basis. Factors affecting earnings include the type of setting the individual is working in, the geographic location and level, size and budget of the ballet company. Other factors include the reputation and experience of the Dancer and the type of part he or she is performing.

Ballet Dancers working in unionized halls have their minimum salaries set by the American Guild of Musical Artists (AGMA). Minimum weekly salaries for the 1998–99 season for individuals working in ballet companies began at $570 for new dancers. Solo Dancers received a weekly minimum of $786. Principal Dancers in a production had a base weekly scale of $852. Individuals receive the same weekly salary for performance or rehearsal weeks. Dancers who travel with a company receive a per diem for room and board.

It should be noted that these figures are minimums. Dancers who are in demand can command much higher earnings.

Ballet Dancers working in nonunionized situations may earn between $300 and $700 or more per week.

Employment Prospects

While employment prospects are poor for Ballet Dancers, talented individuals who have a great deal of determination and drive will usually find jobs. While one can aspire to dance with a troupe that performs in New York or London, Dancers may find opportunities with regional ballet companies throughout the country and the world. Culturally active cities hosting a number of ballet companies offer more opportunities for jobs.

Advancement Prospects

Advancement prospects are poor for Ballet Dancers. There are a number of paths a Ballet Dancer may take to climb the career ladder. The most common path for career advancement is by auditioning for a position in a more prestigious ballet company. Another method of career advancement is to become a lead or Principal Dancer in a ballet.

Education and Training

Training is very important for Ballet Dancers. Individuals usually begin their training early in life. Many Ballet Dancers start taking lessons before they are six years old. By the time Ballet Dancers reach their late teens, they have already had extensive training and lessons in the art of ballet. Ballet Dancers obtain training through intensive lessons, workshops and programs with ballet companies and ballet schools. As mentioned previously, lessons and other training continue throughout the Dancer's career.

Experience/Skills/Personality Traits

Most professional Ballet Dancers have had experience performing in front of audiences when they were amateur Ballet Dancers and students. By the time most of these individuals locate a paying job, they have danced hundreds of times in rehearsals and recitals.

Ballet Dancers must be extremely talented in the art of ballet. Successful Dancers are very dedicated to their profession. Individuals must be willing to practice, train and rehearse on a continuing basis. Ballet Dancers must be physically, mentally and emotionally prepared to dance. They must be graceful in their movement. Creativity in expressing these movements is also helpful. Agility is necessary. Ballet Dancers must have a feeling for the music to which they dance.

Becoming a Ballet Dancer is not easy. Drive, determination and perseverance are necessary for success.

Unions/Associations

Ballet Dancers working in unionized halls must be members of the American Guild of Musical Artists (AGMA). This union negotiates minimum earnings for its members as well as minimum working conditions and standards.

Tips for Entry

1. Look for intern, apprentice and training programs. These can often be found in various ballet companies. The programs are a good way to get your foot in the door and help you obtain necessary experience.
2. Many ballet companies also offer summer workshops and programs. These offer opportunities to get additional training and experience.
3. Training is essential to this type of career. Get the best possible training. You may have to give up a lot of your free time taking classes but it will pay off.
4. Perform whenever you can. Experience in front of audiences is helpful.

CHOREOGRAPHER

CAREER PROFILE

Duties: Developing dances, movements and routines for a theatrical production; assisting in casting of dancers; teaching dancers routines and movements; attending rehearsals.

Alternate Title(s): None.

Salary Range: Impossible to determine due to nature of the job.

Employment Prospects: Fair.

Best Geographical Location(s) for Position: Culturally active cities offer more oppportunities.

Prerequisites:

Education or Training: Training in dance required.

Experience: Experience in theater and dance necessary.

Special Skills and Personality Traits: Ability to teach; technical dance expertise; good communication skills; creativity; ability to conceptualize; assertiveness.

CAREER LADDER

```
┌─────────────────────────────┐
│      Choreographer          │
│      for Larger,            │
│ More Prestigious Production │
└─────────────────────────────┘

┌─────────────────────────────┐
│      Choreographer          │
└─────────────────────────────┘

┌─────────────────────────────┐
│        Dancer               │
│          or                 │
│        Student              │
└─────────────────────────────┘
```

Position Description

The Choreographer of a theatrical production is responsible for staging the movements of the dancers. The individual may have varied responsibilities depending on the specific production.

Choreographers compose dances designed to suggest a story, interpret emotion and enliven a production. The individual may choreograph a variety of different types of shows including ballet, musicals and reviews. The job of the Choreographer begins when a producer or director contacts the individual and sends him or her a script. While the Choreographer is hired and paid by the producer of the show, he or she may be recommended by the director.

After reading the script and discussing specific responsibilities, the Choreographer and the producer negotiate a fee. If they can come to terms, the Choreographer gets the job. In most instances, the individual will sit in on the casting to determine which dancers should be hired for a production.

The Choreographer might meet with the director, musical director, stage manager, lighting, set and costume designers to discuss each individual's concepts. He or she will also study the script and music. The individual will then develop routines and dance movements for the dancers and block them out on stage. A great deal of the Choreographer's job in planning dances is done on paper or in the mind of the individual. This preliminary work uses the Choreographer's most creative powers.

The Choreographer may work with assistants and dancers trying out the routines to make sure that they look good and fit into the time frame of the music.

The Choreographer may spend many hours teaching the dancers the steps and routines that have been developed and created. He or she will be responsible for rehearsing with the dancers until the routines are perfect. The Choreographer will usually begin rehearsing with the dancers separately and then run through the production and include the dancers with the rest of the cast. At this point, the choreography is adapted to changes in lines, entrances, exits and movements by actors and actresses that inevitably occur in rehearsal. The Choreographer meets and discusses changes with the director throughout the rehearsal period. Choreographic changes are made in response to lighting, stage sets and costuming changes.

The individual's job concludes on opening night. At that time, the Choreographer moves on to locate another production requiring the services of a Choreographer.

Salaries

Salaries for Choreographers vary. Factors affecting salaries include the type of production, amount of work the individual does annually, responsibilities, expertise and experience. The Society for Stage Directors and Choreographers sets a minimum fee of $37,130 to be paid to individuals during the rehearsal period for Broadway shows. Choreographers at the top of their profession can earn hundreds of thousands of dollars annually.

Individuals working for theaters that are not unionized, community theaters, experimental theaters, etc. may work for nothing to obtain experience.

Employment Prospects

As with any creative endeavor, employment prospects for Choreographers are fair. Individuals must be willing to work in smaller regional theaters. Prospects become more difficult as individuals aspire to work on major productions such as Broadway shows or for well-known ballet companies.

Individuals may choreograph ballets, musicals, dramas, thrillers, mysteries, etc. They may specialize in ballet, modern, folk, ethnic, jazz, in different dance categories.

Choreographers get jobs in a variety of ways. They may send out their resumes to producers and directors of shows. Others get referrals from producers and directors they have worked with in the past or from organizations such as the Society for Stage Directors and Choreographers (SSDC).

It is important to note that as a rule, Choreographers working in theater work from job to job. Once a production is choreographed and opens, the individual must find another show to work with.

Advancement Prospects

Advancement prospects for Choreographers are difficult to determine. Factors affecting advancement include the individual's drive, determination and experience as well as contacts and being in the right place at the right time. Luck plays an important role too.

Advancement for a Choreographer can take a number of paths. The individual may climb the career ladder by getting the opportunity to Choreograph a larger number of more prestigious productions. Choreographing a Broadway show or major ballet for a prestigious company is a great accomplishment in this profession.

Some individuals advance their career by choreographing television shows or movies. Others find career advancement by moving into directing or producing theatrical performances.

Education and Training

There are no formal educational requirements for Choreographers. Most individuals begin their training as dancers. The best training is a combination of study with dance teachers and professional dancers. Workshops and classes with a number of different teachers give the individual the opportunity to learn a variety of different techniques.

Aspiring Choreographers might also get a college degree in theater or dance.

Experience/Skills/Personality Traits

Most Choreographers have had previous experience in the theater and dancing. While individuals should know a great deal about dance, they do not have to be great dancers to be Choreographers. They should, however, be great communicators with the ability to teach. They must be able to get concepts across to dancers. Technical expertise in dance is imperative, as is a basic knowledge of music and music theory.

The Choreographer should be a team player, for he or she works with a wide variety of people—the producer, director, dancers, set designers, lighting designers, costume designers, etc. He or she should be easy to get along with yet assertive.

The individual should be creative and have the ability to conceptualize ideas. In this way, he or she will develop movements and combinations of movements for the dancers.

Unions/Associations

Choreographers working in unionized theaters must belong to the Society of Stage Directors and Choreographers (SSDC). This group sets minimum fees and working conditions for their members as well as offers professional guidance and support.

If the Choreographer was or is an actor or actress, he or she may also be a member of the actors' union, Actors' Equity.

Tips for Entry

1. Take as many dance and theater classes and workshops as possible with a great variety of teachers. The more classes you take the more you will learn.
2. A great deal of choreography is picked up watching others. Go see different types of plays, musicals and other theatrical productions.
3. Go to the library and find books on choreography. Study the work of others.
4. Volunteer to choreograph your local community theater production. It is great experience.
5. Look for internships in choreography with theater groups, schools and other organizations.

DANCER

CAREER PROFILE

Duties: Using body movements to express ideas, tell stories and entertain.

Alternate Title(s):   None.

Salary Range: Impossible to determine earnings due to nature of the job.

Employment Prospects: Poor.

Best Geographical Location(s) for Position: Culturally active cities will offer more opportunities.

Prerequisites:

Education or Training: Extensive training through schools, private lessons, etc.

Experience: Experience in dance necessary.

Special Skills and Personality Traits: Dedication; creativity; gracefulness; ability to deal with rejection.

CAREER LADDER

```
┌─────────────────────────────────────┐
│   Dancer in More Prestigious Production │
│        or Dance Company              │
└─────────────────────────────────────┘

┌─────────────────────────────────────┐
│              Dancer                  │
└─────────────────────────────────────┘

┌─────────────────────────────────────┐
│          Dance Student               │
│               or                     │
│          Amateur Dancer              │
└─────────────────────────────────────┘
```

Position Description

Dancers use body movement to express ideas and tell stories. They move to sound, music and rhythm with their bodies. Individuals may use traditional moves or improvised ones. Professional Dancers may perform ballet, classical, folk, ethnic, jazz or modern dance. Most individuals specialize in one or two forms.

Professional Dancers working in theater may work in ballets, musicals, comedies, other plays and productions. They may also perform in stage shows. Dancers also might work in other entertainment fields including television, films or music videos.

Competition among professional Dancers is great. Many individuals who aspire to become professional Dancers take on other related jobs and/or responsibilities, including singing and/or acting. Many Dancers also teach to supplement their income.

To become a successful Dancer, an individual needs a great deal of training in the form of classes, private lessons or watching others perform. Dancers practice many hours a day to perfect their movements and keep their bodies in shape.

It is important for the Dancer to say in top physical condition and in good health. A Dancer not only practices and exercises, but eats well too. The lifestyle of a professional Dancer requires self-discipline.

Dancers must audition for jobs. They may have an agent or manager who obtains auditions for them or they may go to open auditions and casting calls. Before going to an audition, the dancer prepares a resume, listing the individual's name, address, phone number, education, training and jobs he or she has had dancing or in the performing arts. The resume also includes any special skills. For example, the Dancer may also be a choreographer or singer. Dancers also bring 8 x 10 color or black-and-white photographs of themselves in a few different poses, including a head shot.

Hundreds of Dancers audition for each job. Even if a Dancer does well at an audition, he or she still may not get the job. Many individuals feel rejected or develop low self-esteem. The difference between a successful dancer and a less successful one is that the former keeps auditioning in spite of the rejections.

Once a Dancer obtains a job, he or she must attend rehearsals. Rehearsals are long and grueling, but are necessary to the success of a performance. At the rehearsal, a choreographer will explain the steps to the Dancers. The individuals will then learn the steps and routines perfecting them as they go.

Dancers will perform at every show. Depending on when performances are scheduled, individuals may work in the afternoon, evening and/or on weekends. If the individual is hired to dance in a road show, he or she must also be prepared to travel.

There can be a lot of stress in this type of job. Most Dancers do not have steady employment. Individuals must also worry about constantly doing their best or someone else may get their job.

Salaries

Due to the nature of the job, it is impossible to estimate earnings. Many variables affect salaries, such as experience, expertise and reputation of the Dancer. Other factors affecting income include the type of dance production the individual is involved in and the amount of time he or she works annually. Many Dancers supplement earnings with other related jobs such as choreography and teaching.

Minimum earnings for those working in unionized situations are set by the unions. Minimum weekly salaries for individuals working in ballet companies or modern productions for the 1998–99 season began around $570. Dancers who travel will also receive a per diem for room and board. Dancers who are in demand can command much higher earnings.

Salaries for Dancers who are working in nonunion situations can vary greatly from $50 a performance and up.

Employment Prospects

Employment prospects for Dancers are poor. There are not a lot of opportunities and there are a great many people who want to fill them. Competition is tremendous.

Individuals may work in a major opera ballet or classical ballet companies. They may also work in stage shows, musical reviews, musicals, comedies and other productions. Other options not involved in theater include television, movies and music videos.

Those aspiring to become professional dancers might find success entering the field through dance groups affiliated with colleges and universities.

Advancement Prospects

Competition is keen in this field and advancement prospects for Dancers are poor. This is not to say that advancement cannot occur, just that it is difficult.

Some Dancers get to the next rung on the career ladder by finding a position with a more prestigious production. Others may advance by becoming better known. This in turn helps them obtain more jobs and demand higher pay.

Education and Training

Educational and training requirements will vary depending on the type of Dancer an individual aspires to become. Ballet Dancers usually start their training early in life. By the time most Ballet Dancers are in their late teens, they have gone through extensive training and lessons in the art of ballet. Many individuals take intensive lessons and attend workshops and training programs with ballet companies and at ballet schools.

Those who aspire to be other types of Dancers must also go through extensive training and constant classes. Individuals may also obtain training through summer programs.

There are colleges offering degrees in dance. A degree can be helpful to the individual by offering training, background and experience.

Experience/Skills/Personality Traits

Dancers must be very dedicated and have a great love for the art of dance. They must have had extensive training in the art form. Individuals need to be creative and graceful in their movements.

Dancers should be physically fit with a great deal of stamina. They need to be flexible, agile and coordinated. Individuals also have a feeling for music.

Dancers should be able to work well with others. They need the ability to learn steps and routines quickly. It is important for individuals to be able to deal with the constant rejection which comes with the various aspects of this type of job.

Unions/Associations

Dancers may belong to a number of different unions. Individuals working with musicals, comedies or other theatrical performances may be members of Actors' Equity. Those performing in ballets, operas or modern dance companies will belong to the American Guild of Musical Artists (AGMA). Dancers working on television or in movies may be members of the American Federation of Television and Radio Artists (AFTRA), the Screen Actors Guild (SAG) or the Screen Extras Guild (SEG).

Individuals may belong to one or a number of unions depending on the type of work they find. They may also be members of trade associations specific to the type of dance they perform including the American Dance Guild (ADG).

Tips for Entry

1. Get as much training as possible. Take classes and workshops from a variety of professional instructors and dancers who teach. This will help you learn additional styles and techniques.
2. Try to perform whenever you can, in school productions, community theater shows, etc.
3. Put together a professional looking resume and photographs.
4. Send your resume, glossies and a letter to professional dance companies requesting information about any training programs that they might offer.
5. If you believe in yourself, do not give up. Your big break will eventually come.

OPERA SINGER

CAREER PROFILE

Duties: Singing and performing in operas.

Alternate Title(s):   Classical Singer.

Salary Range: $10,000 to $100,000+.

Employment Prospects: Fair.

Best Geographical Location(s) for Position: New York City is the opera capital of the country; culturally active cities worldwide hosting opera companies will offer other opportunities.

Prerequisites:

Education or Training: Graduate of music conservatory, college or university.

Experience: Experience singing opera and other classical music necessary.

Special Skills and Personality Traits: Familiarity with operas; physical, mental and emotional stamina; perseverance; drive; determination.

CAREER LADDER

```
┌─────────────────────────────────────┐
│  Opera Singer in More Prestigious    │
│      Production or Soloist           │
└─────────────────────────────────────┘

┌─────────────────────────────────────┐
│                                     │
│          Opera Singer               │
│                                     │
└─────────────────────────────────────┘

┌─────────────────────────────────────┐
│            Student                   │
│     in Music Conservatory,           │
│      College or University           │
└─────────────────────────────────────┘
```

Position Description

Operas are theatrical productions which are set to music. Most, if not all of the dialogue in an opera is sung instead of spoken. Those who perform in operas are called Opera Singers. These Singers are highly trained in classical music. Individuals may be Principal Singers in the opera singing lead, feature or support roles. Singers may also sing in opera choruses.

Each opera is a story. The story is written in a book called the libretto, which means little book. Operas, like many other theatrical plays, can be elaborate productions. They rely on extensive costuming, scenery and lighting.

Individuals go through many years of training to become Opera Singers. Many participate in apprenticeship programs with regional or national opera companies before becoming full-fledged Opera Singers.

In order to get jobs in opera productions, Opera Singers usually have to audition. Individuals may have agents or managers who obtain auditions for them. Others find out about openings in shows through word of mouth, the union or reading about them in the trade papers.

When an Opera Singer does get a part, he or she is required to attend show rehearsals. During this time, the individual will become familiar with the opera and learn the staging of his or her parts. The Opera Singer will also be fitted with costumes. Hairstyle and makeup is also decided.

Many traditional operas are written and performed in other languages, and Opera Singers learn their roles in the particular foreign language. In some situations, the Opera Singer learns the part without being able to speak or understand the meaning of the words. Modern operas by American and British composers are usually written and performed in English. Opera Singers need some acting ability to interpret the story of the opera effectively and dramatically.

Opera Singers are responsible for performing their parts at the actual show. Work hours vary depending on the schedule of performances. He or she may work in the afternoon, evening and/or on weekends.

Salaries

Salaries vary for Opera Singers. Individuals may be paid by the performance or on a weekly basis. Factors affecting earnings include the prestige of the company the individual is singing in, the geographic location, and the size and budget of the opera company. Other variables include the reputation and experience of the individual and the role he or she is singing.

Aspiring Opera Singers, taking part in an apprentice program, earn a weekly salary of approximately $200 to $500 plus housing. Individuals with additional experience such as those involved in a young singer program may earn between $400 and $600 a week.

Opera Singers working in unionized halls have their minimum salaries set by the American Guild of Musical Artists (AGMA). Earnings are based on whether the individual is a principal or a chorus singer. As of September 1998 the minimum salary for a leading part in an opera for three performances is $717. Individuals singing in a featured role receive a minimum of $717 for four performances. Those singing a featured support role or a sole bit will receive a minimum of $596.80 for six performances. Individuals singing in the chorus of an opera will be paid a minimum of $597 per week for seven performances. Opera Singers working in unionized situations are paid extra for rehearsal time. In addition to salaries, AGMA has negotiated required employer contributions to a medical plan for working opera singers.

Opera Singers who are in demand earn $100,000 or more a year. In addition to earnings for live performances, many singers are asked to record certain roles and they receive royalties from recordings.

Employment Prospects

Employment prospects are fair for talented Opera Singers who are determined and driven to be in this profession. The opera capital of the country is New York City. Opera companies do exist, though, in other culturally active cities throughout the world. Individuals with talent who do start their careers as soloists at the Metropolitan Opera in New York can find jobs singing in the choruses of opera companies throughout the country and in other countries.

Many Opera Singers find employment with the help of a manager or talent agent. There are a number of talent agencies specializing in classical music. Most of them are located in New York City.

Advancement Prospects

Advancement prospects are fair for Opera Singers once they get their first role. Individuals advance their career in a number of ways, by practicing, by singing with more prestigious opera companies, and by winning lead or solo roles in a production.

Education and Training

Education and training are extremely important for the aspiring Opera Singer. Individuals must be trained in classical singing. Most Opera Singers are either graduates of a music conservatory or a college or university with a major in classical music. Conservatories and universities offering classical music training are very valuable to Opera Singers. They offer not only training and education but opportunities to perform that the individual may not find elsewhere. Individuals may also take classes from private vocal coaches and teachers to supplement their training.

Experience/Skills/Personality Traits

Opera Singers must have a great deal of experience singing classical music. Many obtain this experience by taking part in young singer and apprenticeship programs sponsored by opera companies.

An individual in this field must have an extraordinary voice. In addition, the Opera Singer must have acting skills. Familiarity with operas is helpful. As noted previously, the majority of operas currently written in this country are in English. However, many of the classic operas are in various foreign languages. It is therefore useful for the Singer to be fluent in other languages.

Individuals must practice their art. To be successful, the Opera Singer should have physical, mental and emotional stamina. Drive, determination and patience are also necessary.

Unions/Associations

Opera Singers working in unionized concert halls, theaters and other venues must be members of the American Guild of Musical Artists (AGMA). This union negotiates minimum earnings for its members as well as minimum working conditions and standards.

Tips for Entry

1. Look for an internship or apprenticeship program. These can often be located through various opera companies. These programs are a good way to get your foot in the door and help you to obtain necessary experience.
2. Training is essential to this type of career. Get the best training you can.
3. Look for summer workshops and programs with opera companies. They offer excellent training experience.
4. Many communities now have local opera companies. Get involved with these groups and take part in their productions.
5. Look into grants and competitions in opera. These will give you opportunities to make contacts.
6. Attend as many operas as you can to learn from other singers.

CHORUS SINGER

CAREER PROFILE

Duties: Singing in the chorus of a theatrical production.

Alternate Title(s): Chorus Vocalist; Chorus Member; Vocalist.

Salary Range: Impossible to determine earnings due to nature of job.

Employment Prospects: Fair.

Best Geographical Location(s) for Position: Culturally active cities will offer more opportunities.

Prerequisites:

Education or Training: No formal educational requirement.

Experience: Experience singing in public helpful.

Special Skills and Personality Traits: Ability to read music; ability to harmonize; ability to deal with rejections; perseverance; drive; determination.

CAREER LADDER

```
┌─────────────────────────────────────┐
│  Chorus Singer in More Prestigious   │
│             Production               │
│          or Solo Singer              │
└─────────────────────────────────────┘

┌─────────────────────────────────────┐
│           Chorus Singer              │
└─────────────────────────────────────┘

┌─────────────────────────────────────┐
│              Singer                  │
│                or                    │
│           Actor/Actress              │
└─────────────────────────────────────┘
```

Position Description

Chorus Singers sing in the chorus of musical productions. The Chorus Singer backs up the lead singers and other performers. He or she acts and/or dances depending on the requirements of the production.

In order to get jobs in theatrical productions, Chorus Singers usually audition. Many individual have agents or managers who obtain auditions for them. Others learn about openings in shows through word of mouth, their union or reading about it in the trade papers, such as *Variety* and *Backstage*.

Chorus Singers audition at open casting calls, so-called because any Singer can try out. Before going to any audition, the Singer prints up a resume listing the individual's name, address and phone number, education and training. It should also include all of the artist's singing, dancing and acting experience, as Chorus Singers may also be required to dance and/or act.

The Chorus Singer also brings professional photographs. In the performing arts industry, these photos are called 8 x 10 glossies and show the performer in different poses, including a head shot. Photographs are in color or black and white. Each photograph includes the Singer's name and phone number stamped on the back of it.

When Singers audition for the chorus, they usually bring a piece of sheet music with them. In most cases, the Singer gives the sheet music to the accompanist who is hired by the producers. In some cases, the Singer brings his or her own accompanist. In smaller shows, the Chorus Singer may also bring a cassette tape of the accompanying music and sing along with the tape.

Depending on the specific production, there may be hundreds of other Singers auditioning for the same job. Singers may not get the part even though they performed well at the audition, because they don't have the right "look" for the show, or do not sing in the style the production requires. The director determines if the Singer fills the dancing or acting requirements that might accompany the job. The important thing is that the individual must keep trying. Singers may be called back to audition a number of times for the same part.

Once a Chorus Singer gets a job, he or she will be required to attend rehearsals. The individual will receive a copy of the script and music. The Singer learns all the words, parts, and music, and any movement that will be necessary on stage. During the rehearsal period, he or she is fitted for costumes, and hairstyles and makeup are set.

The Chorus Singer performs at every show. The individual's work hours vary depending on the schedule of performances. He or she may work in the afternoon, evening and/or on weekends. If the Singer is hired for a touring company, he or she must also be prepared to travel.

There is a great deal of competition in all fields of the performing arts, including the chorus of a theatrical production. In order to make a living while waiting for a big break, many Singers take on related jobs and/or responsibilities, such as acting or dancing in productions without singing. Others may freelance as background singers on recordings, jingles or television commercials. Some may sing backup for performing artists in nightclubs, in concerts or in recording studios.

There is no job security in this type of career. The individual may land a job as a Chorus Singer for a show, go through the rehearsal period and then have the production close in previews. He or she then has to start the job search process all over again. Lack of job security does not seem to deter individuals in the field. Instead, it provides them with the drive and determination necessary for success in this type of career.

Salaries

Due to the nature of the job, it is impossible to determine the annual earnings of Chorus Singers in theatrical productions. Earnings vary greatly depending on a number of factors. These factors include the individual's talent and responsibilities as well as the amount of work they secure annually and the type of productions in which they perform.

Individuals singing in choruses in Broadway productions will have their minimum earnings set by Actors' Equity. In June 1998 the minimum weekly salary for a Chorus Singer was $1,135. Those working in other productions earn less.

Employment Prospects

Employment prospects are fair for Chorus Singers in theatrical productions. Competition for these positions is such that hundreds or even thousands of Singers can audition for the same spot.

The most difficult position to land is one in a Broadway show. Individuals have better prospects working in dinner theaters, regional theaters and stock productions. Those who can act and dance well increase their marketability.

Advancement Prospects

Advancement prospects are poor for Chorus Singers in theatrical productions. Individuals may climb the career ladder in a number of ways. The most difficult path is to become the featured Singer in a production. Another method of career advancement is finding similar work in choruses of larger, more prestigious productions.

Many Chorus Singers advance to work as solo or background Singers in television, recordings or the live performing arts.

Education and Training

There is no formal educational requirement for Chorus Singers in theatrical productions. Individuals should, however, have a broad background in all styles of singing, music and the performing arts. Some individuals are trained in music conservatories. Others go to vocal coaches and private teachers. Many Chorus Singers are self-taught.

Experience/Skills/Personality Traits

Chorus Singers need a good voice and the ability to sing in front of others. The ability to sing harmony and in all styles of music is helpful in obtaining employment. A good vocal range is necessary. Chorus Singers should also be able to read music.

Individuals should be able to deal with rejection without letting it bother them. Perseverance, drive and determination will help the Singer attain success.

Unions/Associations

Chorus Singers working in theatrical productions may be members of the American Guild of Musical Artists (AGMA) or Actors' Equity Association, commonly referred to as Equity.

As many individuals in this field work in other mediums, they may also belong to other unions. These include the American Federation of Television and Radio Artists (AFTRA) and the Screen Actors Guild (SAG).

Tips for Entry

1. When including your phone number on your resume and photograph, remember to use a number where someone can reach you easily or where a message can be left. If you are using a service or an answering machine, check your messages frequently. Directors and casting agents will not wait long for you to call back.

2. Make sure your resume and photographs are neat and professional.

3. The local union offices are full of information on openings. Visit there and become friendly with the people who run the office. You might learn about some good leads.

4. Get as much singing, acting and dancing experience as possible. Take part in school and other amateur productions to gain such experience.

5. Local community theater productions offer valuable experience.

BACKGROUND SINGER

CAREER PROFILE

Duties: Backing up the singing of other vocalists and musicians in live performances or on recordings.

Alternate Title(s): Vocalist; Studio Singer; Chorus Singer.

Salary Range: Impossible to determine due to nature of the job.

Employment Prospects: Fair.

Best Geographical Location(s) for Position: Positions may be located throughout the country; more opportunities may be located in culturally active cities.

Prerequisites:

Education or Training: No formal educational requirement; vocal training may be useful.

Experience: Singing or performing.

Special Skills and Personality Traits: Ability to sing in front of others; wide vocal range; ability to harmonize; versatility; reliability; dependability.

CAREER LADDER

```
┌─────────────────────────────┐
│     Background Singer       │
│  for Prestigious Singers    │
│       and Projects          │
│        or Soloist           │
└─────────────────────────────┘

┌─────────────────────────────┐
│     Background Singer       │
└─────────────────────────────┘

┌─────────────────────────────┐
│          Singer             │
└─────────────────────────────┘
```

Position Description

Background Singers provide background, color and harmony to the performances of other vocalists and musicians. Individuals work in varied professional and theatrical media, at live performances or in recording sessions.

Background Singers work with show groups, single performing artists, lounge acts, touring recording artists, instrumentalists or any other type of musical performers.

The Background Singer sings background vocals for the act's show. If the act tours, he or she will be required to travel and work at all performances.

The Singer attends all necessary rehearsals. He or she learns the act's repertoire. The individual learns exactly when to begin singing his or her part. Background Singers harmonize and learn to blend voices with any other Background Singer in the group.

In certain situations, the Background Singer may be required to have dancing skills. Background Singers who perform may be required to wear costumes provided by the act in order to present a uniform or complementary appearance.

Background Singers who work in theatrical productions are known as Chorus Singers. They must learn parts, attend rehearsals and sing in all productions.

Other employment opportunities for Background Singers in the performing arts are in recording sessions. These individuals are called Session or Studio Singers. Singing for recording sessions is a difficult area to break into until the Background Singer builds a reputation. The individual must be a great singer with a flexible voice and style, and must also be responsible and available when needed.

Background Singers who work in the recording industry often must perform without any rehearsal. They must be able to walk into a studio, pick up the music, go over it quickly and be ready to record without a mistake. This type of work requires the Singer to be able to harmonize with other vocalists with whom he or she has never sung.

In some cases the Background Singer must sing the part exactly as instructed. On other occasions, the individual may be asked to improvise. No matter what type of work the Background Singer is doing, he or she must be versatile. The individual who has a broad vocal range and can sing a variety of styles including show tunes, pop, R & B, country, etc. will find more opportunities for employment.

The individual singing backup for a live act may be employed on a full-time basis or may just be hired for shows when the act performs. Background Singers working in the recording industry usually freelance, although there are a small number of full-time jobs available with record companies. Many Background Singers may work for live acts and in the studio doing session work too.

Background Singers do not usually work regular hours. Those who are employed singing backup with live acts will usually rehearse in the afternoon and work in the evenings and on weekends. Individuals who are involved in theatrical productions will have similar hours. Background Singers doing studio work may have very irregular hours because studio time is often less expensive after midnight.

Salaries

Due to the nature of the job, it is impossible to determine the annual earnings of Background Singers. There are some Background Singers who earn a few hundred dollars a year. There are others who are successful and may earn up to $100,000 and more annually.

A number of factors affect the salary of the individual, including prior success and how much in demand a Background Singer is. Other factors include the amount and type of work the Singer gets and his or her geographic location.

Background Singers working with performing artists in live performances or theatrical productions are either paid by the show or employed on a weekly basis. These individuals may earn between $100 and $1,500 and more a week.

Individuals working as Background Singers in the recording industry usually, but not always, have minimum salaries set by the union. Variables in salaries for those singing backup on recordings include the length of the finished product, how many songs are recorded, what day and time the individual works, how long he or she is in the studio and how many vocalists are singing on the recording.

Employment Prospects

Employment prospects are fair for ambitious Background Singers who are versatile and talented. The best way to enter this field is either in the chorus of a small theatrical production or by singing background for performing artists who are rising to the top of their professions.

Prospects are more limited for those aspiring to work in choruses of Broadway musicals, singing backup for top acts in the performing arts and in recording studios.

Advancement Prospects

Advancement prospects are limited for Background Singers. Many individuals aspire to climb the career ladder by becoming a soloist in the theater, the performing arts and/or on recordings, although advancement in these areas is also limited.

Background Singers may have more luck advancing their career by finding similar work with more prestigious performing arts projects. They can, for example, become Background Singers with a more established act or work in a larger theatrical production.

Those individuals who can get their foot in the door singing backup on recordings, who are talented, can pick up music and learn it quickly and are reliable will be called on a more constant basis and earn more money as a result.

Education and Training

There are no formal educational requirements for a Background Singer. Some Background Singers are graduates of music conservatories. Others have degrees in music or theater arts from colleges and universities. Many individuals take private lessons from vocal coaches and private teachers or are self-taught.

Experience/Skills/Personality Traits

The most important qualification for a Background Singer is a good voice. He or she should also be comfortable singing in front of others.

Background Singers must be versatile in their craft. The ability to sing a variety of styles of music ensures more employment opportunities.

Individuals must be able to harmonize with other singers. The ability to sight-read is essential. Drive and determination and perseverance are necessary for success, as are dependability and reliability.

Unions/Associations

Background Singers are members of various unions depending on the type of work they are doing, and may belong to more than one union. Individuals singing in a theatrical job may belong to the American Guild of Musical Artists (AGMA) or Actors' Equity Association (AEA) also referred to as Equity. Those working in recording studios may belong to the American Federation of Television and Radio Artists (AFTRA). Background Singers working with live entertainment may not have to belong to a union.

Tips for Entry

1. Local performing artists may advertise for a Background Singer in a newspaper's display or classified section. Look under heading classifications of "Background Singer," "Singer," "Vocalist," "Music," "Entertainment," etc.
2. Theatrical productions may hold auditions or casting calls. Find out where these calls are advertised in your area.
3. Read the trades on a regular basis. They will provide you with information on what is happening in the industry as well as where there might be openings.
4. Visit a recording studio. Get to know people who book studio time, producers, engineers, etc. These individuals are often helpful in finding work for you. Make sure you tell them what you do and leave your card with a phone number.
5. The telephone is your lifeline. Make sure that someone always answers your phone or get a beeper or voice mail. If this is not possible, get an answering machine or use an answering service and check in frequently.

CONDUCTOR—SYMPHONY ORCHESTRA

CAREER PROFILE

Duties: Preparing the orchestra for the performance; conducting the orchestra; choosing the orchestra's repertoire.

Alternate Title(s): Musical Director.

Salary Range: $15,000 to $275,000+; individuals working in small orchestras may earn $75 to $500+ per service.

Employment Prospects: Poor.

Best Geographical Location(s) for Position: Culturally active cities will offer the most opportunities.

Prerequisites:

Education or Training: Training in conducting; musical study.

Experience: Practical experience conducting different types of orchestras and/or chamber ensembles is useful.

Special Skills and Personality Traits: Ability to communicate musical thoughts; proficiency at piano and at least one other instrument; thorough knowledge of symphonic repertoire.

CAREER LADDER

```
┌─────────────────────────────────┐
│  Conductor of Major Orchestra   │
└─────────────────────────────────┘

┌─────────────────────────────────┐
│           Conductor             │
└─────────────────────────────────┘

┌─────────────────────────────────┐
│       Assistant Conductor       │
└─────────────────────────────────┘
```

Position Description

The Conductor holds the top musical position in an orchestra. His or her main duty is preparing the orchestra for the finest performances they are capable of presenting.

The job is stressful as well as demanding. Hours are long. The Conductor must often put many hours into rehearsals before a performance. When the orchestra is on tour in cities throughout the country or the world, he or she must travel, too.

Top Conductors possess dynamic, charismatic stage personalities and immense musical talent.

A Conductor must be proficient in at least one musical instrument in addition to the piano. He or she must have the ability to sight-read. Most important, the Conductor must know how to communicate musical thoughts and ideas not only verbally during rehearsals, but also through his or her body movements while involved in a performance.

The Conductor in a symphony is responsible for choosing the orchestra's repertoire. He or she studies the orchestral scores and decides how the works will be played. The same piece of music might sound different depending on who conducts the orchestra. Each Conductor possesses his or her own style.

A good Conductor with a unique technique is often sought out to make appearances as a guest Conductor with other orchestras. As a guest Conductor, the individual's only responsibility is to prepare the program for that particular performance.

While with his or her own orchestra, the Conductor has many other responsibilities. In addition to numerous rehearsals preparing the orchestra for individual performances, the Conductor must plan an entire musical season. He or she is responsible for choosing guest soloists, artists and other conductors to "guest" or fill in with the orchestra.

The Conductor's job includes advising various section leaders and assisting them when auditions are held for section members. The Conductor of an orchestra is also called on for public and private appearances at fund-raising events on behalf of the orchestra. During summers, many leading Conductors teach at seminars, assisting aspiring Conductors to reach their goals, as well as conducting special summer concert series.

The Conductor of a symphony orchestra is usually responsible to the board of directors of that orchestra.

Salaries

Conductors' salaries vary widely. In major orchestras the Conductor may earn $275,000 or more. In smaller orchestras, the individual may earn between $75 and $500 per service. In between there are orchestras where Conductors' salaries range from $15,000 to $70,000 or more. As a rule, Conductors negotiate their salaries with the boards or management of individual orchestras.

Employment Prospects

Jobs are not plentiful for Conductors. The field is very limited. To get a job as a Conductor or even as an assistant Conductor one must have the opportunity to audition. Competition is fierce. Most Conductors work for years as musicians while studying to become Conductors.

Work possibilities for a Conductor include all varieties of orchestras. Not all positions are full-time jobs. Many successful Conductors have agents or managers who seek positions for them. Individuals may also conduct orchestras for theatrical performances or opera or ballet companies.

Advancement Prospects

The Conductor has the top position in an orchestra. Conductors can, however, advance from one type of orchestra to another. For instance, one might obtain a job as a Conductor in a community orchestra and move up to the position of assistant conductor in a larger urban orchestra. In this profession advancement occurs as a result of both great talent and a degree of luck.

Education and Training

Even with a doctoral degree in conducting, a talented musician is still not assured of a job as a Conductor. A conservatory or college degree in conducting is not usually required, but may be helpful. Training similar to that received in an educational setting is required, whether it be through seminars or private study.

Summer seminars in conducting are extremely useful to an individual aspiring to be a Conductor. Through these seminars, one can find out if he or she has the talent to be in this field. The best seminars are led by world renowned Conductors. A seminar given by a skilled Conductor can help an individual bring out his or her own personal style of conducting.

Experience/Skills/Personality Traits

Any practical experience is useful in becoming a Conductor. Conducting chamber ensembles, small community orchestras and youth orchestras gives the individual needed experience. Most conservatories and schools with strong music departments also offer assistant programs where the student is given an opportunity to conduct.

Summer seminars, such as those held in Tanglewood, Massachusetts, also offer individuals a chance to acquire conducting experience.

Unions/Associations

Conductors belong to the American Federation of Musicians (AFM) or the American Guild of Musical Artists (AGMA) depending on their situation. For example, if the Conductor plays or played an instrument, he or she probably belongs to the AFM. If the individual was a soloist, he or she might also belong to AGMA. However many Conductors do not belong to either union.

Tips for Entry

1. Try to attend a summer seminar that has world renowned Conductors associated with it. Aside from the excellent experience gained at these seminars, you can often make important contacts. If you show exceptional talent in the art of conducting, a well-known Conductor may help you and guide you up the ladder of success.

2. There are a number of orchestras that offer internships and fellowships in conducting. Check with orchestras in your area to see what programs they offer and whether you qualify.

3. Positions are advertised in many music-oriented publications, including *The International Musician.*

4. Positions may also be advertised in the newspaper classified or display section. Look under heading classifications of "Music," "Orchestra," "Symphony" or "Conductor."

SECTION MEMBER

CAREER PROFILE

Duties: Playing an instrument in an orchestra of a musical production, symphony, ballet or opera company.

Alternate Title(s):   Section Player; Musician.

Salary Range: Weekly earnings in major orchestra of musical production, symphony, ballet or opera company: $750 to $2,000+; weekly earnings in smaller or less prestigious orchestra of musical production, symphony, ballet or opera company: $300 to $750+.

Employment Prospects: Poor.

Best Geographical Location(s) for Position: Culturally active cities will offer the most opportunities.

Prerequisites:

Education or Training: No formal educational requirement; extensive musical training necessary.

Experience: Experience playing in orchestral situations.

Special Skills and Personality Traits: Musical proficiency; a love of performing in front of audience; dedication to music; perseverance.

CAREER LADDER

```
┌─────────────────────────────────────┐
│   Section Member in Larger or More   │
│      Prestigious Orchestra           │
│         or Section Leader            │
└─────────────────────────────────────┘

┌─────────────────────────────────────┐
│           Section Member             │
└─────────────────────────────────────┘

┌─────────────────────────────────────┐
│        Musician in School or         │
│       Community Orchestra            │
└─────────────────────────────────────┘
```

Position Description

Every orchestra, whether functioning as a symphony, performing for a ballet or opera company or playing as an orchestra for a music production is composed of players known as Section Members. It is the responsibility of Section Members to play the various musical instruments that make up the orchestra. As the size of every orchestra varies, there is no set number of Section Members in an orchestra.

In order to become a Section Member, an individual must be extremely talented at playing his or her musical instrument. A Section Member must audition for the job.

The Section Member auditions in front of a number of people including the conductor, section leaders, concertmaster/concertmistress, personnel director and/or orchestra manager. The individual may be called back a number of times to audition.

Every orchestra does not play the same type of music. Some orchestras play symphonic music. Others may perform classical or operatic pieces. There are orchestras that play the music for ballet, modern or other dance-related performances. Still others play the music for Broadway musicals and other musical productions.

Once an individual becomes part of an orchestra, it is his or her responsibility to become knowledgeable about the orchestral repertoire. The repertoire is the music that the orchestra performs. The Section Member must know and be able to play the music perfectly before going into a scheduled rehearsal.

During rehearsals, the Section Members practice with other members of the orchestra. It is important that the music of the various instruments blend together so that the music is pleasing to the ear.

Section Members may be required to travel to other cities in the country or to foreign lands. When individuals tour, their travel expenses are paid by the orchestra that employs them.

A Section Member with a major orchestra is usually under contract to perform a specific number of concerts and rehearsals per week. The number of performances and rehearsals will vary with the job. The individual is paid extra for any rehearsal or concert over the number specified in the contract.

The Section Member is responsible to the section leader, who determines correct bowings or phrasing in the string section, the correct breathing in the brass section, and who will play what parts.

Salaries

Salaries for Section Members vary from job to job depending on the size, budget, geographic location and type of orchestra that employs the musician. Earnings also depend on the musician's experience, seniority and reputation.

Section Members playing in a major orchestra of a symphony, ballet or opera company earn more than an individual playing in metropolitan or urban companies. The same applies to Section Members playing in musical theater productions, with those performing in Broadway musicals earning more than those playing in regional productions.

Section Members working in unionized orchestras will have their minimum salaries negotiated by the local affiliation of the American Federation of Musicians (AFM). Section Members working in major orchestras of symphonies, ballet or opera companies or Broadway productions earn between $750 and $2,000 or more weekly.

Annual salaries depend on how many weeks per year the company is in session, or how many weeks a musical production runs. In addition to salaries, Section Members receive vacation pay and other benefits. They also receive extra income for playing at recording sessions.

Section Members working in smaller orchestras of symphonies, ballet or opera companies and less prestigious musical productions usually earn considerably less than those playing in major orchestras and music productions. Individuals in these situations earn between $300 and $750 or more weekly.

Some Section Members working in orchestras of smaller companies are paid on a per service basis, that is, Section Members are paid for each rehearsal and concert in which they perform instead of by the week.

Employment Prospects

Employment prospects for Section Members are poor but not hopeless. While competition is keen, talented musicians with drive, determination and perseverance can find a job. The chances of obtaining a position as a Section Member in a major orchestra or a symphony, ballet or opera company, or Broadway musical are limited. However, prospects are brighter for those interested in joining smaller, less prestigious orchestras and musical productions.

Advancement Prospects

Advancement prospects are limited. Once a Section Member obtains a position in an orchestra of a symphony, ballet or opera company, or a musical production, he or she has a chance to advance to section leader. The individual must be very talented to advance to this position.

Another way the Section Member can advance his or her career is by joining a more prestigious orchestra. Some individuals work as a Section Member in a musical production that closes and then find a position as a Section Member in an orchestra of a symphony, ballet or opera company. As many of these orchestras have longer seasons, work is more consistent and secure.

Education and Training

There is no formal educational requirement to become a Section Member in an orchestra. However, extensive musical training is essential. This training is often acquired by studying at music conservatories, colleges and universities and through intensive private study.

Experience/Skills/Personality Traits

Section Members must have experience playing in orchestral settings. Many Section Members play in school and community orchestras and musical productions in order to obtain this experience.

Section Members are excellent musicians, proficient with their instrument. Section Members enjoy performing in front of an audience. There are many excellent musicians who cannot stand playing in front of others and do not work as Section Members.

Section Members are dedicated to their music; they must also have a great deal of drive, determination and perseverance in order to become successful in this career. The ability to deal with rejection is necessary.

Unions/Associations

Section Members working in unionized orchestras must be members of the American Federation of Musicians (AFM). The local affiliation of the AFM negotiates minimum wages and working conditions for its members.

Individuals may also be members of the American Symphony Orchestra League (ASOL) or the National Orchestral Association (NOA).

Tips for Entry

1. Openings for Section Members are listed in music-oriented trade journals and newsletters.
2. Try to locate internships sponsored by orchestra companies of symphonies, opera and ballet companies as well as colleges, universities and trade associations.
3. There are a number of summer programs that aspiring Section Members can participate in. These are also sponsored by orchestra companies of symphonies, opera and ballet companies as well as colleges, universities and trade associations. One such program is offered by the National Orchestral Association (NOA).
4. Play in as many orchestras as possible. Offer to play in school and local theatrical productions, ballets, operas and symphonies.
5. This position is obtained through application and auditions. Become the best possible musician you can. Practice and play in orchestras. Persevere. You will eventually become a Section Member.

STUDIO MUSICIAN

CAREER PROFILE

Duties: Playing instruments to back up the music and/or singing of performing artists on recordings.

Alternate Title(s): Session Player.

Salary Range: Up to $100,000+.

Employment Prospects: Fair.

Best Geographical Location(s) for Position: Culturally active cities hosting large numbers of recording studios; New York City, Los Angeles and Nashville are the recording capitals of the country.

Prerequisites:

Education or Training: No formal educational requirement; training in the form of private study helpful.

Experience: Experience playing instrument in groups, bands, orchestras, etc.

Special Skills and Personality Traits: Ability to sight-read; aggressiveness; ability to get along with others; dependability; reliability; versatility.

CAREER LADDER

```
┌─────────────────────────────────┐
│   Successful Studio Musician     │
│       Who Is in Demand           │
└─────────────────────────────────┘

┌─────────────────────────────────┐
│       Studio Musician            │
└─────────────────────────────────┘

┌─────────────────────────────────┐
│          Musician in             │
│   Group, Band or Orchestra       │
└─────────────────────────────────┘
```

Position Description

When a performing artist goes into a recording studio, he or she usually requires the services of Studio Musicians. These individuals are responsible for playing the instruments that accompany the sounds created by the singer or group.

Studio Musicians are responsible for the sounds heard on the music played on radio, records, tapes and CDs. Even if a group plays the majority of its own instruments in performance it uses Studio Musicians to augment the music on a recording.

Studio Musicians are experts in their field. Those who are flexible and can play a variety of styles and instruments find a lot of work. Studio Musicians are used on all types of recordings from pop, rock and folk to orchestral, operatic and Broadway musicals.

Studio Musicians obtain jobs in a number of ways. They may be hired by a contractor. The contractor is called when musicians are needed for a recording session by a performing artist, the artist's management team or a recording studio. The contractor is told how many Musicians are required and what instruments and style they must play.

The Contractor then calls Musicians who fit the bill. In most instances, the contractor will often call individuals he

or she knows and has worked with before. The Studio Musician then either accepts or rejects the job. If the individual rejects too many jobs, no matter what the reason, the contractor stops calling.

Studio Musicians also obtain jobs through requests by the performing artist, group members or their management team. The recording studio and record producers also recommend various Studio Musicians who have a good reputation.

Once the Studio Musician accepts a job, he or she is told exactly when and where the recording session takes place. The individual may be provided with music to learn ahead of time or may see the music for the first time when he or she arrives at the studio.

It is imperative that the Studio Musician be able to sight-read music. Recording studio time and personnel are expensive. There is usually not a great deal of time for rehearsals and mistakes are not often tolerated.

Studio Musicians do not usually have the opportunity to improvise. At the recording session, the individual is required to play what he or she is told, in the manner and style requested.

In addition to being an excellent musician, the individual must be reliable, dependable and responsible. A Studio Musician who shows up for a session late, or worse not at all, can cost the recording artist a tremendous amount of money. If it happens more than once, such behavior will cost the Studio Musician his or her professional reputation. As there is a great deal of competition in this field, the Studio Musician must also be easy to work with.

Studio Musicians are paid by the hour. Their minimum fees are negotiated by the local affiliation of the American Federation of Musicians (AFM). If individuals are in great demand, they can negotiate and receive higher fees. Successful Studio Musicians can make a good living.

As most artists do not record on a constant basis, Studio Musicians must work for a number of different performing artists. There is not a great deal of job security in this field. Some individuals back up other acts in live concerts on a freelance basis. Others stay in the studio, performing background music for television and radio commercials.

One of the most difficult aspects of being a Studio Musician is that the individual does not have an opportunity to express his particular musical creativity. As mentioned above, he or she is told what to play and how to play it. Some Studio Musicians find it difficult not to get credit for their work and to work in the shadow of other musicians.

Successful Studio Musicians have highly irregular working hours. As studio time is often less expensive in the evening, the individual may work through the night at a recording session.

Salaries

Salaries can vary greatly for Studio Musicians. Factors affecting earnings include the amount of work they get and their geographic location. Other important variables include how often the individual is requested and his or her musical reputation.

The American Federation of Musicians (AFM) sets the minimum fees Studio Musicians receive. Individuals who are in demand can negotiate for more than the minimum rates. Individuals who play more than one instrument during a session will usually receive additional earnings.

Successful, talented Studio Musicians who are in constant demand and are well known in the field earn $100,000 or more annually. Those who are not in that position earn considerably less.

Employment Prospects

Employment prospects for Studio Musicians are fair. The individual must be extremely talented and very aggressive. Contacts are important. Living in a culturally active city which hosts a large number of recording studios helps too. The majority of studio work is located in New York City, Los Angeles and Nashville, although there are studios located throughout the country.

Once a Studio Musician makes contacts or is hired by a contractor who trusts him or her, he or she is usually called continually for jobs. Individuals who can play more than one instrument, are versatile, dependable and reliable have good prospects in this field.

Advancement Prospects

Advancement prospects are poor for Studio Musicians. Individuals may climb the career ladder by being in greater demand, obtaining more jobs and earning higher fees. Other Studio Musicians advance their careers by becoming top recording musicians and performing artists in their own right.

Education and Training

There are no formal educational requirements for Studio Musicians. Individuals must, however, be highly trained on their instruments. This training is obtained through private study or musicians can be self-taught. There are also Studio Musicians who are graduates of conservatories, colleges and universities and have music degrees.

Experience/Skills/Personality Traits

Studio Musicians usually have a great deal of experience playing their instruments. Some have performed in school or local bands and orchestras. Many worked as sidemen or sidewomen with other performing artists in concerts.

Studio Musicians excel at their craft. The ability to play more than one instrument well is helpful. Most Studio Musicians are able to sight-read.

Studio Musicians must be aggressive in order to make the contacts that result in job recommendations. They must also be easy to work with, dependable, responsible and reliable.

Unions/Associations

Studio Musicians are represented by the American Federation of Musicians (AFM). This union negotiates the minimum earnings and working conditions for their members.

Tips for Entry

1. Visit recording studios. Talk to the people who work there and let them know what instrument you play and your past experience. Leave a business card with your name, instrument and phone number.
2. Join the union. There you will hear of job possibilities.
3. Make as many contacts as possible in the performing arts and recording industries. Pass your business cards out regularly.
4. Consider working as a sideman or sidewoman backing up a performing artist or group in concert. This performing experience will give you additional important contacts.

SHOW GROUP

CAREER PROFILE

Duties: Singing, dancing, playing instruments, performing comedy or theatrical skits at theaters, nightclubs, concert halls, etc.; developing and putting together creative shows.

Alternate Title(s):   Show Act; Floor Show Group.

Salary Range: $250 to $15,000+ per show.

Employment Prospects: Fair.

Best Geographical Location(s) for Position: Employment oportunities may be located throughout the country; large, culturally active cities will offer more opportunities.

Prerequisites:

Education or Training: No formal educational requirement.

Experience: Experience performing in public necessary.

Special Skills and Personality Traits: Singing, dancing, acting and/or musical skills necessary; charismatic stage presence; ability to entertain; dependability; reliability; ability to travel.

CAREER LADDER

```
┌─────────────────────────────────────┐
│      More Popular Show Group         │
│                or                    │
│   Show Group Performing at Larger,   │
│      More Prestigious Venues         │
└─────────────────────────────────────┘

┌─────────────────────────────────────┐
│             Show Group               │
└─────────────────────────────────────┘

┌─────────────────────────────────────┐
│          Night Club Band             │
│   or Singers, Dancers, Musicians,    │
│  Actors, Performing in Other Situations │
└─────────────────────────────────────┘
```

Position Description

Show Groups are performing artists who entertain in floor shows at theaters, nightclubs and concert halls. Many of these groups work in hotels and on board cruise ships. Individuals entertain patrons with a variety of forms of entertainment during their act. They may sing, dance, play instruments, perform dramatic skits and/or comedy. Many Show Groups also use extensive light shows, sound and other special effects.

Show Groups must have pizzazz in order to become and stay successful. This act does not merely stand up on stage and play instruments or sing; rather it is creatively developed to suit the setting and the audience. Show sets are planned quite extensively. Ad-libs may sound like ad-libs to the audience but they have usually been rehearsed over and over again. In some situations, the Group will hire outside talent such as choreographers or writers to develop a show for them. In others, the group's members create the show themselves.

Patrons will not come back to see the same show time after time. The Show Group must, therefore, have a number of different shows or sets prepared. Some sets may have the same middle portion but a different opening and closing. Others will be entirely different. The finale of a Show Group's act is usually planned to be rather exciting and leave the audience wanting more.

Many Show Groups have themes for their act. They may do revues of certain eras such as the roaring twenties, the musical fifties, the turbulent sixties, etc. Most Show Groups wear costumes on stage. These will reflect the type of show the act does. Members may often change costumes a number of times during each set.

Some Show Groups perform in a club for one or two nights and then go on to the next club. Other Show Groups may work in the same place for a number of weeks before moving on to another engagement. There is quite a bit of travel involved in this type of career. Individuals must like to live out of a suitcase for months at a time.

The Show Group must continually try to build up its following. One way of accomplishing this is for the club manager to like the show and book the Group back again. Another way is to advertise in the newspaper spotlighting the group's performance. Some groups who appear at the same location time after time develop a fan club of patrons who always come to their show. Show Groups also may acquire a bit of stardom on their circuit where they perform.

Show Groups must appear professional at all times. They must arrive at the correct times for their sets, dressed appropriately, and be ready to work. Members must also be available for any rehearsals or sound checks that are necessary.

Individuals in Show Groups are usually responsible to the club, theater, hall manager or owner. Working hours will be mostly at night and on weekends.

Salaries

Show Groups are usually paid a fee for each engagement or group of engagements. They may earn between $250 to $15,000 or more per show.

Variables regarding earnings include the popularity of the act, whether they work under a union contract, the number of members in the group, the type of establishment where they work, and geographic location.

Earnings of Show Group Members can vary even within groups. Some acts split the money between members equally and some do not. If the act is working under a union contract, the leader of the group earns more than the other members. Earnings also are dependent on how often the group works.

Individuals working for one or more weeks at the same location may be paid weekly or semi-weekly. They may also receive lodging and/or food as part of their fee.

Employment Prospects

Employment prospects for Show Groups are fair. Individuals may work in concert halls, theaters or clubs. They may also find employment on cruise ships and in hotels.

Groups book themselves or may work with agents. Obtaining jobs without an agent is often difficult, especially if the Group has not yet built a steady following. Show Groups may find it profitable to work with agents who have contracts with various venues around the country.

There are some Show Groups who work a specific area of the country such as the upper portion of the East Coast, the Midwest, etc. Others zig-zag around the country wherever they can find employment.

Advancement Prospects

Advancement prospects for Show Groups are determined by a number of factors, including the talent, charisma, drive and determination of the act. Luck also plays a part.

In order for Show Groups to advance their careers and increase earnings they must find similar employment at more prestigious theaters, halls and clubs. Show Groups who build a following and become more popular will be booked on a more frequent basis.

Education and Training

There are no formal educational requirements for members of Show Groups. Individuals must, however, be trained in music, dance, singing and/or acting. This training may be accomplished by attending schools, colleges, private lessons or it may be self-taught.

Experience/Skills/Personality Traits

In order to be successful, members of Show Groups should be extremely talented. There are some members of Show Groups who can sing better than the rest. Others excel at dancing, acting or playing musical instruments.

Show Groups must be exciting. Members need to have good stage presence and a lot of charisma. Show Groups must be able to entertain. Their creativity is key in putting shows together.

Individuals in groups should be articulate. They must also be dependable and reliable. Missing a show or being late will not usually be tolerated by theater club owners or managers.

Unions/Associations

Individuals in Show Groups may belong to the American Federation of Musicians (AFM), Actors' Equity and/or the American Guild of Musical Artists (AGMA). These unions negotiate minimum salaries and working conditions for their members.

Tips for Entry

1. Consider developing brochures to secure new business. Include the group's picture, name and contact phone number. It is also important to include your specialties. Does your act do musical revues? show tunes? comedy? dance? Some Groups include an insert with the names of places where they have performed.
2. Videotaped highlights of your show are also good selling pieces.
3. Have a professional photographer take photos of your group. Be sure to include the group's name and your manager or agent's name and phone number. If your group does not have a manager or agent yet, use a phone number where you know someone will be available to answer the phone most of the time.
4. Be professional. If you have an interview with a talent agent or club manager, show up on time. If you cannot get to an interview on time, managers and agents may be afraid you will also be late for your shows.
5. When you do get bookings, place an advertisement in the newspaper to let people know where you will be appearing. Ads help get your name around.
6. Remember to get commitments in writing in the form of contracts. Make sure dates, times, monies, and all other pertinent information is included. The contract must be signed by both parties to be valid.
7. Contact casinos and casino hotels; they often hire Show Groups for production shows.
8. You may want to get experience by performing in school or community productions.

COMEDIAN

Duties: Attempting to make an audience laugh by telling jokes, delivering comic lines, singing humorous songs, using movements and facial contortions.

Alternate Title(s): Comic.

Salary Range: Impossible to determine earnings due to nature of the job.

Employment Prospects: Fair.

Best Geographical Location(s) for Position: Positions located throughout the country.

Prerequisites:

Education or Training: No formal educational requirements.

Experience: Experience performing in front of audience necessary.

Special Skills and Personality Traits: Ability to see everyday occurrences in life in a humorous manner; ease in performing in front of audiences; articulation; determination; ambition.

> **Successful Comedian**

> **Comedian**

> **Aspiring Comedian**

Position Description

A Comedian is a performing artist who attempts to make an audience laugh. The individual uses many methods to amuse an audience.

The Comedian tells jokes, delivers comic lines or sings humorous songs, although some Comedians never say a word to make people laugh. These individuals perform funny renditions of dances, walks and other movements. They sometimes wear funny costumes or make facial contortions. An example of a famous Comedian who did not speak on stage was Harpo Marx of the Marx Brothers.

Comedians who use movements and facial contortions without speaking are called mimes. There are mimes, however, who are not Comedians.

Comedians have a range of employment opportunities. A stand-up Comedian works in front of a microphone in clubs, halls and on television shows and performs a monologue. He or she may tell stories, jokes or sing songs.

Some Comedians work alone. Others work in pairs with one Comedian feeding off the other's lines. One individual is known as the "straight man" (or woman). Examples of the type of Comedians who worked like this would be George Burns and Gracie Allen and Amos and Andy. One would say something in a serious fashion and the other would react in a humorous fashion.

There are Comedians who work in comedy troupes. These individuals perform in nightclubs, theaters, arenas, halls and on television. Their performance usually contains one or more comedy skits.

Up and coming Comedians must usually do what is known in the performing arts and entertainment industry as "paying their dues." Paying dues may mean different things to different entertainers. For some Comedians it might mean performing in small clubs, going on stage late at night and not being paid or being paid a minimal fee.

Many Comedians get experience performing in front of audiences at showcase comedy clubs. At these shows, they hone their skills and work on their act. This is a good way to determine the audience's reaction to new material. It is usually done solely for experience. As a rule, these individuals are not compensated at all or paid only a small fee.

Comedians may write their own material or may use the services of a comedy writer. Individuals who are starting out usually write their own for a number of reasons. To start with, purchasing material is often expensive. It can run from $100 a minute and up. Another reason is that it is often easier to perform material that comes from personal experience.

Comedians obtain work in a number of ways. They audition live for club owners, managers or promoters. They submit audition tapes to club owners, managers and promoters. People who hire Comedians often visit comedy clubs seeking out new promising talent. Many professional Comedians also seek out agents who obtain work for them.

The length of a Comedian's show varies. Some individuals perform for 10 or 15 minutes. Others have shows ranging from 30 minutes to an hour. Individuals are responsible to the club owner, manager or promoter who hires them.

Salaries

Salaries for Comedians vary greatly depending on a number of factors, including the experience and reputation of the individual and the venue in which he or she is working. Comedians just starting out work in clubs merely for the experience of performing in front of an audience. Other individuals "work for the door," meaning the performer receives a portion or the full amount of the admission paid by patrons of the club.

Comedians who have more experience may earn between $100 and $1,000 or more for a show depending on their reputation and the venue in which they are working.

Very successful Comedians who are well known earn $25,000 or more per show.

Employment Prospects

Employment prospects for Comedians are fair. There are more and more comedy clubs springing up around the country. Talented Comedians work in comedy clubs, hotels, lounges, nightclubs and on cruise ships. Individuals also perform on the college circuit. Some Comedians work as opening acts for singers, musicians and recording artists.

Advancement Prospects

Advancement prospects are determined by the Comedian's talent, ambition, determination and drive. Advancement for a Comedian is based on luck, contacts and being in the right place at the right time.

Comedians advance their careers by performing in more prestigious clubs, halls and arenas. Success for Comedians means they demand higher fees for their performances.

There are performers such as Robin Williams who begin as stand-up Comedians and go on to star in a comedy series on television and then have a successful movie career. Eddie Murphy began as a stand-up and went on to a successful television and film career.

Other paths of advancement for Comedians include writing television scripts, movie screenplays, directing or recording a successful comedy album.

Education and Training

There are no formal educational requirements for Comedians. Some individuals have high school diplomas, others have advanced degrees.

Courses, seminars and workshops in comedy writing and performing are offered throughout the country and are useful to individuals pursuing this type of career.

Experience/Skills/Personality Traits

Most professional Comedians obtain experience trying out their act in comedy clubs and talent showcases. Many Comedians say that their careers really started when they were in school acting as the class clown.

Comedians see life and most things occurring in life in a humorous manner. They must be funny people and be comfortable performing in front of audiences. The ability to write comic material is helpful.

Comedians are articulate with good communications skills. Drive, determination, perseverance and ambition are useful in attaining success. The ability to deal with rejection is useful.

Unions/Associations

Comedians may be members of a number of unions and other organizations depending on the type of work they are doing. Individuals may belong to the American Guild of Variety Artists (AGVA), the Actors' Equity Association (AEA) (better known as Equity), the American Federation of Television and Radio Artists (AFTRA) or the National Mime Association (NMA).

Tips for Entry

1. Get as much experience performing as you can. Volunteer to M.C. school and community variety shows and take part in local talent shows.
2. Find out where in your area the many nightclubs and comedy clubs are. They have talent showcases and open mike nights where new performers can try out material.
3. Practice your act and hone your skills. Do not try to get a paying job in comedy until you are ready.
4. Find an agent who specializes in booking comedy acts.
5. If you know any singers or bands that are performing, talk to them about opening for their act.
6. Watch other Comedians perform live and in different entertainment media and determine what factors—timing, content, costume, gestures—make their acts successful.
7. Videotape your act so that you can see what "works" and what doesn't work with the audience.

CAREER OPPORTUNITIES IN WRITING AND COMPOSING FOR THE PERFORMING ARTS

PLAYWRIGHT

CAREER PROFILE	CAREER LADDER

Duties: Writing scripts for comedies, tragedies, thrillers, mysteries, dramas or musicals.

Alternate Title(s):   Writer; Scriptwriter.

Salary Range: Impossible to determine due to nature of job.

Employment Prospects: Poor.

Best Geographical Location(s) for Position: Positions located throughout the country; more opportunities may be available in culturally active cities.

Prerequisites:

Education or Training: College background or degree helpful, but not required.

Experience: Experience writing useful.

Special Skills and Personality Traits: Excellent writing skills; creativity; resiliency.

```
┌─────────────────────────────────────┐
│  Playwright for Larger, More Prestigious │
│  Production or Hit Broadway Play     │
└─────────────────────────────────────┘

┌─────────────────────────────────────┐
│            Playwright                │
└─────────────────────────────────────┘

┌─────────────────────────────────────┐
│             Writer                   │
│               or                     │
│            Student                   │
└─────────────────────────────────────┘
```

Position Description

A Playwright is the individual responsible for writing the story for a theatrical production. The story is known as a script. Scripts are written in a special manner. The words that the characters speak are written next to or under each character's name. Some parts of the script explain the setting of particular scenes. The Playwright writes both dialogue and setting descriptions.

Playwrights can write a variety of scripts, such as comedies, tragedies, thrillers, mysteries, dramas or musicals. Playwrights write original shows or may adapt themes from fictional, historical or narrative sources.

When working on the script, the Playwright involves the characters in actions that have conflict, purpose and a resolution to the events in the story. The story includes the actors' and actresses' dialogue and directions for actions during the production of the script.

In some instances, a producer requests changes in the script. The Playwright is responsible for revisions. He or she might be required to be present at rehearsals to tighten up lines or make changes from producer or director notes.

Playwrights have an extremely difficult job. They must not only write a good script, but also may have to find a producer willing to finance the production.

In some instances a producer has an idea that he or she wants developed into a script. The producer and writer meet and discuss the idea. The Playwright will then try to write a suitable script.

The life of a Playwright is a solitary one. Most of their work is done alone. Once a script is developed and written, the Playwright shows the script to people until it is accepted for production. This existence leads to a great deal of stress. However, most Playwrights feel that seeing their play produced on the stage is worth the stress and strain.

Salaries

Earnings for Playwrights are difficult to assess. Some individuals never make a cent from their work while others, such as Neil Simon, earn millions.

Playwrights earn money in a number of ways. They may sell their script outright for a specific sum. Others accept option payments on their script. Options allow a producer to "own" the script for a set period of time to see if financing for the production can be obtained. If the producer does find financing, he or she will negotiate with the Playwright or his or her representative for the use of the script. The Playwright then earns money by receiving a royalty each time his or her script is performed.

Employment Prospects

Anyone who has the technical knowledge and means to write a script can write a play. To become a successful Playwright, however, one must find producers willing to use the script and produce the show.

Prospects for production range from poor to fair. It is extremely difficult to get a major producer to use the script of an unknown Playwright because there is a great deal of competition for producers even among those Playwrights who are successful. Sales do occur, however, it is difficult.

Individuals aspiring to be Playwrights have better luck submitting their scripts to experimental theaters, community theaters, college theaters and to producers who are also trying to make a name for themselves.

Another form of possible employment for an individual is to become a Playwright-in-residence for a community, school or repertory theater.

Many aspiring Playwrights have other jobs both in and out of the theatrical world. They write in their spare time until their big break comes along.

Advancement Prospects

Advancement prospects are poor for Playwrights. Career advancement can take a number of different paths. Some Playwrights advance their career by writing for television or movies. Others climb the career ladder by having their scripts produced by a major producer on Broadway.

Education and Training

A college degree gives the Playwright a background that may prove useful but will not guarantee a Playwright's script will be produced and turned into a major production. Majors that an aspiring Playwright might consider include theater, playwrighting, theater arts, acting, journalism, English, communications or liberal arts. Courses, seminars and workshops in scriptwriting, English, writing, theater, stage and acting would also be helpful.

Colleges with degrees in theater, theater arts, playwrighting and acting offer programs where the individual can write or work on a play and have it read aloud or produced within the school. This experience gives the aspiring Playwright an edge over others.

Experience/Skills/Personality Traits

Successful Playwrights have had a great deal of experience writing. Many have written and published short stories, novels, nonfiction articles and poetry before attaining success in theater.

Playwrights have excellent writing skills and a good command of the English language. They are not only able to write well, but have the ability to write dialogue. They have a story to tell and the ability to script it for the stage.

Playwrights are creative people. They can take an idea and make it exciting for others. Writing can often be lonely. Even if the Playwright is collaborating with another author, he or she will be doing a lot of work on his or her own.

Those aspiring to become Playwrights must be thick-skinned and resilient. There is a great deal of rejection in this industry. Scripts are constantly turned down. The individual must have the ability to deal with these rejections without taking them personally and getting depressed.

While there are Playwrights who do not type, typing skills and knowledge of word processing are extremely useful.

An ability to research is imperative for Playwrights. With research, an individual can learn about the language, problems and life of certain time periods that he or she develops in the course of writing.

Unions/Associations

Playwrights are often members of the Dramatist Guild (DG). The Guild offers members assistance in a number of areas including business advice, internships, opportunities to have plays read, contracts and royalties. Playwrights may also be members of the New Dramatist, a service organization for scriptwriters.

Tips for Entry

1. Write as much as you can in all areas of the writing field. The writing experience is invaluable.
2. Look for seminars, courses and workshops in scriptwriting. These will provide you with an opportunity to learn, write and be reviewed.
3. Considering entering playwrighting contests, which are often sponsored by play publishers, regional and community theaters, local and national theater organizations, and colleges.
4. Read a variety of scripts. These will give you inspiration as well as help teach you how scripts are developed.
5. See as many different productions and shows as you can. Include productions put on by school and church theater groups, colleges, community theater, regional theater, summer stock and, if possible, Broadway.
6. Join dramatists' associations and other professional groups. These organizations will help put you in touch with others interested in the same field as well as giving you an opportunity to make important contacts.
7. Search the Internet for Web sites for Playwrights. Many have helpful tips and techniques for writing scripts.

LIBRETTIST

CAREER PROFILE

Duties: Developing a story for an opera; writing the libretto.

Alternate Title(s): None.

Salary Range: $10,000 to $75,000+ per opera.

Employment Prospects: Poor.

Best Geographical Location(s) for Position: New York City is the opera capital of the country; culturally active cities worldwide hosting opera companies will offer other opportunities.

Prerequisites:

Education or Training: No educational requirement necessary; college background may be helpful.

Experience: Experience writing scripts useful.

Special Skills and Personality Traits: Creativity; understanding of opera; good writing skills; sense of the stage; ability to develop a story; perseverance; determination.

CAREER LADDER

```
┌─────────────────────────────┐
│        Librettist           │
│   for More Prestigious      │
│     Opera Production        │
└─────────────────────────────┘

┌─────────────────────────────┐
│        Librettist           │
└─────────────────────────────┘

┌─────────────────────────────┐
│    Amateur Librettist,      │
│   Playwright or Student     │
└─────────────────────────────┘
```

Position Description

Every opera has a story. The story is written in a book called the libretto, which translated means "little book." The person who writes the libretto is called a Librettist.

Operas are theatrical productions which are set to music. Most, if not all the dialogue in an opera is sung instead of spoken.

The Librettist writes the words, which are set to music by a composer. In some instances, the individual will also be the musical composer.

A Librettist may have different responsibilities depending on production requirements. Some individuals develop the entire story. They first come up with an idea for an opera, then write the dialogue, which will be sung and/or spoken by the singers in the production.

Other Librettists are given a basic story to work with. They are then responsible for writing the dialogue of the opera. These individuals are required to write the dialogue for all the singers in the production, including the principal singers who perform the lead, feature and support roles and the chorus singers.

The librettos in operas are really musical scripts, and Librettists are comparable to playwrights or screenwriters. One of the differences between a screenplay or theatrical production script and the libretto is its length. As the majority of the dialogue in an opera is sung instead of spoken, the libretto is about one-third the length of a theatrical play.

Opera has changed over the years. Once, Librettists needed to write like poets using rhyming words. Rhyme is no longer necessary in modern opera.

Another change in the technique of writing modern operas is that they no longer must be written in foreign languages. Modern operas are usually sung in the native language of the composer. If an individual is commissioned to write the libretto of an opera composed in America, he or she will write it in English.

Librettists are hired to write the libretto by either a composer or a producer. He or she may work with others including the composers, and the producers, or may work alone. Librettists write original librettos or adapt themes from other sources.

The Librettist reports either to the producer or to the composer, depending on who commissioned the piece. Librettists do not have normal business hours. They work long hours until the piece is finished. The completion of a libretto can take weeks, months or even years.

Salaries

Librettists may earn between $10,000 and $75,000 or more for writing a full-length opera. Factors affecting earnings include the nature of the specific piece that is commissioned as well as the experience, responsibilities and reputation of the writer and the funding available to produce the work.

Employment Prospects

Employment prospects are very limited for a Librettist. He or she is hired by either a producer or recommended by a composer, and these individuals prefer to work with others who have a track record or whose work they know.

The opera capital of the country is New York City, and it is one of the best cities in which to make contacts in this field. Other cities that support opera companies offer opportunities as well.

Advancement Prospects

Advancement prospects for the Librettist are limited. In order to climb the career ladder, the individual must write a libretto for a more prestigious production.

Education and Training

There are no formal educational requirements necessary to become a Librettist. A college background helps develop skills and contacts and provides experiences the individual might not otherwise have.

Classes, workshops and seminars in all areas of theater arts, opera, script writing, English, music and literature are useful.

Experience/Skills/Personality Traits

Librettists are very creative people with excellent writing skills. An understanding and knowledge of opera is a must.

The ability to develop a good story is mandatory, as is a sense of staging and drama. Librettists write dialogue that sounds good when sung. A good command of the English language is necessary.

Librettists must be very determined. It is often difficult to find a composer or producer willing to take a chance on a new talent. Perseverance is essential.

Typing, computer and word processor skills are helpful to the individual in this profession.

Unions/Associations

There is no specific trade association for Librettists. Opera America (OA), an organization of professional opera companies, is helpful for individuals interested in careers in opera.

Tips for Entry

1. Attend a variety of writers' workshops, as they provide inspiration and education as well as the opportunity to make contacts.
2. Try to meet and get to know a composer. Tell this person of your aspirations. Sometimes a successful composer will provide contacts or the chance to collaborate.
3. Find internships that allow you to work on operatic productions. They are an excellent source of contacts in the field.
4. Go to the library and review librettos from other operas.
5. Attend live operas and watch them on television. Learn as much as you can about the subject.
6. Contact Opera America, an association for professional opera companies. This group sponsors seminars and workshops.

COMPOSER—MUSICAL THEATER/OPERA

Duties: Writing the music for a theatrical musical production or opera; collaborating with lyricist, librettist and/or playwright.

Alternate Title(s):   Songwriter.

Salary Range: Impossible to determine due to the nature of the job.

Employment Prospects: Fair.

Best Geographical Location(s) for Position: Culturally active cities provide the best opportunities.

Prerequisites:

Education or Training: No formal educational requirements; musical training necessary.

Experience: Experience in writing music helpful.

Special Skills and Personality Traits: Ability to play piano and to read and write music; understanding of theater; creativity; aggressiveness; determination; ability to work under pressure; ability to work well with others.

```
┌─────────────────────────────┐
│        Composer             │
│   for More Prestigious      │
│     Musical Theater         │
│ Productions and/or Operas   │
└─────────────────────────────┘

┌─────────────────────────────┐
│ Composer—Musical Theater/Opera │
└─────────────────────────────┘

┌─────────────────────────────┐
│        Songwriter           │
│           or                │
│    Amateur Composer         │
└─────────────────────────────┘
```

Position Description

Composers in musical theater and/or opera write the music for the production. The Composer works alone or collaborates with others on the musical score of a production. The Composer also collaborates with the playwright, lyricists and librettists of the production.

The Composer for musical theater and/or opera is a special type of songwriter. Composing music for a show is not a simple job. It may take weeks, months or even years to complete. Then, as rehearsals demand, a composer turns out songs in a matter of days.

The music of a show is perhaps the one element that audiences remember most. Many songs that become standards have emerged from Broadway musicals. While not everyone has the opportunity to see a production, anyone can turn on the radio or listen to a record or tape of the music from one of these shows.

The Composer of a musical production or opera begins work when given a script and/or the libretto for the show and after consultations with the producer, director and writers, with this information, the composer gets the "feel" of the show and begins to develop ideas for the music. Tunes must fit in with the theme of the play. At times, the Composer adjusts music to fit the talents of various actors or actresses who will be singing the parts. Sometimes the Composer works directly with the lyricist; sometimes the two work independently.

The Composer may put a great deal of time into writing the music only to find out the words will not fit in properly or the director does not like it. He or she will then have to start again. In some instances, the Composer can spend months writing the music for a show which opens and closes quickly.

While composing for musical theater is difficult, it is a thrill to hear one's songs on stage and on recordings.

Salaries

Earnings vary for the Composer working in musical theater and/or opera. Some composers are paid a flat fee for their composition and some receive a percentage of the show and royalties for music and sheet music. Successful Composers earn millions of dollars for the music they write for shows that become popular.

Employment Prospects

Employment prospects are fair for Composers aspiring to work in musical theater and opera. Almost anyone who has talent can become a Composer for a musical production or opera. Talent alone does not ensure success in this field. Composers need to team up with someone to finance the project. Even after composers work with a lyricist and a playwright to come up with an idea for a production, they must then attract the interest of a producer who will fund the project. While finding a producer is difficult, it is not impossible. Composers must be very aggressive, talented, determined and driven.

Another employment prospect is locating smaller theaters and production companies that offer opportunities for new talented composers.

Composers also get involved in projects through producers who have heard their work.

Advancement Prospects

Advancement prospects are impossible to determine for a Composer. Advancement as employment, in this field, depends on the drive, determination and talent of the individual. It also depends to a great extent on having good contacts, being in the right place at the right time, and a generous amount of luck.

Composers climb the career ladder by writing music for more prestigious productions and shows that turn into hits, and receiving good notices of their work. Good reviews lead to more work.

Education and Training

There are no formal educational requirements to become a Composer. Composers are knowledgeable about music. Some are self-trained; most have a musical background, even if it has come exclusively from private teachers.

Many that are interested in pursuing a career in composing for musical theater attend colleges and universities offering majors in music and/or theater arts. Others attend music conservatories.

Experience/Skills/Personality Traits

Composers are very creative people. They see a script, look at some dialogue and develop the music that will fit the script. They can also turn their ideas into music. They then develop that music to suit the lyrics or a libretto.

A complete knowledge of music and music theory is needed. Composers must know how to read music and be able to play the piano. Composers in this field have an understanding of theater as well.

Composers must have the ability to work well with others, as they will collaborate with lyricists, librettists or other composers. They will also have to deal with directors, playwrights and others who create musicals.

Composers work under pressure. Getting a piece of music completed by a set time is often necessary. Composers have the ability to deal with rejection. Aggressiveness is helpful in making contacts and obtaining auditions with producers. In order to become successful, the Composer must usually have a great deal of drive and determination.

Unions/Associations

Composers are members of a number of associations and organizations. These include the American Society of Composers, Authors and Publishers (ASCAP), Broadcast Music, Inc. (BMI) and the Society of European Stage Authors and Composers (SESAC). These performing rights organizations pay composers royalties for public performances of their songs.

Composers might also be members of the Dramatists Guild (DG) or the American Guild of Authors and Composers (AGAC). Composers who are also musicians may be members of the American Federation of Musicians (AFM). Those who have written show tunes which are recorded may also belong to the National Academy of Recording Arts and Sciences (NARAS).

Tips for Entry

1. Attend musical productions and operas. Go to all types of productions, such as stock, amateur and regional in addition to Broadway shows and performances by major companies. Listen to the music of a variety of Broadway musicals and operas on CDs and tapes. This exposure provides you with an insight into what kind of music has been successful.
2. If you are attending school, begin writing for college productions.
3. Compose music for local community productions.
4. Find an internship in musical theater. If nothing else, you will be making good contacts in the industry.
5. Work in summer stock, dinner or regional theaters to become more familiar with the theatrical world and give you the opportunity to make additional contacts.
6. Contact opera companies to see if they offer any training, guidance or internship programs in composing.

SONGWRITER

Duties: Writing the music, lyrics or both for a song.

Alternate Title(s):   Lyricist; Composer; Writer.

Salary Range: 0 to millions.

Employment Prospects: Fair.

Best Geographical Location(s) for Position: Culturally active cities may offer more opportunities to make contacts; any location is suitable for writing songs.

Prerequisites:

Education or Training: No formal educational requirements; workshops, seminars and classes in songwriting are helpful.

Experience: Writing of lyrics, music and poetry are helpful.

Special Skills and Personality Traits: Creativity; knowledge of music and performing arts industry; ambition; drive; determination; ability to deal with rejection; persistence.

```
┌─────────────────────────────────┐
│     Successful Songwriter       │
│        with Hit Songs           │
└─────────────────────────────────┘

┌─────────────────────────────────┐
│          Songwriter             │
└─────────────────────────────────┘

┌─────────────────────────────────┐
│       Aspiring Songwriter       │
└─────────────────────────────────┘
```

Position Description

Songwriters write songs for any style of music, including pop, rock, folk, easy listening, country, and rhythm and blues. Individuals also write songs for Broadway plays, other musical productions and operas. Songwriters are also called composers, writers or lyricists.

Many Songwriters write the lyrics, the melody, or both. Some have an inspiration about a thought, a person, a feeling, and write song about it. Others have a time each day when they sit and write. Others write the music first and then attempt to fit lyrics to it. Others work on the lyrics and try to find the perfect music. In some cases, the Songwriter is talented in one area, either lyrics or music. In those cases, the Songwriter will collaborate with someone who is talented in the other area.

The goal of most Songwriters is to write a song that becomes a hit, then a standard. A standard is a song that becomes popular in all markets and stays that way for a long time. An example of a standard is the song, "Yesterday." After becoming a hit for the Beatles in the pop market, it was recorded and/or performed by many artists for other markets. The song, recorded in the 1960s, is still popular today. After

finishing a song, the Songwriter makes sure it is protected by copyrighting it. Some individuals also use another method of protecting their song: putting the finished music and words into an envelope, sealing it with wax, addressing it and sending it to themselves via registered mail. When the Songwriter receives the envelope from the post office, he or she puts it away without opening it. The official postmark is a type of protection, although industry professionals say the only real protection for a song is a copyright.

Once a song is protected, the Songwriter's next job is to find a music publisher or recording artist to use the song. The Songwriter writes query letters, makes phone calls, sends tapes or knocks on the doors of music publishers, recording acts, producers, Artists and Repertoire people, and managers in order to drum up interest.

When a Songwriter can perform his or her song for any of these people, a more effective way to seek interest is to make a demo record or cassette. Demos do not need to be elaborate but should be as professional as possible and be an accurate showcase of the song.

Once a demo tape is made, the Songwriter makes copies to send out. Each tape is labeled with the Songwriter's name, address and phone number as well as the names and times of each song on the tape.

Once a song is accepted by a music publisher, recording group, record company, or an A & R person, the Songwriter retains a lawyer to go over the details of the contract. The individual may sell the song outright or may sell the rights to it.

The Songwriter receives credit for the song on the record, tape or sheet music but does not receive a lot of attention for writing the song unless he or she also performs it.

Salaries

Salaries for Songwriters can vary greatly. There are some individuals who write songs and never sell them or the rights to the song and do not make a dime. There are others who write the music or lyrics for a Broadway musical or a stream of hit songs that top the music charts and earn millions of dollars.

Earnings for Songwriters depend on a number of factors. These include the number of songs he or she has published and/or sold, the number of times each song is played, used or performed, the general popularity of the song and the type of agreement made for each song.

There are different ways to make money from writing a song. Some Songwriters sell the song outright, some get paid royalties upon performance. If the song or songs are written for a Broadway play, the Songwriter may receive a percentage of the show as well as royalties from the recorded music and the sheet music.

Songwriters who collaborate on the music, lyrics or both will share the earnings of these songs. Splits will differ depending on the individuals and the tunes.

One of the wonderful things about writing a song is that once it is published, the Songwriter may receive royalties from it for the rest of his or her life. A hit or a successful Broadway musical can mean millions of dollars to the Songwriter in his or her lifetime.

Employment Prospects

Employment prospects for Songwriters are fair. Almost anyone with musical talent can write a song. Selling it or publishing it is the key to success in this field.

Individuals may write songs for a performing artist to sing in concert or on a record. They may also write radio or television jingles and music for plays, operas, films or television.

Some Songwriters work full time. Others work part time. A great many Songwriters are also performing artists themselves. Individuals may work for themselves or work with a collaborator. Songwriters can also work for record companies, performing artists, producers or recording groups as staff Songwriters.

Advancement Prospects

Advancement prospects are difficult to determine for Songwriters. Individuals may climb the career ladder by writing a song that turns into a hit. They also advance their career by writing the songs (words or music) for a successful Broadway musical.

Advancement depends as much on luck as it does on talent in songwriting. A song can turn into a hit at any time just as a Broadway musical can become a box office bonanza.

Education and Training

There are no formal educational requirements for Songwriters. For individuals aspiring to write the music of a song, it is helpful to study music theory, harmony, orchestration and/or ear training. Being able to play an instrument is useful. Those who aspire to write the words may benefit from courses in lyric and songwriting.

Courses, workshops, seminars and private lessons are helpful to the Songwriter for their educational value, inspiration and introductions to individuals interested in the same goals.

Experience/Skills/Personality Traits

Songwriters are creative and talented individuals who have songwriting skills. The ability to play one or more instruments is useful for those who write music.

A knowledge of music and the performing arts industry is helpful in marketing, selling and publishing songs. Ambition, drive and determination are essential to success.

Songwriters must be able to handle rejection. They may play their songs for hundreds of people before one likes it enough to record it.

As in many of the careers related to the performing arts, contacts and luck are important factors in one's success.

Unions/Associations

Songwriters may belong to a number of associations and organizations. These include Broadcast Music, Inc. (BMI), the American Society of Composers, Authors and Publishers (ASCAP) and/or the Society of European Stage Authors and Composers (SESAC). These three groups are the performing rights organizations that pay Songwriters royalties for public performances of their songs.

Individuals may also be members of the Songwriters Guild of America (SGA), the National Academy of Recording Arts and Sciences (NARAS), the Nashville Songwriters Association International (NSAI), the Country Music Association (CMA) and the Gospel Music Association (GMA).

Tips for Entry

1. Remember to protect your songs! If you don't, you might write the best song in the world and have it turn into a mega-hit with someone else's name as the writer.

Copyright your songs or send them to yourself by registered, certified mail. Copyrighting is best.

2. Avoid anyone who wants you to pay to publish your songs. Reputable publishers pay you for the right to publish your song, not the other way around.

3. Write as much as you can. Practice does not always make perfect, but it helps develop your craft.

4. Try to find songwriting courses and workshops. These offer helpful advice, tips and inspiration.

5. Join music organizations and associations. These groups will also give you helpful advice.

6. If you are interested in writing music for the theater, look for internships with theater groups, schools and theatrical organizations.

7. Learn as much as you can about every aspect of the music industry and the performing arts. Such exposure helps you become a success as a Songwriter.

8. You may have already written a hit song. Be persistent and persevere.

ARRANGER

CAREER PROFILE

Duties: Determining voice, instrument, harmonic structure, rhythm, tempo, etc., of a song; arranging songs for musical artist.

Alternate Title(s): Adapter; Transcriber; Transcripter.

Salary Range: $15,000 to $150,000+.

Employment Prospects: Fair.

Best Geographical Location(s) for Position: Culturally active cities will offer the most opportunities.

Prerequisites:

Education or Training: Training in music theory, orchestration, composition and harmony required.

Experience: Writing music; playing one or more instruments; copying charts.

Special Skills and Personality Traits: Ability to read music; possession of a good musical ear; proficiency as a musician.

CAREER LADDER

```
┌─────────────────────────────────┐
│  Arranger or Composer of Music  │
│       for Broadway show         │
│      or Successful Arranger     │
└─────────────────────────────────┘

┌─────────────────────────────────┐
│            Arranger             │
└─────────────────────────────────┘

┌─────────────────────────────────┐
│  Writer, Composer or Musician   │
└─────────────────────────────────┘
```

Position Description

An Arranger's primary function is to arrange the various parts of a musical composition. An Arranger determines voice, instrument, harmonic structure, rhythm, tempo and tone balance to achieve the desired effect.

A talented Arranger can take a song and, through creative arranging, turn it into a hit. Often, it is the Arrangers who transform songs of theatrical musicals into hits. A good Arranger is aware of current musical trends, and reworks a song to fit them.

One of the functions of the Arranger is to transcribe a musical composition for an orchestra, band, choral group or individual artist in order to adapt the tune to different musical styles.

The Arranger, in addition to working on new songs, works on new arrangements of old hits or classics. Arranged well, these songs often outsell the original versions.

The Arranger works in a variety of situations in the performing arts including recording and performing artists, theatrical productions and music services such as Muzak.

Music Arrangers also work for music publishers. They develop new and/or different ways to write and play music.

Arrangers also work in television, putting together music for skits or musical guests on comedy or variety shows.

Arrangers also work in the motion picture industry, scoring and/or arranging music for the title theme and the music used throughout the film. Job opportunities are plentiful once an Arranger is established in the field.

Most Arrangers work freelance. The more jobs they obtain, the greater their earnings. Hours for Arrangers are extremely irregular. Staff Arrangers—those who are on the payroll of recording or entertainment production teams—have a more regulated workday.

Arrangers are musicians first. Many Arrangers are performers and also write music as well as arrange it.

Salaries

Arrangers who are not yet established may earn so little from their arranging jobs that they must work other jobs to make a living. Once an Arranger starts to get more work in the field, he or she can expect to make from $15,000 to $20,000 annually.

Others who have attained more success in arranging may earn up to $35,000 annually. Salaries depend, of course, on how much work one gets. Minimum fees for Arrangers of movies, television or recordings are paid according to the scale set by the American Federation of Musicians (AFM).

In some instances, Arrangers are paid a royalty for each sale of a recording to which they have contributed, in addition to their fee.

Top Arrangers who demand and receive fees well over scale payments as well as royalties, may earn between $75,000 and $150,000 or more yearly.

Employment Prospects

It is not difficult for an Arranger to break into the profession on a small scale. Arranging music for local theatrical companies and other regional groups is an example of the work available to Arrangers. These jobs don't pay much, but they give the aspiring Arranger credits in the profession.

Arrangers have opportunities to work for the recording industry, television, theater, motion pictures, music publishers or for print-music licensees. Other opportunities include working for an individual artist or group of artists, arranging materials for recordings or concerts.

Advancement Prospects

Advancement as an Arranger depends on being hired for more prestigious projects. As the Arranger's talent is recognized, more job opportunities will materialize. Composing and arranging one's own material for a Broadway show or a top group is the professional goal of most Arrangers.

Education and Training

No formal education is required to become an Arranger. Some type of musical training—at a conservatory or college or through private study, however, is necessary.

The Arranger must be knowledgeable of and be able to implement all phases of orchestration. Either formally or informally. Arrangers study and are competent in composition, harmony and theory.

Most people aspiring to be Arrangers have studied at least one instrument, either privately, at a conservatory or through college classes, or a combination of both.

Experience/Skills/Personality Traits

Arrangers begin as musicians. They need to play at least one instrument well, and the ability to play and understand the ranges and ability of more than one is a plus.

Most Arrangers compose music either professionally or as a hobby. The Arranger must be able to read and write music. Talented Arrangers—those who become most successful—are creative individuals who can develop their ideas into musical arrangements.

A good musical ear is a necessity, as are versatility and familiarity with current musical trends.

Unions/Associations

Arrangers may belong to the American Federation of Musicians (AFM), a bargaining union that sets payment scales for arrangements.

Arrangers may also be members of the National Academy of Recording Arts and Sciences (NARAS). This organization gives out the Grammy awards each year.

Many Arrangers additionally belong to the American Society of Music Arrangers.

Tips for Entry

1. Join the American Federation of Musicians (AFM). Members receive the organization's publication, *The International Musician*. This newspaper has a number of job opportunities and openings listed in it.
2. Spend spare time around recording studios to learn about the profession and develop contacts.
3. Write as much music as you can. Write for up-and-coming groups, productions and even yourself.
4. Arrange songs and send them to publishers to see what kind of reaction you get.
5. Any type of experience in this field helps. Consider donating your talent (writing and arranging) to a local production or school or college musical. Offer to arrange for a local community theater group.

ORCHESTRATOR

CAREER PROFILE

Duties: Transposing music from one instrument or voice to another in order to accommodate a particular musician or group; writing scores for an orchestra, band, choral group, individual instrumentalist or vocalist.

Alternate Title(s): None.

Salary Range: Earnings depend on how much orchestrating is done; impossible to estimate earnings.

Employment Prospects: Fair.

Best Geographical Location(s) for Position: New York City, Los Angeles, Boston, Philadelphia, Chicago and other culturally active cities offer opportunities.

Prerequisites:

Education or Training: Training in music theory and notation.

Experience: Experience copying music and/or arranging.

Special Skills and Personality Traits: Knowledge of music theory; ability to transpose music; accuracy; reliability; neatness; understanding of music.

CAREER LADDER

```
┌─────────────────────────────────┐
│  Successful Composer or Musician │
│    or Orchestrator Who Is in     │
│        Constant Demand           │
└─────────────────────────────────┘

┌─────────────────────────────────┐
│         Orchestrator             │
└─────────────────────────────────┘

┌─────────────────────────────────┐
│       Arranger, Writer           │
│         or Musician              │
└─────────────────────────────────┘
```

Position Description

The prime function of an Orchestrator is to write the scores for an orchestra, band, choral group, individual instrumentalist or vocalist. In this position, the individual transposes the music from one instrument or voice to another to accommodate a particular musician or musical group. For example, an Orchestrator might be asked to transpose a score for a song into a key more suited to a vocalist.

When accomplishing this function, the individual does not usually alter the musical quality, harmony or rhythm. He or she just scores the composition so that it is consistent with the instrumental and vocal capabilities of the artists.

Although many Orchestrators work with the compositions of composers and arrangers, sometimes the individual is asked to work as the arranger. For instance, the Orchestrator may be asked to transcribe a composition while adapting it to another style of music. An example of this is when the individual changes the style of a pop song to an easy listening, instrumental version. This type of work often requires additional knowledge or training.

The Orchestrator may also function in the capacity of a copyist, transcribing musical parts onto staff or manuscript paper from a score written by an arranger. The individual performing as an Orchestrator can work full time or part time. He or she may be responsible for orchestrating, arranging and/or copying as part of a job.

Salaries

Salaries for Orchestrators will vary depending on how much work they do and under what conditions. Orchestrators may be paid according to fees set by the American Federation of Musicians (AFM). In certain situations, the individual may be paid by the hour. These situations include work where the Orchestrator must do adjustments, alterations, additions or takedowns of the score. Time rates are also used when page rates are not practical.

Effective March 1998 the hourly rate for Orchestrators was $38.63. Four percent vacation pay is added to these rates. These rates are set by the American Federation of Musicians (AFM), the union for Orchestrators.

Rates will vary for work done by the page depending on the type of arrangement orchestrated and what needs to be done. Rates also vary depending on whether the orchestration is done for live performances or recordings.

Employment Prospects

Employment prospects are fair for Orchestrators. They may work for orchestras, bands, choral groups, individual instrumentalists or vocalists. Individuals may work for, with, or as arrangers in the recording field. They may also do orchestration for theater, films and television.

Advancement Prospects

Advancement for an Orchestrator occurs when he or she is constantly kept busy with jobs. The professional goal of some Orchestrators is to become successful composers and musicians in their own right. They may also go on to work in the music publishing field as music editors.

Education and Training

There are no formal educational requirements for Orchestrators. The individual must know all the qualities of voice and the different instruments. He or she must know how to write scores for orchestras, bands, choral groups, etc., and how to transpose them from one instrument to another. This knowledge might be acquired at a conservatory, college or university, through private study, or may be self-taught.

Experience/Skills/Personality Traits

An Orchestrator must have a thorough knowledge of music and music theory. He or she needs the ability to transpose music and must be accurate and have neat handwriting. Reliability and dependability are essential for success in this job.

Unions/Associations

Orchestrators may belong to the American Federation of Musicians (AFM). This union sets the minimum rate scale for Orchestrators.

Tips for Entry

1. Check the classified section of newspapers in major cultural centers for listings for Orchestrators.
2. Make up flyers and business cards. Put them up in music and instrument repair shops.
3. Talk to the orchestra(s), theaters, amateur acting and music groups in your area to see if they have part- or full-time work.
4. If you are just beginning, volunteer to orchestrate for a production of a local theater group putting on a musical. It will give you valuable experience and will add strength to your resume.

COPYIST

Duties: Transcribing musical parts onto staff or manuscript paper from a score.

Alternate Title(s):   None.

Salary Range: Impossible to determine earnings due to nature of the job.

Employment Prospects: Good.

Best Geographical Location(s) for Position: Positions are located through the country; large, culturally active cities will offer the most opportunities.

Prerequisites:

Education or Training: No formal educational requirement; training in music notation and theory necessary.

Experience: Music background helpful; writing music useful.

Special Skills and Personality Traits: Knowledge of musical notation; knowledge of music theory; neatness; accuracy; dependability; reliability.

```
┌─────────────────────────────────────┐
│   Well-Known Writer, Arranger,      │
│   Composer or Orchestrator          │
│   or Copyist with Large Following   │
│   or Music Editor in                │
│   Music Publishing Company          │
└─────────────────────────────────────┘

┌─────────────────────────────────────┐
│              Copyist                 │
└─────────────────────────────────────┘

┌─────────────────────────────────────┐
│   Aspiring Writer, Arranger         │
│   or Composer                       │
└─────────────────────────────────────┘
```

Position Description

A Copyist works in theater, music and other performing arts settings. His or her job is to transcribe the musical parts of a song or arrangement onto staff or manuscript paper. The song is called the score. This score may have been done by an arranger, composer or orchestrator. The individual reproduces the various parts for instruments and/or voices. Writing sheet music is one example of the work of a Copyist.

The Copyist must have a complete knowledge of music notation as well as experience and background in music to do his or her work. Part of the job of the Copyist is to make it easier for the musician or vocalist to play or sing his or her part. It is essential that the individual copy the music in a neat and accurate manner. If not, it will be extremely difficult for the artist to perform well.

The Copyist may be asked to do a number of different things. He or she may, for example, have to copy the various parts of a score for different instruments. Or, the individual may be asked to copy a corrected or changed score.

One of the major tasks a Copyist may have to accomplish in his or her work is to write out the music on paper from hearing a record or tape. Individuals who can do this are always in demand. It is very difficult and requires a knowledge of music theory, notations, harmony, composition and orchestration.

Many individuals now also do electronic or computer music transcribing. This is often done with a computer, electronic instruments capable of MIDI (music instrument digital interface) and software. Transcribing electronically makes it easier and quicker to copy music. As a result, it can be done less expensively. Just a few years ago, equipment to do this was too expensive for most people to buy. Currently, prices on computers, software and electronic MIDI instruments have gone down making this type of transcribing and copying affordable.

The Copyist may work full time or part time. He or she may work either independently or for a music publisher. The individual is responsible to the person or organization utilizing his or her services. As the world of music and theater in any given area is small, the Copyist must do his or her work neatly, legibly, accurately and on time. Otherwise, the word will go out and he or she will not be hired again.

Salaries

Earnings for Copyists will vary depending on how much work they handle in a year and what type of work is done.

The American Federation of Musicians (AFM) sets the minimum fees and wages for Copyists. There are different fee schedules depending on the type of work the Copyist does.

Generally, Copyists are paid by the page copied in relation to the score page. Individuals are usually remunerated per page and a half produced. Rates will vary depending on the parts copied.

In some situations, the Copyist may also be paid by the hour. Rates vary depending on the hour and day the individual works. As of August 1998, the minimum hourly rates ranged from $25.80 to $51.60. Individuals must also be paid scale and one-half after the first 8 hours worked each day, and they must be compensated an additional time and one-half after working 40 hours in one week.

Employment Prospects

Employment prospects are good for Copyists. There are opportunities for individuals who can perform this function in most of the major music, theater and other cultural centers as well as some of the smaller ones.

There are many writers, composers, arrangers and orchestrators who require the services of Copyists. Individuals who can do both manual and electronic copying will be more in demand.

Many Copyists work part time while pursuing a career in music, theater and other performing arts as a composer, singer or musician.

Advancement Prospects

Advancement prospects for Copyists will vary from person to person. Many Copyists become very successful by building up a big client following. Other individuals may advance their careers by becoming well-known arrangers, composers, orchestrators or singers. There are also some Copyists who climb the career ladder by becoming music editors for music publishing companies.

Education and Training

There are no formal educational requirements necessary to become a Copyist. Individuals must, however, know how to transcribe musical parts onto manuscript paper. They should also have a complete knowledge of music notation, music theory and orchestration. This training may be obtained in high school, college, through private music lessons or may be self-taught.

Experience/Skills/Personality Traits

Individuals usually begin their careers with some type of background in music. Many are aspiring writers, composers, arrangers or orchestrators. Most individuals develop a reputation for doing good work and as a result are given references to others who need their services.

Copyists must know how to transcribe musical parts onto manuscript paper. Individuals should have the ability to do this work neatly, accurately and legibly. Copyists must be dependable and reliable always finishing work when promised.

Individuals must have a complete knowledge of music theory, notation and orchestration. A great interest in music is necessary.

Computer skills are necessary for those interested in performing electronic and/or computer copying.

Unions/Associations

Copyists may be members of the American Federation of Musicians (AFM). This union sets the minimum wages and fees that Copyists should be paid. It also sets standards for working conditions for individuals.

Copyists may also belong to the American Society of Music Copyists (ASMC). This organization provides professional guidance and support to members.

Tips for Entry

1. Send your resume and a short cover letter to music publishers. If they don't have any openings, request that they keep your resume on file.
2. Positions may be advertised in the display or classified section of the newspaper. Look under heading classifications of "Copyist," "Music" or "Music Publishing."
3. Consider taking classes or seminars in computer and electronic copying and transcribing. These classes are often offered by computer companies.
4. If you are still in school, take courses in transcribing, notation, orchestration and music theory. The better prepared you are, the more opportunities you will have.
5. Advertise your skills in the newspaper or entertainment magazine in your area.
6. If you are living near a college or university that offers majors in theater arts or music, post signs explaining your talent on the bulletin boards in the school. You may find people who need your services.

CAREER OPPORTUNITIES IN PRODUCTION, DIRECTING AND DESIGN

PRODUCER—THEATRICAL PRODUCTION

CAREER PROFILE

Duties: Finding scripts for productions; locating investors; hiring support staff; making major decisions necessary to producing plays.

Alternate Title(s):   None.

Salary Range: Impossible to determine due to nature of job.

Employment Prospects: Poor.

Best Geographical Location(s) for Position: New York City is the theatrical capital of the country; other culturally active cities may offer additional opportunities.

Prerequisites:

Education or Training: No formal educational requirement; college background or degree may be helpful.

Experience: Experience in theater and business useful.

Special Skills and Personality Traits: Good business sense; knowledge of theater industry and production; negotiation skills; articulateness; creativity; flair for putting projects together; reliability.

CAREER LADDER

```
┌─────────────────────────────┐
│   Producer of More          │
│   Prestigious Productions    │
└─────────────────────────────┘

┌─────────────────────────────┐
│  Producer—Theatrical Production │
└─────────────────────────────┘

┌─────────────────────────────┐
│   Director or Individual     │
│   Working in Some Capacity   │
│ in Theater or Businessperson │
│   Interested in Theater      │
└─────────────────────────────┘
```

Position Description

The Producer of a theatrical production is an important person in the theatrical support team. He or she is ultimately responsible for everything that happens in a production from its inception throughout its run.

Commercial Producers working in legitimate theater are self-employed. If they can find a good script and locate financing, they can put on a production.

Responsibilities and functions of the Producer will vary depending on the specific job. A Producer for a theatrical production for a not-for-profit company, for example, will have different responsibilities than a commercial Producer working with a major Broadway show. No matter what type of show he or she is working with, however, the individual will be responsible for making all the important decisions regarding the production.

A great many of the responsibilities of the Producer are related to the amount the individual knows about the theater. In some instances, the Producer may be a businessperson who is fascinated with the theater. In these cases, individuals often surround themselves with knowledgeable people who can handle specific jobs and limit their production functions to major decision making.

Without a good script, there will usually not be a successful play. One of the initial functions of the Producer is to find the right script or story. If a story has not been scripted, the Producer is responsible for finding a playwright and commissioning that person to write a script. After it is written, the producer pays the playwright for the option of using the script for a certain period of time. During this period, the producer tries to find financing for the production. If, at the end of the option period the Producer has not found financing, the Producer may drop the play altogether or negotiate another option on it.

Before a play opens, a great deal of money is spent getting it ready for the public. Scripts are written and revised, directors, choreographers, general managers, actors and actresses are hired, sets are designed and built, and rent is paid on the theater. One of the major functions of the Producer is to locate money to finance these start-up costs.

Producers seek investors or "angels" as they are often called. These people invest money in the production and hope to make a profit once the play opens. There are no set terms for investors. The Producer is responsible for developing and negotiating terms. After opening, a production may become self-sustaining and earn money or may not be well received and lose money. The Producer is responsible for locating people willing to take that financial risk. In some instances, the Producer is one of the individuals investing money in the show.

Once the Producer has secured financing, he or she locates and hires other important production personnel including the director. The Producer also hires a general manager, press agent, choreographer and set designer. The Producer may also hire a casting director or work with the director on this aspect of the production.

The Producer, the director and the casting director are responsible for choosing actors and actresses for the production. The Producer may have actors and actresses in mind to play specific parts, may sit in on auditions or may just oversee the selections made by the director and the casting director.

As previously noted, the Producer is self-employed, and works extra hard because the success or failure of a production rests on how skillfully and quickly he puts together all the elements of a theatrical production. The Producer puts in long hours and is ultimately responsible to other investors in the show.

Salaries

Producers are not usually paid a salary. Instead they make their money by either receiving a finder's fee for putting together the group of people willing to invest in the show or receive a percentage of the profits earned if the show is successful. Those who produce a hit production such as *The Lion King, Titanic* or *Cats* stand to earn millions of dollars during the show's run. Those who produce shows that don't make it commercially lose money as well as the time they have invested in getting the show ready.

Producers working for other types of theaters such as not-for-profit and community theaters may be paid a salary. These individuals may earn between $12,000 and $38,000 annually. Variables include the length of the season, location, size and prestige of the theater, and the responsibilities, duties and expertise of the individual.

Employment Prospects

Any person with either money, contacts with people who have money to invest in theatrical productions, or business skills, combined with an interest in theater, can become a Producer. However, not everyone who attempts to be a Producer will be successful.

Prospects are poor for those seeking success as a Broadway Producer, because productions on Broadway are very expensive and risky. The Producer may find success producing shows for regional theaters.

Advancement Prospects

Advancement prospects are difficult to determine for Producers. Those producing in smaller regional theaters might advance their careers by doing the same type of work at a larger, more prestigious theater. The top rung of the career ladder for Producers is having a successful show on Broadway while working on another potentially successful show.

A great deal of the success in this job is built on an individual's reputation. If he or she has a success, it enhances the opportunities to produce another show.

Education and Training

Although a college degree is not mandatory to become a Producer, it is helpful. Good choices for majors for aspiring Producers include theater arts, arts management, communications, business, English or liberal arts.

Experience/Skills/Personality Traits

Producers who have a good business sense are more likely to be successful at this job. Business, administrative and math skills are necessary. Producers must also know enough about the theater industry to be able to speak knowledgeably about advantages and risks in investing in a particular production. Negotiation skills are a must.

Producers should be extremely articulate and able to write clearly. They should be exciting, creative people who have a flair for putting projects together.

Unions/Associations

Individuals may belong to such organizations as the Producers Group (PG), the League of Off-Broadway Theatres and Producers (LOBTP) or the League of American Theatres and Producers (LAPT). These groups offer professional guidance and support to their members.

Tips for Entry

1. Become involved in your local community theater. Work in a variety of positions to get experience and learn the different aspects of theater.
2. Volunteer to do fund-raising for a community theater, arts council or not-for-profit theater group. You will be gaining valuable on-the-job training and making contacts that will help you as you advance in your career.
3. Try to locate an internship with a theatrical company. It is another way to become involved in the theatrical world.
4. Look for courses and seminars in theater, business and fund-raising. These will help you in your quest to become a producer.
5. Consider any job in the theater. The more contacts you make and experience you have, the better qualified you become.

DIRECTOR—THEATRICAL PRODUCTION

Duties: Visually interpreting the script; guiding the actors and actresses in their speech patterns and physical movement; coordinating all creative aspects of production; preparing the show for opening.

Alternate Title(s): None.

Salary Range: Up to $200,000+.

Employment Prospects: Poor.

Best Geographical Location(s) for Position: Positions are located throughout the country; culturally active cities may have more opportunities.

Prerequisites:

Education or Training: Four-year college degree helpful but not always necessary.

Experience: Experience working in theater in some capacity from actor to assistant director to stage manager or director.

Special Skills and Personality Traits: Knowledge of theater and stage; creativity; ability to coordinate; detail oriented; patience.

```
┌─────────────────────────────┐
│          Director           │
│     for More Prestigious     │
│         Theatrical          │
│         Productions         │
└─────────────────────────────┘

┌─────────────────────────────┐
│  Director—Theatrical Productions  │
└─────────────────────────────┘

┌─────────────────────────────┐
│     Assistant Director,      │
│     Stage Director or        │
│       Actor/Actress          │
└─────────────────────────────┘
```

Position Description

The Director in a theatrical production is the individual who brings the play to life. He or she takes the words in the script that the playwright has written and helps the actors interpret them visually for the audience. A good Director adds the spark to a production that turns it into a mega-hit. The Director's job can be compared to that of a sports coach. The coach tells the team members what to do and how to do it. The Director does the same sort of thing with actors and actresses. He or she does a combination of guiding, teaching and telling actors and actresses how their lines should be spoken, where they should stand on the stage and the movements they should make.

The Director has input with virtually every creative aspect of the play. He or she will work with the producer and the casting director, if there is one, to choose actors and actresses whose talents will enable the Director's vision of the play to be realized.

The Director coordinates all aspects of the production, from the set, costume and lighting designers to soundmen, production hands and even ushers to give the play a unified look.

The Director works very hard during rehearsals, determining what lines, actions and moves best convey his vision of the script. A Director spends many hours in pre-production, getting the show ready for opening night.

Once the play is rehearsed and ready, it opens. After the opening, the Director's job is essentially done. He or she moves on to another project, although he or she may be called back to rehearse new cast members if the play runs for an extended period.

Salaries

Due to the nature of job, it is impossible to determine the earnings of Directors. They may negotiate a salary for weeks worked or may be offered a set fee to direct a particular show. Some Directors negotiate a deal where they are paid a fee plus royalties derived from each production.

This is not the type of job where individuals are guaranteed work year round. Once the Director has brought the production to its opening, he or she looks for another job. A successful director who is in demand may obtain employment directing the same play in another location or may quickly be hired to direct an entirely new production. Directors are also hired to work for theaters or production companies for an entire season. These Directors are paid a salary.

Aspiring Directors may not earn any income in their profession all year. Others may work consistently. Some Directors whose productions become hits are able to negotiate not only a salary but also a royalty for each production or seat sold. They can earn $200,000 or more a year. Average earnings for Directors can range between $18,000 and $75,000 or more annually with the majority of individuals earning between $20,000 and $32,000 for their directing efforts in one year.

Employment Prospects

Employment prospects for Directors are poor. A lot of people want to be Directors and competition is keen.

Employment is dependent on a number of factors including talent and experience of the individual. Other important factors include contacts an individual has developed, being at the right place at the right time and luck.

Advancement Prospects

Advancement prospects are poor. Most producers would rather hire a known Director or one who has some experience than one who has little background in the field.

Directors advance their careers in a number of ways, by directing more prestigious productions or a show in a more prestigious theater. Individuals might also direct a production which turns into a hit. As success follows success, the Director is usually in greater demand.

Education and Training

While it is not absolutely necessary to have a college degree to become a Director, it is helpful. It gives the Director a certain amount of credibility and better prepares the Director to face both the competition in the industry, and the opportunities that open up.

There are some Directors who have no college background and others who hold bachelor's and master's degrees. Good choices for majors include theater arts, acting and arts management.

In addition to the college education, many Directors get their training watching other Directors do their job.

Experience/Skills/Personality Traits

Directors have some type of theater experience, although there is no one career path. Many individuals work as assistant directors. Others begin their careers as actors, actresses, stage directors or managers.

Directors must be creative people. They need to have the ability to guide actors and actresses in their speech and physical movements. A knowledge of theater, staging and acting is imperative. Knowing stage jargon is also necessary.

Directors must be good at coordinating the various aspects of preparing a production, since much of their job is spent doing that. They need to be detail oriented and have the ability to manage many aspects of a production at one time.

Directors need to have a lot of patience as they must constantly explain their creative vision to those interpreting it. They must also be good working with people.

Unions/Associations

Directors in the theater may be members of the Society of Stage Directors and Choreographers (SSDC). This organization brings together individuals interested in the same field as well as setting guidelines and rules for negotiations and working conditions.

Depending on the specific job, individuals may also be members of Actors' Equity Association and the American Guild of Musical Artists (AGMA).

Tips for Entry

1. Make as many contacts in the theater as possible. You cannot audition to be a Director. Networking is required in this field.
2. When you land jobs, do your best and make a good impression on your co-workers. The theater world is small and a good reputation will follow you everywhere.
3. Get involved with school plays and other theatrical productions.
4. Volunteer to work in your local community theater as an assistant to the director, if possible. If not, work in the theater in any capacity.
5. Try to find an internship working in the theater. Contact schools, colleges, arts councils, theater groups, organizations and associations about availabilities. Once you locate an internship, get involved. Do more than you are asked to and learn as much as possible.
6. Many summer theaters offer part-time or summer jobs to students learning their craft. Send your resume with a short cover letter asking for an interview.

PRODUCTION ASSISTANT

CAREER PROFILE

Duties: Handling production-related secretarial duties; typing production notes and casting lists; typing, duplicating and distributing script revisions.

Alternate Title(s): Production Secretary.

Salary Range: $250 to $550+ weekly.

Employment Prospects: Fair.

Best Geographical Location(s) for Position: Positions are located throughout the country. More opportunities are available in culturally active cities.

Prerequisites:

Education or Training: Minimum of high school diploma; college background or degree helpful to advance in the field.

Experience: Secretarial experience useful but not always necessary.

Special Skills and Personality Traits: Knowledge of theater industry; typing skills; shorthand or speed writing skills; ability to communicate; reliability; organized.

CAREER LADDER

```
+-----------------------------------------------+
|         Production Assistant                  |
|   for More Prestigious Production             |
|   for Larger Number of Productions            |
|   or Various Positions in Production,         |
|     Directing, Writing or Acting              |
+-----------------------------------------------+

+-----------------------------------------------+
|         Production Assistant                  |
+-----------------------------------------------+

+-----------------------------------------------+
|    Entry Level Assistant, Student, or         |
|  Assistant or Secretary in Other Field        |
+-----------------------------------------------+
```

Position Description

A Production Assistant working in theater is responsible for handling production-related secretarial duties. While a Production Assistant works for the producer, the immediate supervisor is usually the director. The Production Assistant has varied responsibilities and functions depending on the specific production or job.

The Production Assistant is in a unique position to learn about all aspects of the theater. A Production Assistant is involved in every aspect of a production from its inception until the show opens and beyond.

During rehearsals, changes occur quite frequently in scripts. Sometimes, the playwright or director does not like the way certain words or phrases sound. In other situations, there may be creative changes. The Production Assistant takes every change that is made and revises the script. In addition, the Production Assistant may be required to type everything from cast lists to contracts. He or she will also be responsible for typing production notes.

After the Production Assistant types and revises the script, the individual makes duplicate copies and distributes them to the cast and crew. Every rehearsal means additional changes and more revisions. Sometimes the changes don't work and the director decides to go back to the previous script and the entire process starts again. Nothing is final until the production opens.

The Production Assistant is responsible for typing the blocking directions and cues for the production into the director's book, a task that may also be done by the stage manager. Blocking, in the theater, refers to the places where actors and actresses are to stand at various times in the production. It also indicates where props and other equipment are located. The director's book is a record of everything that occurs in a production. It is used by the stage manager to adjust props and the lighting manager to ensure proper lighting. It is used to produce revivals of the same play.

The Production Assistant helps the director in every way possible to get the show ready. Other duties besides typing include making or answering phone calls, contacting individuals who are needed for the production and taking notes.

Part of the job entails acting as a sounding board for the director as he or she comes up with possibilities for creative changes. In some instances, the Production Assistant may be asked to offer suggestions.

The Production Assistant is likely to work irregular hours to ensure that script changes are ready for the next rehearsal. The Production Assistant may work during the day, evening or at night.

Salaries

Salaries for Production Assistants vary greatly depending on the number of weeks a year the individual works, the specific production and experience and responsibilities.

Weekly earnings can range from $250 to $550 or more. Those who work steadily can earn from $13,000 to $28,000 annually.

Employment Prospects

Employment prospects are fair for Production Assistants. Individuals may work for various types of theatrical productions. While jobs are located throughout the country, there are many more opportunities available in culturally active cities.

Individuals who have made a lot of contacts in the industry increase their chances of employment.

Advancement Prospects

Advancement prospects for Production Assistants are determined by the skills and drive of the individual. Luck and being in the right place at the right time are also helpful.

Many individuals take jobs as Production Assistants as entry level opportunities in theater and move up the career ladder depending on specific interests. Production Assistants have advanced to positions of directors, stage managers, playwrights and producers.

Another path a Production Assistant takes up the career ladder is to locate a similar position in a television station or film production company. These jobs may offer steadier work resulting in increased earnings.

Education and Training

There are no formal education requirements for Production Assistants, although individuals should have a minimum of a high school diploma. Typing and other secretarial skills are essential and can be learned in high school, by attending a secretarial school or through work experience.

A college degree or background can be very valuable to anyone using this position as an entree into theater and who wants to advance from there.

Majors to consider depend on the specific area the individual wants to specialize in. Production Assistants may have degrees in theater arts, drama or arts management.

Experience/Skills/Personality Traits

This is an entry level position. Contacts in the industry are helpful. A knowledge of theater is useful.

Good typing and word processing skills are essential. The Production Assistant should be able to type quickly and accurately. Good spelling is also necessary. Shorthand or speed writing skills are also important in order to be able to take down what is said rapidly. A Production Assistant should be familiar with other office equipment including dictating machines, photocopy machines and faxes.

The Production Assistant should have good verbal and written communications skills. The ability to speak well on the phone is necessary. A good memory is essential.

Production Assistants must have the ability to get along well with others. They must be personable, compassionate and flexible. Part of the job includes delivering the new scripts and changes to each actor and actress as well as other cast and crew members. In some instances, when a script is changed, an actor or actress may personally lose what they consider to be important lines. The Production Assistant has the ability to deal with frustrating situations like this without getting upset.

Individuals must be dependable and reliable. They should also be organized and have the ability to handle many details at once.

Unions/Associations

Production Assistants in unionized theaters are members of the International Association of Theatrical Stage Employees (IATSE). This organization negotiates minimum wages and working conditions.

Individuals working in non-unionized theaters are not members.

Tips for Entry

1. Learn basic office skills. Practice typing, word processing and shorthand until you work quickly and accurately.
2. Volunteer to act as the Production Assistant for your school or local community theater production.
3. Use any contacts you have in theater to secure jobs.
4. Try to find an internship in any phase of theater production. This will give you valuable experience and help you make more contacts.

STAGE MANAGER

CAREER PROFILE

Duties: Acting as the director's representative; scheduling rehearsals; updating scripts; blocking shows; calling cues; handling paperwork.

Alternate Title(s):   Production Stage Manager; Assistant Stage Manager.

Salary Range: $350 to $1,865+ per week.

Employment Prospects: Fair.

Best Geographical Location(s) for Position: Culturally active cities offer more job possibilities.

Prerequisites:

Education or Training: No formal educational requirement; college degree useful; practical training necessary.

Experience: Experience working in theater required.

Special Skills and Personality Traits: Knowledge of all aspects of theater; personableness; compassion; diplomacy; calmness; detail oriented.

CAREER LADDER

```
┌─────────────────────────────────┐
│        Stage Manager for        │
│   More Prestigious Production    │
│           or Director           │
└─────────────────────────────────┘

┌─────────────────────────────────┐
│          Stage Manager          │
└─────────────────────────────────┘

┌─────────────────────────────────┐
│     Assistant Stage Manager     │
└─────────────────────────────────┘
```

Position Description

The Stage Manager is the individual who takes over the responsibilities of the director when his or her job is completed. The Stage Manager's job usually formally begins two weeks before the production's first rehearsal. His or her main function will then be acting as the representative of the director.

Every production has a Stage Manager. Very elaborate shows may also have assistants. As a Stage Manager, the individual acts as a liaison between the cast and crew, and the management. He or she also coordinates what occurs on stage.

The Stage Manager has many responsibilities. The individual may attend auditions to provide input into casting decisions. He or she will also keep records of the actors, actresses, singers and dancers who have auditioned.

The Stage Manager is required to schedule and plan rehearsals and make sure that actors and actresses are there on time. To do this the individual may prepare a written schedule or might instead verbally inform cast members. The Stage Manager is required to be present at rehearsals.

The individual is responsible for updating the script as changes are made and then making sure that cast members are given the new script.

Another of the functions of the Stage Manager is to block the show. This means he or she will verbally tell or physically tape the stage to illustrate where actors or actresses should be at certain times and where props and scenery should be placed.

Part of the responsibility of the Stage Manager is making sure that the show goes on the way the director intended it to. If, during rehearsals or the actual production, the Stage Manager sees that an actor or actress is performing his or her part differently than agreed upon, he or she will talk to the individual to get things back on track.

The Stage Manager also must be on hand to make sure that things are running smoothly among the cast and crew members. He or she may be required to settle both professional and personal disputes.

The Stage Manager has a great many responsibilities during a performance. The individual does what is referred to as "calling the show." He or she will call cues for the sound, lighting and scenic technicians. If actors or actresses need a line, he or she will give it to them. The Stage Manager will make absolutely sure that everything goes according to the script and schedule.

During the performance, the Stage Manager is responsible for everything that goes on backstage. He or she will make sure that everybody does their job and does it properly.

After each performance the Stage Manager will write a report regarding the show. In this report, he or she will document activities and discuss things that went well, things that went wrong and other occurrences. Any accidents or injuries must also be reported. The Stage Manager's job ends about one week after closing. In the time period between the last performance and the final day of work, he or she will do all required paperwork, get necessary files in order and load the show out of the theater.

The Stage Manager works many hours in his or her job. When finished, the only people who know if the Stage Manager performed well or not are the cast, crew and director.

Salaries

Salaries can vary greatly for Stage Managers depending on a number of variables. These include the individual's experience, responsibilities and reputation. Salaries are also dependent on the type of theater and production the individual is working for. Minimum earnings are higher for those involved in Broadway musicals than those working in summer stock.

For example, a Stage Manager working in a Broadway musical can earn a minimum salary of approximately $1,865 a week. Stage Managers who work in summer stock will earn minimums of approximately $500 to $600 weekly. Individuals employed by off Broadway shows or by nonunionized theater productions may work for $350 weekly or less depending on how much they want the job.

It is important to note that if a Stage Manager is in demand or highly regarded in the profession, the individual can earn a great deal more. The figures given are just minimums.

Employment Prospects

Employment prospects are fair for Stage Managers who are willing to work in a variety of theaters in various locations. These venues might include summer stock, regional theaters, off Broadway and off-off Broadway. Prospects become more difficult for individuals when they aspire to work as Stage Managers in Broadway productions.

While New York City is the major theatrical capital, there is so much competition that it may be easier to find work in other culturally active cities.

Advancement Prospects

Advancement prospects are good for Stage Managers who are proficient at their jobs. Individuals may take a number of paths to advancement.

Stage Managers who want to stay in their profession may advance their careers by obtaining similar jobs with more prestigious productions. They may also find a steady stream of employment possibilities resulting in higher annual earnings.

Another method for Stage Managers to climb the career ladder is by becoming a director. There are also a number of former Stage Managers, who, after obtaining experience, went on to become producers.

Education and Training

There is no formal educational requirement for a Stage Manager. A college degree is not mandatory, but may be helpful in the individual's career. A degree offers a basic background, opportunities for experience and making contacts and a degree of credibility. Good choices for majors include theater arts or arts management.

Training, in the form of practical experience, is necessary to get a job and be successful at it. This experience can be obtained by working as an intern, assistant or in almost any area of the theater. School, summer stock and regional theaters are all good training grounds.

Experience/Skills/Personality Traits

Stage Managers must have a great deal of experience working in the theater. Individuals may gain this by working in various capacities. Most, but not all, have acted as assistant Stage Managers before obtaining their first position.

Stage Managers must know at least a little about everything in the theater. They must know something about acting, directing, set design, lighting and costuming. The more knowledgeable the Stage Manager is, the more successful he or she will be in the job.

Individuals must be personable and get along well with people. In many circumstances, the Stage Manager must deal with others who are tense, worried and/or nervous about openings. The individual must be compassionate and have the ability to calm people down and make them feel comfortable. He or she must be diplomatic in all situations.

The Stage Manager should be detail oriented and have the ability to work on many projects at once. He or she should be able to remain calm in the eye of a storm.

Unions/Associations

Stage Managers working in unionized settings must belong to Actors' Equity. This union negotiates minimum salaries and working conditions for their members.

Tips for Entry

1. Learn as much as you can about all aspects of theater. This knowledge will be useful in obtaining a job and being successful.
2. Look for internships to obtain on-the-job training.
3. Try to locate a job in summer stock. It doesn't matter what type of position you get. The experience will help you learn as well as provide an opportunity to make important contacts that may help you during the rest of your career.
4. Become involved in your school's theater production.
5. Volunteer at your local community theater. This is another way to learn more about the theater industry.

CASTING DIRECTOR

CAREER PROFILE

Duties: Casting the roles in a theatrical production; auditioning actors and actresses.

Alternate Title(s):   Casting Agent.

Salary Range: Impossible to determine earnings due to nature of the job.

Employment Prospects: Poor.

Best Geographical Location(s) for Position: Culturally active cities offer the most opportunities.

Prerequisites:

   Education or Training: No formal educational requirement.

   Experience: Experience working in theater required.

   Special Skills and Personality Traits: Ability to match an actor or actress with the right part; organized; detail oriented; knowledge of theater industry; communication skills.

CAREER LADDER

```
┌─────────────────────────────────────┐
│         Casting Director            │
│  for More Prestigious Productions   │
└─────────────────────────────────────┘

┌─────────────────────────────────────┐
│         Casting Director            │
└─────────────────────────────────────┘

┌─────────────────────────────────────┐
│   Apprentice to Casting Director    │
│                or                   │
│     Assistant Casting Director      │
└─────────────────────────────────────┘
```

Position Description

The Casting Director is responsible for casting actors for the roles in a theatrical production. Good casting can mean the difference between a great production and a mediocre one. Without the proper characters acting out the script, the power of a play can be diminished.

The Casting Director works with the producer, the playwright and the director of the production. He or she first reads the script. In this way, the Casting Director determines the characters that are needed for the play.

Once the Casting Director finds actors and actresses to fill the parts, he or she brings them to the attention of the producer, director and playwright who then make the final decisions.

In order to begin casting, the Casting Director must understand the character's personality and physical appearance. The Casting Director chooses actors and actresses who look like the characters the playwright describes and who can make particular characters come to life on stage.

Depending on the situation, the Casting Director is responsible for creating, mailing or delivering display or classified advertisements for newspapers or the trades announcing casting requirements for specific productions.

The Casting Director keeps records on file cards or in a computers of all talent who audition as well as actors and actresses who merely sent in resumes with photographs. This information includes an actress's or actor's name, address, phone number, agent affiliation and professional acting credits. It also contains data about the individual's hair and eye color, height, weight, age, personality type and skills. If the actor auditioned or was interviewed, the date is indicated with any comments made by the Casting Director. This information is useful when searching for a certain type of face, look, personality or talent.

The Casting Director is responsible for arranging preliminary casting calls or auditions. Casting calls are events where many actors and actresses come in with their resumes and photographs (commonly known in the business as 8 x 10 glossies). During a preliminary casting call, the Casting Director or an assistant eliminates those who do not fit the look or talent type of the specific role. Actors and actresses are found not to be suitable for a particular part for any number of reasons, from being the wrong age, to having the wrong hair color, body type or even accent, or because they do not sing or dance as well as they can act.

The Casting Directors or an assistant takes resumes and photos from all applicants. After reviewing them and deciding who he or she wants to see, the Casting Director or the assistant is responsible for calling the actors, actresses or their talent agents back for another audition or interview.

In some cases, the Casting Director has a specific actor in mind to play a part, and approaches that actor or his agent.

Sometimes, established actors hear that productions are being cast and have their agents call the Casting Director to inquire about the possibility of a role. If these individuals are right for a part, they often get the job without auditioning for it.

Sometimes, the Casting Director holds open auditions. He or she will advertise the parts that are available for a production and the types of actors or actresses needed to fill each part. The Casting Directors may see hundreds or even thousands of people in this manner.

The Casting Director may be hired to handle the casting for just the major stars of the show or for all the parts. If the production also has a road company production, the Casting Director may be required to fill the parts in those shows too.

Casting Directors are responsible to the production company or theater that hires them. In some instances, Casting Directors may handle the casting requirements for television, film and commercials as well as for theatrical productions.

Salaries

Salaries for Casting Directors vary depending on the specific production to be cast as well as the Casting Director's experience and reputation in the field. Earnings also depend on whether the Casting Director is on staff at a theater or is acting as a consultant.

Casting Directors working on a consulting basis are paid a fee for their services ranging from $2,500 to $25,000 or more per production. Some Casting Directors receive a fee plus royalties on the show and earn $150,000 or more per year.

Employment Prospects

Employment prospects are poor for Casting Directors seeking consulting positions. Every production does not employ a Casting Director, because casting sometimes falls on the shoulders of the director, the producer, or both. Usually only larger, more prestigious productions use Casting Directors. However, individuals aspiring to have a career in this field can join the production staffs of regional or dinner theaters and concentrate on casting the shows.

Advancement Prospects

Casting Directors advance in their field by their own drive, determination, contacts and reputation. Individuals take a number of different paths to climb the career ladder, by finding similar positions in a greater number of productions, or by becoming Casting Director of more prestigious productions. Still other Casting Directors advance their careers by becoming directors.

In some cases individuals find similar jobs casting parts for television or films.

Education and Training

There is no formal education requirement for Casting Directors. While it is not necessary to have a college degree, it is helpful. Good choices for majors include theater arts, drama and arts management. A degree gives the individual a certain amount of credibility while the education offers experiences he or she may not otherwise have. There are some Casting Directors who have no college background at all.

Many individuals obtain training by assisting other Casting Directors, directors and producers who handle the job.

Experience/Skills/Personality Traits

Casting Directors usually need some experience working in theater, working as assistant casting directors, apprentices, stage managers or assistant directors. There are also Casting Directors who worked as actors or actresses before landing their job. There is no one way to obtain experience.

Casting Directors must have good communication skills and must be good listeners. In some situations, the producer or director may tell the Casting Director what type of actor or actress he or she is looking for. The Casting Director must have the ability to match up the actor or actress with the right part and the contacts to be able to supply the right actors.

A knowledge of the workings of theater—stage and acting—is imperative. Casting Directors are very organized and detail oriented. They have the ability to do many things at one time. A good memory is essential.

Unions/Associations

Casting Directors may belong to the Casting Society of America, a trade association for those working in the field. Trade associations such as this one often hold seminars, conferences and offer valuable information for individuals in the field.

Tips for Entry

1. Volunteer to cast a school or community theater production.
2. Find an apprenticeship or intern program in this field. It will offer an excellent way to obtain on-the-job training and important contacts.
3. Get involved in your community theater. Learn all you can about the industry.
4. Consider a job as an assistant at an advertising agency handling accounts that produce television commercials, then get involved in learning the casting process for those commercials.
5. Attend casting calls. Facing the rejection that most actors routinely face gives you valuable insight into the demands of the job of Casting Director.

ASSISTANT CASTING DIRECTOR

CAREER PROFILE

Duties: Helping the casting director cast parts in a theatrical production; clerical work; running preliminary auditions; keeping records of auditioning talent.

Alternate Title(s):   Assistant Casting Agent.

Salary Range: $15,000 to $35,000+ annually.

Employment Prospects: Fair.

Best Geographical Location(s) for Position: Culturally active cities will offer the most opportunities.

Prerequisites:

Education or Training: No formal educational requirement; college degree in theater arts, drama or arts management helpful.

Experience: Experience working in theater useful but not always necessary.

Special Skills and Personality Traits: Energetic; enthusiastic; organized; detail oriented; knowledge of theater industry; communication skills; ability to perform clerical tasks.

CAREER LADDER

```
┌─────────────────────────────────────┐
│          Casting Director           │
└─────────────────────────────────────┘

┌─────────────────────────────────────┐
│      Assistant Casting Director      │
└─────────────────────────────────────┘

┌─────────────────────────────────────┐
│   Apprentice to Casting Director,    │
│    Intern, Clerk or Secretary in     │
│          Casting Office              │
└─────────────────────────────────────┘
```

Position Description

The Assistant Casting Director works with the casting director selecting the talent for theatrical productions, for movies, television shows and commercials.

Responsibilities vary for people in this position depending on the experience of the Assistant as well as the specific casting director the individual is working with.

Assistant Casting Directors with little experience are often responsible for clerical duties. They are required to write and type memos and letters to talent agents and managers regarding casting for specific parts. They phone agents about casting calls and auditions or to arrange to have talent come back for additional interviews.

The Assistant Casting Director attends casting calls and auditions with the casting director. Being present at the auditions helps the Assistant learn more about choosing the correct actor or actress for a particular part. The Assistant usually is asked his or her opinion of a particular actor or actress's work.

The Assistant is required to keep records on all the talent who audition for parts. The individual is also required to keep records of actors and actresses who send resumes with pho-

tographs to the casting director. The Assistant keeps information such as the actor's name, address, phone number, agent affiliation and professional acting credits on file cards or enters the data into a computer. The data includes the individual's hair color, eye color, height, weight, age, personality type and skills. If the talent was auditioned or interviewed, the date is indicated with any comments offered by the casting director. This information is useful when the casting director is searching for a certain look in an actor or actress.

In some instances, the Assistant is responsible for creating display or classified advertisements for newspapers or the trades announcing casting requirements for specific parts. Sometimes the Assistant is required to mail or deliver finished advertisements.

The Casting Assistant is responsible for arranging or running preliminary casting calls or auditions where many actors and actresses come with their resumes and photographs (commonly known in the business as 8 x 10 glossies). During a preliminary casting call, the Assistant is required by the casting director to eliminate people who do not fit the part to be filled. For example, the casting director will instruct the Assistant to look for actresses who can sing and dance. When the Assistant talks to potential actresses or reviews their resume, he or she will eliminate those who do not sing and dance.

The Assistant takes resumes and photos from all suitable applicants and gives them to the casting director. After the casting director reviews them and decides who he or she wants to see, the Assistant is responsible for calling the actors, actresses or talent agents representing these people back for another audition or interview.

When the casting director finds an actor or actress that looks promising for a part, the Assistant is responsible for calling or notifying the producer, the director and the playwright. He or she will also be responsible for setting up further auditions for the people involved.

Once the talent is chosen, the Assistant Casting Director is responsible for booking it through the proper agent or agency. The Assistant is required to type contracts. He or she may be responsible for delivering the finished contracts and any other material to the talent or the talent agent and then getting the contracts signed and returned. If the actors or actresses are union employees, the Assistant obtains union membership numbers and takes care of any other union-related business.

The Assistant Casting Director handles a great deal of telephone work for the casting director. He or she is required to make calls on behalf of the individual as well as answer the phone. The individual is required to buffer calls from talent agents, directors and producers when the casting director has not decided on the casting of a particular project.

The Assistant Casting Director is responsible to the casting director and usually works long hours. The Assistant regularly attends new and nonunion productions to report on new talent.

Salaries

Salaries for Assistant Casting Directors can range from $15,000 to $35,000 or more annually depending on a number of factors, such as his or her responsibilities, experience and geographic location. Earnings also depend on whether the Assistant Casting Director is on staff at a theater or working as a consultant.

Assistant Casting Directors working in New York City and Los Angeles earn more than individuals employed in other cities.

Employment Prospects

Employment prospects are fair for Assistant Casting Directors. While every production does not employ a casting director, Assistants land jobs with those who are handling the casting responsibilities in those productions.

Assistant Casting Directors work for consultants or on the staffs of regional or dinner theaters. More opportunities for Assistant Casting Directors are available in major cultural centers.

Advancement Prospects

Assistant Casting Directors may have difficulty finding their first job and from there, their careers advance along a number of different paths. Some Assistant Casting Directors move up the

career ladder by becoming casting directors in theater. Others become casting consultants for either theater, television or film. In order to advance, the Assistant must have a great deal of determination, drive and ambition.

Education and Training

There are no formal educational requirements for Assistant Casting Directors. A college degree for this position is helpful but not necessary. Previous experience in theater arts, drama or arts management offers an opportunity to make contacts and obtain hands-on experience.

Experience/Skills/Personality Traits

Assistant Casting Directors should be energetic, enthusiastic people with a great deal of personality.

Depending on their experience level and duties, Assistants may be required to perform a number of clerical tasks and should have typing and word processing skills and be able to file and keep records. Assistants should be detail oriented and highly organized.

A knowledge of theater and acting is helpful. Good communications skills are necessary. A pleasant phone manner is essential. The Assistant will be both making and taking calls from agents, actors and actresses, and managers. The ability to take instructions and follow them is a must.

The ability to match up the actor and actress with the right parts is a plus. Some individuals have an innate sense of this skill, while others can learn it by watching professionals in the field select actors and actresses for various parts.

Assistant Casting Directors obtain jobs in this field by working in clerical jobs for casting directors or consultants. Others work as interns or apprentices.

Unions/Associations

Assistant Casting Directors belong to the Casting Society of America, a trade association for those working in the casting field.

Tips for Entry

1. If you are still choosing your college, try to locate one with a theater arts or broadcast department. In addition to the courses, participate in extracurricular activities that will help prepare you for this job.
2. Participate in school plays and productions.
3. Volunteer your services to a nonprofit or local theater group to gain hands-on experience.
4. Try out for a few casting calls yourself. This experience enables you to see the casting process from the other end and brings you into contact with actors.
5. Seek a part-time or summer job as a clerk, secretary or assistant in a theatrical agent's office. You'll gain valuable experience and make important contacts.
6. Try to locate an internship or training program in a theater. This position will help you get established on this career path.

SCENIC DESIGNER

Duties: Creating the set design for a theatrical production; conceptualizing the ideas necessary for sets.

Alternate Title(s):   Set Designer.

Salary Range: Impossible to determine earnings due to nature of job.

Employment Prospects: Fair.

Best Geographical Location(s) for Position: Culturally active cities such as New York, Los Angeles, Chicago, Atlanta and Philadelphia.

Prerequisites:

Education or Training: No formal educational requirement; undergraduate or postgraduate degree helpful; on-the-job training necessary.

Experience: Experience working in theater helpful.

Special Skills and Personality Traits: Creativity; ability to conceptualize; knowledge of theater, staging and color; drawing and painting skills; reliability; ability to work well with others.

```
┌─────────────────────────────────────┐
│        Scenic Designer              │
│  for More Prestigious Production     │
└─────────────────────────────────────┘

┌─────────────────────────────────────┐
│        Scenic Designer              │
└─────────────────────────────────────┘

┌─────────────────────────────────────┐
│     Assistant Scenic Designer        │
│                or                    │
│        Apprentice or Intern          │
└─────────────────────────────────────┘
```

Position Description

Scenic Designers working in theater and the performing arts are responsible for creating stage sets. The Scenic Designer works with the director, lighting designer and one or more assistants.

The word "set" in theater means the physical look of the stage. Stage settings are very important to a production. They help create the mood for a show and visually explain to the audience where a specific scene is taking place. The Scenic Designer produces a variety of effects using different backdrops, props and lighting.

In many productions, the Scenic Designer creates more than one set depending on the requirements of the play. For example, an individual may develop an opening set for a scene in a living room. The next set may have to illustrate a backyard. The Scenic Designer determines how each set will be changed. When using multiple sets, it is important that the scenery and props are designed so that they can be moved easily and replaced quickly with new sets.

One of the major responsibilities of the Scenic Designer is to formulate the look of the show. He or she meets with the director to get a sense of the director's thinking. The Scenic Designer also researches a specific time period to make sure props are appropriate.

The Scenic Designer determines what equipment, props and backdrops are needed to produce the desired effects, working with a lighting designer to achieve the necessary effects. Once the Scenic Designer has some ideas, he or she may produce sketches or create models to illustrate them to the director.

Once the director has agreed to the set designs, the Scenic Designer is responsible for writing all the information on paper including plans, ideas and necessary equipment. He or she may also create models of each set. After the documentation and models are completed, the Scenic Designer is responsible for soliciting bids on building the sets from scenery shops. After the production's general manager approves the bid, the scenery shop builds the sets under Scenic Designer's direction.

When a shop is chosen and the price has been agreed upon, it is the responsibility of the Scenic Designer to check on the progress of the scenery shop to make sure that everything is on schedule. If there are any problems with the scenery, or if the costs are escalating, the Scenic Designer must sometimes change his designs to keep costs within the production's budget.

Sometimes, a Scenic Designer of a Broadway production designs sets for a number of theaters because the show may go into previews in other theaters before it actually opens in New York. The scenery must be adaptable to every theater, as all stages are not the same. The Scenic Designer finds a way to make every set fit in every theater.

Once built, the sets are checked on stage. The Scenic Designer makes sure that the sets change smoothly, and that the lighting is right. Once the play opens, the Scenic Designer's job is usually over. He or she may, however, be contracted to handle the scenic design for any road shows. The Scenic Designer is responsible to the director of the production.

Salaries

Scenic Designers working in the theater are usually paid a fee for each production they work on. Individuals may also receive a percentage of the profits in addition to or instead of a fee.

Salaries for Scenic Designer vary greatly depending on the individual's experience, expertise and reputation. Earnings also depend on the specific production the individual is working with, the type of theater and its location.

Individuals working in unionized theaters have minimum fees set by the United Scenic Artists (USA). The minimum fee in 1998 for designing the sets for a Broadway multi-set musical was $21,259 plus a guaranteed royalty advance of $4,530. This guarantee is paid in case the show does not open or closes quickly. In addition, the individual receives 13% for pension and welfare.

Those working in nonunionized settings may receive fees ranging from $500 to $25,000 or more for designing the sets for a production. Established Scenic Designers who are in demand for Broadway shows may earn $100,000 plus if their compensation includes a large percentage of the box office gross.

Employment Prospects

Employment prospects are fair for Scenic Designers who are willing to work on a variety of smaller, less prestigious productions in different types of theaters. Prospects are difficult for those aspiring to be Scenic Designers for Broadway productions.

Advancement Prospects

Advancement is difficult for Scenic Designers. It takes ambition, talent and determination.

A beginner in the field works with a Scenic Designer which can keep him employed on a regular basis. The young Scenic Designer advances his career by taking on more responsibility in more prestigious productions. Creating the set design for a major Broadway show is a giant career step on the ladder of success.

Education and Training

A college degree or background is not always necessary to become a Scenic Designer but is helpful in obtaining training. Most individuals who are professionals in this field have at least a bachelor's degree in theater arts, design or a related field. Many Scenic Designer also hold graduate degrees. There are colleges located throughout the country which offer degrees or courses in theater arts, scenic design, art, lighting and architecture. These schools usually offer hands-on-training and experience.

Courses and/or seminars in art history, drawing, mechanical drawing, painting, architecture, lighting and stagecraft are useful.

Experience/Skills/Personality Traits

Scenic Designers need to be extremely creative, artistic people. They should have the ability to take an idea from its inception and turn into a reality on stage.

Experience working on sets for school plays and community theater is helpful for aspiring Scenic Designer. Work in any aspect of theater is useful to obtain experience and help make important contacts. Some individuals intern or apprentice with other Scenic Designers in order to get additional valuable experience.

Scenic Designers should be able to work well with others, for the job demands good working relationships with the producer, director, lighting designer, carpenters, electricians, engineers and assistants.

Scenic Designers should be reliable and be able to complete work in a timely fashion. The ability to work under pressure is necessary.

Unions/Associations

Scenic Designers working in unionized theaters must be members of the United Scenic Artists (USA) union. In order to become a member of this group, an individual must go through an interview process and pass an examination. United Scenic Artists negotiates and sets the minimum fees and working conditions for their members.

Tips for Entry

1. Get involved with school plays and other theatrical productions.
2. Volunteer to work with your local community theater. Get experience designing sets, painting, constructing and working with the theater lighting.
3. Try to locate an internship working in a theater in the scenic design department. If a position isn't open in that department, take any available internship you can find. Ask questions and keep your eyes and ears open.
4. Many summer theaters offer part-time or summer jobs to students learning their craft. Send your resume with a short cover letter asking for an interview.
5. Contact the local affiliation of the United Scenic Artists (USA) to learn more about membership requirements.

ASSISTANT SCENIC DESIGNER

CAREER PROFILE

Duties: Helping the scenic designer create the set design for a theatrical production; locating props; drafting plans to build a prop; doing research.

Alternate Title(s):   Assistant Set Designer.

Salary Range: $300 to $1,000+ per week.

Employment Prospects: Fair.

Best Geographical Location(s) for Position: Culturally active cities offer more opportunities.

Prerequisites:

Education or Training: No formal educational requirement; undergraduate or postgraduate degree helpful.

Experience: Experience working in theater helpful.

Special Skills and Personality Traits: Creativity; research skills; ability to develop ideas for props; knowledge of theater and staging; drawing and drafting skills; reliability; ability to work well with others; organized.

CAREER LADDER

```
┌─────────────────────────────────────┐
│          Scenic Designer            │
└─────────────────────────────────────┘

┌─────────────────────────────────────┐
│      Assistant Scenic Designer       │
└─────────────────────────────────────┘

┌─────────────────────────────────────┐
│     Student, Apprentice or Intern    │
└─────────────────────────────────────┘
```

Position Description

Every theatrical production has at least one set. The word "set" in theater means the physical look of the stage. Stage settings are very important to a production as they visually explain to the audience where a specific scene is taking place on stage. The Assistant Scenic Designer in a theatrical production helps the designer create the sets that the audience sees onstage. Individuals will have varied responsibilities depending on the specific job.

One of the responsibilities of the Assistant Scenic Designer will be to find props that are necessary to complete the look of sets in a play. This task is sometimes passed onto a propman or propwoman.

Props, or properties, are the articles used on stage by the actors and actresses. They are used to decorate a set in order to make it look more realistic. Examples of props might be sofas, chairs, telephones, pens, fruits, flowers, etc. Props may also include costume props for the cast members such as umbrellas. Props are not always easy to find. In some instances, needed items are antiques or other items from bygone eras. One of the interesting parts of the job of an Assistant Scenic Designer is looking for a prop or coming up with solutions for finding props that are easily located.

Sometimes, props can be purchased. Other times, props are rented from warehouses, museums or rental companies. The Assistant Scenic Designer must know where to go to find needed items. A great deal of the individual's job is looking, shopping and calling around to find just the right piece that will complete a stage set. Experienced individuals in this line of work develop lists over the years of where specific items can be located. In some cases, the scenic designer cannot buy or rent a certain prop and must design it personally.

In some situations, the Assistant Scenic Designer will be responsible for drafting the plans to build a prop. He or she will then give the plans to a propmaker or carpenter to build. At other times, the individual may be responsible for building models of sets or scenery at the request of his or her superior.

Once the scenic designer has come up with some ideas, he or she may give them to the Assistant to sketch or make models of so that the ideas can be illustrated for the director.

The Assistant Scenic Designer may sit in on meetings with the scenic designer and the director. He or she may be asked to help develop ideas when the scenic designer is conceptualizing thoughts for show sets.

The Assistant Scenic Designer will be expected to do a lot of the legwork for the scenic designer. He or she may be required to do research about specific time periods to determine what types of items might be used in a production from a certain time period. The individual may do this research in libraries, through books and magazines or by visiting museums.

The Assistant Scenic Designer will help the scenic designer and lighting designer work on ideas that can be used for props, backdrops and other scenery. He or she may be required to locate equipment that is needed to produce certain effects.

The Assistant will also be required to do a great deal of the necessary paperwork. This may include documentation of set designs or detailing plans. The Assistant Scenic Designer will be responsible for helping the scenic designer check the props and set designs on the actual stage. He or she will work with the individual making sure that scenery moves smoothly off and on the stage and that each set design is as perfect and problem-free as is possible.

The Assistant Scenic Designer is responsible to the scenic designer of the production.

Salaries

Earnings for Assistant Scenic Designers can range greatly depending on a number of factors including the type of production the individual is working in, his or her experience, responsibilities and reputation. Assistants are usually paid by the week in contrast to their superiors who are paid fees for projects. Assistant Scenic Designers working in unionized theaters will have their minimum earnings set by the United Scenic Artists union. Minimum weekly salaries for those working on Broadway in 1998 were $947 plus 13% pension and welfare for a five-day week. Assistant Scenic Designers working in nonunionized theaters may earn between $300 and $700 or more per week.

Employment Prospects

Employment prospects for Assistant Scenic Designers are fair. Most productions have at least one if not more people in this position. Individuals may work in any type of theatrical production using sets including operas and ballets. There are opportunities in dinner theaters, stock theaters and resident theaters.

Advancement Prospects

Advancement prospects for Assistant Scenic Designers are determined to a great extent by the determination, ambition, skills and luck of the individual. The path most individuals take toward career advancement is becoming a full-fledged Scenic Designer.

Other Assistant Scenic Designers may advance their careers by locating similar positions in more prestigious theat-

rical productions. Some individuals climb the career ladder by doing similar work in television or films.

Education and Training

While there is no formal educational requirement for Assistant Scenic Designers, most individuals in this profession do have a college background or degree. Many hold postgraduate degrees. A major in theater arts or scenic design is helpful in obtaining experience, honing skills and making contacts necessary for success.

Experience/Skills/Personality Traits

Individuals interested in becoming Assistant Scenic Designers should get experience working in theater. A good way to do this is to work in community or school theatrical productions doing such things as building scenery or finding props. Additional experience can also be obtained by working as an apprentice or intern.

Assistant Scenic Designers should be creative. They must possess the ability to develop ideas and to locate solutions. Individuals should have the ability to take an idea from its inception and know how to make it into an onstage reality. Drafting and drawing skills are needed.

Knowing how to fix and build props and scenery is helpful. Knowledge of the theater and stage are necessary.

Assistant Scenic Designers should be highly organized with good record keeping skills. Individuals should also enjoy searching through shops, warehouses, factories and antique stores for props.

Unions/Associations

Assistant Scenic Designers working in unionized theaters must belong to the local affiliation of the United Scenic Artists (USA). This union sets the minimum salaries and working conditions for its members.

Tips for Entry

1. Get involved in your school and community theater. Offer to build sets, create scenery or find props.
2. Attend as many productions of all types that you can and study their set designs. If possible, try to go backstage to see up close what is entailed in each set.
3. Try to locate an internship working in a theater in the prop or scenic design department. If one isn't open in that department, take any internship you can find that is available. Ask questions and keep your eyes and ears open.
4. Many theaters, opera and ballet companies offer parttime or summer jobs to students learning their craft. Send your resume with a short cover letter asking for an interview.

LIGHTING DESIGNER

CAREER PROFILE

Duties: Creating the stage lighting for a theatrical production; conceptualizing the ideas necessary for lighting; determining necessary equipment; charting light boards; mapping out light placement.

Alternate Title(s): Lighting Director.

Salary Range: Impossible to determine earnings due to nature of job.

Employment Prospects: Poor.

Best Geographical Location(s) for Position: Culturally active cities such as New York, Los Angeles, Chicago, Atlanta, Boston and Philadelphia.

Prerequisites:

Education or Training: No formal educational requirement; undergraduate or postgraduate degree helpful; on-the-job-training necessary.

Experience: Experience working as electrician.

Special Skills and Personality Traits: Creativity; ability to conceptualize; knowledge of theater, staging and color; electrician skills; communications skills; ability to work under pressure.

CAREER LADDER

```
┌─────────────────────────────────┐
│   Lighting Designer for More    │
│     Prestigious Production       │
└─────────────────────────────────┘

┌─────────────────────────────────┐
│       Lighting Designer          │
└─────────────────────────────────┘

┌─────────────────────────────────┐
│          Electrician             │
└─────────────────────────────────┘
```

Position Description

The Lighting Designer is responsible for creating the onstage lighting and lighting effects for a theatrical production. This work is extremely important in creating the mood of the show. With proper lighting, a Lighting Designer can create sunrise, a cloudy day, a moonlit night or the lighting of the interior of a house, all on the same set. Lighting is also necessary in theaters so that the audience can see the actors' and actresses' faces and movements.

The Lighting Designer produces a variety of effects by using different lights, filters and colors, and by placing lights in certain positions in the theater. In some circumstances, the Lighting Designer is also required to spotlight certain actors or actresses on stage.

One of the major responsibilities of the Lighting Designer is to create the lighting that conveys the mood of the show. He or she then determines what equipment—spotlights, floodlights, colored filters—will be needed to produce the desired effects.

The Lighting Designer meets with the director of the show to determine what type of lighting ideas he or she has. The individual meets with the scenic designer to learn more about the sets to be used.

The Lighting Designer writes down all lighting information, including details of plans, ideas and equipment. He or she also documents the methods that must be used to obtain the proper lighting. A schedule is prepared so that people manning the lighting boards will know when to turn on the proper lights. A chart illustrating which knobs on the light board relate to which lights is also prepared. The Lighting Designer also draws a map of where each light is placed and lists the wattage of every light.

Once everything is documented, the Lighting Designer works with a master electrician to put the plan into action. During this period, the Designer will instruct the electrician on how lights are to be focused, what colors are to be used, and where lights are to be located. In some productions, the Lighting Designer acts as his or her own electrician performing these tasks.

The lighting is then checked with the scenery and costumes. Lighting often looks fine until it hits a different color costume. The Designer adjusts the lighting until it is as perfect as possible.

After everything is set up, the Lighting Designer is responsible for checking the system again during the dress rehearsal. If problems develop, he or she must take care of them. Once the play opens, the Lighting Designer's job is over. The lighting of each performance of the show is then the responsibility of the person working the light board and an electrician.

Salaries

Lighting Designers working in the theater are usually paid a fee for each production they work on. Individuals may also receive a percentage of the profits in addition to or instead of a fee.

Salaries for Lighting Designers vary greatly depending on the individual's experience, expertise and reputation. Earnings also depend on the specific production the individual is working with, the type of theater and its location.

The United Scenic Artists (USA) sets minimum fees for Lighting Designers working in union shops. The minimum fee in 1998 for designing the lighting for a single set dramatic production on Broadway was $5,851.

Lighting Designers working in nonunionized settings receive fees ranging from $500 to $3,500 or more per production. The few Lighting Designers who are in demand for Broadway shows may earn $150,000 plus, because they receive a fee plus a percentage of the box office gross.

Employment Prospects

The job of Lighting Director is usually a freelance position. Employment prospects are poor for Lighting Designers aspiring to work in theatrical productions. Some productions do not have a Lighting Designer and instead use a production assistant to handle the responsibilities of the Lighting Designer as well as other positions.

Those seeking employment can find opportunities in universities, colleges, off Broadway or off-off Broadway, or theaters that belong to LORT (League of Regional Theaters).

Advancement Prospects

Advancement prospects are poor for Lighting Designers. As noted previously, there are limited opportunities for work. Producers and directors usually would rather work with a Lighting Designer who they have worked with before and who has performed satisfactorily. Because of this, openings do not occur frequently.

Lighting Designers may advance in their profession by broadening their experience, working on diffferent kinds of productions. The Lighting Designer might also advance his or her career by handling the lighting for a more prestigious production. Creating the lighting for a major Broadway show would be a career pinnacle.

Education and Training

There are no formal educational requirements to become a Lighting Designer. There are some Lighting Designers who have no college background at all and others who have undergraduate and graduate degrees. Good choices for majors include theater arts and design.

Other training can be obtained by watching Lighting Designers and electricians at work or becoming an apprentice, assistant or intern.

Experience/Skills/Personality Traits

Lighting Designers working in theater must have a great deal of creativity. They must also have the ability to conceptualize what a particular scene should look like to achieve the desired effect. Individuals must have the capability and expertise to turn ideas into reality.

Lighting Designers should have a thorough knowledge of theater, staging and color, as well as the skills of an electrician. They need the ability to communicate their ideas to others.

Lighting Designers should work well with people, such as directors, scenic designers and electricians. Individuals should be detail oriented and able to work under pressure.

Unions/Associations

Lighting Designers working in unionized theaters are members of the United Scenic Artist (USA) local. Some individuals are also members of the International Brotherhood of Electrical Workers (IBEW) and/or the International Alliance of Theatrical Stage Employees (IATSE). These groups set minimum fees and working conditions for their members.

Tips for Entry

1. Internships are a great way to learn as well as to make contacts. Try to locate them through schools, theater groups and organizations. You might also ask a Lighting Designer if he or she will let you intern.

2. Apprenticeships are another method of learning the trade. Contact appropriate unions for information.

3. Go to as many plays and productions as possible and study the lighting techniques.

4. Read the numerous books that are published on the subject. These will help you understand and learn more about lighting design.

5. Offer to act as the Lighting Designer or his or her assistant for your school or local community theater production. This position will give you good hands-on experience.

COSTUME DESIGNER

CAREER PROFILE

Duties: Developing and creating costume designs for clothing worn in theatrical productions.

Alternate Title(s):   Designer.

Salary Range: Impossible to determine earnings due to nature of job.

Employment Prospects: Poor.

Best Geographical Location(s) for Position: Culturally active cities such as New York, Los Angeles, Chicago, Atlanta and Philadelphia.

Prerequisites:

Education or Training: College degree or background in theater, fashion or costume design helpful, but not always required.

Experience: Experience in designing clothing necessary.

Special Skills and Personality Traits: Knowledge of fashion, colors and fabrics; expertise in designing; sketching skills; fashion drawing skills; creativity; ability to work under pressure.

CAREER LADDER

```
┌─────────────────────────────────┐
│  Costume Designer for More      │
│  Prestigious Production         │
└─────────────────────────────────┘

┌─────────────────────────────────┐
│  Costume Designer               │
└─────────────────────────────────┘

┌─────────────────────────────────┐
│  Clothing Designer or Apprentice│
└─────────────────────────────────┘
```

Position Description

The Costume Designer in a theatrical production is responsible for developing and creating the costumes worn in the show. Depending on the size and type of the production, the Costume Designer has varied responsibilities. The Costume Designer is usually hired by the producer at the request of the director.

The Costume Designer is an important part of the production. Costumes help the characters come to life on stage. Without them, a great deal of the allure of the performance is not present.

In some productions the Costume Designer creates and executes elaborate designs. In others, he or she is responsible for locating clothing "off the rack" that fits into the production.

A Costume Designer first becomes familiar with the script. He or she then discusses costuming ideas with the director. Together they will determine how elaborate a production will be. For example, the Costume Designer determines the number of times the actors and actresses change costumes and the number of costumes needed. The Costume Designer also meets with the scenic and lighting designers to learn more about their ideas for the production.

If the production is set in a certain time period, the Costume Designer researches clothing, fabrics and styles of the era by reading, by watching television or movies, by checking museums, and by looking through periodicals. He or she then begins developing ideas for costumes by sketching them and bringing them to the director for approval.

A lot of thought goes into developing costumes for productions. If, for instance, an actor must make quick changes, costumes are designed so that they are easy to get in and out of. Costumes are designed so that they look as good from the back of a theater as they do from the front. As the same costumes are used for every performance, fabrics and designs must be made to withstand heavy wear.

The responsibilities of the Costume Designer depends on the production. In some productions, the costumes are sent out to companies for construction. Other productions hire workers to make the costumes under the direction of the

Designer. In other instances, the Costume Designer makes the costumes either alone or with the help of one or two assistants.

In most productions, when all the costumes are ready, there is what is known as a "dress parade," a dress rehearsal for actors and actresses in costume. Each person walks across the stage in their costume to see how it looks under the lights and with the sets. If the actors have problems with the costumes such as a button that doesn't remain closed or a seam that inhibits movement, the Designer fixes it.

In addition to designing the actual costumes that the actors and actresses wear in a production, the Costume Designer is also responsible for designing, selecting or finding accessories to go with each outfit. These include items such as shoes, stockings, socks, jewelry, hats and purses. He or she is also responsible for undergarments to be worn by the actors and actresses with their costumes. Nothing is left to chance.

The Costume Designer is responsible for handling all the details related to costuming. He or she must make sure that all costumes are complete and ready for the production. The Designer also discusses care and maintenance of costumes with actors and actresses and with members of the wardrobe department.

Once costumes are turned over to the wardrobe department, the clothing becomes their responsibility and the job is completed.

Salaries

Earnings for Costume Designers can range greatly depending on a number of factors, including how often the individual works, and the location and type of production he or she is working with. Other factors include the individual's expertise, experience, reputation and responsibilities.

Costume Designers working in nonunionized settings may negotiate any type of fee. Those that are working in unionized theaters will have their minimum fee set by the United Scenic Artists (USA). In 1998, the minimum fee for a Costume Designer designing costumes for a large Broadway production with a cast of 36 or more people was $21,259 plus a guaranteed royalty advance of $4,530. Individuals also receive a 13% pension and welfare fund.

Employment Prospects

Employment prospects are poor for Costume Designer in the theater. There are a large number of people seeking positions and competition is great. Many producers and directors feel more comfortable hiring people who have proven themselves in the field.

Most Costume Designers work on a per project basis, that is, after they finish one project they must find another one to stay employed. Some theaters have Designers who work on staff.

Aspiring Costume Designers often break into the profession by designing the costumes for productions at dinner and regional theaters.

Advancement Prospects

Advancement prospects are poor for Costume Designers. Those working with smaller productions may advance their careers by finding similar jobs with more prestigious productions. A major accomplishment for a Costume Designer is designing the costumes for a Broadway musical.

Others may climb the career ladder by designing costumes for television shows or films.

Education and Training

A college degree does not guarantee an individual a position as a Costume Designer, but it may help in getting work in the theater.

There are colleges that offer degrees in costume design. Aspiring Costume Designers may also major in theater or fashion. Classes in drawing, art history, sewing, designing, history, theater, costuming, fashion, sketching and design are also useful.

Experience/Skills/Personality Traits

Costume Designers must have a great deal of knowledge about fashion, colors, and fabrics, and expertise in all facets of designing. They must be able to sketch and do fashion drawing. A sense of style is necessary to success. While it is not imperative to be an expert seamstress or tailor, it helps to have the ability.

Creativity is a must. A knowledge of art history and costuming is useful.

The Costume Designer works with a great many different people from directors and producer to actors and actresses to seamstresses, assistants, scenic and lighting designers. He or she must be personable and easy to work with.

Costume Designers should have the ability to work on a number of different projects at one time without getting flustered. He or she should be reliable and be able to finish projects within budgets and on time. The Costume Designer must have the ability to work under pressure.

Unions/Associations

Costume Designers belong to a number of organizations and unions. Individuals working in unionized situations must be members of the United Scenic Artists (USA). This group negotiates minimum fees and working conditions for its members. Costume Designers may also be members of the Costume Designers Guild.

Tips for Entry

1. Many museums have costume exhibits from different eras. Visit these exhibits often.
2. Learn how to sew well. While you might not have to sew garments as a Costume Designer, knowing how will give you an edge over others and over pressured situations once productions are under way.

3. Take as many classes as you can in art history, fashion design, theater and costuming. They will be useful in bringing you together with others interested in the field.

4. Offer to act as the Costume Designer for a school production or a local community theater. This work will give you good hands-on experience.

5. Try to find an internship in costume design, fashion design or costuming within the theater, another opportunity for hands-on experience and for developing important contacts.

SOUND DESIGNER

CAREER PROFILE

Duties: Handling sound requirements for theatrical productions; determining sound mix; blending and amplifying sound; designing sound effects.

Alternate Title(s): Master Sound Technician.

Salary Range: Impossible to determine earnings due to nature of the job.

Employment Prospects: Poor.

Best Geographical Location(s) for Position: More opportunities can be found in culturally active cities.

Prerequisites:

Education or Training: No formal educational requirement; training in electronics and sound.

Experience: Experience as apprentice necessary in many positions.

Special Skills and Personality Traits: Understanding of acoustics; complete knowledge of electronics; creativity; supervisory skills; communication skills; ability to work under pressure.

CAREER LADDER

```
┌─────────────────────────────────────┐
│         Sound Designer               │
│  for More Prestigious Production     │
└─────────────────────────────────────┘

┌─────────────────────────────────────┐
│         Sound Designer               │
└─────────────────────────────────────┘

┌─────────────────────────────────────┐
│           Apprentice                 │
└─────────────────────────────────────┘
```

Position Description

The Sound Designer is responsible for the acoustics for a theatrical production. He or she makes sure that everyone can hear what is going on and that the sound is pleasing to the ears of the audience.

Sound Designers work in Broadway theaters as well as dinner and summer stock theaters. They also work in concert halls, arenas or other venues. Their job is to design the sound for the production before the show opens. Sound requirements and responsibilities are then passed on to other sound technicians. Many theaters, however, give the responsibilities of the Sound Designer to a soundman or soundwoman who will stay with the show once it opens and also handle the soundboard.

Sound Designers do with sound what lighting designers do with lights. The sound of a show, like the lighting, helps create the mood of a production. With proper sound, a scene can include a thunderstorm, or a quiet night, or a noisy dance hall. Without good sound control, the playwright's words may not be heard and sound effects may not create the mood the director wants.

As each theater has different acoustics, obtaining good sound with the proper effects is difficult. The sound for each production is examined, thought out, developed and executed in a unique way for each theater.

The Sound Designer has varied responsibilities depending on the specific production. In some instances, he or she will be supervising other sound specialists. In others, the Sound Designer handles all sound-related tasks personally.

The Sound Designer meets with the director to determine what type of sound and effects are needed and then works toward achieving these effects. For example, if the sound of thunder is required, the Sound Designer must find something that can imitate the sound. He or she then decides if the effect will be used live for each performance or if a recording will work as well.

The Sound Designer also determines if the production requires any recorded music. If it does, he or she is responsible for recording it or assigning the task to a sound technician.

The Sound Designer produces a variety of sound effects with different equipment and is responsible for determining what equipment is needed and making sure it is available. He or she must also decide where equipment, such as microphones and amplifiers are placed to obtain optimum sound.

The Sound Designer makes the sound the audience hears appear normal and lifelike. This is accomplished by mixing and blending the various sounds that come from all the microphones used on stage and backstage. The Designer decides what amplification each microphone should have. When music is playing, for instance, the Sound Designer will want to make sure the audience can still hear on-stage voices.

A great deal of this work is accomplished by determining how the controls should be adjusted at the soundboard. The Sound Designer will try various levels until he or she comes up with the perfect mix.

The Sound Designer documents all sound information on paper, including all equipment used and its placement. He or she also prepares the schedule that will be used by technicians operating the soundboard during a performance. From the schedule, the sound technician knows how to adjust controls to appropriate levels.

The Sound Designer reports to the director of the production.

Salaries

Sound Designers working in the theater are paid a fee for each production, or on a weekly salary. Earnings vary depending on the individual's experience, expertise and reputation. The earnings also depend on the specific production, the type of theater and its location.

Those working in unionized settings have minimum earnings set and negotiated by the local affiliation of the International Alliance of Theatrical Stage Employees (IATSE).

Earnings for Sound Designers can range from $350 to $1,000 or more per week on a salary basis, or they may be paid a fee for the production ranging from $750 to $20,000 or more. Some individuals who are in demand for Broadway shows earn $100,000 or more if they have worked out deals where they receive a fee plus a percentage of the gross at the box office. There are, however, not many people in the field earning this type of money.

Employment Prospects

Employment prospects are poor for individual aspiring to work as Sound Designers in theatrical productions. Job prospects increase for those who do the technical work as well as the sound design.

All productions do not have a Sound Designer. Some use other sound technicians to handle the responsibilities of Sound Designer.

Advancement Prospects

Advancement prospects are limited for Sound Designers. Individuals may climb the career ladder by finding a greater number of productions to design the sound for or by doing similar work for more prestigious productions. Another method of career advancement is to do similar work for major popular music acts, which in turn may lead to more a permanent position and increased earnings.

Many producers and directors hire Sound Designers they have worked with before and who have performed satisfactorily. Openings in this field do not occur that frequently.

Education and Training

There are no formal educational requirements for becoming a Sound Designer. Training in electronics and sound techniques is necessary. There are vocational schools that teach this. Some Sound Designers pick up necessary skills by watching others.

A college background is not required, but it gives the individual a well-rounded education, opportunities to gain experience in the field, and a way to make important contacts. Majors for those interested in sound design include theater arts or design.

Sound Designers who work in unionized settings must be members of the local affiliation of the International Alliance of Theatrical Stage Employees (IATSE). In order to become a member of this union, individuals must go through an apprenticeship program.

Experience/Skills/Personality Traits

Sound Designers for theatrical productions obtain experience by taking part in apprenticeship programs. Others get experience by handling the sound requirements for school and community productions. Still others work in the music industry doing sound design for groups and singers.

Sound Designers working in theater must have an understanding of acoustics plus a full knowledge of electronics and the use of all sound equipment.

Sound Designers are creative. While to the layperson "sound is sound," the Designer uses it to create a mood in the theater. Designers need the ability to understand how to produce a desired sound effect and then make it happen.

Sound Designers also need supervisory skills. The ability to communicate is necessary. Individuals should be able to work under pressure without getting flustered.

Unions/Associations

Sound Designers working in unionized theaters are members of the International Alliance of Theatrical Stage Employees (IATSE). Some individuals may also be members of the International Brotherhood of Electrical Workers (IBEW). These organizations negotiate and set minimum fees and working conditions for their members.

Tips for Entry

1. Internships are a great way to learn, as well as to make contacts. Try to locate them through schools, theater groups and other organizations.
2. Apprenticeships are another method of learning the trade. Contact the appropriate unions for information.
3. Offer to act as the Sound Technician or assistant for your school or local community theater production. This will give you good hands-on experience.
4. Work with a local music group that needs a Sound Technician.

CAREER OPPORTUNITIES IN THEATRICAL ADMINISTRATION AND BUSINESS

COMPANY MANAGER

CAREER PROFILE

Duties: Overseeing the day-to-day activities and operations of a theatrical production; record keeping; keeping production moving smoothly; setting up and dispersing payroll funds; overseeing ticket sales; documenting sales of tickets and cash flow after each performance.

Alternate Title(s): None.

Salary Range: $400 to $2,000+ per week.

Employment Prospects: Fair.

Best Geographical Location(s) for Position: Culturally active cities offer the most opportunities.

Prerequisites:

Education or Training: College background or degree useful, but not always required; apprenticeship usually necessary.

Experience: Experience as assistant or apprentice.

Special Skills and Personality Traits: Detail oriented; reliable; personable; knowledge of theater business; bookkeeping, payroll and math skills; articulate.

CAREER LADDER

```
┌─────────────────────────────────┐
│      Company Manager for        │
│  More Prestigious Production     │
│     or General Manager          │
└─────────────────────────────────┘

┌─────────────────────────────────┐
│       Company Manager           │
└─────────────────────────────────┘

┌─────────────────────────────────┐
│  Assistant to Company Manager   │
│             or                  │
│          Apprentice             │
└─────────────────────────────────┘
```

Position Description

The Company Manager of a production represents the show's producer and oversees day-to-day business operations. Company Managers supervise everything that relates to the business of running the show, including record keeping, documentation and the negotiation of contracts.

The Company Manager's job begins when rehearsals for the production start, although some Managers start a short time prior to rehearsals. He or she attends every rehearsal and performance.

The Company Manager makes sure that the production proceeds on schedule. If things have stalled, the Manager talks to the director about getting the schedule back on track.

The Company Manager is required to check on the progress of sets, costumes and lighting design to make sure that production is moving along smoothly and on schedule. When there is a problem, the Company Manager determines where and what it is and then fixes it quickly.

One of the major responsibilities of a Company Manager is to set up the payroll. To do this, the Manager goes over each contract and determines salaries while the show is in rehearsal as well as when it is in production. The Manager also determines the daily allowances for room and board if they are included. He or she is then responsible for dispersing funds to each member of the production. The Manager also requires each performer to file the proper tax forms.

Another function of the Company Manager is to oversee production expenses. The Manager keeps tabs on expenses to make sure that the production does not go over budget. If expenses are running over budget, the Manager notifies the general manager and tries to find ways to cut costs.

Ticket sales are vital to a production and it is the Company Manager who oversees ticket sales and finds ways to increase both single and groups sales. The Company Manager works directly with the ticket office or with the assistance of a theatrical press agent. The Manager is responsible for keeping a number of seats available for reviewers and other members of the press and media.

After each performance, the Company Manager determines how much money was taken in for each performance, checking the number of tickets sold, the price category and the number of discounted and free tickets. A report is then written to document this information.

The Company Manager is required to be with the production for each performance and travels with the company if it goes on a road tour. He or she is also responsible at the close of a show for taking care of any necessary last minute details, including the return of rental equipment and storing scenery.

The Company Manager works long, hard hours at his or her job and is responsible to the general manager of the production company.

Salaries

Salaries for Company Managers vary depending on the size of theater and its geographic location, and the experience and specific responsibilities of the Manager. Weekly earnings of Company Managers range from $400 to $2,000 or more.

Company Managers working in unionized settings have minimum salaries that are set by the Association of Theatrical Press Agents and Managers (ATPAM). The minimum base weekly earnings for a Company Manager as of 1998 was $1,393. Company Managers also receive vacation pay, a welfare fund and pension.

Employment Prospects

Employment prospects are fair for Company Managers. Once a Manager gets the proper training by acting as an assistant or going through an apprenticeship program, he may work in any unionized theatrical setting.

Advancement Prospects

Advancement prospects are fair for Company Managers and are determined by the individual's expertise, experience and reputation. Drive and determination are crucial to advancement in this field.

There are two different paths a Company Manager can take in career advancement, either as a Company Manager for a more prestigious production or becoming a general manager of a production.

Education and Training

A college degree does not guarantee a job as a Company Manager, but it does give the individual good background, experience and credibility. Good choices for college majors include theater arts or arts management.

Classes in all areas of theater, theater management, lighting, sound and scenic design are useful. Courses in bookkeeping, math, entertainment law, business and payroll are also useful.

Company Managers working in unionized theaters go through an internship program.

Experience/Skills/Personality Traits

Company Managers working in unionized theaters get job experience by entering an internship program run by the Association of Theatrical Press Agents and Managers (ATPAM). These programs provide on-the-job training by requiring an intern to work as an assistant to a Company Manager or general manager.

Company Managers must be detail oriented and able to work on a great many projects at once without getting flustered. They should be honest and reliable, and have a great deal of knowledge about the theater and its workings. They need to know and enforce union rules and regulations.

Bookkeeping, math and payroll skills are necessary, as are negotiations skills. Company Managers must work well with a variety of people and should be articulate and have good communications skills.

Unions/Associations

Company Managers are members of the Association of Theatrical Press Agents and Managers (ATPAM). This union sets minimum fees, working conditions and standards for their members. It also regulates and runs an apprenticeship program that Company Managers take part in.

Tips for Entry

1. Work in as many areas of theater as possible. The more experience, the better prepared you are for this career.
2. Volunteer to work in your local community theater to get experience in production.
3. Get involved with your school productions to learn every aspect of theater.
4. Find an internship with a Company Manager or general manager of a theatrical company. Internships provide excellent hands-on experience as well as helping you make contacts.
5. Contacts are extremely important in this job. The more people you make a good impression on, the more job opportunities you will have.
6. Apprenticeships are available through the Association of Theatrical Press Agents and Managers (ATPAM) as well as a number of other theater groups.

BOX OFFICE TREASURER

CAREER PROFILE

CAREER PROFILE

Duties: Managing box office operations; selling tickets; filling requests for mail order tickets; determining seating arrangements; counting money after performance; preparing statements detailing tickets sold and money received.

Alternate Title(s): Box Office Manager.

Salary Range: $18,000 to $50,000+.

Employment Prospects: Fair.

Best Geographical Location(s) for Position: Culturally active cities offer most opportunities.

Prerequisites:

Education or Training: Educational requirements vary from high school diploma to college background or bachelor's degree.

Experience: Experience working in box office necessary.

Special Skills and Personality Traits: Organizational and communication skills; detail oriented; ability to keep accurate records; bookkeeping skills; supervisory skills.

CAREER LADDER

```
┌─────────────────────────────────┐
│      Box Office Treasurer in     │
│    More Prestigious Theater      │
│       or House Manager           │
└─────────────────────────────────┘

┌─────────────────────────────────┐
│       Box Office Treasurer       │
└─────────────────────────────────┘

┌─────────────────────────────────┐
│  Assistant Box Office Treasurer  │
│               or                 │
│           Apprentice             │
└─────────────────────────────────┘
```

Position Description

The Box Office Treasurer or Box Office Manager is responsible for managing the box office that sells tickets that in turn makes money for the production. The Box Office Treasurer is employed by the theater and schedules hours when patrons can purchase show tickets. The Box Office Treasurer handles everything that occurs in the ticket office. He or she oversees the entire office and staff. If the theater is small and hires only one person for the ticket office, the Box Office Treasurer sells tickets. If the theater is larger, the Box Office Treasurer assigns sales duties to staff members who sell the tickets, obtain payment and assign seats.

The Treasurer or staff who is responsible for selling tickets at the theater's box office window puts credit card purchases through the system and authorizes ticket sales made by check. The Treasurer learns how to spot counterfeit tickets and counterfeit money.

The Treasurer is responsible for selling tickets in advance of the performance for the night or day of the event. Even if the Box Office Treasurer is not selling tickets, he or she must be at the theater for each performance.

The Box Office Treasurer is responsible for ordering the printing of the tickets, although sometimes the producer of the show may handle this task. When tickets arrive, the director examines them to be sure they have been printed correctly.

There is no room for error in the box office. All tickets must be accounted for. The Box Office Treasurer counts the tickets to make sure that the same number that were ordered are received. It is important that the Box Office Treasurer keep track of each ticket sold by number and the payment received. In some theaters the use of computerized ticket machines make this task easier.

The Box Office Treasurer is aware of the various sections of seating in the theater and the prices for tickets in each of these sections. In most theaters, the Box Office Treasurer has a chart of the seats and marks off seats as they are purchased by patrons. This chart, on computers in some theaters, helps the Box Office Treasurer see at a glance which seats are available and their locations. The Box Office Treasurer is responsible for fulfilling telephone requests for tickets, giving callers information regarding the various price breakdowns, availability of seats and the times of performances.

Many patrons purchase tickets well in advance of the opening of a production. The Box Office Treasurer is responsible for handling and filling all requests for advance ticket sales. He or she must make sure that all tickets are mailed in time for patrons to receive them or hold the tickets at the box office for pickup.

Handling group ticket sales is another function of the Box Office Treasurer, who is responsible for informing theater parties and school groups about discounts for tickets purchased in blocks. He or she makes the necessary arrangements for the blocks of seats to be sold sometimes working through an agency that solicits orders from theater parties.

The Treasurer is busy before the opening of a production. During this time, he or she is responsible for handling requests for tickets for friends of the cast, critics and reviewers. One of the more difficult jobs of the Box Office Treasurer is juggling the seating arrangements for opening nights among celebrities, dignitaries, critics and reviewers.

The Treasurer is responsible for holding and dispersing tickets to patrons who have ordered tickets prior to a performance but have not picked them up. The Treasurer also gives out complimentary tickets or passes issued by the producers, cast and press agents.

After each performance, the Box Office Treasurer prepares a statement detailing the number of tickets sold and the prices they were sold at. He or she must also count the money, checks, credit card slips and money owed by ticket agents and computer ticket sales. Each ticket not sold must be counted, also. When the entire process is completed, the Treasurer can account for every ticket in the house for that night and at the end of the week document in a financial statement, the amount of money the production earned in any time period.

Salaries

Earnings of Box Office Treasurers vary according to the responsibilities and experience of the individual and the size and prestige of the theater. Treasurers working in unionized theaters earn a minimum salary set by the union.

Box Office Treasurers working in nonunionized theaters earn from $18,000 a year for those working smaller theaters to $50,000 or more a year for those handling a lot of responsibilities in the box offices of larger theaters.

Employment Prospects

Employment prospects are fair for Box Office Treasurers, who can look to theaters, performing arts centers, orchestra, ballet or opera company box offices for employment.

While positions are located throughout the country, prospects are better in culturally active cities that support a large number of theaters.

Advancement Prospects

Box Office Treasurers advance by finding similar positions in more prestigious theaters that result in increased earnings and responsibilities. Treasurers also climb the career ladder by becoming house managers.

Education and Training

Educational requirements vary for Box Office Treasurers. Some theaters offer the position to an individual with a high school diploma and prior experience working in a box or ticket office. Other theaters require that the individual have a college degree or background.

A major in theater arts management is helpful. Useful courses, seminars and workshops include arts management, box office management, accounting, math, bookkeeping and computer science.

Experience/Skills/Personality Traits

Box Office Treasurers must be highly organized and able to deal with many details at the same time. The ability to keep accurate records is essential.

Bookkeeping and math skills are mandatory. A good memory is necessary, as well as the ability to supervise and work well with others.

Treasurers need both verbal and written communications skills and must be very patient and diplomatic, since box office patrons sometimes express displeasure with their seats or the prices. The Treasurer must remain cool and calm to resolve disputes.

As many box offices are now computerized, computer skills are essential.

Unions/Associations

Box Office Treasurers working in a Broadway theater must be members of the International Alliance of Theatrical Stage Employees (IATSE). This organization offers on-the-job training in the form of an internship. The union also negotiates minimum earnings and working conditions for its members. Those working in nonunionized theaters need not be members of a union.

Tips for Entry

1. Work in the box office of your college's activity department selling tickets to entertainment or sporting events or doing clerical work in the activities office.

2. Consider a summer or part-time job in a movie or theater ticket office to gain on-the-job experience.

3. Make sure that you have computer training and know how to work and feel comfortable with these systems. Many offices are automated. Computer literacy gives you an extra edge in the job market.

4. Volunteer to help sell tickets and run the box office for a community theater. It's a good way to gain experience.

5. Look in the classified ads under headings for "Box Office," "Tickets," "Theater" or "Sales" for jobs working in the box office of theaters.

6. Contact the local affiliation of the appropriate unions to determine specific membership requirements.

7. Try to locate an internship program with the help of your school or by contacting theaters directly.

THEATRICAL PRESS AGENT

CAREER PROFILE

Duties: Publicizing theater productions such as Broadway and off Broadway shows, regional theater groups; compiling press kits; writing press releases; arranging press conferences; developing publicity and promotional campaigns.

Alternate Title(s): Press Agent.

Salary Range: Minimum salary for individuals working on Broadway shows, $1,588 per week plus benefits.

Employment Prospects: Poor.

Best Geographical Location(s) for Position: New York City, Hollywood and Los Angeles offer most opportunities; Chicago, Atlanta, Philadelphia, Washington, D.C. or any large and culturally active city may hold additional possibilities.

Prerequisites:

Education or Training: Three-year Apprentice program required.

Experience: Experience in publicity or public relations a plus.

Special Skills and Personality Traits: Creativity; innovation; good writing skills; communications skills; ability to work under pressure; knowledge of entertainment industry.

CAREER LADDER

```
┌─────────────────────────────────┐
│      Theatrical Press Agent     │
│       Working with More         │
│      Prestigious Projects       │
└─────────────────────────────────┘

┌─────────────────────────────────┐
│      Theatrical Press Agent     │
└─────────────────────────────────┘

┌─────────────────────────────────┐
│  Theatrical Press Agent Apprentice │
└─────────────────────────────────┘
```

Position Description

A Theatrical Press Agent works with theater productions such as Broadway plays, off Broadway shows and regional theater groups. His or her main function is to publicize the production in order to get as much exposure as possible. Such exposure makes people aware of the show and generates audiences. A Press Agent develops various forms of publicity and promotion to keep the production in the public eye as much as possible.

Much of the Theatrical Press Agent's work is done before a show opens. During this time, Agents work on creating ideas, putting programs and concepts together and developing pre-opening publicity.

The Theatrical Press Agent has many responsibilities. Once he or she is hired to work on a production, they develop a publicity and promotional campaign that includes writing

and producing a press kit, getting information about and photographs of the talent for fact sheets, and planning press releases, interviews and feature articles.

The Agent deals with media, arranging press conferences, press parties, opening night parties and media events. He or she does this by setting up television and radio interviews with the stars to help publicize the production locally, regionally and nationally.

The Theatrical Press Agent calls editors and reporters with feature stories and article ideas. With luck and a good idea, the Agent can convince a writer or producer to cover the show on television and radio, as well as in magazines and newspapers.

A Press Agent uses every avenue possible to obtain press coverage for a show. The Agent calls theater critics and reporters of newspapers, magazines, radio and television. He or she may also contact cooking editors, fashion editors, or financial editors to offer interesting tie-in possibilities with the show and its stars. For example, the Agent may place an actress on a television talk show during the cooking segment. The Theatrical Press Agent may arrange an interview with a financial reporter of a newspaper and the financial backer of a successful play. The idea is to get as much publicity reaching as many different people as possible.

If the show features well-known stars, the Theatrical Press Agent arranges for a photographer to take pictures of the stars attending a media event, party or fund-raiser. He or she may also pass information along to a television, radio or publication columnist about the celebrity.

The Theatrical Press Agent contacts critics and other members of the media to invite them to show openings, prepares a guest list ahead of time, and then arranges for tickets, assigns seats and distributes appropriate press material prior to the opening.

The Theatrical Press Agent puts in long hours. They often start in the morning contacting media people, writing press releases, developing and implementing publicity and promotional strategies, and attending performances.

Theatrical Press Agents work under a lot of pressure and stress. There are constant deadlines to meet and new, clever, creative and innovative ideas to develop that will result in publicity for the show.

Salaries

Theatrical Press Agents belong to the Association of Theatrical Press Agents and Managers, AFL-CIO (ATPAM), a union that negotiates salaries and working conditions with theatrical producers.

In 1998, the minimum salaries allowed for Theatrical Press Agents working on Broadway shows were $1,588 per week, plus $134.98 vacation, 8% pension and $130 per week for a welfare fund. Minimum salaries for individuals working on off Broadway productions are determined by the seating capacity of the theater.

It is difficult to estimate earnings of Theatrical Press Agents because these individuals may not work every week of the year. They are usually hired for a specific project and there is no way to tell how long each production will last.

Individuals who are in demand command weekly salaries that are higher.

Employment Prospects

Employment prospects are poor for Theatrical Press Agents. To get into this profession, an individual must first apprentice with a press agent who is a member of the Association of Theatrical Press Agents and Managers (ATPAM). This apprenticeship takes three years to complete. During this time, the Theatrical Press Agent must show talent, creativity and an aptitude for the profession.

After becoming a member of ATPAM, the individual will have to build a good reputation in order to find work.

Advancement Prospects

Advancement prospects are fair for Agents who are good at their job, create a lot of excitement for theatrical productions in the media and have built up their professional reputation.

Theatrical Press Agents move up the career ladder by obtaining more prestigious projects to work on. These could include shows that are produced, directed or written by famous producers, well-known directors and established authors, as well as shows that spotlight major stars.

Education and Training

There are no educational requirements for the position of Theatrical Press Agent. Individuals must, however, go through a three-year apprenticeship working with an ATPAM member.

Those who are considering college should take courses in writing, communications, journalism, public relations, advertising, marketing, English, theater arts and business. Seminars and courses in publicity and promotion are also useful in honing skills.

Experience/Skills/Personality Traits

Theatrical Press Agents need to be creative, innovative people who write well. A good command of the English language, word usage and spelling is necessary in order to produce factual, accurate press releases, feature stories and other materials with unique angles or "hooks" to catch an editor's eye.

Theatrical Press Agents should be articulate and possess excellent communications skills. A good phone manner is essential, as much of the Press Agent's work is done on the telephone.

The ability to create excitement through unique publicity and promotional campaigns is imperative to a Theatrical Press Agent's success, so a good working relationship with the press and media is helpful.

Unions/Associations

As noted previously, the bargaining union of Theatrical Press Agents is the Association of Theatrical Press Agents and Managers, AFL-CIO (ATPAM). This organization negotiates and sets the minimum salary that can be paid to Theatrical Press Agents. It also set standards for the profession and provides a welfare fund for members.

Theatrical Press Agents might also belong to trade associations, including the Public Relations Society of America (PRSA). This organization offers seminars, booklets, periodicals and other helpful information to those in the industry.

Tips for Entry

1. Publicize and promote productions for school or local theater groups.
2. Take courses in all facets of writing. Honing your skills now will help in the future.
3. Become a member of Public Relations Society of America (PRSA). The organization offers student memberships. You will have the opportunity to attend seminars and conferences which will be helpful in learning skills.
4. Find an ATPAM member who will sponsor you through a three-year apprentice program. Contact the appropriate union if you have any questions or want to find the closest branch office.

THEATRICAL PRESS AGENT APPRENTICE

CAREER PROFILE

Duties: Assisting senior press agent in publicizing and promoting theatrical productions; learning techniques of the trade.

Alternate Title(s):   Press Agent Apprentice.

Salary Range: $350 per week, first year of apprenticeship.

Employment Prospects: Poor.

Best Geographical Location(s) for Position: New York City, Hollywood and Los Angeles offer most opportunities; Chicago, Atlanta, Philadelphia, Washington, D.C. or any large and culturally active city may hold additional possibilities.

Prerequisites:

Education or Training: No educational requirement.

Experience: Experience with publicity helpful.

Special Skills and Personality Traits: Good verbal communications skills; good writing skills; ability to handle details; innovation; creativity; aggressiveness.

CAREER LADDER

```
┌─────────────────────────────────────┐
│      Theatrical Press Agent          │
└─────────────────────────────────────┘

┌─────────────────────────────────────┐
│      Theatrical Press Agent          │
│           Apprentice                 │
└─────────────────────────────────────┘

┌─────────────────────────────────────┐
│  Entry Level or Publicity Assistant in │
│         Other Industry               │
└─────────────────────────────────────┘
```

Position Description

The Theatrical Press Agent Apprentice is a full-time paid assistant who works in the office of a senior theatrical press agent, and who helps publicize and promote theatrical productions.

The Apprentice works as an assistant for a three-year period. During this time, he or she will work with one specific press agent at a time, although he or she may change employers during their apprenticeship. The employer, however, must be a certified, union member of the Association of Theatrical Press Agents and Managers (ATPAM).

When an individual decides to enter the profession of theatrical press agents, he or she will apply to work with a senior theatrical press agent who is a member of ATPAM. If the senior press agent feels that the applicant is dedicated to the profession, he or she will sponsor the individual who can them become an Apprentice.

The individual will be a Theatrical Press Agent Apprentice for the next three years. He or she will take this time to learn everything possible from the senior press agent about publicizing and promoting theatrical productions.

The Theatrical Press Agent Apprentice will learn the techniques of the profession. Everything he or she does will be under the strict supervision of the senior press agent. It is important for the Apprentice to work with an individual he or she both likes and respects professionally. The two will be spending many hours together. A lot of the future success of the Apprentice will be the result of the training received from his or her superior.

A great amount of the Apprentice's time will be spent watching the senior press agent do his or her job. As the Apprentice monitors the mentor's techniques, he or she will find that many of the techniques used in publicity are similar. For example, every time the press agent arranges and runs a press conference, he or she will follow the same basic steps. The press agent may create new promotions but a location must always be chosen for the program, the media must be invited and there has to be a reason to hold an event.

The Theatrical Press Agent Apprentice will learn how to write a press release, put together a press or media kit and prepare biographies. At this point in the educational process, the individual will just be learning. He or she might gather information for the senior press agent or check the accuracy of facts, but probably would not do much of the actual writing. As time goes by in the apprenticeship, the individual will begin by writing simple press releases or bio copy.

The individual will also learn how to stage media events. This might include the development of ideas which attract media attention as well as the implementation of the actual event. The Apprentice will assist with many of the details involved in the running of these events. He or she may do a lot of the legwork including reviewing the media guest list, checking to make sure that press kits are compiled and brought to the event location, or helping to greet media people. The Theatrical Press Agent Apprentice will learn to put press lists together and may be responsible for making sure that names, addresses and phones numbers are kept accurate. He or she may make calls on behalf of the senior press agent to the media and others.

The Theatrical Press Agent Apprentice will do a lot of running around. He or she may deliver press kits, press releases or photographs. The individual might accompany one of the stars of the production to a press interview or television appearance.

On opening nights, the Theatrical Press Agent Apprentice will help the senior press agent with his or her duties. The individual may call critics or reviewers to make sure that they will be attending, put names on seats so that the reviewers will know where to sit or pass out press kits and media information.

The Theatrical Press Agent Apprentice's main function is to assist the senior press agent in every way while learning everything the individual knows about publicizing and promoting theatrical productions.

The Theatrical Press Agent Apprentice is responsible directly to the senior press agent. He or she will work long hours. This is not a 9-to-5 job. After the apprenticeship, the individual will be ready to strike out on his or her own and become a full-fledged theatrical press agent.

Salaries

Minimum salaries for Theatrical Press Agent Apprentices are set by the Association of Theatrical Press Agents and Managers, AFL-CIO (ATPAM).

In 1998, the minimum salary was $350 per week for the first year of their apprenticeship.

Employment Prospects

Employment prospects are extremely limited for a Theatrical Press Agent Apprentice. To obtain this position, an individual must first locate an Association of Theatrical Press Agents and Managers union member who is willing to sponsor him or her. He or she will then work with the senior Theatrical Press Agent learning the ropes.

Advancement Prospects

Advancement prospects are good for individuals who become Theatrical Press Agent Apprentices. The Apprentice will go through a three-year program where he or she learns as much as possible about performing the functions of the job. Those who make it through the program and are creative, innovative and aggressive will likely become successful Theatrical Press Agents.

Education and Training

There is no educational requirement for a Theatrical Press Agent Apprentice. The individual must go through a three-year apprentice program learning the skills of the trade.

Those who are considering college first, may want to take courses in public relations, writing, communications, journalism, advertising, marketing, English, theater arts and business.

Experience/Skills/Personality Traits

Individuals have to possess good communications skills to excel in this position. They should be able to verbalize clearly, intelligently and articulately. The ability to make and take phone calls and to obtain the correct information is essential.

The Theatrical Press Agent Apprentice must have excellent writing skills.

In order for the individual to succeed, he or she should be an innovative, creative person; someone who can "brainstorm" and come up with unique ideas and concepts for publicity and promotion. They should be aggressive, persuasive and able to get along well with others.

Unions/Associations

Theatrical Press Agent Apprentices are members of the Association of Theatrical Press Agents and Managers, AFL-CIO (ATPAM). This a bargaining union which negotiates and sets minimum salaries for members, sets standards for the profession and provides a welfare fund for members.

Individuals may also belong to trade associations which offer professional and educational guidance and other information. The most prominent trade association for those working in publicity is the Public Relations Society of America (PRSA). This organization also offers a student membership.

Tips for Entry

1. Contact the Association of Theatrical Press Agents and Managers (ATPAM) to get information regarding the union, branch offices, members who might sponsor you and specifics about Apprentice applications.
2. Get as much experience as you can ahead of time doing publicity and promotion. If you're in school, work on your school theater productions. If you aren't, you might consider doing publicity for a local theater group.

3. You might also want to take seminars in publicity, promotion and writing. These will help you learn the basics.

4. Join the Public Relations Society of America (PRSA) or their student chapter to take advantage of their seminars, courses, literature and professional guidance.

Look in the appendix for their address and phone number.

5. You might consider getting a summer or part-time job working in the administrative end of local theater groups or summer stock to give you a partial understanding of the theater industry.

CAREER OPPORTUNITIES IN ORCHESTRA, OPERA AND BALLET COMPANY ADMINISTRATION

BUSINESS MANAGER—ORCHESTRA, OPERA OR BALLET COMPANY

CAREER PROFILE

Duties: Supervising the financial affairs of an orchestra, opera or ballet company; preparing and distributing payroll.

Alternate Title(s):   Comptroller.

Salary Range: $20,000 to $65,000+ a year.

Employment Prospects: Fair.

Best Geographical Location(s) for Position: Culturally active cities offer the most opportunities.

Prerequisites:

Education or Training: Educational requirements vary; four-year college degree preferred, but not required for all positions.

Experience: Bookkeeping or accounting experience helpful.

Special Skills and Personality Traits: Ability to work well with figures; accuracy; accounting and bookkeeping skills; detail oriented; communications skills.

CAREER LADDER

```
┌─────────────────────────────┐
│     Business Manager        │
│  of Larger, More Prestigious│
│         Company             │
└─────────────────────────────┘

┌─────────────────────────────┐
│     Business Manager        │
└─────────────────────────────┘

┌─────────────────────────────┐
│        Bookkeeper           │
│           or                │
│        Accountant           │
└─────────────────────────────┘
```

Position Description

The Business Manager of a symphony orchestra, opera or ballet company is in charge of supervising its financial affairs. Depending on the size and budget of the organization, the Business Manager may work alone or have an assistant and a staff.

The Business Manager is responsible for checking all bills the organization receives. If they are correct, he or she issues checks to pay the bills on time. If they are wrong or if there is any discrepancy, the Business Manager or comptroller rectifies the problem.

The Business Manager looks at prices of various items—for example, the prices of music stands—to establish the best price. The Business Manager works out deals with airlines and with hotel or motel chains for transporting and housing the singers, orchestra or ballet members while on tour. As the budgets for most organizations are extremely tight, the Business Manager continually tries to find ways to save money.

Accurate records are kept on all expenditures paid out for the organization and include payment dates, check numbers and lists of items purchased.

The Business Manager is responsible for preparing and distributing the payroll both for staff members and visiting artists. These payments are disbursed in accordance with any applicable union regulations. The Business Manager makes sure that the proper deductions are taken from everyone's salary and that these monies are correctly deposited and reported to the government.

The Business Manager works closely with the organization's director of development, keeping account of money raised by donations. The Business Manager oversees the bookkeeping for the fund-raising department.

The Business Manager also works with the managing director in putting together an annual budget for the organization. After the budget is approved by the board of directors, the Business Manager is responsible for keeping costs within bounds.

The Business Manager works fairly regular hours. Depending on the specific job structure of the organization, he or she may report to the orchestra, opera or ballet's general manager or to a board of directors.

Salaries

Salaries of Business Managers of orchestra, opera and ballet companies vary depending on a number of factors including the classification, size and budget of the organization, as well as the candidate's responsibilities, expertise, experience and qualifications. Earnings of full-time Business Managers may range from $20,000 to $65,000 or more annually.

Employment Prospects

Employment prospects are fair for Business Managers. In major cultural centers, full-time work is available. In other regions the jobs may consist of part-time work.

Advancement Prospects

Advancement prospects for Business Managers working in orchestras, ballet or opera companies are limited. Candidates climb the career ladder by moving to similar positions with more prestigious organizations that offer increased responsibilities and increased earnings. A Business Manager may also be promoted to the position of company manager.

Education and Training

Educational requirements vary from position to position. A four-year college degree is recommended and preferred, but not always necessary. College majors include business, accounting, finance, theater arts or arts management.

Experience/Skills/Personality Traits

Business Managers working in the performing arts should have a good sense of business. The primary skills a Business Manager needs is an ability to work with numbers and to keep immaculate records. Accuracy is essential.

The ability to set up a payroll and disperse funds is necessary. Bookkeeping skills and/or accounting experience are helpful.

The Business Manager must be able to handle many details at once without becoming flustered. The ability to communicate well is necessary.

Unions/Associations

The Business Manager belongs to different organizations depending on the specific job. The candidate may be a member of local arts councils, the American Symphony Orchestra League (ASOL), Metropolitan Opera Association (MOA), Metropolitan Opera Guild (MOG), National Opera Association (NOA), Opera America (OA) or the Ballet Theater Foundation (BTF). These organizations offer professional guidance and support to their members.

Tips for Entry

1. Check for jobs in the classified ads sections of newspapers. Most of these jobs open at the end of a season. Organization and trade association newsletters also list job openings.
2. Find an internship in the business department of a performing arts company.
3. Send a resume and a cover letter to orchestra, ballet and opera companies. Ask that they keep your resume on file if there is no current opening.

DIRECTOR OF FUND-RAISING AND DEVELOPMENT—ORCHESTRA, OPERA OR BALLET COMPANY OR NOT-FOR-PROFIT THEATER

CAREER PROFILE

Duties: Raising funds for not-for-profit theater, orchestra, opera or ballet company to sustain organization; creating and developing fund-raising programs; implementing programs; cultivating potential donors.

Alternate Title(s): Fund-Raising and Development Director; Fund-Raising Director; Development Director; Director of Development.

Salary Range: $15,000 to $80,000+ a year.

Employment Prospects: Good.

Best Geographical Location(s) for Position: Positions may be located throughout the country; large, culturally active cities offer more possibilities.

Prerequisites:

Education or Training: Requirements vary from high school diploma through bachelor's degree.

Experience: Experience in fund-raising, public relations and marketing may be preferred.

Special Skills and Personality Traits: Communication and interpersonal skills; enthusiastic; aggressiveness; persuasiveness; organizational skills; creativity.

CAREER LADDER

```
┌─────────────────────────────────────┐
│            Director of              │
│   Fund-Raising and Development      │
│    for More Prestigious Company     │
└─────────────────────────────────────┘

┌─────────────────────────────────────┐
│            Director of              │
│    Fund-Raising and Development     │
└─────────────────────────────────────┘

┌─────────────────────────────────────┐
│  Assistant to Fund-Raising Director │
│                 or                  │
│     Fund-Raising and Development    │
│        Department Staff Member      │
└─────────────────────────────────────┘
```

Position Description

Running a not-for-profit theater, orchestra, ballet or opera company is expensive. Ticket sales usually do not cover the costs of running such an organization. Most not-for-profit organizations augment the monies earned from ticket sales with fund-raising activities. The person responsible for directing these efforts is called the Director of Fund-Raising or the Development Director.

Director of Fund-Raising is an important administrative position in an orchestra, opera or ballet company or a not-for-profit theater. The individual's main responsibility is to raise money to run the company.

Finding donations is not easy, especially when the country is in a recession. Many organizations and causes vie for funds donated by the public. However, many people take a special interest in their community's cultural and performing arts organizations, and it is the Director's job to find ways to urge these people to donate money.

The Fund-Raising Director is responsible for developing programs to raise funds to keep the company solvent. The candidate is expected to find ways to raise money not only for large capital campaigns to pay for new buildings or performing arts centers, but also for other sustaining programs of the organization.

The Director creates and develops these programs and is then responsible for their implementation. The individual coordinates the annual giving activities, sustaining campaigns, capital campaigns and deferred giving opportunities for donors and potential donors. These programs may increase attendance and result in increased revenue from ticket sales. They may also help develop direct financial support for the organization.

Some Fund-Raising and Development Directors run special events or create huge annual fund-raising dinners, auctions and dances to raise money. Other activities launched by the Director of Fund-Raising and Development include direct mail campaigns, telephone fund-raisers, telethons, galas and cocktail parties. Many Fund-Raising and Development Directors will also look for benefactors or grants to raise needed funds.

The Fund-Raising and Development Director is responsible for cultivating potential donors. To do this, he or she might attend luncheons, dinners, meetings, parties and other affairs on behalf of the performing arts organization. The Director also speaks to groups of people about the theater, orchestra, ballet or opera.

A large amount of money for not-for-profit theaters, orchestras, operas and ballet companies is raised through grants, foundations, corporations and endowments for the arts. The Fund-Raising and Development Director keeps up with the latest information on these programs and applies for grants, writes proposals and follows up in order to receive the largest possible gifts.

The Director handles a great deal of paperwork including reports describing the progress of fund-raising projects, press releases and publicity programs to promote specific fund-raising events. Other writing responsibilities include direct mail pieces, advertising copy, fliers, fund-raising letters, invitations, speeches and brochures about the company.

The Director is responsible for keeping accurate records of donor activities and resource development. He or she also develops and writes newsletters advising patrons of the organization's programs, new artists performing with the company and other highlights of the season.

In addition to regular job requirements, the Director attends community meetings, volunteer meetings and special events. The Director reports to either the company's manager, managing director or the board of directors.

Salaries

Annual earnings range from $15,000 to $80,000 or more. Salaries for Fund-Raising and Development Directors can vary greatly depending on a number of factors, including the size, prestige, budget and geographic location of the company. Variables also include the individual's experience, duties and record.

Employment Prospects

Employment prospects for Fund-Raising and Development Directors in the performing arts are good, as there is always a demand for individuals who can produce results. Candidates may find positions in not-for-profit theaters, performing arts centers, orchestras, or ballet or opera companies.

Advancement Prospects

Advancement prospects for Fund-Raising and Development Directors are good for those who are good at their jobs. An individual who is knowledgeable in the field and gets results can move on to positions with more prestigious theater, orchestra, ballet or opera companies.

Education and Training

Educational requirements vary for Directors of Fund-Raising and Development. Some positions require a high school diploma, others a college degree or background. A college degree is useful both for its educational value, and for the experience and the opportunities to make contacts.

Good choices for majors include arts administration, arts management, marketing, business, public relations and liberal arts. Courses, workshops or seminars in fund-raising, public relations, marketing, business, arts administration and arts management are also helpful.

Experience/Skills/Personality Traits

Experience is helpful in attaining a job as the Director of Fund-Raising and Development for a performing arts company. Many individuals work as assistants or staff members in a fund-raising department before obtaining their current jobs. Other individuals get experience volunteering to chair an organization's fund-raising drive. Other candidates work in public relations, fund-raising, development or marketing in either the performing arts or in another industry.

The Director must be articulate with excellent verbal and written communication skills. He or she also should have good organizational and interpersonal skills, and the ability to work well with volunteers.

Fund-Raising Directors have an interest and an understanding of the performing arts. Success in raising funds comes from talking to others interested in the same areas.

Unions/Associations

Directors of Fund-Raising and Development working for not-for-profit theaters, orchestra, opera or ballet companies may belong to the Associated Council of the Arts and local arts councils. Depending on the specific performing art the individual is working in, he or she may also be involved with the American Symphony Orchestra League (ASOL), Metropolitan Opera Association (MOA), Metropolitan Opera Guild (MOG), National Opera Association (NOA), Opera America (OA) or the Ballet Theater Foundation (BTF).

Tips for Entry

1. Send your resume and a short cover letter to not-for-profit theaters, orchestras, ballet and opera compa-

nies. These organizations often have assistant or trainee positions open.

2. Find an internship program in the fund-raising and development office of a performing arts company.

3. Check newspaper classified ads for positions for Fund-Raising and Development Directors under headings of "Fund-Raising," "Development," "Performing Arts," "Not-For-Profit," "Theater," "Orchestra," "Ballet" and "Opera."

4. Look for lists of jobs in the various newsletters and publications put out by arts councils and trade associations.

DIRECTOR OF AUDIENCE DEVELOPMENT—ORCHESTRA, OPERA OR BALLET COMPANY OR NOT-FOR-PROFIT THEATER

CAREER PROFILE

Duties: Finding ways to increase the size of a company or theater's audience through single-ticket and annual subscription sales.

Alternate Title(s): Subscription and Ticket Service Director.

Salary Range: $15,000 to $39,000+.

Employment Prospects: Fair.

Best Geographical Location(s) for Position: Cities hosting symphonies, operas, ballets and not-for-profit theaters.

Prerequisites:

Education or Training: High school diploma, minimum requirement. Some positions may prefer or require college degree.

Experience: Experience working in the administrative end of theater or performing arts helpful.

Special Skills and Personality Traits: Detail oriented; creativity; administrative ability; communication skills; writing skills; basic understanding of theater and performing arts; organized.

CAREER LADDER

```
┌─────────────────────────────────────┐
│   Director of Audience Development   │
│    in Larger, More Prestigious       │
│       Company or Theater             │
│              or                      │
│  Director of Funding and Development │
└─────────────────────────────────────┘

┌─────────────────────────────────────┐
│   Director of Audience Development   │
└─────────────────────────────────────┘

┌─────────────────────────────────────┐
│       Assistant Director of          │
│      Audience Development            │
│              or                      │
│            Student                   │
└─────────────────────────────────────┘
```

Position Description

The Director of Audience Development finds ways to increase the size of a company's or theater's audience through single-ticket and annual subscription sales. This position is found in nonprofit theaters, orchestras, opera and ballet companies. The candidate is also called a Subscription and Ticket Service Director.

The Director develops a variety of programs in an effort to increase the number of tickets sold, seeking new subscribers and new markets to sell tickets. The Director also works with schools, theater groups and other organizations to develop group sales.

The Director runs a variety of campaigns to find potential subscribers. These programs include telemarketing, mailing and telethons. The individual also works with the company's advertising department in designing and running advertisements and brochures to obtain new subscribers. He or she works with the public relations department sending out press releases and feature articles about upcoming events.

The Director of Audience Development tries to target specific audiences. If the theater is presenting children's plays, he or she develops sales letters, brochures and fliers targeted to schools and parents' groups. The individual might also develop mailings and special pricing schedules for senior citizens groups and theater clubs.

The Director of Audience Development may be required to do research to find out what types of people have come to the theater or performing arts center previously on other occasions. The individual may also need to determine the demographics of annual subscribers to the theater. With this in mind, he or she can develop strategies to bring in more of the same types of people and find ways to open markets of new audiences.

The Director of Audience Development often works with other departments in the organization. These include public relations, advertising and the box office. In some situations, the Director of Audience Development is responsible for the box office and all its activities.

The Director of Audience Development is responsible for keeping track of current subscribers. The individual may personally send out renewal forms to current subscribers or pass the duty on to an assistant, secretary or volunteer.

Depending on the situation, the Director of Audience Development may be responsible for handling the coordination of individual theater tickets sales. Tickets for theatrical events are often sold on location at the box office, at schools, stores or through a ticket service such as Ticketron, and the Director may be required to keep records of how many tickets are sold at each location. In many instances, especially when the theater is a small one operating with a skeleton staff, the Director will be responsible for making sure they receive monies owed to them for ticket sales.

The Director of Audience Development must keep clear, concise records of everything thta is done in the department. This includes records of subscribers, logistics, new markets, phone calls, letters, renewals and promotions.

As a rule, the Director of Audience Development will work fairly regular hours. He or she may, however, also be required to be in attendance at theatrical performances. The Director of Audience Development knows he or she has been successful, when the majority of seats for all performances are sold out ahead of time.

Salaries

Salaries for Directors of Audience Development will vary greatly depending on the specific job, including the size, budget and prestige of the theater or company and its geographic location, as well as the responsibilities and experience of the individual.

Earnings may range from $15,000 a year for an individual working in a small theater, orchestra, opera or ballet company to $39,000 or more a year for someone working in a larger, more prestigious setting in a major city.

Employment Prospects

Employment prospects for positions as the Director of Audience Development are fair, as the duties of this position may be handled by the director of fund-raising and development. The great majority of the available jobs are with smaller theatrical companies, orchestras, ballet or opera companies.

Advancement Prospects

Advancement prospects are fair for the Director of Audience Development. Directors climb the career ladder by finding a position in a larger more prestigious theater or by becoming the director of funding and development.

Education and Training

Educational requirements differ from job to job. Some positions require only a high school diploma while others require or prefer a college degree or background. Good choices for college majors include theater arts, communications, marketing, business and liberal arts.

Courses and seminars in theatrical development, audience development, bookkeeping, computers and marketing are also useful.

Experience/Skills/Personality Traits

In some cases, the Director of Audience Development is an entry level position someone fills after performing similar duties in a voluntary capacity or in an internship. Some people also enter this position after earning a degree in theater arts in college. Some people obtain experience working as an assistant director of audience development.

The Director of Audience Development should be detail oriented and organized. An ability to keep accurate records is a must.

The Director should be a creative individual who has the ability to come up with unique ways to market the theater to potential audiences. The Director of Audience Development requires good verbal communications skills as well as written ones. A basic understanding of the theater and performing arts is necessary.

Unions/Associations

The Director of Audience Development belongs to any number of associations depending on the type of theater he or she is working with. The Director may be a member of local arts councils. The Director working in orchestras, ballet or opera companies may belong to the American Symphony Orchestra League (ASOL), Metropolitan Opera Association (MOA), Metropolitan Opera Guild (MOG), National Opera Association (NOA), Opera America (OA) and the Ballet Theater Foundation (BTF). These organizations offer professional guidance and support to their members.

Tips for Entry

1. Find an internship with a symphony, ballet, opera or nonprofit theater group.
2. Volunteer with a local community theater group or symphony in the development or ticket services department. This job provides good hands-on experience and helps you make useful contacts.

3. Look in the classified ads under heading such as "Theater," "Community Theater," "Symphony," "Orchestra," "Opera," "Dance," "Arts Council" or "Audience Development." Openings may also be listed in arts council newsletters, theater group newsletters and the American Symphony Orchestra League (ASOL) newsletter.

4. Send your resume and a short cover letter to community and other nonprofit theater groups, orchestras, ballet or opera companies.

PUBLIC RELATIONS DIRECTOR— ORCHESTRA, OPERA OR BALLET COMPANY

CAREER PROFILE

Duties: Handling the promotion and public relations activities for an orchestra, opera or ballet company; writing press releases.

Alternate Title(s): P.R. Director; Director of Public Relations.

Salary Range: $18,000 to $60,000+ a year.

Employment Prospects: Fair.

Best Geographical Location(s) for Position: Positions may be located through the country; culturally active cities will offer more opportunities.

Prerequisites:

Education or Training: Educational requirements vary; smaller companies may prefer, but not require, a college degree; bachelor's degree may be required in larger companies.

Experience: Experience in public relations, publicity or as a journalist.

Special Skills and Personality Traits: Creativity; good writing skills; articulate; verbal communication skills; organized; supervisory skills; interest in and knowledge of orchestra, ballet or opera.

CAREER LADDER

```
┌─────────────────────────────────────┐
│        Public Relations Director     │
│       at Larger, More Prestigious    │
│    Orchestra, Opera or Ballet Company│
└─────────────────────────────────────┘

┌─────────────────────────────────────┐
│        Public Relations Director     │
└─────────────────────────────────────┘

┌─────────────────────────────────────┐
│   Assistant Public Relations Director,│
│              Publicist               │
│                 or                   │
│              Journalist              │
└─────────────────────────────────────┘
```

Position Description

The Public Relations Director handles the promotion and public relations activities of a performing arts organization. Specific responsibilities depend on the size and prestige of the company.

If the orchestra, ballet or opera company is large and prestigious, it supports a large public relations department. The Director of the department is responsible for supervising the staff, the size of which varies. In very small organizations, the Public Relations Director works alone.

All orchestras, operas and ballet companies have specific seasons, during which they put on performances. One of the duties of the Public Relations Director is to make sure that the community knows about the performances during any given season. The Director does so by notifying the press and other media so that they can publicize the company's activities. The Public Relations Director writes press releases about the performers and the performances. He or she also invites the press to press conferences or press parties. During these events, the media learns about the various activities that the organization has planned for the season. The press, in turn, writes about the events and activites in their newspapers and magazines and talks about them on radio and television programs.

The Public Relations Director obtains additional publicity by promoting special activities that the company has planned for the season including children's performances, educational activities and holiday shows.

The Public Relations Director is responsible for building up a media contact list. This list consists of names, addresses and phone numbers of newspapers, magazines, television and radio stations along with contact names of editors and reporters.

In order to obtain the maximum amount of publicity for the organization, the Public Relations Director writes press releases with a variety of slants about the organization, including the hiring of new members of the company, interesting stories about the organization, performance schedules, guest soloists, dancers or conductors.

After writing and sending out press releases, the Public Relations Director follows up by calling individual editors to find out if they need more information or photographs.

The Director is required to set up interviews with members of the company and various media on a regular basis to coincide with special events. It is the Director's job to call radio or television stations to set up dates for guest appearances of members of the company on various shows.

The Public Relations Director works with other departments in the organization, such as the fund-raising and development department during a fund-raising drive.

The Public Relations Director is also responsible for placing advertising about the company in the various media, working with the organization's advertising director or an outside agency.

The Public Relations Director is responsible for developing, writing and printing the publications used for promotion, education or fund-raising. The Director assigns these tasks to others and supervises the project.

Although the Public Relations Director has a relatively normal work schedule, he or she sometimes works long hours, since his or her attendance at press parties, functions and affairs after hours is required. The Public Relations Director is responsible to the company manager, managing director or the organization's board of directors.

Salaries

Salaries of Public Relations Directors working in orchestras, opera or ballet companies vary depending on the size, prestige, geographic location and budget of the company. Other factors affecting earnings include the responsibilities and experience level of the individual.

Public Relations Directors earn between $18,000 and $60,000 or more annually with the lower salaries going to those with less experience and those working in smaller companies.

Employment Prospects

Employment prospects are fair for Public Relations Directors who aspire to work with orchestras, opera or ballet companies. Individuals may, however, work in smaller organizations or relocate to find positions. Jobs are located throughout the country. However, culturally active cities offer more opportunities.

Advancement Prospects

Advancement prospects are poor for Public Relations Directors in orchestras, opera or ballet companies. The career path many individuals attempt is to find similar positions with more prestigious companies, although there are not a lot of openings in the more prestigious companies. When someone does leave a position, it is usually filled from within the ranks of the organization. Another route up the career ladder for a Public Relations Director is to become the Director of Development.

Education and Training

Educational requirements vary for Public Relations Directors in orchestras, ballet or opera companies. In very small companies, the Public Relations Director is not required to hold a college degree although one may be preferred. In larger companies, however, a bachelor's degree is often required. Good college majors for this type of job include public relations, communications, liberal arts, English, marketing and music or theater arts management.

Courses, workshops or seminars in journalism, theater and music arts, communications, public relations, publicity and marketing are also helpful.

Experience/Skills/Personality Traits

Public Relations Directors in orchestras, opera and ballet companies are required to have some promotion experience, either as publicists in a similar organization or in an unrelated field, or as an assistant in the marketing or development department. Some P.R. Directors work as assistant public relations directors prior to their current jobs; others work as journalists in either the print media, television or radio.

Public Relations Directors must be creative. A significant part of their job involves writing, and they should be able to write clearly and concisely.

Public Relations Directors must be articulate and have good communications skills, as they speak on a one-to-one basis and in front of large groups regularly.

Supervisory skills are often necessary. The Director learns to work under pressure without becoming flustered. Public Relations Directors must be very organized and have the ability to work on many projects at one time.

Unions/Associations

Public Relations Directors working in orchestras, ballet or opera companies belong to a number of organizations related to the specific performing art they are working with. These organizations include the American Symphony Orchestra League (ASOL), Metropolitan Opera Association (MOA), Metropolitan Opera Guild (MOG), National Opera Association (NOA), Opera America (OA) and the Ballet Theater

Foundation (BTF). They offer professional guidance and support to their members.

Directors also belong to the Public Relations Society of America (PRSA).

Tips for Entry

1. Find an internship program where you gain valuable on-the-job training as well as opportunities to make valuable contacts. Internships are offered through organizations, associations, colleges, orchestras, ballet or opera companies.

2. Look for openings in the newspaper classified or display section under the headings "Public Relations," "P.R.," "Orchestras," "Music," "Ballet," "Dance," "Opera" or "Publicity." Jobs are also advertised in the trade journals of the various organizations and associations.

3. Check the newsletters of regional arts councils for lists of job openings.

4. Send your resume and a short cover letter to the personnel directors of orchestras, opera and ballet companies. Request that your resume be kept on file if there are no current openings.

ORCHESTRA MANAGER

CAREER PROFILE

Duties: Assisting orchestra's managing director in various management duties; negotiating contracts with musical orchestra personnel.

Alternate Title(s): Assistant Manager; Operations Manager.

Salary Range: $20,000 to $65,000+ a year.

Employment Prospects: Poor.

Best Geographical Location(s) for Position: Culturally active cities hosting orchestras offer more opportunities.

Prerequisites:

Education or Training: College degree preferred or recommended for most positions.

Experience: Positions in supervisory capacities useful.

Special Skills and Personality Traits: Management, supervisory and negotiating skills.

CAREER LADDER

```
┌─────────────────────────────────────┐
│         Managing Director            │
└─────────────────────────────────────┘

┌─────────────────────────────────────┐
│         Orchestra Manager            │
└─────────────────────────────────────┘

┌─────────────────────────────────────┐
│      Director of Development         │
│               or                     │
│            Publicity                 │
│               or                     │
│      Public Relations Position       │
└─────────────────────────────────────┘
```

Position Description

The Orchestra Manager is the assistant to the orchestra's managing director. A primary duty of the individual is negotiating with the musician's union on behalf of the orchestra's management. An Orchestra Manager tries to get the best deal for the orchestra management from the union while keeping the players happy.

The Orchestra Manager also arranges any concert tours for the orchestra, arranging the details to make it easy for the orchestra. The Manager is responsible for handling the problems that are not directly music related; from a musician's instrument that arrives late to an auditorium with bad acoustics; a musician who becomes ill in the middle of a tour or a dispute caused by hot tempers erupting on the road.

The Orchestra Manager also oversees the orchestra's administrative employees including the director of development, director of public relations, music administrator, business manager, director of educational activities and director of ticket subscriptions. He or she is knowledgeable about these positions and the problems that might occur. The Manager also understands the needs of the community or area in which the orchestra is based. As Orchestra Manager, he or she negotiates contracts for guest soloists and guest conductors.

The Orchestra Manager is responsible to the managing director of the orchestra and works very long hours. Enjoyment of symphonic music makes the long hours and hard work worthwhile.

Salaries

Symphony orchestras are classified into different groups depending on size, budget and other factors. There are major orchestras, such as the Boston Symphony or the Cleveland Orchestra; regional orchestras, for example, the Birmingham Symphony Orchestra or the Memphis Symphony Orchestra; and metropolitan, urban, community, college and youth orchestras. Salaries of Orchestra Managers vary according to the classification and location of the orchestra. Salaries range from $20,000 to $65,000 or more annually. Orchestra Managers of urban, community, college or youth orchestras often donate services or work on a per-service basis.

Employment Prospects

There are a limited number of major and regional orchestras in the country. Therefore, employment prospects at this level are poor. Positions are sometimes available at the metropolitan, urban and community levels. However, these jobs are not always full-time.

Advancement Prospects

The position of an Orchestra Manager is not an entry-level job. Positions that contribute to the Orchestra Manager's experience include public relations director, fund-raising director, business manager, or assistant in one of these fields. Once an individual has proven him- or herself in the position of Orchestra Manager, he or she is a valuable commodity to the orchestra and has the opportunity to move up to the position of managing director or to a position as Orchestra Manager in a more prestigious orchestra.

Education and Training

A college degree is preferred or recommended for most positions as Orchestra Manager. Individuals may find a few positions without this requirement, usually with smaller orchestras.

Courses in music management, administration and/or business are helpful. Classes in publicity, labor negotiations, fund-raising and psychology are useful too. There are also seminars given around the country in arts administration. These seminars put the individual in touch with others already in the field and help develop contacts.

Experience/Skills/Personality Traits

A good sense of business is important to the Orchestra Manager. An understanding of and sensitivity to musicians and their problems and pressures are equally important. To do the job well, a Manager must be able to deal effectively with problems and people under pressure. Hands-on experience is helpful. Many conservatories and universities have internship programs that provide practical experience. Enjoying music makes it all worthwhile.

Unions/Associations

The Orchestra Manager belongs to the American Symphony Orchestra League (ASOL) and may also belong to a local arts council.

Tips for Entry

1. Find an orchestra or school that has an internship in orchestral management. The American Symphony Orchestra League (ASOL) sponsors a variety of intern programs.
2. Attend seminars on orchestra management. Seminars are sponsored by various universities and orchestras in addition to the ASOL.
3. Check openings listed in the ASOL newsletter, the Associated Council of the Arts newsletter and many regional arts organization publications.
4. Look for job openings in the classified or display section of the newspaper under the headings of "Performing Arts," "Orchestra," "Symphony" or "Music."
5. Job openings may also be located on the Internet. Look for orchestra sites, which often list employment opportunities.

DIRECTOR OF EDUCATIONAL ACTIVITIES—ORCHESTRA, OPERA OR BALLET COMPANY OR NOT-FOR-PROFIT THEATER

CAREER PROFILE

Duties: Developing young people's concert series, ballets and/or plays; coordinating activities for students; planning learning activities related to the theater and performing arts.

Alternate Title(s): Director of Education; Manager of Educational Activities; Education Director.

Salary Range: $12,000 to $40,000+ a year.

Employment Prospects: Poor.

Best Geographical Location(s) for Position: Major cultural centers offer more opportunities.

Prerequisites:

Education or Training: High School diploma is the minimum requirement; some positions may require or prefer a college degree.

Experience: Experience working in theater, orchestra, ballet or opera company in some capacity helpful; administrative and business experience useful.

Special Skills and Personality Traits: Good writing and communications skills; ability to get along with young people; basic knowledge of the workings of theater, ballet, opera and orchestra companies.

CAREER LADDER

```
┌─────────────────────────────────────┐
│   Director of Educational Activities │
│      in Larger, More Prestigious     │
│         Company or Theater           │
│                 or                   │
│    Director of Public Relations,     │
│      Funding and Development         │
└─────────────────────────────────────┘

┌─────────────────────────────────────┐
│   Director of Educational Activities │
└─────────────────────────────────────┘

┌─────────────────────────────────────┐
│        Assistant Director of         │
│      Educational Activities,         │
│       Publicist or Student           │
└─────────────────────────────────────┘
```

Position Description

The Director of Educational Activities in a performing arts setting is responsible for coordinating activities for students and other young people in the community where the company performs. As a rule, this position is found in the not-for-profit performing arts sector.

The Director of Educational Activities is responsible for coordinating programs with the schools in the area surrounding the theater, orchestra, ballet or opera company's base of operations. The Director meets with school district personnel as well as music supervisors or teachers, dance or physical education teachers or supervisors, and English teachers regarding programs that are available for students.

The Director of Educational Activities offers various programs to the schools. For example, the Director might bring the entire orchestra or just parts of it directly into the school to perform. The Director might offer actors, actresses, directors, playwrights, dancers and musicians as guest speakers at a school assembly. He or she might also gather various members of an ensemble for a theater and the performing arts career day.

The Director of Educational Activities works closely with other departments in the theatrical organization. If the Director is working with an orchestra, he or she works with the music administrator, managing director and/or orchestra manager designing young people's concerts. If the Director is working with a ballet company, he or she works closely with the managing director, dance company manager and other administrators designing programs for young people. After these performances, the Director sets up question-and-answer periods for the performers and students.

The Director recommends reduced prices for student tickets and makes sure that students, parents and school administrators are aware of the special activities and ticket prices by designing and sending brochures or posters to the schools, placing them in the surrounding areas, sending out press releases to newspapers and mailing notices to current subscribers of the performing arts company.

Other activities the Director plans include coordinating tours for students of their performing arts center, including backstage and/or business offices. The Director of Educational Activities is also responsible for the development and preparation of booklets and pamphlets explaining the different career opportunities in the field. He or she may be asked to counsel students about educational and training requirements of various positions.

The Director of Educational Activities works long hours that include regular business hours as well as the performances at schools and meetings with administrators to develop programs.

Salaries

Salaries for the Director of Educational Activities working in a theatrical or performing arts setting vary depending on a number of factors, including the size, prestige, budget and geographic location of the company as well as the individual's responsibilities and experience. Earnings can range from $12,000 a year for a person with little or no experience working in a small theatrical situation to $40,000 or more a year for an experienced Director working for a more prestigious theater group, orchestra, ballet or opera company.

Employment Prospects

Employment prospects are poor for those seeking positions as Director of Educational Activities. As the majority of these jobs are found with nonprofit companies, budgets often can not be stretched to include this position. Many times, the duties of the Director of Educational Activities are absorbed by the director of public relations, director of audience development or director of subscriptions and ticket services.

Advancement Prospects

Advancement prospects are fair for those who get their first job in this position. The Director of Educational Activities climbs the career ladder in a number of ways—finding a similar position in a larger, more prestigious theater group, orchestra, ballet or opera company or by becoming the director of public relations, development or fund-raising for a similar organization.

Education and Training

Educational requirements vary from job to job. Some positions require a high school diploma, others a college degree. Good choices for college majors include theater arts, liberal arts, communications, education or public relations.

Experience/Skills/Personality Traits

Directors of Educational Activities should have a working knowledge of the organization that employs them. If working for an orchestra, the Director should understand the workings of the orchestra and have a knowledge of music in general. If the person works with a theatrical group, he or she should have a basic knowledge of theatrical arts and business.

Some Directors obtain their jobs without a lot of experience, although they probably have worked for a theater, orchestra or ballet company in another capacity—such as administrative assistant, publicist, journalist, musician, dancer or actor—prior to their appointment as Director.

The Director of Educational Activities should be articulate and well groomed. He or she should have the ability to develop and write clear, concise and creative copy, letters and brochures. The Director needs good verbal communications skills both in person and on the telephone.

An ability to get along well with young people is necessary. A basic understanding and ability to describe the specific type of performance group is essential.

Unions/Associations

There are no unions or associations that the Director of Educational Activities must belong to. The Director of the company may be a member of various arts councils, the American Symphony Orchestra League (ASOL), Metropolitan Opera Association (MOA), Metropolitan Opera Guild (MOG), National Opera Association (NOA), Opera America (OA), the Ballet Theater Foundation (BTF) or the Public Relations Society of America (PRSA).

Tips for Entry

1. Find an internship with an orchestra, ballet, opera or theatrical company. This job gives you hands-on experience working with a group as well as leads you to important contacts. Find these positions by contacting the companies themselves, through colleges and universities or local arts councils.

2. Look for jobs advertised in the classified or display section of newspapers under headings of "Educational Activities," "Arts," "Theater," "Orchestra," "Symphony," "Ballet," "Opera" or "Music." Openings are also listed in various arts council newsletters. For those interested in working with an orchestra, the American Symphony Orchestra League's (ASOL) newsletter also lists openings.

3. Call the theatrical department of your local college or university, arts councils, or ballet, opera, orchestra or theatrical companies to find seminars, workshops and courses on management and administration of a theater or other performing arts that will be useful in obtaining information and making contacts.

4. Send your resume with a short cover letter to the Personnel Director of symphony orchestras, opera, ballet and theatrical companies.

ORCHESTRA, OPERA OR BALLET COMPANY PERSONNEL MANAGER

CAREER PROFILE

Duties: Hiring all employees on both the business and the artistic side of the company; sending out notices of job openings; placing advertisements; interviewing applicants.

Alternate Title(s): Personnel Director.

Salary Range: $18,000 to $50,000+ a year.

Employment Prospects: Poor.

Best Geographical Location(s) for Position: Culturally active cities hosting orchestras, ballet and opera companies offer more possibilities.

Prerequisites:

Education or Training: Requirements vary from high school diploma to bachelor's degree.

Experience: Experience working in personnel useful.

Special Skills and Personality Traits: Ability to put the right person in the right job; interviewing skills; organized; detail oriented; communication skills.

CAREER LADDER

```
┌─────────────────────────────────────┐
│ Personnel Manager for More Prestigious │
│  Orchestra, Opera or Ballet Company   │
└─────────────────────────────────────┘

┌─────────────────────────────────────┐
│  Orchestra, Ballet or Opera Company   │
│          Personnel Manager            │
└─────────────────────────────────────┘

┌─────────────────────────────────────┐
│        Personnel Staff Member         │
└─────────────────────────────────────┘
```

Position Description

Many often wonder how people are chosen to work in an orchestra, opera or ballet company. The individual responsible for hiring staff is the company's Personnel Manager, who has a variety of duties depending on the specific position.

The Personnel Manager is responsible for all the hiring and firing decisions in the organization. In some situations the Personnel Manager supervises a staff, and, if so, delegates many of these responsibilities.

One of the main functions of the Personnel Manager is to send out notices whenever there are openings in either the business or the artistic end of the organization. These notices are sent to a number of places, including schools, colleges, conservatories, newsletters, associations, organizations and unions.

The Personnel Manager is also responsible for writing and placing classified advertisements in the print media for job openings and for determining which magazines and

newspapers will bring responses from the most qualified candidates for the jobs.

Once people respond to notices or advertisements, the Personnel Manager is responsible for screening their applications and setting up preliminary interviews with applicants. The Personnel Director then calls back the best candidates for further interviews with others in the company. The Personnel Director has ability to put people into the jobs for which they are best suited.

When there are openings for dancers, musicians or singers, the Personnel Manager works with others who handle the auditions. For example, in an orchestra, the Personnel Director works with the conductor or concertmaster; in a ballet company, with the balletmaster or mistress.

In addition to looking for applicants and holding interviews for full-time artists, the Personnel Manager is often responsible for finding substitutes often needed on the spur of the moment. The Personnel Manager develops and maintains a list of backup people in all performance areas, knows exactly how they perform, what they are capable of and where they are at all times. Names, addresses and phone numbers are updated constantly. A substitute performer who cannot be located is of no value to a company.

The Personnel Manager makes sure that all those who are hired understand the orchestra, ballet or opera company's policies, rules and regulations. He or she negotiates or assists in the negotiation of salaries and working conditions. While not given a free hand regarding salaries, the Personnel Director is given a range within which to work and finds the most competent, talented person to fill the position at the lowest price.

Another responsibility of the Personnel Manager is to make sure that all necessary forms are filled out, since many of the jobs are filled by members of various unions. These organizations have very strict rules and regulations that must be adhered to with proper documentation. The Personnel Manager also makes sure all contracts are signed, dated and filed in the appropriate place.

The Personnel Manager of an opera, orchestra or ballet company is responsible for keeping track of employee attendance and punctuality.

One of the more difficult responsibilities of the Personnel Manager is handling the firing of employees.

Salaries

Salaries for Personnel Managers working in ballet, orchestra or opera companies vary depending on the size of the company, its budget and the geographical location. Other variables affecting salaries include the Personnel Director's experience, responsibilities and qualifications.

Annual earnings for Personnel Managers range from $18,000 to $50,000 or more, with the higher salaries going to those with more experience and responsibilities working in larger ballet, opera or orchestra companies.

Employment Prospects

Employment prospects are poor for those aspiring to be Personnel Managers in orchestras, ballet or opera companies, as there are a limited number of companies large enough to hire Personnel Managers. Smaller companies that tour assign the duties of the Personnel Manager to another staff member in the organization.

Advancement Prospects

Advancement prospects are limited for Personnel Managers due to the limited availability of jobs. When people secure these positions, they tend to keep them.

Though difficult, advancement is not impossible. Individuals climb the career ladder in a number of ways, such as finding a similar position with a larger, more prestigious company. Personnel Managers also advance to other departments in the company if they are qualified, or some move into

labor relations in either the performing arts or an unrelated field.

Education and Training

Educational requirements vary for Personnel Managers in orchestras, opera and ballet companies. A few positions require a high school diploma, others require a four-year college degree.

While some Personnel Directors have degrees in any subject matter, major orchestras, ballet and opera companies prefer or require degrees in personnel administration or human resources.

Experience/Skills/Personality Traits

Personnel Managers may have experience working in personnel in either the performing arts or an unrelated field. It is usually necessary for the Personnel Director to have a background in or basic knowledge of music, dance and the performing arts.

One of the most important skills Personnel Managers can have is the ability to match the right people with the right jobs. The Personnel Manager must be skilled at interviewing techniques, screening applications and reading between the lines.

Personnel Managers must be very organized and detail oriented and have an ability to keep records. A good memory is helpful. Personnel Managers should have good verbal and written communication skills.

Unions/Associations

Personnel Managers working in orchestras, opera or ballet companies are members of various organizations depending on their specific job, including the Associated Council of the Arts, the American Symphony Orchestra League (ASOL), Metropolitan Opera Association (MOA), Metropolitan Opera Guild (MOG), National Opera Association (NOA), Opera America (OA) or the Ballet Theater Foundation (BTF). Individuals may also be members of local arts and councils.

Tips for Entry

1. Look for an internship program through schools, organizations, associations, orchestras, ballet or opera companies. Once you are working with a company, you have an easier time finding or creating this position.

2. Look for openings for Personnel Manager in the various association and organization newsletters and trade journals.

3. Look for other job possibilities in the classified ads or display section of the newspaper under the headings of "Arts," "Personnel," "Opera," "Symphony," "Orchestra," "Ballet," "Dance," "Theater Arts," "Performing Arts" or "Human Resources."

4. Stay in school to get the highest degree you can. The more qualified you are the better. Education gives you the edge in securing and keeping this position.

5. Send your resume and a short cover letter to orchestras, opera and ballet companies. Request that they keep your resume on file if there are no current openings.

6. Job openings may also be located on the Internet. Look for orchestra, opera or ballet sites that list employment opportunities.

ORCHESTRA, OPERA OR BALLET COMPANY MUSIC LIBRARIAN

CAREER PROFILE

Duties: Cataloging and ordering music for an orchestra, ballet or opera company; assisting conductor in copying scores and parts; handing out and collecting music before and after performances.

Alternate Title(s): None.

Salary Range: $18,000 to $38,000+ a year.

Employment Prospects: Poor.

Best Geographical Location(s) for Position: Culturally active cities hosting larger orchestras, ballet or opera companies.

Prerequisites:

Education or Training: Bachelor's degree in music history or theater and library sciences; master's degree in music or library science often required.

Experience: Experience as assistant to music librarian helpful; internship useful.

Special Skills and Personality Traits: Organized; detail oriented; ability to copy conductor's markings; interest in music and the performing arts.

CAREER LADDER

```
┌─────────────────────────────────────┐
│        Music Librarian for          │
│        More Prestigious             │
│  Orchestra, Opera or Ballet Company │
└─────────────────────────────────────┘

┌─────────────────────────────────────┐
│  Orchestra, Opera or Ballet Company │
│         Music Librarian             │
└─────────────────────────────────────┘

┌─────────────────────────────────────┐
│      Music Librarian's Assistant    │
└─────────────────────────────────────┘
```

Position Description

Music Librarians involved in the performing arts work with orchestras, opera and ballet companies and have varied responsibilities depending on their specific job.

Working with orchestra, opera and ballet companies, Music Librarians combine their skills as librarians with their love for and comprehensive knowledge of music and the performing arts. The responsibilities of the Music Librarian include cataloging the organization's printed music and ordering new music when needed. In cases where the company decides not to purchase certain pieces of music, the Librarian locates the sheet music, rents it and returns it when the company has finished with it.

The Music Librarian needs to be able to copy musical markings, as he or she often assists the conductor of the orchestra in this task. The Music Librarian copies parts for the different section members, makes the necessary corrections and adds bowings or phrasing where indicated.

Another function of the Music Librarian working with orchestra, opera or ballet companies is to organize and then hand out the music. He or she is responsible for collecting the music after the rehearsal or the performance has concluded.

The Music Librarian travels with the company when it goes on tour or has special performances. On the road, the Librarian is responsible for all of the sheet music.

The Music Librarian is also responsible for contacting guest conductors or soloists to find out about the music needed for the artist's performance.

A Music Librarian working at a school or a library has some of the same responsibilities as a company Music Librarian, but usually less involvement with the performer and performance but more contact with students. One of the big differences between a company Music Librarian and those working other settings is the working hours. Music Librarians working with orchestras, ballet or opera companies do not work regular hours. Instead, they are required to do routine tasks in the morning and afternoon and attend rehearsal or performance at night or on weekends. Music Librarians for performance troups are responsible to the orchestra conductor.

This job can be quite enjoyable for those who have the skills and enjoy being in a performing arts setting. Music Librarians attend every rehearsal and performance and thus have the opportunity to see a production evolve from its beginning to the final performance.

Salaries

Salaries vary for Music Librarians as they do for most jobs in the performing arts. Factors affecting earnings include the experience and responsibilities of the individual as well as the specific company, its size, prestige and geographic location.

A Music Librarian working for a major orchestra, ballet or opera company earns between $24,000 and $38,000 or more annually.

An individual working for a regional or metropolitan orchestra, opera or ballet company earns an annual salary between $18,000 and $30,000. In smaller orchestras, ballet and opera companies, duties of the Music Librarian are often assumed by a section member of the orchestra, and thus there is no paid position with these organizations.

Employment Prospects

Employment prospects for Music Librarians working in orchestras, ballet or opera companies are poor. There are a limited number of these companies in the country, and as previously noted, some companies do not employ paid Music Librarians. In very small opera or ballet companies they often do not even use an orchestra, relying instead on recorded music.

Advancement Prospects

Advancement prospects are limited for Music Librarians working in orchestras, ballet or opera companies. Because jobs are so hard to find, once an individual does land a position, he or she usually does not leave it. Those who do advance find similar jobs in larger, more prestigious companies. Others move into positions in other settings such as universities, colleges or libraries.

Education and Training

The educational requirements for Music Librarians vary from job to job. Some positions require an undergraduate degree in music theory or history. Others require a dual major in music and library sciences. Still others require a master's degree in either music or library sciences.

Music Librarians also have training in copying musical parts and scores.

Experience/Skills/Personality Traits

Music Librarians working in orchestras, opera or ballet companies often get experience prior to obtaining their current job by working as assistants to music librarians. These jobs are usually available only in larger orchestras, opera and ballet companies. Individuals may also get experience through internship programs.

Music Librarians should be very organized, detail oriented, dependable and reliable.

Music Librarians working in these settings must have the ability to copy conductor's markings on scores in neat, legible handwriting.

Music Librarians must have the ability to get along well with others and should have a great interest in music and a love for the performing arts.

Unions/Associations

Music Librarians belong to a number of associations depending on their specific job. These organizations provide professional guidance and support to their members. They offer seminars, newsletters and other valuable information.

Organizations include the American Library Association (ALA), the Special Libraries Association (SLA), the American Federation of Musicians (AFM), the American Symphony Orchestra League (ASOL), Metropolitan Opera Association (MOA), Metropolitan Opera Guild (MOG), National Opera Association (NOA), Opera America (OA) and the Ballet Theater Foundation (BTF).

Tips for Entry

1. Find an internship as a Music Librarian with a major orchestra, ballet or opera company.
2. Volunteer to act as the Music Librarian of your college or school orchestra or band. This position will provide you with good hands-on experience.
3. Write to orchestras, ballet and opera companies to find out if they employ music librarian assistants. If they do, send your resume and a short cover letter.
4. Work as a Music Librarian in a radio station. While the duties vary from performance work, the experience is useful.
5. Job openings may be located on the Internet. Look for orchestras, ballets and opera company sites; they often list employment opportunities.

ORCHESTRA, OPERA OR BALLET COMPANY TOUR COORDINATOR

CAREER PROFILE

Duties: Coordinating all facets of the company's appearances when away from home city; overseeing everything that is done on the road; organizing schedules.

Alternate Title(s): Tour Coordinator; Road Coordinator.

Salary Range: $32,000 to $80,000+ a year.

Employment Prospects: Poor.

Best Geographical Location(s) for Position: Culturally active cities hosting orchestras, ballet and opera companies offer more possibilities for employment.

Prerequisites:

Education or Training: Requirements vary from high school diploma to preference for college degree.

Experience: Experience working with orchestra, opera or ballet company useful; experience on the road helpful.

Special Skills and Personality Traits: Coordination skills; ability to work under pressure; understanding of performing arts industry; organized; detail oriented; communication skills; supervisory skills; dependability; reliability.

CAREER LADDER

```
┌─────────────────────────────────────┐
│         Tour Coordinator            │
│       for More Prestigious          │
│ Orchestra, Ballet or Opera Company  │
└─────────────────────────────────────┘

┌─────────────────────────────────────┐
│   Orchestra, Ballet or Opera Company │
│         Tour Coordinator            │
└─────────────────────────────────────┘

┌─────────────────────────────────────┐
│     Assistant Tour Coordinator      │
│                or                   │
│  Orchestra, Ballet or Opera Company  │
│           Staff Member              │
└─────────────────────────────────────┘
```

Position Description

Orchestra, ballet and opera companies have a home city where they perform during their regular season. Most companies also schedule appearances in other cities. These performances take the form of a tour that lasts from one day to a few months or more depending on the specific company. The person in charge of arranging the tour and handling all details while the company is on the road is called the Company Tour Coordinator.

The Coordinator is responsible for all facets of the touring company's appearances and for overseeing everything that is done while the company is on the road. The Coordinator handles details for the performers as well as for all staff members, crew and equipment.

In some situations, the Company Tour Coordinator works with a road manager. In others, he or she is the road manager. He or she must coordinate the efforts of every person on the road to make sure that the tour and all appearances are successful.

The Company Tour Coordinator begins his or her job before the company leaves its home city. He or she works with the company manager, production manager, booking agents, publicists and public relations people to determine the locations, date and time of each performance.

Many times, when symphony orchestras, ballet or opera companies are performing in other cities, receptions, galas or charity events are scheduled to coincide with the performances. Members of the company are invited and expected to be on hand for these events. The Company Tour Coordinator also determines what additional appearances are made in radio interviews, television spots, print media interviews and special events promoting the tour.

When the Tour Coordinator has compiled all this information, he or she makes up a schedule of appearances, rehearsals and performances. Most Coordinators prepare schedules for each member of the company and crew and hands them out before a tour begins.

The Company Tour Coordinator is also responsible for arranging transportation. Depending on the number of people traveling and the distance, the individual may rent busses, vans or cars or use train service. If the company is traveling a great distance, the Tour Coordinator arranges air travel.

The Company Tour Coordinator is responsible for making reservations for accommodations or for contacting a travel agent to handle the task. He or she also arranges for meals for the company. In some cases meals are catered at the hall or at a restaurant or hotel. In others, company members receive a per diem allotment for food.

While on the road, the Company Tour Coordinator has a great deal of responsibility and must coordinate all the activities of the company. In this job, everybody else's problems become the problems of the Company Tour Coordinator.

The Coordinator maintains close contact with the company's main office, and advises it about the schedule or any problems that develop.

Before a performance, the Tour Coordinator makes sure all the equipment has arrived and is in place. The Company Tour Coordinator is in charge of getting everybody to rehearsals and performances on time. After a performance, he or she is responsible for making sure all the equipment is packed up and loaded to go to the next destination.

In some situations, the Company Tour Coordinator is responsible for handing out per diems and paychecks. He or she is also required to keep expense sheets.

The Company Tour Coordinator is present at all performances on the road. If something goes wrong, he or she takes care of it on the spot. The Coordinator stays with the company until it returns home.

Salaries

Salaries for Company Tour Coordinators vary depending on the size and prestige of the company. The Coordinator's responsibilities and previous experience influence earnings as well.

Earnings for Company Tour Coordinators range from $600 to $1,500 or more per week. Coordinators also receive a per diem or are reimbursed for expenses.

In some instances, when the Company Tour Coordinator is not on the road, he or she may receive a reduced salary.

Employment Prospects

Employment prospects are poor for Company Tour Coordinators. While there are orchestras, opera and ballet companies throughout the country, they do not all go on the road. Even the ones that do tour do not always hire a Company Tour Coordinator.

Advancement Prospects

Advancement prospects are limited for Company Tour Coordinators, as there are more people looking for these positions than there are openings.

A Company Tour Coordinator advances his or her career by finding a similar position with a larger or more prestigious company.

Education and Training

Educational requirements vary for Company Tour Coordinators depending on the specific position. Some jobs require a high school diploma, others require a college background or diploma.

As competition is stiff for these jobs, those aspiring to work with major orchestras, ballet or opera companies should have a four-year degree. Good choices for college majors include arts management, theater arts, music, business administration, communications or liberal arts.

Experience/Skills/Personality Traits

Company Tour Coordinators usually have experience working with orchestras, ballet or opera companies in other capacities. Some have worked on the road with music groups or on road tours for theatrical productions.

Company Tour Coordinators should have a background and understanding of the particular performing art they are working with. Coordinators must enjoy traveling, as they are away from home for sometimes extended periods of time.

Company Tour Coordinators should be extremely organized and detail oriented. Supervisory skills are needed and coordination skills are a must. Individuals must be articulate and able to communicate effectively. Dependability and reliability are essential to this position.

Coordinators should be personable and easy to talk to, since people come to them with problems that need to be solved. Coordinators must be able to deal with crises effectively without panicking. Individuals must also be able to work under a great deal of pressure and related stress.

Unions/Associations

Company Tour Coordinators belong to a number of organizations related to the specific performing art they are working with, including the American Symphony Orchestra League (ASOL), Metropolitan Opera Association (MOA), Metropolitan Opera Guild (MOG), National Opera Association (NOA), Opera America (OA) or the Ballet Theater Foundation (BTF).

Tips for Entry

1. Contact associations and organizations to find out if they offer any training programs. This is a good way to get your foot in the door and make valuable contacts.

2. Look for an internship program through schools, organizations, associations, orchestras, ballet or opera companies.

3. Try to get some experience on the road even if it is not with an orchestra, opera or ballet company. Consider touring music groups, musical revues and theatrical road tours.

4. Send your resume with a short cover letter to orchestras, opera and ballet companies that you know tour and perform in other cities.

CAREER OPPORTUNITIES
BEHIND THE SCENES

SOUND PERSON

CAREER PROFILE

Duties: Making sure the theater audience can hear the dialogue and sound effects during a production; mixing and blending sound; amplifying sound; playing sound effects.

Alternate Title(s): Soundman/Soundwoman; Master Sound Technician; Sound Operator; Sound Mixer.

Salary Range: $350 to $2,000+ a week.

Employment Prospects: Fair.

Best Geographical Location(s) for Position: Positions can be located throughout the country; more opportunities can be found in culturally active cities.

Prerequisites:

Education or Training: No formal educational requirement; training in electronics and sound.

Experience: Experience as apprentice necessary in many positions.

Special Skills and Personality Traits: Complete knowledge of electronics; skill at using soundboard; ability to work well with others; ability to follow written and verbal directions; reliability.

CAREER LADDER

```
+-----------------------------------+
|         Sound Designer            |
|               or                  |
|  Sound Person for Larger Number   |
|          of Productions           |
+-----------------------------------+

+-----------------------------------+
|           Sound Person            |
+-----------------------------------+

+-----------------------------------+
|           Apprentice              |
|     or Amateur Sound Person       |
+-----------------------------------+
```

Position Description

The main function of a Sound Person, working in a theater setting, is to make sure that everyone in the house can hear what is going on. This is not always an easy job because of the acoustics of a theater.

Sound People may also be referred to as Master Sound Technicians, Sound Operators or Sound Mixers, and may work in a variety of situations ranging from Broadway theaters to dinner and summer stock theaters. They may also work in concert halls, arenas or other venues. Duties will vary depending on the specific job.

Individuals working in situations where there are a number of Sound People have more specialized duties. Those working in jobs where they are the only Sound Person will perform more general duties.

If actors and actresses had to yell out every line in a play, it would take away from the production and would not be pleasing to the ear. Part of the job of a Sound Person working in a theater is to make the sound lifelike to those listening in

the audience. To accomplish this, the Sound Person will do what is called mixing or blending the sound. He or she must put the sounds from all the sources together. These sources might include microphones used to amplify the voices of actors or actresses, background noises, special effects and music.

The Sound Person uses various machines and equipment to mix the sound and amplify it. He or she may also be responsible for doing the mixing for the "house" or the "stage." (The house refers to the audience and the stage to the area where the actors, actresses and musicians are situated.)

The Sound Person strives to obtain the type of sound effect that the director indicates. In large productions, the Sound Person is told what to do and how to do it by a sound designer. In smaller productions, the Sound Person may be the sound designer.

The Sound Person is responsible for making sure that microphones and speakers are placed in a way that will produce the best sound. He or she may be required to physically install them or may have someone else perform this task.

During a performance, the Sound Person is required to work at a control board, where he or she adjusts the sound. In most instances, they remain in contact with the stage manager who alerts them to cues for using various sound effects or playing recorded music.

The Sound Person will work varied hours depending on performance times. He or she will also be responsible for readying and placing equipment, and in some instances performing sound checks before a performance.

The Sound Person is responsible to either the sound designer, stage manager or director, depending on the specific show.

Salaries

Salaries for Sound People vary depending on a number of factors, including experience and responsibilities. Other factors include the size, type and location of the theater the individual is working in. Weekly earnings for Sound People can range from $350 to $2,000 or more per week.

Those working in unionized situations have their minimum salary dictated by the International Alliance of Theatrical Stage Employees (IATSE).

Employment Prospects

Employment prospects are fair for qualified Sound People. Work in this area can be found in a variety of situations including dinner theater, stock, Broadway, off Broadway, off-off Broadway, experimental theater or university theater. Work can also be found on road tours or with orchestras, opera or ballet companies.

Jobs can be located throughout the country. However, more opportunities exist in culturally active cities.

Advancement Prospects

Sound People can advance their careers in a number of ways. These include becoming sound designers for theatrical productions, doing a satisfactory job and being recommended for additional positions with increased annual earnings and by locating similar positions for more prestigious productions.

Education and Training

There are no formal educational requirements for Sound People. Individuals must, however, be trained in electronics and sound technology. Those who plan on working in unionized settings, which include most professional theaters, must be members of the International Alliance of Theatrical Stage Employees (IATSE). In order to become a member of this union, individuals must go through an apprenticeship.

Other training may be obtained by attending a college or university with classes in sound, electronics and staging. There are also many vocational schools offering training in sound and electronics throughout the country.

Experience/Skills/Personality Traits

Sound People need a complete knowledge of electronics, the soundboard and other sound equipment. Most people get this experience handling the sound requirements for school productions or community theater productions. Others get this experience from watching technicians at work.

Sound People must be able to work well with people. At one time or another, they will have to work with lighting designers, sound designers, actors, actresses, directors, stage managers and a variety of other technicians. They must have the ability to follow written or verbal directions supplied by a lighting designer or stage manager.

Sound People must be responsible; they must be at the job when they are supposed to be there. A show cannot wait for them to show up.

Unions/Associations

Sound People working in unionized situations must be members of the International Alliance of Theatrical Stage Employees (IATSE). This is a bargaining union for individuals working in theater that negotiates and sets the minimum salary and working conditions for its members. Sound People working in nonunion facilities, obviously, do not have to be members of this group.

Tips for Entry

1. Contact IATSE to find out how you can become an apprentice. Involvement in this union will help you make valuable contacts.
2. Get experience by volunteering to do the sound for your local community theater production.
3. Obtain additional experience by working for musical acts handling their sound.
4. Contact clubs in your area to see if they need a resident sound technician.
5. Take classes, courses, seminars and workshops in all areas of theater, staging, sound and lighting. These will be useful for the educational value and for making contacts.

LIGHTING PERSON

Duties: Working the lighting control board during a theatrical performance; checking to see that lighting equipment is in working order.

Alternate Title(s): Lightman/Lightwoman.

Salary Range: $350 to $3,000+ per week.

Employment Prospects: Fair.

Best Geographical Location(s) for Position: Culturally active cities offer more employment opportunities.

Prerequisites:

Education or Training: No formal educational requirement; training in lighting and electronics.

Experience: Experience working with lighting in theatrical situations.

Special Skills and Personality Traits: Knowledge of lighting and electronics; background in theater; ability to follow written instructions; reliability; dependability.

```
┌─────────────────────────────────────┐
│         Lighting Designer           │
│                 or                  │
│  Lighting Person for Larger Number of│
│   Productions or More Prestigious   │
│            Productions              │
└─────────────────────────────────────┘

┌─────────────────────────────────────┐
│          Lighting Person            │
└─────────────────────────────────────┘

┌─────────────────────────────────────┐
│            Apprentice               │
│                 or                  │
│       Amateur Lighting Person       │
└─────────────────────────────────────┘
```

Position Description

The Lighting Person is responsible for the lighting of a theatrical stage. While the lighting designer creates the lighting for the production, the Lighting Person will be the one working at the lighting control board.

The Lighting Person is required to be at the theater for all performances. His or her duties usually start an hour or so before the show begins. At that time, the Lighting Person is responsible for checking that all lights and lighting equipment are in proper working order. He or she must make sure that every bulb is ready, that filters are in place as well as making other lighting checks. The individual also sees that every light is in the correct position.

The Lighting Person works from the documentation prepared in the pre-production period by the lighting designer. In smaller productions, the individual may have done the documentation of lighting instructions him or herself.

Documentation includes all lighting information necessary to duplicate the lighting effects that the designer created. A written schedule is used by the Lighting Person during the production so he or she will be able to man the lighting board. The schedule contains cues so that the person working the lighting or control board will know which lights should be used and at what time during the production.

By following the schedule, the Lighting Person produces a variety of effects with different lights, filters and colors. He or she may, for example, turn the spotlight on an actor or actress at a specific time or make the light on the stage fade to darkness.

Depending on the specific production, the Lighting Person is responsible to the stage manager or to a head lighting technician.

Salaries

Salaries for Lighting People vary greatly depending on the individual's experience, expertise and reputation. Earnings will also depend on the specific production the individual is working with, the type of theater and its location. Lighting People earn weekly salaries set by the union. Those working in nonunionized settings must negotiate their own salaries.

Employment Prospects

Employment prospects are fair for Lighting People working in theatrical productions. Almost every production uses the services of a professional in this field. Jobs may be found handling the lighting requirements in any type of production or theater including dinner theaters, Broadway, off Broadway, off-off Broadway, regional theaters or resident theaters.

Advancement Prospects

Advancement prospects are fair for Lighting People. Individuals can climb the career ladder in a number of ways including finding more frequent work, finding similar work for more prestigious productions or becoming a lighting designer.

Education and Training

There are no formal educational requirements for becoming a Lighting Person. There are some who do not have a college background and others who have undergraduate and graduate degrees. Good choices for college majors include theater arts or design.

A lot of the necessary training can be learned watching other Lighting People, lighting designers and electricians at work. Interested individuals should consider becoming an apprentice, assistant or finding an internship.

Experience/Skills/Personality Traits

Lighting People working in theater should have a background in theater and a complete knowledge of lighting, staging and electronics. Experience handling the lighting for school plays or community theater productions is useful.

Individuals must know how to follow written instructions for the lighting requirements developed by the lighting designer. They must also be able to follow the directions of the stage manager who may call lighting cues. They should be reliable and dependable. A Lighting Person who does not show up for a production can ruin a show.

Unions/Associations

Lighting People working in unionized theaters must be members of the local affiliation of the International Alliance of Theatrical Stage Employees (IATSE). If they also assume duties of the lighting designer they may be members of the United Scenic Artists (USA). Some may also be members of the International Brotherhood of Electrical Workers (IBEW). These groups set minimum fees and working conditions for their members.

Lighting People working in nonunionized theaters may or may not be members of these organizations.

Tips for Entry

1. Learn as much as you can about lighting and electronics. Take classes in school, or find courses offered through vocational programs.
2. Workshops in theatrical lighting, staging and other related subjects will also be useful for their educational value and to help make contacts.
3. Internships are another good way to learn, make important contacts and obtain hands-on experience. Locate them through schools or theater groups.
4. Apprenticeships are another method of learning the trade. Contact the appropriate union for information.
5. Offer to handle the lighting at your school or local community theater production.
6. Attend a variety of productions to see how the lighting requirements are handled.

PROPERTY PERSON

CAREER PROFILE

Duties: Locating the necessary props for stage sets; moving props; handing props to actors or actresses; making minor repairs on props.

Alternate Title(s):   Property Man/Property Woman; Stage-hand.

Salary Range: $300 to $1,500+ per week.

Employment Prospects: Fair.

Best Geographical Location(s) for Position: Culturally active cities offer more opportunities.

Prerequisites:

Education or Training: No formal educational requirement; on-the-job training helpful.

Experience: Internship or apprenticeship useful.

Special Skills and Personality Traits: Creativity; handiness with tools; knowledge of building props; good memory; organizational skills; knowledge of theater.

CAREER LADDER

```
┌─────────────────────────────────────┐
│        Property Master               │
│             or                       │
│  Property Person for More Prestigious│
│           Production                 │
└─────────────────────────────────────┘

┌─────────────────────────────────────┐
│                                      │
│        Property Person               │
│                                      │
└─────────────────────────────────────┘

┌─────────────────────────────────────┐
│          Student,                    │
│     Apprentice or Intern             │
└─────────────────────────────────────┘
```

Position Description

The Property Person working in a theatrical production is a stagehand and has varied responsibilities depending on the specific job. One of these responsibilities is to assist the scenic designer or the assistant scenic designer to locate props for a stage setting. Props, or properties, are the articles used on stage sets to make a setting appear more authentic. Examples of props might be furniture, telephones or dishes. Props also include costume props for the cast members. Some props are not easy to find and in some instances may be antiques or other items from different eras. One of the interesting parts of the job of a Property Person is finding difficult to locate props.

Sometimes props can be purchased and other times they are rented from warehouses, museums or rental companies. The Property Person must know where to find needed items. A lot of the job involves shopping and calling around to find just the right piece that will complete a stage set. Part of the art of doing this is knowing where to find needed items. Sometimes, a scenic designer will be looking for an antique chair which might cost $1,000 in an antique store, and meanwhile the Property Person may have seen a chair that would fit the bill in a Goodwill store for $5.00. Those experienced in this field develop lists over the years of where specific items can be located. The Property Person must keep accurate records of everything he or she rents or purchases and will be required to submit bills to the scenic designer in a timely manner.

In some cases, the Property Person cannot buy or rent a certain prop that a scenic designer requests and must construct it or have it made. In some instances he or she may be responsible for actually building a prop or may just be responsible for assembling the pieces of props to get them ready for the stage.

One of the major functions of a Property Person is to make sure props are in the correct place on stage. To accomplish this, they must know exactly which scenes use which specific props. After a scene takes place, they may also be required to remove the props from the stage and replace them with the new props for the following scene.

Another function the Property Person will be responsible for is physically handing props to actors and actresses during a performance. For example, they may hand an actor or actress an umbrella or bouquet of flowers before he or she walks on stage for a scene.

When actors or actresses appear to be drinking alcoholic beverages on stage, it is the Property Person who is responsible for mixing liquids that resemble these drinks. He or she is also responsible for cooking any food that the actors or actresses will be using as props during a scene.

All props must be kept clean and in good condition. The Property Person, depending on the production, may be responsible for handling minor repairs on props. For example, he or she may fix the leg of a table that is unsteady. Or hammer a picture frame back together. If the repair is a major one, the Property Person will be required to have it fixed or must obtain a duplicate prop.

In the event that the Property Person is working on a road tour, he or she will be responsible for packing and unpacking all props, and arranging them where they belong.

Salaries

Earnings for Property People can range greatly depending on a number of factors. Weekly salaries can run from $300 to $1,500 or more. Factors affecting earnings include the type of production an individual is working in, his or her experience, responsibilities and reputation. Property People working in unionized theaters have their minimum earnings set by the local affiliation of the International Alliance of Theatrical Stage Employees (IATSE).

Employment Prospects

Employment prospects for Property People are fair. Most productions have more than one person in this position. Work can be found in any type of theatrical production that uses sets including operas and ballets. There are opportunities in dinner and resident theaters as well as stock productions.

Advancement Prospects

Advancement prospects for Property People are determined to a great extent by the determination, ambition, skills and luck of the individual. The next step up the career ladder for many individuals is to become property masters.

Careers may be advanced by locating similar positions in more prestigious theatrical productions such as Broadway musicals. Other Property People climb the career ladder by doing prop work in television or films.

Education and Training

While there is no formal educational requirement for Property People, individuals with college degrees are not uncommon in this field. A college education may be helpful in obtaining experience, honing skills and making contacts necessary for success.

Experience/Skills/Personality Traits

Individuals interested in becoming Property People should get experience working backstage in theater. Many people obtain experience in community or school theatrical productions building scenery and finding props. Additional experience can also be obtained by working as an apprentice or intern.

Property People should be creative individuals. They must possess the ability to develop ideas for solutions to finding props that are difficult to locate. Individuals who are handy with tools will be more employable. Knowing how to fix and build props is helpful. Knowledge of the theater and stagecraft is important.

Property People should have a good memory. Individuals should also enjoy searching through shops, warehouses, factories and antique stores for props. The ability to get along well with others is necessary.

Unions/Associations

Property People working in unionized theaters must belong to the local affiliation of the International Alliance of Theatrical Stage Employees (IATSE). This union sets the minimum salaries and working conditions for its members. It also provides apprenticeship programs for those seeking memberships.

Tips for Entry

1. Get involved in your school and community theater. Offer to build sets, create scenery and find props.
2. Try to locate an internship working in a theater in the prop or scenic design department. If one isn't open in that department, take any internship you can find that is available. Ask questions and keep your eyes and ears open.
3. Many theaters offer part-time or summer jobs to students learning their craft. Send your resume with a short cover letter asking for an interview.
4. Don't forget to contact opera and ballet companies about jobs in the prop or scenic design department.

WARDROBE DRESSER

CAREER PROFILE

Duties: Keeping costumes used in theatrical productions in good condition; assisting actors and actresses into costume; making minor repairs on costumes.

Alternate Title(s):   Dresser; Day Worker.

Salary Range: $30,000 to $55,000+ for full-time employment.

Employment Prospects: Fair.

Best Geographical Location(s) for Position: Culturally active cities including New York City and Los Angeles.

Prerequisites:

Education or Training: No formal educational requirement.

Experience: Prior experience in theater in some capacity necessary.

Special Skills and Personality Traits: Basic sewing skills; knowledge of laundering and pressing; personableness; dependability; reliability.

CAREER LADDER

```
+-----------------------------+
|     Personal Dresser        |
|            or               |
|    Wardrobe Supervisor      |
+-----------------------------+

+-----------------------------+
|     Wardrobe Dresser        |
+-----------------------------+

+-----------------------------+
|     Actor/Actress or        |
|   Individual Working in     |
|  Theater Behind the Scenes  |
+-----------------------------+
```

Position Description

A Wardrobe Dresser working in the theater is responsible for making sure that the costumes used in a production are in good condition. The Dresser has varied duties depending on the specific situation and works under the supervision of a wardrobe supervisor. As a rule, he or she is assigned one or more actors or actresses to help costume during a production.

If the Dresser works in the daytime before a performance, he or she is called a Day Worker. Wardrobe Dressers may work during the day and/or immediately before and during a theatrical performance. Many Dressers work both shifts, increasing their earnings considerably. The Dresser is responsible for maintaining the complete wardrobe that the actors and actresses wear in the production including dresses, pants, blouses, shirts, suits, hats, glasses, shoes, underwear and jewelry.

Before a performance, the Dresser makes sure that every piece of the costume is available and in good condition. He or she is responsible for attending to any minor repairs such as sewing on buttons, sequins or beads, fixing a hem or repairing a seam. In the event that a costume is in need of a major repair, he or she reports this situation to the wardrobe supervisor. The Dresser then makes sure that the repairs are made and the costume is available for the next performance.

In addition to other duties, Dressers are required to help actors and actresses into their costumes during performances. In elaborate productions, the actors and actresses change costumes frequently and the Dresser makes sure they change quickly and helps them dress properly. The Dresser also checks that the actor or actress is wearing the correct hat, shoes, jewelry and other accessories.

After a performance, the Dresser is required to check the condition of the costume. He or she makes repairs, cleans a costume at that time or makes note of a problem for the attention of the day worker.

A career as a Dresser allows an individual to work behind the scenes. Dressers have the satisfaction of knowing that they have performed an important function in making a performance aesthetically pleasing to patrons. In addition, many Dressers have a unique relationship with the actors and actresses who they help costume and work with.

Salaries

Minimum salaries are set for Dressers working in unionized theaters by the local affiliation of the International Alliance of Theatrical Stage Employees (IATSE). Salaries for Dressers vary depending on the amount of work the individual performs, his or her responsibilities and experience level, and the specific local he or she is affiliated with.

As of August 1998 the minimum salaries set by the IATSE Local 764 for Dressers working eight performances was $596.51 per week. If the Dresser works by the hour, he or she receives a minimum of $21.27 per hour for a minimum of a four-hour call. Individuals who are paid by performance receive a minimum of $74.56. In addition, union members receive 8% vacation pay, 11% welfare fund, 7% annuity and 6% pension.

Dressers working full time earn between $30,000 and $55,000 or more a year. It is important to remember, however, that not all Dressers work all 52 weeks a year.

Employment Prospects

Employment prospects are fair for Dressers who are ambitious and good at their jobs. While opportunities are found throughout the country, major cultural centers such as New York and Los Angeles that have a great number of theaters provide the most jobs.

Advancement Prospects

A Dresser climbs the career ladder in a number of ways, including landing a position with the star of the show. He or she may also rise to the position of wardrobe supervisor. Others move up the career ladder by becoming Dressers in television, commercials or films.

Advancement prospects depend on the skills, personality and qualifications of the Dresser. As in other facets of the entertainment industry, advancement also depends on luck, being in the right place at the right time and contacts.

Education and Training

There are no formal educational requirements for becoming a Wardrobe Dresser. In order to be successful, however, individuals should have basic sewing, pressing and laundering skills.

Experience/Skills/Personality Traits

Most Dressers have prior experience working in the theater in some capacity. Some have been actors or actresses in theater or have worked in other capacities behind the scenes.

Dressers must have basic sewing skills. They must know how to make costume repairs including fixing hems, seams and sewing on buttons, sequins and beads. Individuals must also know how to launder and press costumes.

Successful Dressers are personable and get along with everyone. They are good listeners and know how to make the actors and actresses comfortable in their costumes. Dressers learn to keep all conversations between themselves and the actors and actresses they dress confidential.

Dressers see actors and actresses in situations that other people do not. Dressers must be careful not to make negative comments on costumes or the way the actor or actress looks in them.

It is imperative that Dressers be dependable and reliable.

Unions/Associations

The union responsible for Wardrobe Dresser is the International Alliance of Theatrical Stage Employees (IATSE). The local affiliation of this union negotiates minimum salaries and working conditions. In order to work in a unionized theater, Dressers must be either a member of the union or in the process of becoming a member.

Tips for Entry

1. Volunteer your services as a Dresser in a local community or school play. This position give you hands-on experience.
2. Take classes in basic sewing skills.
3. If you are near a college or university that offers a major in theater arts, take courses or seminars in theater and theatrical costuming.
4. Contact IATSE to find out what the membership requirements are in your area.
5. Contacts are important. If you know anybody in this field, ask for their help.

STAR DRESSER

CAREER PROFILE

Duties: Checking costumes of production's star to make sure the costumes are ready and in good condition; laying out costumes; assisting star to dress and change.

Alternate Title(s): Dresser; Personal Wardrobe Dresser; Personal Dresser.

Salary Range: $35,000 to $75,000+.

Employment Prospects: Poor.

Best Geographical Location(s) for Position: New York City.

Prerequisites:

Education or Training: No formal educational requirements.

Experience: Experience as wardrobe dresser usually necessary.

Special Skills and Personality Traits: Easy to get along with; basic sewing skills; knowledge of laundering; ability to work under pressure; organized; dependable; reliable.

CAREER LADDER

```
┌─────────────────────────────────┐
│         Star Dresser            │
│   for More Prestigious Stars    │
│              or                 │
│       Wardrobe Supervisor       │
└─────────────────────────────────┘

┌─────────────────────────────────┐
│         Star Dresser            │
└─────────────────────────────────┘

┌─────────────────────────────────┐
│       Wardrobe Dresser          │
└─────────────────────────────────┘
```

Position Description

A Star Dresser works with a featured star in a major production and has a number of responsibilities, primarily overseeing the star's costumes to make sure that they are in good condition and ready for the actor or actress to wear at show time and assisting with costume changes.

To do this, the Star Dresser must be completely familiar with the script of a show and may be required to attend rehearsals to determine when, where, how quickly and in what order the star will have to change costumes. A quick change may not always take place in the star's dressing room but, depending on the requirements of the script, may occur in the wings, backstage or in another dressing room. The Star Dresser must make sure that the correct costume and any accessories are available wherever the changes occur, and be there, ready to assist. As a featured star is generally onstage through much of a show, a Star Dresser must be well organized and prepared to help the star make each change smoothly and—in most instances—rapidly.

The Star Dresser is responsible for maintaining all the star's costumes for each production, from dresses, pants, blouses, shirts, suits and underwear to hats, shoes, glasses and jewelry.

The Star Dresser must check costumes before and after each performance and do what is necessary to keep each costume piece clean, pressed and in good condition. He or she will be responsible for attending to minor repairs such as sewing on buttons, sequins or beads, or fixing hems or seams, and, when necessary, reporting major repairs to the costume or wardrobe supervisor. The Star Dresser must then follow up to make sure that repairs are completed before the next performance.

To keep costumes clean, the Star Dresser will spot clean or launder some items, and take others to a dry cleaner or Laundromat to have them cleaned, washed and pressed. The Star Dresser may also be responsible for polishing or repairing the dye on the star's shoes, checking stockings or socks for holes, and buying replacements or spares as necessary.

Many Star Dressers are also required to put the star's makeup on the dressing table in the order in which it will be used. Some may also put out wigs, hairpieces or hair ornaments that are to be worn in the production though this is more often the function of a wigmaster or hairdresser.

Before each show, the Star Dresser will help the star put on the first costume and check to make sure the star looks right and that all costume pieces are on.

After each change or at the end of the show, the Star Dresser will check the costumes for any repairs that are required and make notes on what the repairs are. He or she will then hang up each costume. The Star Dresser may repair and launder costumes after final curtain or the next day.

The Star Dresser may have additional duties that other dressers do not. A star often requires special attention and may have a variety of more personal needs that their dresser must attend to such as keeping the star's dressing room neat and comfortable, providing a favored beverage, seeing that flowers received from friends and fans are put in water and arranged around the dressing room, writing thank you notes to people who send the star gifts, flowers or correspondence, or passing this task on to the star's personal assistant or secretary.

Becoming a dresser to a Broadway star can be exciting and glamorous. It is also demanding. A Star Dresser who fulfills his or her wardrobe duties and develops a personal rapport with the actor or actress with whom they are working may establish a bond that will last for years.

Salaries

Minimum salaries for individuals working in unionized theaters are set by the local affiliate of the International Alliance of Theatrical Stage Employees (IATSE). Salary ranges for Star Dressers are determined by their level of responsibility and experience. If a star requests the services of a particular dresser, he or she may be paid more.

In August 1998, the minimum salaries set by the IATSE Local 764 for Dressers working eight performances was $596.51 pe week, or a minimum of $21.27 per hour for a minimum four-hour call. Those working per performance receive a minimum of $74.56 per performance. In addition, union members also receive 8% vacation pay, 11% welfare, 7½% annuity and 6% pension. It is important to note that Star Dressers usually receive more than the minimum. Individuals working full time may earn between $35,000 and $75,000 plus annually.

Employment Prospects

Employment prospects are poor for Star Dressers. Many productions do not use Star Dressers, relying instead on the services of wardrobe dressers who handle the costuming needs of the general cast.

Obtaining employment as a Star Dresser depends on many things including their experience and expertise. Other factors include the Star Dresser's personality, luck and being in the right place at the right time. Contacts also help.

The best location for an individual seeking this type of position is New York City.

Advancement Prospects

Advancement prospects are fair for Star Dressers who have determination, drive and ambition. Those who make the stars most comfortable, are good at their jobs and have developed pleasant business relationships will be requested again and again. This factor can lead to increased earnings.

Individuals may also advance their careers doing similar work for stars in television and film. Those who prefer to stay in theater may become wardrobe supervisors. As previously noted, advancement, like employment, is dependent on luck, being in the right place at the right time and contacts.

Education and Training

There are no formal educational requirements necessary to become a Star Dresser. In order to be successful, however, individuals should have at least basic sewing, pressing and laundering skills.

Experience/Skills/Personality Traits

Star Dressers usually have prior experience working as wardrobe dressers. Many have had exposure to other kinds of theater craft as well.

To be successful, Star Dressers need to be easy to get along with because they work closely with the star. If the star is not happy and comfortable with the Star Dresser, he or she will either be replaced or not requested again.

Star Dressers must have basic sewing skills and be able to make basic costume repairs including fixing hems and seams, and sewing on buttons, sequins and beads. They should also have a knowledge of how to launder and press costumes.

The ability to work quickly and well under pressure is essential, as is dependability and reliability. Star Dressers must be organized and able to perform a number of tasks at one time without getting flustered.

Unions/Associations

To work in a unionized theater, Star Dressers must be either a member of the union or in the process of becoming a member of the local. The union to which Star Dressers belong is International Alliance of Theatrical Stage Employees (IATSE) whose local affiliate negotiates minimum salaries, working conditions, etc.

Tips for Entry

1. Contacts are important in for Star Dressers. If you have any, use them.
2. You might consider having business cards printed to give to people who might either hire you or know someone who is in a position to help you.
3. A resume is another important tool that may help you find employment. Put all theater-related experience on your resume and list any references. Make sure your resume is neatly typed and duplicated.
4. Send actors and actresses your resume with a cover letter requesting that they consider you for the Star Dresser position. It won't cost you anything, and you might even obtain an interview or, better yet, the job.
5. Courses in basic sewing, theatrical costuming, wardrobe, etc. will be useful.
6. Contact the union to find out what the membership requirements are in your area.

MAKEUP ARTIST

CAREER PROFILE

Duties: Creating or changing the appearance of actors and actresses through the use of makeup.

Alternate Title(s):   Makeup Designer.

Salary Range: $14,000 to $100,000+ a year.

Employment Prospects: Fair.

Best Geographical Location(s) for Position: Culturally active cities offer more employment opportunities.

Prerequisites:

Education or Training: Requirements vary from position to position; some require an ability to handle theatrical makeup, others proficiency in theatrical hairstyling and makeup; some positions may require completion of a cosmetology course.

Experience: Experience doing theatrical makeup useful.

Special Skills and Personality Traits: Cosmetology skills; knowledge of lighting, staging and costume design; creativity; ability to get along well with others.

CAREER LADDER

```
┌─────────────────────────────┐
│      Makeup Artist          │
│      for Larger,            │
│  More Prestigious Production │
└─────────────────────────────┘

┌─────────────────────────────┐
│      Makeup Artist          │
└─────────────────────────────┘

┌─────────────────────────────┐
│  Makeup Artist Apprentice,  │
│   Assistant or Student      │
└─────────────────────────────┘
```

Position Description

A Makeup Artist working in a theatrical situation is responsible for the physical appearance of actors and actresses in a production. Makeup Artists use makeup as their medium and an actor's or actress's face as their canvas.

The Makeup Artist is responsible for helping to convey the persona of a character in a play. He or she applies makeup so that the performer looks the part and their faces and expressions can be seen by the audience. When doing this, the Makeup Artist takes into account the lighting in the theater as well as the lighting used for the various scenes.

In some productions, the Makeup Artist may be required to design a look. For example, Makeup Artists in the popular production of Cats had to make actors and actresses look like cats. Along with the costumes, the makeup created the feline look. Makeup also gave each "cat" a distinct personality.

In other productions, the Makeup Artist is responsible for taking a beautiful young actress and turning her into an old hag through the magic of makeup. Makeup Artists also use makeup to age actors to show the passage of time.

The Makeup Artist works with the costume designer and the hairstylist. Together, they determine the type of look for each actor and actress, then the Makeup Artist coordinates the colors of makeup with the individual's costumes, hair color and style. In some instances, the Makeup Artist is also the production hairstylist.

Depending on the production, the Makeup Artist is responsible to either the costume designer or to the director.

Salaries

Minimum salaries for Makeup Artists working in theatrical settings vary depending on a number of factors including the specific production and the experience, responsibilities and reputation of the individual. Annual earnings range from $14,000 to $100,000 or more.

Individuals working in Broadway productions must be members of the local affiliation of the International Alliance of Theatrical Stage Employees (IATSE). In New York the local is 798. This union sets minimum salaries and working conditions for its members. As of August 1998, the minimum weekly earnings for individuals was $888.15. Those who work as assistants had minimum weekly earnings of $807.40. Individuals can, of course, negotiate higher salaries.

Makeup Artists working in other theatrical settings set their own salaries. They may be paid by the performance or by the week depending on the type of production. Earnings can range from $300 to $700 or more per week.

Employment Prospects

Employment prospects are fair for individuals seeking employment as theatrical Makeup Artists. They may find work in off Broadway, off-off Broadway, stock productions and dinner theaters. Prospects are more difficult for individuals aspiring to work in major theatrical productions such as Broadway plays.

Some Makeup Artists work in the cosmetics and hairstyling industries in fields other than theater and the performing arts to augment their earnings.

Advancement Prospects

Advancement prospects are difficult to determine in this profession since so much depends on the reputation that the Makeup Artist builds for him- or herself. Makeup Artists who are good at their jobs become a commodity and are requested. They advance their careers by being sought out to work in larger, more prestigious productions. Depending on their aspirations, Makeup Artists also advance their careers by doing the same work in television and films.

Education and Training

There are no formal educational requirements for theatrical Makeup Artists. Requirements will vary depending on the specific position. Some productions want the Makeup Artist to have previous experience working with theatrical makeup and techniques. Others prefer the Makeup Artist to have had courses, workshops or seminars in theatrical makeup.

Those who attend college with a major in theater arts find courses in theatrical makeup, hairstyling, costuming, staging and lighting useful.

In many areas, Makeup Artists hold a state cosmetology or hairstyling license. To obtain this, individuals attend a licensed school of cosmetology and hair styling for a specified number of hours. They then take a state examination that usually consists of a written section and a practical portion.

Individuals who want to become members of the International Alliance of Theatrical Stage Employees local take a practical exam in order to be admitted. During this examination, Makeup Artists must show that they can perform certain makeup techniques such as applying scars and bruises and laying mustaches.

Experience/Skills/Personality Traits

Makeup Artists must have the ability to get along well with others and make them feel comfortable. Makeup Artists should be creative, artistic people, skilled in cosmetology and theatrical makeup and hairstyling. They should also have a knowledge of theater, lighting, staging and costume design.

Unions/Associations

The local affiliation of the International Alliance of Theatrical Stage Employees (IATSE) is the major bargaining union for Makeup Artists working in Broadway theater. In the East, it is local 798. This union negotiates minimum salaries and working conditions. Individuals may also be members of a number of trade associations including the National Hairdressers and Cosmetologists Association (NHCA). Groups such as this provide professional guidance, support and educational opportunities to their members.

Tips for Entry

1. Try to find an internship as a Makeup Artist in a theater. Look into community, regional, stock and dinner theaters.
2. Volunteer as a Makeup Artist for school or college productions.
3. Find an apprenticeship with a theatrical Makeup Artist as a method of entering the field.
4. Contact the local affiliation of the appropriate union to determine membership requirements.
5. Take classes, workshops and seminars in theatrical makeup staging, lighting and costume design.

PRODUCTION HAIRSTYLIST

CAREER PROFILE

Duties: Creating hairstyles for actors and actresses in theatrical productions; washing, cutting, styling and coloring hair and wigs for cast members.

Alternate Title(s):   Hairstylist; Hairdresser.

Salary Range: $14,000 to $100,000+ a year.

Employment Prospects: Fair.

Best Geographical Location(s) for Position: Culturally active cities will offer more job possibilities.

Prerequisites:

Education or Training: Requirements vary from position to position; some may require an ability to work well with hair; others may require completion of a cosmetology/hairstyling course and still others may prefer classes in theatrical hairstyling and makeup; many states require a license in hairstyling or cosmetology.

Experience: Experience in hairstyling necessary; experience in theatrical hairstyling helpful.

Special Skills and Personality Traits: Hairstyling skills; ability to research; personableness; knowledge of theatrical lighting, makeup and costuming.

CAREER LADDER

```
┌─────────────────────────────────┐
│   Production Hairstylist        │
│   for Larger,                   │
│   More Prestigious Production    │
└─────────────────────────────────┘

┌─────────────────────────────────┐
│   Production Hairstylist         │
└─────────────────────────────────┘

┌─────────────────────────────────┐
│ Hairstylist Apprentice or Assistant │
│              or                  │
│  Hairstylist in Unrelated Field  │
└─────────────────────────────────┘
```

Position Description

A Production Hairstylist working in a theatrical setting is responsible for the appearance of the hair of the actors and actresses in a production. The Hairstylist works with the actual hair of the cast members or with wigs. He or she is also responsible for the styling of facial hair.

The Production Hairstylist works with the costume designer and the makeup artist. Together they are responsible for creating the look of the characters in the production. In many instances, the Production Hairstylist also acts as the makeup artist.

The Hairstylist determines many things before creating a hairstyle for an actor or actress, such as the time period of the production. If, for example, the Hairstylist is working on a production that was supposed to have taken place 50 years ago, he or she researches the hairstyles from that period. This research is conducted by visiting museums or libraries or by looking through books and magazines, or by watching movies.

In some productions, the Hairstylist is required to design special looks for cast members that also require research. The Hairstylist has to handle various hairstyling situations within a production. For instance, the production may have characters who age as the scenes change. The Hairstylist develops styles that can change as quickly as scenes do.

The Hairstylist knows how to wash, style, cut and color hair to fit the look of characters created by the playwright and the director. He or she must also be familiar with working with wigs. Through the use of wigs, a character can change his or her hairstyle within minutes. Wigs allow the actor or actress to have perfectly styled hair at all times.

Depending on the budget of the production, wigs are purchased or are custom made by a wigmaker. In instances where they are custom made, the Hairstylist is responsible for making appointments for fittings for cast members with the wigmaker. After the fitting, the Hairstylist is required to cut and style the wig appropriately for the actors or actresses.

The Production Hairstylist may be responsible for all the cast members' hair or for only a few. In some situations, he or she is the Hairstylist for the star of the show only.

Other responsibilities of the Hairstylist include determining what equipment and supplies are required and ordering or purchasing them. Expenses are reimbursed if the Production Hairstylist pays for these items.

The Hairstylist works in the pre-production period of the show designing hairstyles. He or she may also work before, during or after performances styling the hair and wigs of cast members.

Depending on the production, the Production Hairstylist is responsible to either the costume designer or the director.

Salaries

Minimum salaries for Production Hairstylists working in theatrical settings vary with the specific production and the experience, responsibilities and reputation of the individual. Annual salaries for Production Hairstylists working fairly frequently can range from $14,000 to $100,000 or more. Individuals augment earnings by styling hair outside the theater industry.

Production Hairstylists working in Broadway productions are members of the local affiliation of the International Alliance of Theatrical Stage Employees (IATSE) for Makeup Artists and Hairstylists. On the East Coast, the local for this group is local 798.

This union sets minimum salaries and working conditions for its members. The minimum weekly earnings for individuals in August 1998 were $888.15. Those who work as assistants earned a minimum salary of $807.40. Many individuals negotiate higher salaries.

Production Hairstylists working in off Broadway or regional theatrical productions negotiate their own salaries. They are paid by the performance or by the week depending on the demands and budget of the job. Earnings range from $300 to $700 or more per week.

Employment Prospects

Employment prospects are fair for Production Hairstylists. They find work in off Broadway, off-off Broadway, stock productions and dinner theaters. Prospects are more difficult for individuals aspiring to work in major theatrical productions such as Broadway plays.

Advancement Prospects

Advancement prospects are poor for Production Hairstylists and most select a couple of different career paths. One way to climb the career ladder is by doing similar work for more prestigious productions. Another method is to perform similar work in television, commercials or films.

Advancement prospects depend to a great extent on the reputation the Hairstylist builds for him or herself. Those who are reliable, qualified, do a great job and make people feel comfortable are consistently requested.

Education and Training

Educational requirements vary for Production Hairstylists depending on the state they work in. Some positions require that an individual know how to work well with hair and wigs. In may areas, Production Hairstylists are required to hold a state cosmetology or hairstyling license and they obtain this by attending and graduating from a licensed school of cosmetology and hairstyling. They are then required to take a state examination which usually consists of a written section and a practical portion.

Individuals who want to become members of the International Alliance of Theatrical Stage Employees local also take a practical exam in order to be admitted. During this examination, Production Hairstylists illustrate that they can perform certain hair techniques and do styling for various eras in time.

Courses, workshops and seminars in theatrical hairstyling, makeup, costuming, staging and lighting are useful. A college degree with a major in theater arts gives the individual a well-rounded background and the opportunity to obtain experience in theatrical hairstyling and makeup procedures.

Experience/Skills/Personality Traits

Production Hairstylists need to have a flair for working with hair. Individuals must be able to wash, style, cut and color hair and wigs. They must have the ability to create hairstyles for all types of hair and wigs that might be used on stage. Those who are also skilled at theatrical makeup techniques will be more marketable.

Production Hairstylists need to get along well with others and make them feel comfortable.

Production Hairstylists should have an interest in and knowledge of the theater. An understanding of lighting, staging and costume design is helpful in their work, and an ability to research is useful.

Unions/Associations

Production Hairstylists working on Broadway must be members of the local affiliation of the International Alliance of Theatrical Stage Employees (IATSE). This union negotiates minimum salaries and working conditions for its members. The East Coast affiliation for Broadway's Production Hairstylist is local 798.

Individuals may also be members of a number of trade associations including the National Hairdressers and Cosmetologists Association (NHCA).

Tips for Entry

1. Get experience in theatrical hairstyling by offering to be the Production Hairstylist for your local school or community theater group.
2. Consider an internship in theatrical hairstyling. Contact associations, schools or theatrical groups for information.

3. Consider an apprenticeship with a Production Hairstylist. It is a good way to learn the trade and make contacts.

4. Take as many classes, workshops and seminars in theatrical hairstyling and makeup as possible. Participation in these groups is important for learning techniques as well as for making important contacts.

5. Become a licensed hairstylist. While it isn't always necessary to have a license, it gives you the opportunity to earn extra money outside the theater while waiting for your big break in the industry.

CAREER OPPORTUNITIES
IN SUPPORT SERVICES
FOR PERFORMING ARTISTS

PERSONAL MANAGER

CAREER PROFILE

Duties: Representing a client; overseeing and guiding all aspects of his or her career.

Alternate Title(s): Manager; Artist's Representative.

Salary Range: 10% to 50% of a client's earnings; impossible to determine exact salary due to nature of the job.

Employment Prospects: Good.

Best Geographical Location(s) for Position: Positions are located throughout the country; culturally active cities may offer more opportunities.

Prerequisites:

Education or Training: No educational requirement; college background useful.

Experience: Experience in entertainment industry preferred.

Special Skills and Personality Traits: Knowledge of and contacts in entertainment industry; aggressiveness; creativity; ability to work under pressure.

CAREER LADDER

```
┌─────────────────────────────────────┐
│      Personal Manager               │
│ for Large Roster of Prestigious Clients │
└─────────────────────────────────────┘

┌─────────────────────────────────────┐
│        Personal Manager             │
└─────────────────────────────────────┘

┌─────────────────────────────────────┐
│         Entry Level or              │
│  Assistant to Personal Manager,     │
│  Entertainer or Performing Artist   │
└─────────────────────────────────────┘
```

Position Description

A Personal Manager can represent one or more clients. His or her main function is to oversee all aspects of a client's career. Managers may represent actors and actresses, dancers or singers in theater, film, television, music, dance or a combination of these arts. Some entertainments prefer a Manager who specializes in one type of client area such as theater or dance. Others prefer that their Manager represent entertainers in a different field to eliminate the possibility of conflicts.

In his or her job, the Personal Manager deals with and advises the client on all business decisions and many of the creative decisions that must be made. While doing this, the Manager attempts to guide the artist to the top of his or her profession.

Some Managers develop a plan for an entertainer's career. Others plan as they go. The Manager can be the single most important person assisting an artist.

Part of the Manager's job is surrounding the client with people who can help him or her become successful. The Manager will advise the client on the hiring or firing of important support personnel such as agents, public relations firms, publicists, photographers, accountants, business managers, record companies or choreographers.

The Manager must oversee all the support personnel and their jobs in relation to the client. The Manager might feel, for instance, that the finances of a project do not sound right. He or she would make sure that the business manager or accountant look into the potential problem.

Managers must work hard on behalf of their clients. However, a hard working Manager does not ensure that the client will become a superstar. It is extremely helpful for the Personal Manager to have a variety of industry contacts that can make a major difference in a client's success.

When an actor or actress is rehearsing for the reading of a part, or a client is polishing an act, many Managers help in a creative sense. Individuals, for example, may help their clients choose songs when auditioning for a musical.

Personal Managers may be given what is called power of attorney by their clients. This may be a complete power of attorney or a limited one. Whatever the case, the Manager usually is given authority to approve dates and monies for employment and publicity materials.

The Manager and the actor, actress or other entertainer being represented should be compatible. He or she must be available on a day-to-day basis to discuss any problems the client has or develops. In addition, the two must meet on a regular basis to discuss new methods to advance the career of the client.

In some instances, the Manager will put up money to finance some of the expenses of a client in hopes of making the money back later. In other cases, he or she may search for a financial backer.

The Manager must be in constant communication with all the people working with the client. He or she must call agents to see what type of work is available and when casting calls and auditions are being held. The Manager may also work closely with the client's public relations firm or publicist in an attempt to promote the individual.

Managers are responsible directly to the client. Although the terms of each contract are different, most run for a specified number of years. Some have option clauses that the Manager can pick up if he or she desires.

Salaries

Earnings for Personal Managers are impossible to determine due to the nature of the job. Managers receive a percentage of the client's earnings. This percentage varies with the individual and the Manager. It can range from 10% to 50%, although the usual amount is 15% to 20%. In some situations, the Manager may earn a higher percentage as his or her client attains greater success or makes more money.

Managers receive their earnings, also called a fee, off the top. Fees can be received from all personal appearances, theatrical engagements, television shows, films, concerts, performances, recordings, merchandising, commercials and endorsements.

For a Manager representing a major star, 20% of all the star's earnings can add up to a great deal of money. As Managers can represent more than one client, they can earn a million dollars or more annually. However, most Manager do not represent major clients and receive only a fraction of this sum.

Employment Prospects

There are thousands of people who aspire to be actors and actresses in the theater, television and films. Countless others want to be dancers, singers or musicians. Some think that they can do it by themselves. Others feel that a Manager will make the quest quicker and more successful.

Employment prospects are good for Personal Managers. Almost anyone who wants to be a Personal Manager can be one if they find one or more clients to represent. However, not everyone can be a successful Manager. In order to be successful, they must have important contacts and the ability to guide a client's career.

Advancement Prospects

Advancement prospects are difficult to determine for Personal Managers. A great deal of the advancement has to do with the experience and expertise of the individual as well as luck, contacts and being in the right place at the right time.

Personal Managers attain advancement in a number of ways, by developing a roster of more prestigious clients that results in increased earnings; by starting with a relatively unknown actor or actress and successfully guiding their rise to stardom; by working for a management firm and taking on more management responsibilities for more prestigious clients.

Education and Training

There are no formal educational requirements for Personal Managers. A college degree or background often is helpful to lend credibility to the individual and for contacts.

Good choices for college degrees include theater, theater arts, arts management, business, communications, liberal arts or law. Courses, seminars and workshops in publicity, theater, promotion, public relations, arts management, music, marketing, negotiation, psychology, business, writing and law are also useful in the Manager's career.

Experience/Skills/Personality Traits

Managers must have a broad knowledge of the entertainment industry. Many learn as they go. Some have been entertainers and find they are more successful in the business end of the industry.

Business skills are a must for Personal Managers. Contacts are especially important. The more prestigious contacts a Manager has, the better the opportunities are for his or her clients.

Personal Managers must be extremely aggressive on behalf of the people that they represent. Individuals need good communications skills and should be very articulate.

The ability to negotiate is essential. Creativity is helpful in building a client's image. Individuals must be able to offer their clients constructive advice in a positive manner.

Successful Managers are hard working people who are confident enough in their abilities to surround themselves with a good team. They offer advice to their clients on the retention of attorneys, agents and publicists. Managers must also have the ability to see the raw talent of a performer and develop that talent in ways that enhance their career.

Unions/Associations

Managers of actors are familiar with the rules and regulations of Actor's Equity as well as any other union that their clients come under the auspices of. Those working with musicians are familiar with the American Federation of Musicians (AFM).

Managers may be members of the Conference of Personal Managers (CPM), an organization that sets the standards for the conduct of Personal Managers.

Tips for Entry

1. Find an internship in any facet of the theater gives you a good background in the industry.
2. Consider working for a management agency in an entry-level position to learn the ropes.
3. Go to the library and find books on entertainers who have made it. Read all you can on their struggle to the top to get an insight into the business.
4. If you are interested in becoming a Manager of a singer, dancer or musician, try to break in on a local level. There are many acts that need guidance from someone willing to help.

PRESS AGENT

CAREER PROFILE

Duties: Getting the name or project of a performing artist better known and more familiar to the public; compiling press kits; writing press releases; arranging press conferences; plotting publicity campaigns.

Alternate Title(s): Publicist.

Salary Range: $18,000 to $150,000+ a year.

Employment Prospects: Fair.

Best Geographical Location(s) for Position: New York City, Los Angeles, Hollywood, Chicago, Atlanta, Philadelphia, Washington D.C. or any large and culturally active city will offer opportunities.

Prerequisites:

Education or Training: College degree in communications, journalism, English, advertising, marketing, public relations preferred.

Experience: Experience as journalist or critic for newspaper or magazine helpful; experience in publicity or public relations a plus.

Special Skills and Personality Traits: Creativity; good writing skills; persuasiveness; ability to work under pressure; knowledge of entertainment industry; aggressiveness.

CAREER LADDER

```
┌─────────────────────────────────┐
│   Independent Press Agent       │
│            or                   │
│  Press Agent with Large Roster  │
│    of Prestigious Clients       │
└─────────────────────────────────┘

┌─────────────────────────────────┐
│        Press Agent              │
└─────────────────────────────────┘

┌─────────────────────────────────┐
│      Press Agent Trainee        │
└─────────────────────────────────┘
```

Position Description

The basic duty of a Press Agent or publicist working in the performing arts field is to create methods of making an entertainer's name or their project better known. The best way to do this is to keep the entertainer or the project in the public eye as much as possible. The more popular and well known personalities and projects in show business are, the more successful they will be.

Press Agents work with many types of entertainers, including performing artists, movie stars, television stars, actors, disc jockeys, radio commentators, models, comedians, singers, musicians or magicians. They also work with theatrical revues.

The Press Agent must not have a big ego and must be willing to accept the fact that if a client is successful, the client will take and get the credit, and if he or she is unsuccessful, the Press Agent will often be blamed.

The Press Agent must be able to come up with creative campaigns for placing their clients in the public eye. This is accomplished in any number of ways including inducing magazine and newspaper editors to do feature stories and articles on their client or scheduling television or radio appearances. The Press Agent sometimes uses some type of advertising campaign featuring their client. Press Agents often create something called "hype" to gain notoriety for their client. Hype is a super-saturation of publicity in the media which is used to promote people and projects in the entertainment business. While publicity should be true, hype sometimes exaggerates facts.

Press Agents write creative press releases for the press to use. The successful Press Agent has the ability to come up with a good hook or angle for a press release. The hook is what will draw attention to that particular press release as it sits on a desk with dozens of others. Press kits, consisting of press releases, biographies, pictures and reprints or reviews and articles are also compiled by the Agent. The Press Agent is responsible for sending the press kits or media kits, as they are sometimes known, to editors, TV and radio producers, talent coordinators and column planters. The individual knows how to get through to these people in order to place their client on television, radio, or to have feature articles written. The Press Agent also has the ability to work under the constant pressure of deadlines.

Press Agents are responsible for calling and arranging press conferences for their client. He or she knows what type of event is important enough to call a press conference for, how to put one together and how to have the right people attend.

Often the media isn't really interested in a client until he or she is so well known that publicity will be self-generating. In these types of cases, the Press Agent has the ability to come up with unique ideas and angles to gain attention from the media.

Some acts are so well known that every editor, television and radio show, journalist and reporter wants an interview and appearance. In these cases, the Press Agent must be selective and decide which opportunities are in the best interest of the client. For example, a well-known entertainer would gain more media attention from an appearance on the *The Tonight Show* than from a local morning talk show.

The Press Agent also has to act as a shield to keep the press away from a client if he or she feels it would harm a client's image to give interviews. The Press Agent might also not allow an interview if he or she feels it would overexpose the client in the media.

Press Agents often attend press parties, dinners, luncheons and other social events on a client's behalf or to make important contacts. These contacts are important for a number of reasons including helping to promote the client and helping to build a client list for either the individual Press Agent or the company he or she works for.

As a Press Agent the individual is usually responsible directly to the client. He or she may also be responsible to the client's management representative. If the Press Agent is working for a company, he or she will be answerable to his or her supervisor, or the owner or president of the company.

Salaries

Salaries for Press Agents are dependent on a number of variables including experience, the type of client, whether the Agent is self-employed or working for a radio station, television station or for an agency. The individual may also be working part time for one or more clients.

A Press Agent may earn anywhere from approximately $18,000 to $80,000 a year. Press Agents working with major stars or projects in the performing arts industry might make $150,000 or more a year.

Employment Prospects

Press Agents in this field can work for theatrical companies, public relations firms, television stations, radio stations, record companies, film companies, publicity firms or other press agents. There are a fair amount of jobs available for qualified individuals at public relations firms and publicity organizations. Positions at major television and radio stations, film companies and record companies are harder to come by. A Press Agent can also work as an independent which means that he or she must get their own clients. Press Agents working as independents usually have to have a proven track record with clients in order to get other clients and to be successful.

Advancement Prospects

Press Agents can advance their careers in a number of ways. As one example, they can advance at the firm or organization they are working at by seeking opportunities to work with better, more established clients. The interesting thing about advancement in this field is that it really can happen at any time. For example, a Press Agent might move up the ladder of success by working with a relatively unknown client like a new actor on a television pilot which hits it big; or he or she might be working with a client who lands a part in a big Broadway musical production. Anything can happen.

Education and Training

Although there are exceptions, the most qualified person applying for the job will usually get it. While a Press Agent doesn't really need a college degree it helps. Courses in communications, journalism, public relations, advertising, marketing, English or business are helpful in honing the skills necessary for the job. Seminars and courses in publicity and promotion are also useful.

Experience/Skills/Personality Traits

A Press Agent must come up with creative angles for a client's press releases, media events and feature stories. He or she must be articulate and able to write enticing press releases to persuade the media to use his or her ideas to for articles and appearances.

The Press Agent must also be able to work under the constant pressure of not only deadlines, but also of clients who feel that they are not getting the exposure they deserve.

In order for Press Agents to gain a good reputation with reporters, journalists, producers, TV and radio people, they must be credible or they will lose their contacts.

Press Agents often have prior experience as journalists, producers, reviewers or talent coordinators.

Unions/Associations

Press Agents may belong to the Association of Theatrical Press Agents and Managers (ATPAM), the National Entertainment Journalists Association (NEJA) or the Public Relations Society of America (PRSA). These organizations offer seminars, booklets, periodicals and other helpful information to those in the industry.

Tips for Entry

1. Try and get an internship with one of the larger entertainment public relations firms, record labels or television stations. Most internships it should be noted are very low-paying or unpaid positions.
2. Send your resume, a short cover letter and samples of your writing to entertainment oriented public relations companies in areas where you are interested in working.
3. Work with a local theater, television station, or entertainer as an independent publicist to get some experience for yourself and for your resume. At this level you probably will have to work at a nominal fee.
4. Work as a reviewer for your local newspaper or magazine entertainment section. This will help you build contacts.

PRESS AGENT TRAINEE

CAREER PROFILE

CAREER LADDER

Duties: Assisting a senior press agent in getting the name or project of an entertainer into the media and before the public; compiling press kits; writing press releases; assisting press agents in arranging press conferences; handling detail work for press agent.

Alternate Title(s):   Junior Publicist; Junior Press Agent; Assistant Publicist; Assistant Press Agent.

Salary Range: $14,000 to $20,000+ a year.

Employment Prospects: Fair.

Best Geographical Location(s) for Position: New York City, Los Angeles, Chicago, Atlanta, Philadelphia, Washington, D.C. or any large and culturally active city will offer most opportunities.

Prerequisites:

Education or Training: College degree in communications, journalism, English, advertising, marketing, public relations preferred.

Experience: Writing experience helpful; knowledge of entertainment business useful but not always necessary; experience in publicity or public relations a plus.

Special Skills and Personality Traits: Creativity; good writing skills; articulateness; ability to work under pressure; aggressiveness.

```
┌─────────────────────────────────────┐
│         Senior Press Agent          │
└─────────────────────────────────────┘

┌─────────────────────────────────────┐
│         Press Agent Trainee         │
└─────────────────────────────────────┘

┌─────────────────────────────────────┐
│ Intern Newspaper or Magazine Reporter│
│                 or                  │
│         Entry Level Position        │
└─────────────────────────────────────┘
```

Position Description

The Press Agent Trainee or junior publicist assists the senior press agent in making an entertainer's name or entertainment project better known. This entry level position is a good way to break into the entertainment business.

The Press Agent Trainee may work with any type of entertainer or performing artist including actors, actresses, movie stars, television stars, disc jockeys, models, comedians, singers, musicians or magicians, He or she might also work with theatrical productions, television shows, movies or other types of special programs.

The Press Agent Trainee might sit in on a creative meeting with a client but will usually not contribute any campaign ideas to the client directly. If he or she does come up with some concept, it is discussed with the senior press agent in a private meeting.

The Press Agent Trainee does a lot of the detail work for the press agent. He or she might types releases, calendar event sheets, and prepare envelopes for the press. The Trainee is the one who puts together the various parts of the press kits—stapling, compiling and placing information into folders.

The Press Agent Trainee spends a lot of time on the phone calling important members of the press on behalf of the senior press agent and answering routine calls from the media.

As the Trainee gets more experience, he or she begins writing press releases or bio sheets of the client. Most of this writing however, will have to be checked with the senior press agent before it goes out to the media. With more experience, the Press Agent Trainee will begin to find hooks or angles for press releases. These are the ideas that make a press release exciting and capture the attention of editors or talent coordinators.

The Press Agent Trainee learns how to plan press conferences. He or she addresses envelopes for invitations, makes calls, learns who is to be invited and decides on the correct time to hold a conference. During the press conference, he or she will give press or media kits to the people attending, mingle and make sure that everything is going according to schedule.

At times, the Press Agent Trainee will act as a buffer for the press agent. For example, when the press agent is preparing to break a big story that he or she isn't ready to let the media in on, the Trainee might answer the phones and keep the media at bay.

The Press Agent Trainee usually has opportunities to attend press parties, dinners, luncheons and other social events with the Press Agent. These events are necessary to attend in order to make important contacts that will help the Press Agent Trainee meet people in the media and in the industry. Contacts will not only help the Trainee do a better job at this stage in his or her career, they will be of assistance in finding better jobs or potential clients down the road.

The Press Agent Trainee often seems like a glorified secretary. There is a lot of typing, stuffing envelopes, answering phones, tracking bills and running around involved. Eventually, Trainees begin writing releases, talking to the clients and handling more and more work without supervision.

The Press Agent Trainee will get little recognition and he or she must accept this fact, much as a senior press agent does. The Press Agent Trainee is getting paid to help keep someone else's name, image or product in the public eye. When and if a press or publicity campaign works, the press agent won't get much credit; the Press Agent Trainee will get even less. If the Trainee does come up with a good campaign idea, in many cases the senior press agent may take full credit. Ego cannot play a big part in the Press Agent Trainee's career.

Salaries

Salaries for a Press Agent Trainee are relatively low. It is important to remember, though, that as the individual gains experience, salaries will go up. Press Agent Trainees may begin their careers earning as little as $14,000 a year. This figure could go up to $20,000 annually.

Employment Prospects

Press Agent Trainees may find work in public relations firms, television stations, radio stations, record companies, film companies, publicity firms or with independent Press Agents. An individual who is willing to work in any of the above mediums and is also willing to work in a major city will have a fair chance at finding employment.

Advancement Prospects

As mentioned previously, a Press Agent Trainee's position at times seems like a glorified secretary. Fortunately, though, the trainee phase does not last forever. If the individual is lucky, he or she will soon gain the experience necessary to become a full-fledged publicist.

Advancement can move in many directions for the Press Agent Trainee. It can mean becoming a Senior Press Agent for a company or going out and locating clients for working on a freelance basis; both of which usually means a dramatic rise in salary.

Press Agent Trainees who show a flair for publicity and who are aggressive will move up the career ladder.

Education and Training

Although there are some successful press agents who haven't even finished high school, a college degree in business, marketing, advertising, English, journalism or liberal arts is usually required to get a job as a Trainee. Any type of course or seminar in public relations, publicity or marketing will also be useful.

Experience/Skills/Personality Traits

A Press Agent Trainee must be creative, articulate and be able to develop persuasive press releases to entice the media to use his or her ideas for articles.

The Press Agent Trainee must have the ability to work under the constant pressure not only from deadlines but from the senior press agent who is in turn being put under pressure by his or her clients.

The Press Agent Trainee must be credible or the individual will not have the ability to build a list of contacts. In order to advance his or her career, it is important for the Press Agent Trainee to be aggressive in a non-threatening way. Press agents are often concerned that the Trainee will become too capable and take their list of clients when they establish their own practice.

Unions/Associations

Press Agent Trainees do not have to belong to any union. They may belong to trade associations which put them in contact with others in their field as well as providing professional guidance and support. These could include The Association of Theatrical Press Agents and Managers (ATPAM), the Public Relations Society of America (PRSA) or its student chapter or the National Entertainment Journalists Association (NEJA).

Tips for Entry

1. Try to find an internship program. While most of these internships are very low-paying or even non-paying positions, getting involved in one is a good idea. Once someone invests time in your training, you are likely to remain with the company. Internships can be found at many of the larger entertainment public relations firms, record labels and television stations.

2. Work at a local theater, performing arts center, television or radio station during the summer to gain some type of experience in the entertainment industry.

3. Work as a reviewer for a local or school newspaper or magazine entertainment section. This will give you needed experience and help build contacts.

THEATRICAL AGENT

Duties: Finding parts for actors and actresses in theatrical productions; contacting producers and casting directors to fill openings; setting up auditions for clients; negotiating contracts.

Alternate Title(s):   Agent.

Salary Range: $20,000 to $1,000,000+ a year.

Employment Prospects: Poor.

Best Geographical Location(s) for Position: New York City offers the most employment prospects; other culturally active cities offer additional opportunities.

Prerequisites:

Education or Training: Educational requirements vary from high school diploma to college background or bachelor's degree.

Experience: Experience working in theatrical or other booking agency necessary.

Special Skills and Personality Traits: Knowledgeable about theatrical industry; good phone skills; articulateness; selling skills; aggressive; organization; negotiation skills; ability to work under pressure; determination; drive.

```
┌─────────────────────────────────────────┐
│        Theatrical Agent                  │
│   with Large Roster of Clients           │
│              or                          │
│  Working for More Prestigious Agency     │
└─────────────────────────────────────────┘

┌─────────────────────────────────────────┐
│        Theatrical Agent                  │
└─────────────────────────────────────────┘

┌─────────────────────────────────────────┐
│        Assistant to Agent                │
└─────────────────────────────────────────┘
```

Position Description

Theatrical Agents specialize in finding jobs for actors and actresses in theatrical productions.

Theatrical Agents representing well-known clients are called often by producers to determine if a specific actor or actress is interested in playing a part in an upcoming Broadway show. In some cases, the actor or actress learns about a certain production and asks his or her Agent to find out if the lead part has been cast. If it has not been cast yet, the Theatrical Agent determines if his or her client might be considered.

Theatrical Agents representing less well-known clients work hard finding parts and obtaining auditions. To accomplish this, the Theatrical Agent researches the productions that are being planned by reading about them in trade papers or by talking to productions, casting directors and others in the industry.

Theatrical Agents socialize with others in the theatrical world in hopes of hearing news about new productions, auditions and casting calls. They also spend a lot of time talking on the telephone in the hopes of making contacts, locating possible parts and setting up auditions.

Contacts are essential to the Theatrical Agent. The more contacts he or she has, the better. Agents also must have good working relationships with producers and casting directors. When an opening for a part occurs, he or she places a call and requests an audition for a client.

The Theatrical Agent is careful to send only actors and actresses that fit the part. The Agent knows the strong points and limitations of the clients he or she represents.

The Agent's duties also include helping the actor or actress put together a portfolio or press kit to bring to auditions, developing or writing their resume and suggesting professional photographers to take the necessary pictures.

At open auditions, thousands of actors and actresses may try out the same part. Those who are represented by an Agent often receive more attention from the casting director or producer, especially if the Agent has contacted the producer or casting director about a particular client.

Theatrical Agents act as the intermediary between actors and actresses and producers. If the producer is interested in an actor, he or she calls the Theatrical Agent to set up another audition. The Theatrical Agent then calls the actor or actress with the good news about the call-back.

Once a producer or casting director has decided to hire an actor or actress, the Theatrical Agent handles the financial negotiations.

Negotiations for theatrical artists include areas other than money. A big point of negotiation for many actors and actresses is billing, that is, where the actor's or actress's name is placed on the marquee, in advertisements and on the program. Other negotiating points include length of the contract, dressing room size and extra perks.

Once everything is successfully negotiated and a deal is struck, the Theatrical Agent is responsible for preparing contracts and seeing that they are signed and returned.

Theatrical Agents can be self-employed or may work for an agency. Some agencies employ many Agents who represent all types of clients. Other Agencies represent only theatrical artists.

Theatrical Agents working for an agency are assigned clients and are responsible for bringing in new clients. To accomplish this, the Agent attends talent showcases and small theatrical productions.

Theatrical Agent have a difficult job and work under a great deal of pressure. They must constantly produce auditions, parts and jobs for the actors and actresses they represent. Theatrical Agents are responsible either to the actor or actress who employs them or to the manager of the agency.

Salaries

Earnings for Theatrical Agents vary greatly. Annual salaries range from approximately $20,000 to $1,000,000 or more. Individuals starting out or those handling clients who are not yet well known will be paid at the lower end of the scale. Successful Agents handling well-known actors earn more.

Factors affecting earnings include the number and prestige of clients that the Agent represents as well as the fees clients receive for performances. Other factors include whether the Agent is self-employed or works for an agency. Theatrical Agents are paid in a number of ways. If they work for an agency, they earn a salary or a salary plus a commission on business brought in. In some agencies, Theatrical Agents are paid a bonus plus a commission on new clients signed up.

Theatrical Agents are paid on a commission or percentage basis, that is, a percentage off the top of the fee that the actor or actress is paid. Commissions vary from agent to agent, ranging from 10% to 25% of a client's gross earnings.

Depending on the situation, the Agent may receive a percentage of earnings from the client's participation in pro-

ductions, personal appearances, engagements, commercial endorsements or recordings.

Employment Prospects

Employment prospects are poor for Theatrical Agents. While Theatrical Agents who produce results are in demand, there is a great deal of competition for these jobs and too few top performers to sustain high earnings for all those who seek to be Agents.

Advancement Prospects

Advancement prospects for Theatrical Agents vary with the specific agency an Agent works for, as well as their aggressiveness, ambition, drive and determination.

Theatrical Agents climb the career ladder by building up a large client roster of successful actors and actresses. Other Agents advance by locating similar positions in more prestigious agencies or starting their own agency.

Theatrical Agents also climb the career ladder by handling a relatively unknown actor or actress who zooms to the top of their profession in a relatively short time.

Education and Training

Educational requirements vary for Theatrical Agents.

A number of colleges around the country offer majors in arts management. Classes, workshops and seminars in all areas of arts management, business, contract negotiation, contract law, theater, theater arts and booking entertainment are also useful.

In some states, Theatrical Agents, like other booking agents, must be licensed. These licenses are similar to those required at other employment agencies. They are usually obtained through the state's department of licensing.

Experience/Skills/Personality Traits

Theatrical Agents should have some experience working in a theatrical or other talent agency, either as an assistant, secretary or intern to other agents.

Theatrical Agents should be knowledgeable about the theatrical industry and all its components. They should have extensive contacts in the industry, well-practiced negotiation skills and an understanding of the rules and regulations of the various unions involved in theater.

Theatrical Agents should be articulate and have the ability to communicate well on the phone. They should be very organized as they frequently work on a variety of projects at one time.

Successful Theatrical Agents are very determined, ambitious and hard working.

Unions/Associations

Theatrical Agents may work with a number of unions. The union for actors working in theater is Actors' Equity, which sets minimum earnings and working conditions for its members. Agents must adhere to all union rules and regulations when representing their clients.

Tips for Entry

1. Try to find a training program with one of the larger booking agencies. Even if the agency does not specialize in theatrical clients, the job gives you an opportunity to make important contacts and learn the trade.

2. Consider an entry level position in a theatrical agency as an assistant, secretary, receptionist or mail room clerk. These jobs are often advertised in the classified or display section of the newspaper under the headings of "Entertainment," "Theatrical," "Theater," "Talent," "Agent," "Administrative Assistant" or "Secretary."

3. Look for an internship program in a theatrical booking agency through the agency itself or with the help of a school offering a degree in arts management.

BOOKING AGENT

Duties: Securing work for performing artists; negotiating contracts; locating and signing up new talent.

Alternate Title(s): Agent; Booking Manager; Booker; Booking Representative.

Salary Range: $18,000 to $850,000+ a year.

Employment Prospects: Fair.

Best Geographical Location(s) for Position: Major booking agencies are located in New York City and Los Angeles; other culturally active cities offer the most opportunities; smaller cities offer other opportunities.

Prerequisites:

Education or Training: Educational requirements vary from high school diploma to college background or bachelor's degree.

Experience: Experience working in performing arts or entertainment industry helpful.

Special Skills and Personality Traits: Marketing ability; communications skills; aggressiveness; organization; good phone manner; negotiation skills; understanding of performing arts and entertainment industry.

CAREER LADDER

```
┌─────────────────────────────────┐
│        Booking Agent            │
│             for                 │
│   Large Roster of Prestigious   │
│          Clients                │
└─────────────────────────────────┘

┌─────────────────────────────────┐
│        Booking Agent            │
└─────────────────────────────────┘

┌─────────────────────────────────┐
│   Assistant to Booking Agent,   │
│  Intern or Agent for Local Talent │
└─────────────────────────────────┘
```

Position Description

Booking Agents help performers find jobs. Agents represent a variety of performing artists, including musicians, singers, dancers, actors, actresses and comedians.

Booking Agents may be self-employed or may work for an agency. There are a variety of agencies that employ Booking Agents, including theatrical and various types of talent agencies. Talent agencies work with a number of different clients in the performing arts or may specialize in one or two areas. For example, an agency may handle only classical artists. Very large talent agencies such as the William Morris Agency handle all types of entertainers and performing artists. Some agencies handling a variety of performing artists separate their Agents into categories, assigning one to the classical singers and musicians, another to the comics, and a third to dancers.

Booking Agents are assigned clients by their agency. They may also be responsible for bringing in new clients, both established and new. The Agent accomplishes this by attending showcases, clubs, concerts and recitals. Booking Agents also receive audio- and videotapes of performing artists seeking representation. Depending on the specific job, the Agent may be responsible for reviewing these tapes and contacting the performing artists or their management to let them know if the agency is interested in booking them.

The Booking Agent obtains engagements or jobs for his or her clients in a number of ways. If the client is a well-known performing artist such as Itzhak Perlman, the world famous violinist, concert halls and arena booking managers and promoters often seek out and contact the Agent to determine booking information such as dates the performing artist is available and fees for an appearance.

In some situations the Booking Agent actively seeks places for a performing artist to be booked. This is done by sending out literature, brochures and photographs of the performing artists represented by the agency to a mailing list of clubs, concert halls, arenas and theaters.

The telephone is the lifeline of the Booking Agent, who also spends most of the working day calling promoters negotiating and talking to the performing artist's management.

The Booking Agent is responsible for negotiating prices for client appearances. Sometimes, the performer takes less for an appearance if it coincides with another appearance in the area, or if the appearance provides good exposure. Fees are not the only negotiating point. Other items the Agent must negotiate include the type of accommodations, instrumental augmentation, background singers, food and expenses.

Once a deal has been struck, the Booking Agent is responsible for preparing and sending copies of contracts to the promoter or buyer. These contracts include all the information required by both parties. The Booking Agent sees to it that contracts are signed and returned.

The contract also includes riders, which are the parts of contracts that stipulate the extras the act is supposed to receive. Depending on what is negotiated, the riders may stipulate limousines, first-class air travel to and from a particular city, refreshments in the dressing rooms, extra background singers or instrumental augmentation.

The performing artist is often paid a percentage of the fees when the contract is signed and the rest at the performance. The Booking Agent is responsible for collecting the money, taking the agency percentage and paying the act.

The Booking Agent may book appearances individually across the country or may set up an entire tour, such as a summer tour or an East Coast tour.

Booking Agents usually represent more than one client. They can represent clients either exclusively or non-exclusively. Agents may also represent clients exclusively in one field, such as concerts and non-exclusively in another such as personal appearances.

Booking Agents usually work long hours. They must constantly try to sell the services of their clients to talent buyers, booking managers and promoters. The Agent is responsible to either the performing artist or his or her management team.

Salaries

Salaries for Booking Agents can vary greatly depending on the number and prestige of clients the Agent handles as well as the fees clients receive for performances and other appearances. Very successful Agents can earn between $200,000 and $850,000 or more a year. Individuals just starting out, or those working with clients who are not well known, may earn considerably less. Some earn as little as $18,000 a year.

Booking Agents are paid on a commission basis. That means that they receive a percentage off the top of the fee that the performing artist is paid. Commissions vary from Agent to Agent, ranging from 10% to 25% of a client's gross earnings. Depending on the situation, the Agent may receive a percentage of earnings from personal appearances, engagements, commercial endorsements or recordings. Booking Agents who work in agencies may be paid a salary plus a percentage of the money that they bring in.

Employment Prospects

Employment prospects are fair for Booking Agents if they are willing to work in smaller, regional agencies with less well-known clients. Booking agencies are located throughout the country in culturally active cities.

Prospects are more competitive for Agents aspiring to work in large well-known booking agencies in New York and Los Angeles.

Advancement Prospects

Advancement prospects are fair for aggressive and ambitious Booking Agents, who climb the career ladder by building up a large client roster of more prestigious performing artists or by starting their own booking agencies.

Booking Agents also move to similar positions in more prestigious agencies.

Education and Training

Some agencies require their Agents to be high school graduates and have the ability to perform the job well. Other agencies prefer that their Agents have college backgrounds or degrees. There are degree programs offered in performing arts management that are helpful in this field. Classes, seminars or workshops in booking entertainment, arts management, performing arts, business, contracts and contract law are also useful.

In some states, Booking Agents must be licensed. These licenses are similar to those required at other employment agencies and are obtained through the state's department of licensing.

Experience/Skills/Personality Traits

Many Booking Agents get experience by working as assistants or secretaries to other Agents. Some work as interns, others book local talent into clubs, working with arts councils or placing talent in other regional projects.

Booking Agents must have a good understanding of the performing arts and entertainment industry and a basic knowledge of contracts.

Booking Agents must be excellent sales people and have a well-practiced ability to negotiate. Communications skills are also mandatory. Agents must be aggressive without being obnoxious.

Unions/Associations

Booking Agents work with various unions and must adhere to their rules and regulations, depending on their clients' fields, these unions include Actors' Equity, the American Federation of Musicians (AFM), the American Federation of Television and Radio Artists (AFTRA), the American Guild of Variety Artists (AGVA), the American Guild of Musical Artists (AGMA) and the Screen Actors Guild (SAG).

Tips for Entry

1. Volunteer to work with your local arts council booking acts for the organization.
2. If you are still in school, get involved with the student activities department.
3. Investigate training programs offered by many of the larger booking agencies. These are a good way to get your foot in the door, make important contacts and learn the trade.

LITERARY AGENT

Duties: Marketing playwrights' scripts to producers; reading scripts; suggesting revisions; negotiating contracts.

Alternate Title(s): Writers' Agent; Agent.

Salary Range: $18,000 to $500,000+ a year.

Employment Prospects: Fair.

Best Geographical Location(s) for Position: New York City offers the most opportunities; other culturally active cities may offer other opportunities.

Prerequisites:

Education or Training: Educational requirements vary from high school diploma to bachelor's degree.

Experience: Experience working in publishing, theater or the entertainment industry helpful.

Special Skills and Personality Traits: Ability to see raw talent; communication skills; aggressiveness; marketing skills; organizational skills; contacts in theatrical industry.

```
┌─────────────────────────────────────┐
│     Literary Agent with More        │
│       Prestigious Clients           │
│ in Larger, More Prestigious Agency  │
│                 or                  │
│          Self-Employed              │
└─────────────────────────────────────┘

┌─────────────────────────────────────┐
│          Literary Agent             │
└─────────────────────────────────────┘

┌─────────────────────────────────────┐
│       Assistant Literary,           │
│   Theatrical or Talent Agent,       │
│ Editor, or Playwright or Producer   │
└─────────────────────────────────────┘
```

Position Description

The text of a play—the script—is written by a playwright and contains the story of the production, the words the characters speak, the settings where the scenes take place and the stage directions. When playwrights finish writing their scripts, they must find someone to either buy them or buy the rights to use them. Literary Agents are used by many playwrights to find buyers for their works.

Literary Agents are either self-employed or they work for an agency. There are a variety of agencies that employ Literary Agents. These include theatrical, talent and literary agencies and they may work with a number of different types of clients ranging from performing artists to authors and playwrights.

Agents usually specialize in one or two types of clients. Literary Agents may also handle authors, and theatrical agents may assume the responsibilities of Literary Agents.

The duties of Literary Agents vary depending on whether they are working alone or are employed by an agency. Their primary function, however, remains the same: the Literary Agent must market as many scripts or other literary works as possible for the greatest amount of money.

Selling a work outright means that the playwright is paid a one-time fee for his or her script. Limited rights, called options, may also be sold, meaning the buyer has the exclusive right to use the script for a specified amount of time.

Sometimes Agents actively pursue authors or playwrights. Writers may also send scripts to a Literary Agent to review, and if the Agent thinks the script or the writer has talent, he or she attempts to acquire the client.

Successful Literary Agents read hundreds of scripts, often finding it difficult to tell if they show promise. Agents must have the ability to read a script and envision an entire production. In some instances, the Agent reads a script and suggests that the playwright make revisions before trying to market it.

In order for Agents or agencies to make money, they must sell their client's work. Literary Agents working with playwrights must have a great many contacts in the theatrical world. It is the responsibility of the Literary Agent to bring the work of his or her client to the attention of the proper people. In this business, theatrical producers are the lifeline of Agents.

Playwrights are constantly urging producers to read their scripts. Many producers do not have time to read every script.

Because of possible legal problems, some producers will not read scripts unless they come through an agent. It is the responsibility of the Literary Agent to contact producers about clients' scripts. In some cases, the Agent first needs to peak the interest of the producer. If the producer is interested, the Agent then sends the script to the producer.

Sometimes a producer is looking for a certain type of script and will contact a number of Agents to see if any of their clients have suitable scripts. The producer may also be looking for a playwright to write a specific script he or she has in mind. In some cases, a producer may contact the Agent of a playwright to see if the author is willing to sell the rights of the play for a movie production.

Another responsibility of the Literary Agent is to negotiate contracts. The Agent must try to get the best possible terms for his or her client. Money is not always the only consideration in a contract. Other things that must be considered include length of time for which a script is under option, the billing of the author if the play is produced and the control the playwright has over changes to the script.

Literary Agents representing playwrights spend a lot of time on their job. While they may work regular hours, they may also have to entertain and socialize with producers, clients and others in the theatrical industry.

Salaries

Earnings for Literary Agents representing playwrights can vary tremendously. Individuals may earn between $18,000 and $500,000 or more a year.

Literary Agents usually receive a percentage of the monies earned by their clients. If Agents are working for an agency, they may earn a salary plus a commission for each new client brought in. They may also receive a percentage of all deals negotiated.

Employment Prospects

Employment prospects are fair for Literary Agents. They may work for large literary, theatrical or talent agencies or be self-employed. Being self-employed, however, means that they must obtain all their own clients.

The best location for a Literary Agent in the theatrical field is New York City. However, other culturally active cities also offer opportunities.

Advancement Prospects

Advancement prospects for Literary Agents in the theatrical field depend to a great extent on the drive, determination and luck of the individual. Literary Agents advance their careers by obtaining a position with a larger, more prestigious agency, or by being assigned more prestigious clients in the agency for which they currently work. Some Literary Agents climb the career ladder by becoming sufficiently well known to open their own literary agency.

If an Agent sells the work, or the rights to the work, of a client to a producer who turns it into a success, that Agent will earn more money and will be sought out by more prestigious clients.

Education and Training

Educational requirements vary for Literary Agents. Some individuals hold high school diplomas. Others have college degrees with majors in arts management, theater arts, English or business.

Experience/Skills/Personality Traits

Literary Agents may start their careers as assistants to other agents, although many obtain experience in other fields prior to becoming Literary Agents. Agents sometimes work in publishing as editors or writers. Others gain experience working in the theatrical field as playwrights, producers, theatrical or talent agents or assistants.

Literary Agents must have the ability to see raw talent. They must be able to read a script and envision the play.

Literary Agents must be aggressive without being so pushy that producers will not want to talk to them. Marketing skills are necessary, as it is an Agent's job to sell his or her client's work to other individuals.

Agents should be organized and detail oriented. They must be able to work on many different projects at once without becoming confused.

Contacts in the theatrical world are essential. If the Agent does not have contacts, he or she must be able to make them.

Unions/Associations

Literary Agents may be members of the Authors Guild (AG) or the Association of Authors' Representatives (AAR). These organizations bring others in the same field together, provide educational guidance and professional support.

Tips for Entry

1. Find an internship in one of the larger literary or theatrical agencies. This is a good way to obtain experience and make important contacts.

2. Take classes, workshops or seminars in playwriting and other aspects of theater.

3. Try to find a job as an assistant or secretary to a producer. In this position, you make contacts with others in the theatrical world as well as with Literary Agents who are attempting to contact the producer you are working with.

4. Look for a job as an editor or assistant editor with a book publishing company. You will be able to make contact with Literary Agents trying to sell their clients' work.

PLACEMENT SPECIALIST

Duties: Placing clients on radio and television shows; scheduling media tours; preparing clients for interviews; arranging for clients to be interviewed for print media.

Alternate Title(s): Placement Professional.

Salary Range: Up to $150,000+ a year.

Employment Prospects: Fair.

Best Geographical Location(s) for Position: Positions are located throughout the country.

Prerequisites:

Education or Training: College background is useful but not always required.

Experience: Experience in publicity, public relations, advertising or selling helpful.

Special Skills and Personality Traits: Good phone manner; persuasiveness; articulateness; good communications skills; excellent writing skills.

```
┌─────────────────────────────────────┐
│      Placement Specialist           │
│     for Prestigious Clients         │
│              or                     │
│   Press Agent or Publicist in       │
│         Large Agency                │
└─────────────────────────────────────┘

┌─────────────────────────────────────┐
│      Placement Specialist           │
└─────────────────────────────────────┘

┌─────────────────────────────────────┐
│      Publicity Assistant            │
│              or                     │
│      Press Agent Trainee            │
└─────────────────────────────────────┘
```

Position Description

A Placement Specialist places people as guests on television and radio shows, and also arranges for clients to be interviewed for print media. There are many television and radio stations throughout the country with scheduled talk, news and variety shows and programs. These shows must have guests booked on a constant basis.

The Placement Specialist or Placement Professional, as he or she is frequently called, may work for a variety of clients. He or she may work for celebrities such as theatrical actors and actresses, movie or television stars, singers, dancers, musicians or other show business personalities. These performers or their management team often use the services of a Placement Specialist to promote the opening of a new play, a concert tour or recital.

The Placement Specialist decides whether the client will be placed on a local, syndicated, national or cable show. While most clients want to get on *The Tonight Show* or the *Late Show with David Letterman,* this is not always feasible. The Placement Specialist must decide on the most effective booking.

Local shows are television or radio shows which have a local listening or viewing audience. There is a difference, however, between small-market local and major-market lo-

cal. New York City would be an example of a local major broadcast market. Middletown, New York would be an example of a small local broadcast market. The Placement Specialist usually finds it easier to place guests on shows in small local markets than larger local markets.

Placement Specialists often find that syndicated shows are good avenues to place clients. Syndicated shows are bought by local stations and may be shown at different times in a number of different locations. There can be small syndicated shows which only go to two or three areas, or large ones, such as *The Oprah Winfrey Show,* which is bought by local stations throughout the country.

The Placement Specialist frequently uses cable shows when arranging interviews for clients because they are plentiful and have specialized audiences.

National shows broadcast throughout the country on the affiliate stations of networks such as ABC, CBS or NBC. Placing guests on national shows is difficult unless the guest is a very well-known celebrity or personality.

To do their job, Placement Specialists must obtain a biography of the client, press kits, news releases, photographs and any other pertinent information. In some cases, the Placement Specialist will put these together for an additional fee. In others, the information is supplied by a publicist or manager.

The Placement Specialist must also find out if the client wants to do a media tour, just one or two placement shots.

The Placement Specialist then goes to work by looking at specific cities and making a list of potential shows. Placement Specialists know what radio and television stations are in an area as well as what type of programming is available. They then write cover letters and send them with press information to either the program producer or guest coordinator. If the Placement Specialist does not hear from a program within a reasonable amount of time, he or she may call the producer or guest coordinator asking about the possibilities of an interview for the client.

If the Placement Specialist is booking a media tour, he or she must make sure that the scheduling is both cost and time efficient. With new technology, the client can, however, do phone interviews for radio or satellite hookups for television without leaving the house. In some instances, the Placement Specialist accompanies clients to shows or arranges for someone else to accompany them. In other situations, the Placement Specialist prepares a list of shows, the dates and times of appearances, contact names at the stations and phone numbers and addresses and then gives the list to the client. The Placement Specialist also sends confirmation letters to the program personnel.

The Specialist may work with clients to prepare them for interviews. He or she sets up mock interviews to make sure that the individual can answer questions easily and feel comfortable in front of a microphone or television camera.

Placement Specialists work long hours. If they have many clients, or are placing people in different time zones, they may stay on the phone for hours. The Placement Specialist who is consulting or freelancing will usually be responsible to the client who has done the hiring.

Salaries

Earnings are almost impossible to estimate for Placement Specialists. The individual may work on a per-project or freelance basis. He or she may also be retained for weeks, months or longer by clients.

Placement Specialists earn from $25 to $7,500 or more per placement on a show depending on the specific program and whether it is local, syndicated or national. Individuals might receive a flat fee per week, month or city at a flat rate that can range from $50 to $20,000 or more.

Earnings increase if the Placement Specialist performs other services such as writing press releases, compiling press kits, preparing clients for interviews or accompanying them to shows. Successful Placement Specialists can earn up to $150,000 or more annually.

Employment Prospects

Individuals who are interested in becoming Placement Specialists on a consulting or freelance level will have to find clients. There are performing artists, singers, dancers, actors and actresses, as well as people in other fields who want media exposure. Aspiring Placement Specialists may have to advertise or do publicity and promotions in order to make people aware of their business, but they can usually find clients to get started.

This job can be accomplished successfully by seasoned pros and those just entering the field. Success depends on persistence, perseverance, persuasiveness and personality.

Advancement Prospects

Anyone can become a Placement Specialist, but everyone will not be successful. Those who enlist clients and get them booked on shows will have little problem finding additional clients.

Placement Specialists who climb the career ladder advance by obtaining a larger client list and more prestigious clients.

Education and Training

While there are no educational requirements for Placement Specialists working on a freelance or consulting level, some training helps. If the individual is in college, a major in public relations, communications, journalism, English, liberal arts, marketing or advertising is useful.

Seminars and courses in publicity and media placement are also helpful in honing skills and making contacts.

Experience/Skills/Personality Traits

The Placement Specialist must be persuasive and persistent. Her or she needs to be articulate and have good communications skills and an excellent phone personality.

The Placement Specialist should know how to write press releases, compile press kits and prepare effective letters.

A good working relationship with the media is important to the Placement Specialist's success.

Unions/Associations

There are no unions that the Placement Specialist must belong to. He or she may become a member of the Public Relations Society of America (PRSA). This organization provides useful seminars, educational materials and guidance to those working in publicity of public relations.

Tips for Entry

1. Begin by volunteering to place people from a local nonprofit theater group on television or radio shows to publicize an event that the group is holding. This will give you hands-on experience.
2. Place a small display ad in a local publication. Keep it running regularly. When people need your service, they will remember seeing your advertisement.
3. Use your skills to get yourself on television or radio to publicize your own business.

4. You may not find performing artists, celebrities and other entertainers to work with right away, so try to place people in other fields on television or radio.

Send out a brochure or letter to corporations and trade associations in your area letting them know about your service.

CAREER OPPORTUNITIES
IN HALLS, ARENAS
AND OTHER VENUES

HALL MANAGER

CAREER PROFILE

Duties: Managing theater, concert hall, arena or other facility; overseeing all activities in venue; supervising employees.

Alternate Title(s): Theater Manager; Concert Hall Manager; Arena Director; Facility Director; Director of Hall Operations.

Salary Range: $22,000 to $85,000+ a year.

Employment Prospects: Fair.

Best Geographical Location(s) for Position: Positions may be located in all geographic locations; culturally active cities offer more opportunities.

Prerequisites:

Education or Training: High school diploma minimum; some positions may require additional education.

Experience: Working in concert halls, clubs, theaters or arenas in various positions helpful; experience as assistant hall manager useful.

Special Skills and Personality Traits: Knowledge of theater, entertainment or music business; responsible; ability to handle crises.

CAREER LADDER

```
┌─────────────────────────────────┐
│   Hall Manager in Larger, More  │
│        Prestigious Venue        │
└─────────────────────────────────┘

┌─────────────────────────────────┐
│          Hall Manager           │
└─────────────────────────────────┘

┌─────────────────────────────────┐
│      Assistant Hall Manager     │
└─────────────────────────────────┘
```

Position Description

A Hall Manager is in charge of managing the hall and overseeing all activities occurring in the facility. The individual has diverse duties to perform depending on the facility and the position held. He or she may work in large concert halls hosting major symphonies or smaller halls hosting concerts, ballets, plays and other types of theatrical entertainment.

The individual is also called an Arena Manager, Arena Director or Concert Hall Manager. One of the functions of the Hall Manager is to supervise all employees of the facility. These workers include electricians, sound technicians, lighting technicians, ticket sellers, ushers, security, maintenance personnel and a host of others. In some situations, the Manager also hires a publicist, public relations firm or advertising agency to handle promotion. In other circumstances, the hall owner might handle this portion of the project. As a rule, the Hall Manager has the authority to hire and fire employees. In

directing the activities of all these workers, the Manager tries to ensure the most efficient operations possible for theater management.

Another function of the Hall Manager is to oversee the financial business of the hall. The Manager tries to keep the hall or theater booked; sometimes buying the talent, sometimes renting out the hall to various promoters. Whatever system is used, the Manager must negotiate to get the best price. When promoters rent the hall, the Hall Manager obtains the best rental fee, giving away the least possible extras.

The Hall Manager may also be responsible for payroll. In some cases if a union is involved (and they frequently are), the Manager sees that all union regulations are enforced at the hall. Unions involved might include the musicians union, the electricians union and others.

After an event has been planned, the Manager is in charge of advertising and publicizing the program in order to maximize attendance. This might be accomplished with the assistance of an advertising agency or a public relations firm, or the hall may have its own in-house advertising agency or publicist. The Hall Manager ideally must obtain the most exposure for an event at a minimum cost.

It is the responsibility of the Hall Manager to make sure that the facility is in good condition and clean at all times. If there are items requiring repair, he or she oversees the work. On occasion, the hall may be refurbished. The Hall Manager, once again, is in charge of these projects.

The Hall Manager handles all types of crises effectively and without panicking. Potential problems include an act not showing up for a performance, union workers going on strike before a show, inclement weather on the night of a performance when tickets are being sold at the door or a patron getting unruly during a show.

The Hall Manager sees to it that the money paid to the acts is available on the night of a show. He or she must also be sure to fulfill any contract riders exactly as they are written.

The Hall Manager works closely with all the media in the immediate area. Most of the time the press is offered press or backstage passes. Maintaining a good relationship with the press and other media goes a long way toward helping the theater become successful.

The Hall Manager works long irregular hours and is responsible to the owner of the theater, hall or arena.

Salaries

The salary of a Hall or Arena Manager or Director varies greatly depending on the size of the venue, the location, the prestige of the hall, qualifications of the individual and the duties.

Someone managing a small concert theater in a small city will not earn as much as one who is managing a large, prestigious hall in a major metropolitan area. Those managing small theaters might earn from $22,000 to $35,000 yearly. Those who manage larger, more prestigious halls in major metropolitan areas earn from $36,000 to $85,000 or more annually.

Employment Prospects

Employment prospects for a Hall Manager are fair. There are different types of theaters and halls that vary in size and location. Major cities have the greatest number of concert halls, theaters and arenas. However, it may be more difficult to obtain a job in these locations.

Smaller cities have fewer opportunities, but jobs are usually easier to obtain due to less competition.

Advancement Prospects

Advancement prospects are fair for Hall Managers. In order to move up the career ladder, individuals must find positions in larger or more prestigious facilities.

While there is usually a correlation between the size and prestige of a hall and the difficulty in obtaining jobs at these larger facilities, individuals who do move into better positions, as a rule, continue advancing their careers.

Education and Training

Most positions as Hall Manager require a high school diploma. Many people who hold these positions have degrees in music, theater or business. A large number of these individuals originally aspired to be musicians, actors or actresses. When the opportunities fell through, these individuals went into managing concert halls as a way of maintaining contact with the theater industry.

Courses that may prove useful include theater management, business, bookkeeping, accounting, communications, marketing and public relations.

Experience/Skills/Personality Traits

Hall Managers need previous experience. Usually the individuals have worked in a theater, entertainment or music business in some capacity for a period of time. A job as assistant manager of a concert hall is often extremely helpful to the individual.

In managing a hall, one must be adept at reading entertainment contracts and the long riders that sometimes accompany them. One must have the ability to handle crises effectively, and have considerable knowledge about the theater, entertainment or music industries as well as concert hall and arena affairs.

Supervisory skills and responsibility are imperative for this position as well.

Unions/Associations

Hall Managers may belong to the International Association of Auditorium Managers (IAAM). They may also have to deal with a variety of performing arts unions, including the American Federation of Musicians (AFM).

Tips for Entry

1. Look for a job at a smaller facility or in a smaller city, if you are not experienced.
2. Look for jobs for theater or concert Hall Managers in the classified or display section of newspapers under the heading classifications of "Theater," "Concert Hall," "Arena" or "Venue."
3. Try to find a job as an assistant manager in a small venue. The employee turnover is higher in these halls and you will have a better chance of promotion in a shorter span of time.
4. Seek out Hall Managers in other facilities. Many openings are advertised in a word-of-mouth fashion.
5. Find an internship through your college or other theatrical program in hall management.
6. Surf the World Wide Web for job openings. Check major job and career sites under key words including "entertainment," "venue," "arena" or "concert hall management."

RESIDENT SOUND TECHNICIAN—THEATERS, HALLS, ARENAS OR CLUBS

CAREER PROFILE

Duties: Overseeing the sound requirements of a facility; providing the sound for performances at concert halls, arenas, theaters and clubs; working the soundboard; keeping sound equipment in good working condition.

Alternate Title(s): Sound Technician; Sound Tech; Audio Technician; Sound Man/Sound Woman; Sound Engineer.

Salary Range: $15,000 to $40,000+ a year.

Employment Prospects: Fair.

Best Geographical Location(s) for Position: Employment prospects are located throughout the country; culturally active cities may offer more opportunities.

Prerequisites:

    Education or Training: No formal educational requirement; some positions may require formal or self-taught electronic or sound training.

    Experience: Experience working soundboards, sound equipment and electronic equipment necessary.

    Special Skills and Personality Traits: Knowledge of electronics; knowledge of soundboard; ability to work well with others; dependability; reliability.

CAREER LADDER

```
┌─────────────────────────────────┐
│   Resident Sound Technician in  │
│    Larger, More Prestigious     │
│   Theater, Club, Arena, Hall    │
│    or Resident Stage Manager    │
└─────────────────────────────────┘

┌─────────────────────────────────┐
│   Resident Sound Technician     │
└─────────────────────────────────┘

┌─────────────────────────────────┐
│  Sound Technician Apprentice    │
│          or Student             │
└─────────────────────────────────┘
```

Position Description

The main function of a Resident Sound Technician is to attend to the sound requirements of a facility. He or she is responsible for making sure that everything sounds as good as possible. Individuals may work in a variety of facilities, including theaters, clubs, concert halls, arenas and schools.

The Technician must fully understand the sound in the facility. He or she must be aware of any acoustical problems that occur and then be able to resolve these difficulties, often by moving certain pieces of equipment or adjusting controls on the soundboard to compensate for problems.

The Resident Sound Technician is responsible for overseeing the set-up of the facility's sound equipment. In some situations, such as when performing artists bring their own sound equipment, the Technician is responsible for advising and assisting them with this task. He or she also oversees their sound set up.

The Resident Sound Technician works closely with the resident lighting technician and stage manager. He or she also works closely with the performing artist or group, and their sound, lighting and road crews.

Sound requirements change depending on the type of act that is appearing in the facility. A theatrical production, for example has different sound requirements than a rock concert; a ballet requires different sound than a comedian does.

The Resident Sound Technician is required to attend all rehearsals and sound checks. During these times, the Technician talks to the performing artists themselves, their manager, road manager or sound technician to determine what type of sound they require and if the show has any special sound effects.

In certain locations, sound is not allowed to exceed a certain level. If the performing artist or group is handling its own sound, the Technician is responsible for letting the artist or group know what the volume requirements of the facility are. If he or she is responsible for the sound and the performers have planned to use louder sound than permitted, the Technician must regulate it.

Sound Technicians are required to check all sound equipment and make sure it is in good working condition. If something is missing or not working properly, they are responsible for locating a replacement.

One of the major functions of the Resident Sound Technician is to run the sound or control board during the performance. The soundboard is usually set up in the middle of the front of the stage, although this depends on the specific facility. From this location, the individual can best hear the sound and make the proper adjustments. He or she must be sure that the sound is properly balanced and regulated. If special effects are required, the Technician adjusts the soundboard for them. If, during the performance, there are any sound problems, the individual must attend to them immediately.

After each performance, the Resident Sound Technician is responsible for checking each piece of equipment for any problems. If repairs are required, the technician either makes them or arranges for others to take care of them immediately.

The Resident Sound Technician is responsible to either the stage manager or the manager or owner of the facility. Individuals in this job work afternoons, evenings and on weekends.

Salaries

Salaries for Resident Sound Technicians vary greatly. Individuals may work on either a full-time or part-time basis. Those who are working part time are usually paid by the hour or by the show. Rates can range from a minimum wage up to $85 per hour.

Resident Sound Technicians working full time may earn between $15,000 and $40,000 or more annually. Factors affecting salaries include the size, prestige and location of the theater, club, arena or hall. Other factors include the experience and responsibilities of the individual. Resident Sound Technicians working in a unionized facility have minimum earnings set by their union.

Employment Prospects

Employment prospects are fair for Resident Sound Technicians. Individuals may find opportunities throughout the country. Culturally active cities usually have more prospects.

Virtually any facility that hosts performing artists uses the services of a Resident Sound Technician. Technicians are hired by all types of theaters, clubs, arenas and concert halls. Positions are also found on cruise ships and in hotels.

Advancement Prospects

Advancement prospects are limited for Resident Sound Technicians. Individuals may climb the career ladder by locating similar positions in larger, more prestigious theaters, halls, arenas, clubs or other facilities.

Some individuals advance their career by becoming the facility's resident stage manager. Others are hired by major touring artists seeking qualified sound technicians.

Education and Training

There are no formal educational requirements for Resident Sound Technicians. Various positions may require, however, that applicants have some sort of training, formal or informal, in electronics and sound.

There are vocational and technical schools that teach electronics throughout the country. Most individuals pick up the basics of sound engineering by watching and listening to others.

Experience/Skills/Personality Traits

Resident Sound Technicians must be able to work well with a variety of people. As noted, the individual may work with the facility's lighting technicians and stage managers as well as the performing artist or group and their sound technicians, lighting people, management and road crew.

The Technician must be responsible and dependable. Without proper sound a show can be ruined. He or she must attend all sound checks, rehearsals and performances on time.

The Resident Sound Technician needs a knowledge of electronics, the soundboard and sound equipment. As the individual must be at every performance, he or she should enjoy music, dance, theater and all aspects of the performing arts.

Unions/Associations

Resident Sound Technicians may be members of the International Alliance of Theatrical Stage Employees (IATSE). This union negotiates minimum salaries and working conditions for its members.

Individuals working in nonunionized facilities do not have to belong to a union.

Tips for Entry

1. Checks the classified or display section of the newspaper for ads for Resident Sound Technicians. Look under "Resident Sound Technician," "Sound Technician," "Sound Engineer," "Audio Technician," "Facility," "Hall" or "Club" for this position.
2. Find an apprenticeship with a Resident Sound Technician as a good way to obtain on-the-job experience.
3. Don't be afraid to ask other Resident Sound Technicians if they know of any openings.
4. Send your resume and a short cover letter to clubs, theaters, arenas and concert halls inquiring about openings. Request that your resume be kept on file if there are no current openings.

RESIDENT STAGE MANAGER— CONCERT HALLS, CLUBS OR ARENAS

CAREER PROFILE

Duties: Supervising activities that occur on stage and backstage during a performance at a concert hall, club or arena.

Alternate Title(s): Stage Manager.

Salary Range: $15,000 to $55,000+ a year.

Employment Prospects: Fair.

Best Geographical Location(s) for Position: Jobs can be located throughout the country; culturally active cities offer more employment possibilities.

Prerequisites:

Education or Training: No formal educational requirement; training in lighting, sound and electronics helpful.

Experience: Experience as a lighting or sound technician or assistant stage manager useful.

Special Skills and Personality Traits: Knowledge of lighting and sound technology; ability to get along well with people; organized; supervisory skills; dependability.

CAREER LADDER

```
┌─────────────────────────────────────┐
│      Resident Stage Manager         │
│  at Larger, More Prestigious Facility│
│                 or                  │
│          Facility Manager           │
└─────────────────────────────────────┘

┌─────────────────────────────────────┐
│      Resident Stage Manager at      │
│   Concert Halls, Clubs or Arenas    │
└─────────────────────────────────────┘

┌─────────────────────────────────────┐
│         Sound Technician,           │
│        Lighting Technician,         │
│      Assistant Stage Manager        │
│                 or                  │
│           College Student           │
└─────────────────────────────────────┘
```

Position Description

The Resident Stage Manager works in concert halls, clubs or arenas. He or she is responsible for supervising everything that happens both on stage and backstage during a performance.

This job is not always easy. Concert halls, arenas and clubs do not book the same entertainment every night. As a result, the Stage Manager has to work with new people every few days. The Resident Stage Manager may work with a classical soloist one night, a modern dance troupe the next and a rock band the day after. He or she must be able to deal well with individuals in every aspect of the performing arts.

The Resident Stage Manager has a lot of responsibility. Depending on the size of the facility, he or she may work alone or may supervise a large staff. The Stage Manager must attend all rehearsals. At this time, he or she will inquire about sound and lighting requirements.

In some cases, the performing artist travels with his or her own lighting and sound technicians. The Stage Manager is responsible for helping and advising them about the require-

ments of the hall. In other situations, the facility has its own resident sound and lighting technician who the Stage Manager supervises. In facilities that are very small, Stage Managers themselves may be responsible for handling the sound and lighting requirements. They must also check to see that all the equipment that is required is available and working properly. If the facility is unionized, the Stage Manager must be sure that all union rules and regulations are adhered to.

In many jobs, the Resident Stage Manager is also responsible for assigning dressing rooms to the performers. He or she must find out how many dressing rooms and what amenities are needed.

One of the duties of the Stage Manager is to keep the backstage area as clear as possible. Some time before the performance, the Stage Manager obtains a list of people allowed backstage, including the performers as well as any backup singers, musicians and crew members. The Stage Manager will then issue backstage passes to each individual who is permitted there during and after the performance. The Stage Manager also obtains the names of business associates, journalists and family members who will also be allowed backstage. The Stage Manager is responsible for checking that everyone who is backstage is authorized to be there. If not, he or she must clear the area as quickly as possible.

During the performance, the Stage Manager is responsible for almost everything that occurs backstage and must make sure that everybody does his or her job properly. The Stage Manager is responsible for telling the performers how long they have before show time and indicating when it is actually time to go on stage.

Stage Managers are in charge of curtain changes. They must find out exactly how long the show will last and when intermissions will be held. In order to do this, he or she must discuss the length of the show with the performer or the road crew. During the show, the Stage Manager is responsible for opening the curtains at the proper times and cueing the performers when there is an intermission or when the show has ended.

If there are any problems during the show, the Stage Manager handles them. He or she may cue the sound and lighting technicians or the curtain operators. The Manager is also responsible for documenting any accidents, injuries or other mishaps that occur before or during the performance.

Resident Stage Managers are usually responsible to the facility manager or owner. They do not usually work regular hours. They may work split shifts attending rehearsals in the morning or afternoon and the performances in the evening or on weekends.

While Resident Stage Managers do work hard, they have the opportunity of seeing a variety of performing artists. Individuals also have the opportunity of making important contacts in the industry.

Salaries

Salaries vary greatly for Resident Stage Managers depending on a number of factors including experience, responsibilities and qualifications. Salaries are also dependent on the size, type and prestige of the facility as well as its geographic location.

Individuals can earn between $15,000 and $55,000 or more annually. As a rule, the larger and more prestigious the facility, the higher the Stage Manager's earnings are.

Employment Prospects

Employment prospects are fair for Resident Stage Managers. Individuals can work almost anywhere in the country. There will, however, be more opportunities in larger, more culturally active cities.

Resident Stage Managers can work in a variety of locations from large arenas to concert halls and clubs.

Advancement Prospects

Advancement prospects are limited for Resident Stage Managers. Individuals may advance their career by locating

a similar position at a larger, more prestigious facility. There are also some Stage Managers who go on to become facility managers.

Education and Training

There is no formal educational requirement for Resident Stage Managers. Some positions may require training in sound, lighting and electronics. This training is often secured working as an apprentice, intern or by watching others working in the position.

Experience/Skills/Personality Traits

Resident Stage Managers should have a basic knowledge of lighting, sound equipment and electronics. They either have to handle the lighting and sound requirements or advise technicians.

The Resident Stage Manager should be dependable and reliable. The ability to get along well with people is helpful. Supervisory skills are often necessary if the individual is working with an assistant or crew.

The Resident Stage Manager must be detail oriented and have the ability to work on many projects at once. He or she should be able to remain calm in situations where others might panic.

Many Resident Stage Managers get experience as sound or lighting technicians, while others work as Resident Stage Managers. Some learn the ropes while participating in theater, music and other performing arts productions in school.

Unions/Associations

Resident Stage Managers in arenas, concert halls and clubs may belong to the International Alliance of Theatrical Stage Employees (IATSE), a bargaining union which negotiates minimum salaries and working conditions. If the individual is working in a theatrical setting, he or she may belong to Actors' Equity. The Resident Stage Manager might also belong to the American Guild of Musical Artists (AGMA) under certain conditions. Individuals not working in unionized facilities might not belong to any union.

Tips for Entry

1. Volunteer to act as the Stage Manager in a community, school or church concert or theatrical production. This will provide you with good hands-on experience.
2. Learn all you can about lighting, sound, electronics and stage techniques. Take any relevant courses, workshops or seminars. These will provide you will skills and help you make important contacts.
3. Look under heading classifications of "Resident Stage Manager," "Stage Manager," "Concert Hall," "Arena" and "Clubs" in the display or classified sections of newspapers and jobs as Resident Stage Manager.

4. Send your resume and a short cover letter to the personnel director, owner or manager of clubs, arenas and concert halls. Request that your resume be kept on file if there are no current openings.

5. Find an internship that will give you on-the-job training and help you get your foot in the door for a job.

USHER

CAREER PROFILE

Duties: Helping patrons to get to their seats in a theater, hall, arena or performing arts center; handing out programs; directing patrons to rest rooms, telephones and refreshments; settling disputes between patrons; handling complaints.

Alternate Title(s): Usherette.

Salary Range: $250 to $500+ weekly.

Employment Prospects: Excellent.

Best Geographical Location(s) for Position: Positions may be located throughout the country; culturally active cities offer more prospects.

Prerequisites:

Education or Training: No formal educational requirements; high school diploma preferred.

Experience: Experience as usher in school or community theaters helpful, but not required.

Special Skills and Personality Traits: Pleasant; friendly; outgoing; good verbal communication skills; ability to remain on feet for long hours; ability to remain calm.

CAREER LADDER

```
┌─────────────────────────────────┐
│         Head Usher,             │
│   Usher in More Prestigious     │
│   Theater, Hall or Arena        │
│             or                  │
│    Other Position in Theater    │
└─────────────────────────────────┘

┌─────────────────────────────────┐
│             Usher               │
└─────────────────────────────────┘

┌─────────────────────────────────┐
│  Usher in Amateur Theater or    │
│   Aspiring Actor or Actress     │
└─────────────────────────────────┘
```

Position Description

Ushers in theaters, halls or performing arts centers help patrons locate their seats for performances. The number of Ushers in a venue depends on the size of the facility. Very small theaters may have only two or three Ushers, larger theaters often have 10 or more, and halls, arenas and large performing arts centers may have more than 30.

Seating in theaters and other venues is often separated into sections designating the various price categories of tickets. Ushers are usually assigned a certain section of the theater to work in.

Ushers stand in their section of the theater or other facility waiting for patrons to come in. The Usher may be assigned a position at the entrance of the theater. If this is the case, he or she may be responsible for looking at the patron's tickets and directing them toward the proper section.

Ushers determine where patrons' seating is by looking at their ticket stub. The stub contains information such as a seat number, letter, or symbol, or may be color coded. The Usher matches the information on the ticket stub with the proper number or letter of a seat.

Usher responsible for specific sections look at patrons' tickets and guide them to their seats. While doing this, they may be required to hand out programs to the patrons. The Usher may be responsible for walking patrons directly to their seats or may indicate where the seats are.

Ushers are responsible for directing patrons to rest rooms, refreshment stands, telephones and other areas within the theater. If a patron gets up and leaves his or her seat during a performance, the Usher will also direct the individual back to the proper seat.

The Usher is required to enforce any rules and regulations of the theater, hall or facility. For example, in some theaters, the patrons are not allowed to go to their seats after the curtain goes up until there is a pause in the performance or until intermission.

After the performance, the Usher is required to help people locate the most convenient exits. The Usher is also responsible for assisting patrons looking for lost articles or items that were left in their seats after the performance such as purses, glasses, packages, wallets or umbrellas.

Other functions of the Usher include resolving the complaints of patrons. In some instances, patrons might not like their seats and want to change them. In others, two people may insist that they are both supposed to be sitting in the same seat. The Usher must solve the problem calmly, quietly and quickly.

In the event of a fire, accident or emergency, the Usher is responsible for coordinating the exit of patrons. He or she is also required to help break up fights that might occur in the theater.

Salaries

Earnings vary for Ushers depending on their responsibilities and the type of theater they are working in. Salaries can range from minimum wage to $10 per hour or more. Individuals working full time may earn between $250 and $500 or more a week. In some situations, Ushers are volunteers and not paid anything.

Ushers working in unionized theaters have their minimum salaries set by the union.

Employment Prospects

Employment prospects for Ushers are excellent. Individuals may work in a variety of settings, including theaters, performing arts centers, concert halls and arenas.

Jobs for Ushers are located throughout the country. However, larger, culturally active cities offer more prospects.

Individuals interested in becoming Ushers for theatrical productions on Broadway may have a more difficult time finding employment.

Advancement Prospects

Advancement prospects for Ushers depend to great extent on what career direction an individual wants to take.

Those that want to continue working as Ushers can find similar positions in more prestigious theaters and facilities. Individuals may also seek the position of head usher.

Ushers aspiring to work in theatrical situations may advance to a job working in a Broadway theater. Ushers who take the job as a means of getting their foot in the door of a theater or performing arts career may take varied paths when climbing the career ladder. Advancement depends on the drive, determination, ambition and skills of the individual.

Education and Training

As a rule, there are no formal educational requirements for Ushers, although many theaters prefer their employees have at least a high school diploma. There are a great many people who become Ushers as a way of getting their foot in the door of a career in theater and the performing arts. There are, therefore, Ushers who have college degrees in everything from theater arts to liberal arts.

Experience/Skills/Personality Traits

In most instances, the job of an Usher is an entry level position. Ushers should be pleasant and friendly people with outgoing personalities. An ability to deal with others is necessary. Individuals should be articulate.

Ushers need to have the physical stamina to be on their feet for many hours. They will either be standing or walking for a good portion of their work time.

Ushers should also have the ability to remain calm in a crisis. They must be able to deal with occasional irate patrons who are too loud or do not like the location of their seats.

Unions/Associations

Ushers working in Broadway theaters must be members of the International Alliance of Theatrical Stage Employees (IATSE). This organization sets the minimum salaries and working conditions for its members.

Individuals working in nonunionized situations need not belong to a union.

Tips for Entry

1. Volunteer to act as an Usher for your school or local community theater production.
2. Look in the newspaper classified or display section under heading classification of "Theater," "Performing Arts," "Arenas," "Halls" or "Ushers."
3. Send your resume with a short cover letter to the personnel director of theaters, concert halls, performing arts centers or arenas. Inquire about openings and ask for an interview. Request that your resume be kept on file if there are no current openings.
4. Find a summer or part-time job as an Usher in a movie theater. It provides good hands-on experience.

CAREER OPPORTUNITIES IN PERFORMING ARTS EDUCATION

THEATER ARTS PROFESSOR— COLLEGE/UNIVERSITY

CAREER PROFILE

Duties: Teaching courses in theater and the performing arts including drama, acting, staging, scenic design, scriptwriting, dance and music.

Alternate Title(s): Instructor; Educator.

Salary Range: $24,000 to $65,000+ a year.

Employment Prospects: Fair.

Best Geographical Location(s) for Position: Positions may be located throughout the country.

Prerequisites:

Education or Training: Minimum of master's degree; some positions require doctoral degree.

Experience: Teaching experience helpful; experience in theater or the performing arts.

Special Skills and Personality Traits: Knowledge of theater and performing arts industry; teaching skills; good communications skills; enthusiasm.

CAREER LADDER

```
┌─────────────────────────────────────┐
│   Tenured Theater Arts Professor     │
│                 or                   │
│      Professor at More Prestigious   │
│         College or University        │
└─────────────────────────────────────┘

┌─────────────────────────────────────┐
│      Theater Arts Professor          │
└─────────────────────────────────────┘

┌─────────────────────────────────────┐
│   Theater Arts Teacher in Lower      │
│  Level of Education or Private School,│
│                 or                   │
│     Performing Artist, Director      │
└─────────────────────────────────────┘
```

Position Description

College or University Theater Arts Professors are hired for a variety of different positions. They may be brought into a school as a general theater educator or may teach in specialized areas of theater arts management, theater history, acting, staging, lighting, scenic design, drama or playwriting. Some educators are also responsible for teaching dance or music. Individuals may work in colleges and universities with majors in theater and the various performing arts or they may work in a school that doesn't. They may teach undergraduate classes, postgraduate classes or a combination.

Professors are also called Educators or Instructors. Those teaching in institutions of higher learning, especially those schools specializing in theater degrees, generally teach students hungry to learn all they can, and who are seriously considering professional careers in theater.

It is the duty of the Professor to be as knowledgeable and informed about his or her subject matter as possible, and to help the students learn all they can.

Many Professors in theater-related subjects have worked in theater and the performing arts in some capacity. Some were actors, actresses, dancers or singers, while others worked in production, direction and a variety of behind-the-scenes careers. A great many of the Educators are still active in various theatrical projects.

Professors working in a college setting usually participate in the cultural programs of the school. A great deal of this responsibility depends on the demands of the school. Those teaching in educational institutions with theater arts, drama, dance and music degrees may have duties relating to their specialty. For example, those teaching theater-related courses may be required to guide students in putting on campus productions.

An Educator cannot walk into a classroom or lecture hall and begin teaching without preparation. Preparation for each class takes a great deal of time especially for the beginning Instructor or for someone who is teaching a particular course for the first time.

In addition to teaching courses, Professors set aside specific hours each week to meet with students. The individual's other duties might require reading students' papers and grading exams.

The Professor, working in a community college setting, probably teaches about 18 hours a week. An individual working at a four-year college or university spends fewer hours teaching, usually from 9 to 12 hours per week. Additional hours are spent in preparation, student meetings, grading and evaluation. Those working on productions may put in extra time. The total working time may end up considerably over 40 hours per week.

The Professor is responsible to the head of his or her department or to the administrator of the school.

Salaries

Earnings for Professors working in colleges and universities can vary greatly depending on a number of factors including the specific school, its reputation and geographic location. Salaries also depend on the professional status of the Instructor and his or her experience and responsibilities.

Salaries for Assistant Professors can begin at $24,000 annually. Full Professors earn $65,000 plus a year.

Individuals who have achieved acclaim in theater and other performing arts may earn more than other Professors. Educators teaching at more prestigious universities will also earn larger salaries than those with similar duties at a smaller college.

Employment Prospects

Employment prospects are fair for those aspiring to teach theater or the performing arts in colleges and universities. Applicants, however, must be willing to relocate to areas that have openings.

There may also be more opportunities for those willing to teach in smaller schools. Those who are qualified in a number of different subject areas increase their employment prospects.

Advancement Prospects

Advancement prospects are fair for college or university Theater Arts Professors. Individuals may climb the career ladder by finding similar positions in larger, more prestigious schools.

An Educator starting out as an Assistant Professor may teach for a few years and be promoted to an Associate Professor. Associate Professors advance their careers through promotion to a Full Professor position. Individuals working in a school for a number of years may also be granted tenure, assuring them of security in that position.

Education and Training

Most college and university Professors are usually required to hold a master's degree. Many positions may require a doctoral degree.

The Educational requirement is sometimes waived if an individual has achieved acclaim in the theatrical world. An example of this might be a famous actor or actress teaching a drama course or an accomplished playwright teaching a playwriting course.

Experience/Skills/Personality Traits

Experience for College and University Professors teaching theater and other performing arts classes can vary. Most but not all individuals, have had some experience teaching on some level prior to their appointment at a college or university. Others have had actual experience working in the theater in various capacities.

Professors must have a tremendous knowledge of the performing arts or theater industry as well as his or her own specialization. A genuine love of the performing arts is important.

Individuals should be good communicators and should be enthusiastic about the subject matter with an ability to teach others.

Unions/Associations

Instructors in the theater arts at colleges and universities may belong to a number of associations depending on their specialization. Those teaching dance may be members of the Congress on Research in Dance (CORD), World Congress of Teachers of Dancing (WCTD) or Dance Educators of America (DEA).

Individuals involved in theater may be members of the Organization of Professional Acting Coaches and Teachers (OPACT) or the American Alliance for Theatre and Education (AATE). Their schools can be members of the University Resident Theatre Association (URTA).

Those teaching music-related subjects may be members of the College Music Society (CMS) or the American Musicological Society (AMS).

Tips for Entry

1. Obtain experience teaching theater and other performing arts subjects to local community youth groups.
2. Look in the display or classified sections of newspapers under headings of "Education," "Educators," "Instructors," "Professors," "Theater Arts," "Performing Arts," "Music" or "Dance."
3. Check with your school's placement office. They often know of openings.
4. Send your resume with a short cover letter to a college or university personnel office. Request that your resume be kept on file if there are no current openings.
5. Many colleges and universities have web sites advertising job openings.

PRIVATE DANCE TEACHER

CAREER PROFILE

Duties: Instructing students in the techniques of various forms of dance.

Alternate Title(s): Instructor.

Salary Range: $10 to $250+ per class.

Employment Prospects: Good.

Best Geographical Location(s) for Position: Positions can be located throughout the country; culturally active cities may offer more opportunities.

Prerequisites:

Education or Training: No formal educational requirement; training in dance necessary.

Experience: Experience as a dancer.

Special Skills and Personality Traits: Knowledge of dance techniques; excellent teaching skills; patience; good communication skills; reliability.

CAREER LADDER

```
┌─────────────────────────────────┐
│        Dance Teacher            │
│  with Large Roster of Students  │
└─────────────────────────────────┘

┌─────────────────────────────────┐
│        Dance Teacher            │
└─────────────────────────────────┘

┌─────────────────────────────────┐
│           Dancer                │
└─────────────────────────────────┘
```

Position Description

A Private Dance Teacher, as the name implies, teaches students how to dance. Individuals teach the fundamentals as well as advanced techniques and a variety of dancing styles. Some students are eager to learn, while others may have been forced to take lessons by parents. Students who take classes under these circumstances can be quite frustrating for a teacher.

Many of the students of Private Instructors already know how to dance and want to learn additional dance skills and techniques. Instructors may teach beginners or advanced students. One of the opportunities for expert Instructors is the chance to teach professionals.

Teachers may provide instruction in all forms of dance including ballet, folk, ethnic, modern, jazz and ballroom. Most individuals specialize in one or two forms of dance and become recognized in the field for classes in these specialties.

Private Instructors work in a variety of settings. Some teach in private studios, while others work for organizations or schools offering private lessons. Some Instructors have studios in their home.

Good Dance Teachers have the ability to make a lesson exciting, an important skill when teaching a youngster who is being forced to take lessons. It is also important for those who are experienced dancers seeking knowledge about another's style and technique.

Private Dance Teachers may teach small groups of students at one time or may offer private lessons to individual students. Lessons can run from 45 minutes to an hour or more. Students may take one lesson a week or two or three. Some serious dance students take lessons six days a week.

Private Dance Teachers may be self-employed or may work on staff for a studio or school. Those who are self-employed must not only be very knowledgeable about dance techniques and be good teachers, but must also know how to run a business. He or she must make such decisions as how much to charge for lessons, how and when the fee will be paid and how to run the classes.

Other responsibilities for Private Dance Teachers include putting on dance programs and recitals with their students. These activities give students confidence as well as the opportunity to showcase their talents.

Private Dance Teachers, working with professional dancers, often help them prepare for auditions. Individuals may also work with dancer in productions, providing assistance in perfecting their techniques and styles.

Private Dance Teachers may be responsible to a number of different people depending on the specific situation. If he or she is self-employed, the individual is responsible to the student, or, in the case of children, to the parents. Those working for private studios, schools or organizations are responsible to the director or supervisor of the program.

Salaries

Salaries for Private Dance Teachers vary greatly depending on a number of factors including the skills, experience and expertise of the Teacher. Another factor determining earnings is whether the individual is self-employed, in which case earnings will depend on the fees charged and the number of students receiving lessons, or whether the individual works for schools, studios or organizations. In that case, fees are paid by the class, by the number of students, on a weekly basis, or a combination of these factors.

Fees for Private Dance Teachers can range from $10 per class up to $100 or more depending on the Instructor. Fees are higher for Teachers who have achieved fame and are well known in the field.

Those working for studios, schools or organizations may charge a flat fee ranging from $25 per hour up to $250 or more. Private Dance Teachers working on a weekly salary may earn $250 to $1,000 or more.

Employment Prospects

Employment prospects are good for Private Dance Teachers. Individuals may work freelance, be self-employed or work for private schools, organizations or studios.

Private Teachers may instruct students in any age bracket and in all forms of dance. While employment can be found throughout the country, culturally active cities offer more opportunities.

Advancement Prospects

Advancement prospects are fair for Private Dance Teachers. Advancement is determined to a great extent by the determination and drive of the individual as well as by his or her expertise and experience.

Private Dance Teachers may advance their careers in a number of ways. They may work for a studio or school and decide to open their own studio. Another path for career advancement is to increase the number of students and collect more earnings. Dance Teachers who have a good reputation and are sought out will also be able to increase their fees for lessons.

Education and Training

There is no formal educational requirement for Private Dance Teachers. Individuals must, however, have training in the various forms of dance that they teach. This training may be in the form of professional training from a school of dance, private lessons, self-taught skills or a combination.

Experience/Skills/Personality Traits

While Private Dance Teachers need to know how to dance well, they do not have to be excellent dancers themselves. They must, however, be excellent teachers.

Teachers must know the basic techniques and styles and be able to perform them. They must also have the capability to communicate instructions so that others can fully understand. They must also have the capability to communicate instructions so that others can fully understand. They must also be able to see areas where students need improvement and know how to correct technical flaws.

Private Dance Teachers must be dependable. Forgetting a lesson or habitually canceling a class is not tolerated.

One of the most important traits a Private Dance Teacher can have is patience. It often takes a while for a student to grasp a step or a concept. The Teacher should also be enthusiastic and excited about the craft of dance whether the student is an amateur or professional.

Unions/Associations

There is no union for Private Dance Teachers. Individuals may belong to a number of associations with others interested in the same goals and subjects. Some of these organizations provide educational support and professional guidance and include the Dance Educators of America (DEA), Ceccetti Council of America (CCA), Dance Masters of America (DMA), World Congress of Teachers of Dancing (WCTD), the National Dance Council of America (NDCA) and the Professional Dance Teachers Association (PDTA).

Tips for Entry

1. Volunteer to teach dance for your local community youth organization. This will give you good hands-on experience and help you make local contacts.
2. Make up business cards, fliers and posters. Distribute these on store bulletin boards, community centers and to local civic organizations. Include information such as your name, phone number, any accomplishments in your field of dance, and other pertinent information.
3. Contact local dance studios to see if they need a teacher. You may call or write. Either way, send your resume with a short cover letter. Ask that it be kept on file if there are no current openings.
4. Continue taking classes, courses and workshops. Just because you are teaching does not mean you should stop learning yourself.
5. Join trade associations. These will put you in touch with others interested in your field and offer a variety of other opportunities.

DRAMA COACH

CAREER PROFILE

Duties: Coaching actors and actresses in acting techniques; instructing performers in stage movements; evaluating the performance of an actor or actress.

Alternate Title(s): Drama Teacher; Theater Coach.

Salary Range: $14,000 to $85,000+ a year.

Employment Prospects: Fair.

Best Geographical Location(s) for Position: New York City, Los Angeles or other culturally active cities offer the most opportunities.

Prerequisites:

Education or Training: No formal educational requirement; college degree or background in theater is helpful.

Experience: Acting or directing experience necessary.

Special Skills and Personality Traits: Knowledge of acting skills and techniques; good communication skills; ability to teach; ability to critique students; enthusiasm.

CAREER LADDER

```
┌─────────────────────────────────┐
│   Drama Coach with Large Roster  │
│         of Students or           │
│    More Prestigious Students     │
└─────────────────────────────────┘

┌─────────────────────────────────┐
│           Drama Coach            │
└─────────────────────────────────┘

┌─────────────────────────────────┐
│         Actor, Actress           │
│          or Director             │
└─────────────────────────────────┘
```

Position Description

Drama Coaches are individuals who coach actors and actresses in their acting techniques. Coaches teach students how to better interpret scripts and place themselves in character roles. They also instruct performers in stage techniques that may help their performances. Sometimes a Drama Coach teaches a student how to project his or her voice differently, or use other accents.

Drama Coaches may work in a variety of situations, including colleges, universities and schools that supplement the teaching of instructors and professors. Coaches may also work with theatrical groups and movie and television production companies. Many Drama Coaches are self-employed. They have workshops or studios where they coach either groups of students or one actor or actress at a time.

A Drama Coach has varied responsibilities depending on the situation he or she is working in. His or her major function is to develop the acting skills of the performer. This may be accomplished in a number of ways.

The Drama Coach first evaluates the abilities of the actor or actress by asking the individual to read a portion of a script. Some Coaches have students do readings while other students evaluate and comment on their performance. Other Coaches do the evaluation of performances themselves. With camcorders, many

Coaches film the performance and have the students themselves do the evaluation.

After the evaluation process is completed, the Coach works on training techniques. He or she may read the script him or herself, illustrating changes that can be made in inflection, vocalization and movement. The Coach may also instruct the student on changes that may improve the reading.

Another function of the Drama Coach is to teach the students stage presence and techniques. Stage presence is the way an actor or actress stands and moves while on stage. If the individual is working in television or film, he or she must also coach the students about where to stand and how to look to take advantage of various camera angles.

A Drama Coach may work with an actor or actress who is auditioning for a part. If this is the case, the Drama Coach works on the audition script with the student.

After the actor or actress reads the script, the Coach evaluates the student's performance. He or she then suggests techniques and methods that the student can incorporate into the performance. The Coach works with the actor or actress until the audition script is mastered.

Many well-known actors and actresses who appear in theatrical productions, television shows or movies also use the services of a Drama Coach. The two may work with the script, perfecting the performance before rehearsals begin.

Another function of the Drama Coach is to prepare students for their professional careers as actors or actresses. This preparation may include advice on wardrobe, hairstyle and makeup for auditions for acting jobs. Some Drama Coaches prepare audition tapes for their students to send to casting directors and producers.

Drama Coaches work varied hours depending on the times that their classes and workshops are scheduled. The Drama Coach working in a school, university or college is responsible to the department chairperson. The Coach who is self-employed is responsible to his or her students.

Salaries

Earnings can vary greatly for Drama Coaches depending on a number of factors, including the specific situations the individual is working in as well as his or her responsibilities, experience and reputation.

Drama Coaches working in schools, colleges or universities may earn between $14,000 and $45,000 or more annually. Those who are self-employed may have annual earnings of $85,000 or more.

Individuals who are self-employed may charge students a monthly fee for group lessons. The fees can run between $100 and $500 or more a month. Drama Coaches teaching individual students may charge the student on a hourly, daily, weekly or per-project basis. Fees can range from $25 to $500 or more.

Many Drama Coaches are actors, actresses or directors who augment their earnings by teaching.

Employment Prospects

Employment prospects are fair for Drama Coaches. Individuals may work in schools, universities, colleges or for theater groups. Coaches may also open up their own drama or acting workshops and be self-employed.

Some Drama Coaches specialize in working with children, while others work with actors or actresses of any age. Opportunities for Drama Coaches in theatrical situations are greater in New York City, Los Angeles and other culturally active areas. However, individuals may find opportunities for self-employment throughout the country.

Advancement Prospects

Drama Coaches advance their careers in a number of ways. If they are working in a school, college or university, they find a similar position in a larger or more prestigious facility. This move usually results in increased earnings.

Drama Coaches may also climb the career ladder by building either a larger roster of students or of more prestigious students. Some individuals start out as Theatrical Drama

Coaches and advance their careers by coaching actors and actresses in movies or television.

Education and Training

There are no formal educational requirements for self-employed Drama Coaches. Schools, universities and colleges may require a bachelor's or master's degree in theater arts or drama.

While a college degree or background may not always be required, it may be helpful for the educational value, experience and contacts.

Drama Coaches should be trained in acting through the formal education offered by a college, private acting classes or on-the-job experience.

Experience/Skills/Personality Traits

Drama Coaches should possess a full range of acting skills and techniques. While it is not imperative that they be excellent actors or actresses themselves, they must have the ability to teach others the craft. Good communication skills are helpful in this profession.

Acting experience is essential for the Drama Coach. Without it, he or she will have a difficult time explaining concepts and techniques. There is no substitute for on-the-job training. Many Drama Coaches are currently or were previously actors, actresses or directors.

Drama Coaches should have a great deal of integrity, they must have the ability to critique students honestly and gently. Enthusiasm towards a student's progress is helpful.

Unions/Associations

There is no union for Drama Coaches. There is, however, a group called the Organization of Professional Acting Coaches and Teachers (OPACT) which provides guidelines of professional conduct for those in this profession.

Tips for Entry

1. Volunteer to coach actors and actresses taking part in your school or community theater productions.
2. Work as a drama counselor in a children's camp.
3. Develop contacts. If you have a good working relationship with casting directors, producers and directors, let them know what you do.
4. Offer to teach a mini-course at the local community college on drama, acting or theater. This will help you obtain hands-on experience.
5. Get as much performance and directing experience as you can.
6. Take classes, workshops and seminars from others. This will help you learn new techniques.

CAREER OPPORTUNITIES IN PERFORMING ARTS JOURNALISM

CRITIC—BROADCASTING

CAREER PROFILE

Duties: Viewing plays, theatrical productions, movies and television shows; writing, preparing and broadcasting reviews for on-air execution.

Alternate Title(s): Journalist; Reviewer; Reporter; Cultural or Entertainment Editor.

Salary Range: $15,000 to $1,000,000+ a year.

Employment Prospects: Poor.

Best Geographical Location(s) for Position: Positions may be located throughout the country; large, culturally active cities offer more possibilities.

Prerequisites:

Education or Training: Four-year college degree required for most positions.

Experience: Journalism or broadcasting experience necessary.

Special Skills and Personality Traits: Excellent writing skills; comfortable in front of a microphone or a camera; articulate; clear, pleasant speaking voice; pleasing appearance; ability to work under pressure; objectivity; interest in and knowledge about theater and the performing arts.

CAREER LADDER

```
┌─────────────────────────────┐
│      Critic for Larger,     │
│       More Prestigious      │
│  Television or Radio Station│
└─────────────────────────────┘

┌─────────────────────────────┐
│           Critic            │
└─────────────────────────────┘

┌─────────────────────────────┐
│  Television, Radio Journalist│
│             or              │
│       Print Journalist      │
└─────────────────────────────┘
```

Position Description

A Critic working in the broadcasting media reviews plays, theatrical productions, movies and TV shows for broadcast on television or radio. As is true in print media, a good review by an objective, respected Critic can mean success or failure for a production.

Critics working in the broadcasting field may work in either television, radio or both. Most radio stations, however, do not have their own Critics. Instead they rely on an entertainment reporter or purchase a series of reviews from a syndicate. Depending on the size of the television station, the Critic may also function as an entertainment reporter or be responsible for reporting on non-entertainment, but related feature stories.

Critics in major television markets such as New York, Los Angeles, Chicago, Washington and Boston attend plays, operas, symphonies, concerts or movies and review the shows. In some cases, they may also review new television shows.

In smaller television markets, the Critic reviews productions that come through the area. He or she is also responsible for reviewing local theatrical productions including summer stock, community theater, concerts by local artists, and school and college productions.

The Critic may be responsible for nightly entertainment news or may be assigned three or four shows a week to review. As individuals move into positions in larger markets, their jobs usually become more specialized. Critics may review plays, operas or symphonies, or may review only movies or television shows.

Examples of well-known broadcast Critics are Siskel and Ebert. They present movie reviews in different media including television shows, radio reports and in syndicated newspapers and magazines.

After watching a show, Critics write their own copy for the review. When doing this, the individual has to be objective, honest and fair. The review gives the viewers or listeners an idea of how well the production was done. It may include information on the specific show, story, production, actors and actresses. Many Critics may also give the play or production a rating such as one star, two stars, etc.

The next step in the Critic's job is reading the review on air. They may do this live on a broadcast or may tape the review. Critics are also responsible for obtaining a clip or short piece of film of the production. While reading the review, the clip is often shown on air.

The more the Critic knows about the medium to be reviewed, the better the review will be. For example, it may be difficult for a Critic to review a production of *Romeo and Juliet* unless he or she is familiar with other productions of the play and with all of Shakespeare's work.

Critics must watch and review all shows without bias. They cannot let their personal opinions of certain actors or actresses or specific shows get in the way of honestly critiquing a particular production.

One of the perks Critics enjoy is getting invited to openings of theatrical productions or screenings of new movies or television shows. Those working for television stations in New York and Los Angeles may also be invited to opening night parties and galas to meet and mingle with the stars.

It may appear that all a Critic does is go to a play or movie and then show up to broadcast his or her review, but that is not the way it happens. A Critic's working hours may vary depending on the specific shift they are working, on-air schedules and the times productions and shows have to be viewed.

Salaries

Earnings for Critics working in the broadcasting field will vary greatly. Factors affecting salaries include the size, market and prestige of the television or radio station at which an individual works. The Critic's salary will also depend on his or her experience level, responsibilities and fame.

Individuals working for national or major-market television or radio stations can earn $1,000,000 or more annually. Critics working in smaller and medium markets may earn between $15,000 and $65,000 or more.

Employment Prospects

Employment prospects for Critics working in broadcasting are generally poor. There are a great many people who want this type of job and competition is keen. The larger and more prestigious a station or market is, the harder it is to find employment. Prospects are slightly better in smaller markets.

Jobs are located throughout the country. Major markets are located in large cities such as New York, Chicago and Los Angeles.

Advancement Prospects

Advancement prospects are fair for Critics in broadcasting once they get their foot in the door. Most people who aspire to be Critics move from station to station, trying each time to find similar jobs at larger, more prestigious stations.

As in most broadcasting jobs, advancement prospects are more difficult as individuals obtain positions working at larger and more prestigious stations.

Education and Training

Critics working in broadcasting are usually required to have a minimum of a four-year college degree. Good choices for major include journalism, English, liberal arts, broadcasting, mass media, theater and the performing arts, and communications. Any additional writing and broadcasting courses and seminars are useful.

Experience/Skills/Personality Traits

Most Critics working in television have experience in broadcasting. Often, they have come up through the ranks in college serving as interns and reporters covering non-entertainment subjects. Most have some type of journalism background either in college or writing for a newspaper, magazine or for broadcast news.

Critics usually have a great interest and a basic knowledge and understanding of different forms of entertainment, theater and the performing arts before becoming involved in this career.

Individuals should have excellent writing skills with a good command of the English language and should be comfortable in front of a microphone and cameras. The broadcast Critic must be articulate and have a clear, pleasant speaking voice. Those aspiring to be Critics on television should be well groomed and have a pleasing appearance.

The Critics must be objective and interesting when presenting a review. The ability to perform well under pressure is necessary for those working on a deadline.

Unions/Associations

Critics working in television or radio may belong to a number of unions, organizations and trade associations. Some of these include the Writers Guild of America (WGA), American Federation of Television and Radio Artists (AFTRA), the National Critics Institute (NCI) and the American Theatre Critics Association (ATCA).

Tips for Entry

1. Join your school's radio or television station. Get as much experience as possible in all aspects of broadcasting.
2. Find an internship in a television station. This will be a good learning experience and will help you make important contacts.
3. Learn to write well. Obtain experience critiquing performances of all types by reviewing plays, music events, concerts, records, movies and television shows for your school paper.
4. Look for and take seminars in journalism, broadcasting and writing. These programs will help prepare you for your career in addition to putting you in touch with others interested in the same field.

CRITIC—PRINT MEDIA

Duties: Viewing plays, theatrical productions, movies and television shows and then writing reviews for publication in newspapers and magazines.

Alternate Title(s):   Journalist; Reviewer; Performing Arts Critic.

Salary Range: $15,000 to $1,000,000+ a year.

Employment Prospects: Fair.

Best Geographical Location(s) for Position: Positions may be located throughout the country; culturally active cities offer more possibilities.

Prerequisites:

Education or Training: Bachelor's degree required or preferred for most positions.

Experience: Journalistic experience helpful.

Special Skills and Personality Traits: Excellent writing skills; ability to work under pressure; objectivity; interest and knowledge in theater and performing arts.

```
┌─────────────────────────────┐
│      Critic for More         │
│   Prestigious Publication     │
└─────────────────────────────┘

┌─────────────────────────────┐
│          Critic              │
└─────────────────────────────┘

┌─────────────────────────────┐
│         Reporter             │
└─────────────────────────────┘
```

Position Description

Critics in the print media are responsible for reviewing plays and other theatrical productions, movies and television shows for a newspaper or magazine. A good review by a respected Critic can mean financial success to a show. A bad review can close it quickly.

Critics work in many different outlets from small weekly publications to large, prestigious daily newspapers and weekly or monthly magazines. Depending on the situation, a Critic might be responsible for writing reviews on any plays, shows, concerts and theatrical productions in the area. The Critic might also write a weekly, biweekly or monthly column on the performing arts. In some small circulation papers, the Critic might also be responsible for writing and reporting on non-entertainment subjects.

As individuals move into positions with larger newspapers and magazines, their jobs typically become more specialized. The Critic may review plays, operas or symphonies, or may review only movies or television shows.

The more specialized the job, the more the Critic must know about the subject being covered. For example, Critics reviewing plays must have a good working knowledge of theater in general as well as a familiarity with similar produc-

tions, actors, actresses, halls, lighting and set designs. The more he or she knows about the subject area being covered, the better the Critic will be able to review a show.

Critics must review a show without any bias. They cannot let their personal opinions of certain actors or actresses or specific shows get in the way of honestly critiquing a particular production.

After attending a play or show the Critic will be required to write a review, in which he or she will give an idea of how well the production was done. The review includes things such as whether the show, story, production, actors or actresses were good or bad, and why the Critic thinks so. In some instances, the Critic might think the production was bad but the acting of one or two actors was excellent.

Critics may be invited to openings of theatrical productions or screenings of new movies or television shows before the general public has the opportunity to view it. Those working for newspapers and magazines with large circulations in cities such as New York and Los Angeles may also be invited to opening parties and galas to meet the stars.

Critics work irregular hours; many work a full day at the office writing and researching and then in the evening go to the theater to review a play or the movies to critique a film.

Critics are usually responsible to the entertainment editor of their publication.

Salaries

Salaries for Critics vary greatly depending on a number of factors including the type of production employing the Critic, and the individual's experience level and responsibilities.

Individuals working full time may earn between $15,000 and $65,000 or more a year. There are a few nationally known Critics who earn one million dollars or more annually.

There are also some Critics who work for smaller local publications on a review-by-review basis. Earnings for these reviews may range from a few cents a word to a flat fee of $100 or more.

Employment Prospects

Employment prospects for Critics working in the print media are fair for those who don't mind starting at the bottom of the career ladder. Prospects become more limited as individuals seek positions with larger newspapers and publications.

Jobs are located throughout the country, although those aspiring to review Broadway and other major theatrical productions must move to New York City or other large, culturally active cities.

Almost every newspaper and a great many magazines have entertainment sections. Local newspapers and magazines are no exception and provide those entering the field with a good place to find employment.

Advancement Prospects

Advancement prospects are fair for Critics who start out at smaller, local newspapers and publications. The next rung up the career ladder for these individuals is a similar position at a larger, more prestigious publication. Individuals may also advance their careers by becoming specialists in one area of the arts such as plays, movies or television.

Advancement prospects become more difficult for individuals working at larger and more prestigious publications. At this point, there is a great deal of competition for each job.

Education and Training

Most larger publications now require at least a bachelor's degree in order to be considered for employment. There are, however, smaller, local newspapers which may hire individuals who do not have a college education. Advancement in these cases is usually difficult.

Good college majors for aspiring Critics include journalism, English, liberal arts, theater and the performing arts, or communications. Writing courses are helpful.

Experience/Skills/Personality Traits

Most Critics have journalistic experience in either high school, college or on a small local newspaper. Many individuals have written on a variety of subjects before becoming involved in entertainment, theater and the performing arts.

Critics must have excellent writing skills with a good command of the English language. They should be able to turn out clear, concise, objective and interesting reviews in a timely fashion. The ability to type or use a computer or word processor is necessary. The ability to work well under pressure is essential for those working on a deadline.

An interest and knowledge of the type work being reviewed is needed whether it be theater, television or films. In order to become successful in this field, the Critic's views must be respected for their honesty and objectivity over a long period of time.

Unions/Associations

Many newspapers and magazines are unionized. Individuals working as Critics may therefore be members of the specific union the publication is affiliated with.

Critics may also be members of a number of trade associations and other organizations. These might include the Music Critics Association (MCA), the New York Drama Critics Circle (NYDCC) and the Outer Critics Circle (OCC).

Tips for Entry

1. Obtain experience by reviewing plays, concerts, records, movies and television shows for your school paper.
2. Call the entertainment editor at your local newspaper and see if you can review a play or concert on spec, which means that if the editor likes the review he may run it. If not, you have gained some experience writing a review as well as making an important contact.
3. Find an internship in a newspaper or magazine in the entertainment department. If this is not possible, find an internship in any area of journalism.
4. If you are in college, try to get on the school newspaper. Every bit of experience is important: The more you obtain, the better journalist and Critic you will be in the long run.
5. Send your resume, a short cover letter and samples of your writing to the editors of publications you are interested in working for. Names and addresses of daily newspapers are available in the *Editor and Publisher International Year Book*. This publication is available in many libraries and larger newspaper offices around the country.

MISCELLANEOUS CAREERS IN THEATER AND THE PERFORMING ARTS

ARTS COUNCIL DIRECTOR

CAREER PROFILE

Duties: Managing the affairs of an arts council; fund-raising; auditioning, reviewing and selecting talent for performances; writing grants; performing public relations duties; working with volunteer committees.

Alternate Title(s): Executive Director; Chief Executive Officer.

Salary Range: $18,000 to $55,000+ a year.

Employment Prospects: Fair.

Best Geographical Location(s) for Position: Culturally active cities offer more opportunities.

Prerequisites:

Education or Training: Requirements vary from high school diploma to bachelor's degree; some positions require a master's degree.

Experience: Experience working in the performing arts, public relations, fund-raising or marketing.

Special Skills and Personality Traits: Knowledge of the performing arts industry; business skills; fund-raising, organizational coordination and communications skills.

CAREER LADDER

```
┌─────────────────────────────────────┐
│       Arts Council Director         │
│  for Larger, More Prestigious Council│
└─────────────────────────────────────┘

┌─────────────────────────────────────┐
│       Arts Council Director         │
└─────────────────────────────────────┘

┌─────────────────────────────────────┐
│    Assistant Arts Council Director  │
│                 or                  │
│  Individual Involved in Fund-Raising,│
│      Publicity, Public Relations,   │
│             Marketing or            │
│         the Performing Arts         │
└─────────────────────────────────────┘
```

Position Description

Arts councils are usually private, not-for-profit agencies established by people interested in the arts. In very small organizations all work is handled by volunteers from the membership. Other arts councils employ a number of people to run the organization. The person who coordinates the activities of the arts council is called the Arts Council Director. He or she may also be called the Executive Director or Chief Executive Officer.

The main function of the Arts Council Director is to manage the affairs of the organization. Responsibilities will vary depending on the job. In smaller organizations, the Director may handle everything with the help of committees of volunteers. In larger arts councils, the Director may have assistants and a staff to work with who handle the various duties. In these councils, the Director serves as a coordinator.

Arts councils bring a variety of events in the performing arts to the community, including a full range of performers, singers, dancers, musicians, theatrical, ballet or opera productions, symphonies, mimes, lecture or concert series, and comedians.

The Director, sometimes in conjunction with a committee from the council, determines the type of events the council wants to schedule for the coming year.

Once the type of shows are decided upon, the Arts Council Director finds the talent for these performances. One of the primary responsibilities of the Director is to audition, review and select the talent. The Director may travel to various locations or may simply view audio or videotapes from booking agents, managers or directly from performing artists.

When making a decision on booking any performance, Arts Council Directors must keep a number of things in mind, including the potential community audience and the policies and preferences of the council. They must also work within the budget of the organization.

The Arts Council Director also handles contract negotiations with the performers or their booking agents. The individual arranges the terms of the contract, schedules the dates and determines fees to be paid for each engagement. He or she is responsible for seeing that all contracts are signed by all parties concerned. The Director may also be required to make sure that checks are made out for deposits or fees and paid to the proper people at the correct times.

The Arts Council Director is heavily involved in the budget and finances of the organization. One of the responsibilities of the individual may be the preparation of an annual budget. This is generally difficult because many arts councils work with limited funds.

In order to help increase the funds of an organization, the Arts Council Director is responsible for fund-raising. The individual develops, implements and runs a number of special events during the year to raise needed money. These events may include annual dinner dances, membership drives, auctions, galas or special performances.

Grants are another source of money that many arts councils depend on. The Arts Council Director is responsible for locating grants from federal, state or local agencies and from private industry. They must then write and prepare the grant application. If the council receives grant money, the Arts Council Director makes sure that all rules and regulations of the grant are adhered to.

The Director is also responsible for handling the council's public relations and advertising for activities and performances, as well as internal publicity within the organization.

The Director is also responsible for handling the council's public relations and advertising for activities and performances, as well as internal publicity within the organization.

The Director is required to write and prepare press releases, calendar schedules and newsletters, and is responsible for developing, writing and producing all brochures, leaflets, and booklets.

Most not-for-profit groups, such as arts councils, depend on the help of volunteers. The Arts Council Director is responsible for coordinating the efforts of all the volunteer groups and committees in the council.

The Arts Council Director usually works regular hours. He or she may work overtime, however, to finish a project, audition talent or attend a performance. The individual is responsible to the council's board of directors or trustees.

Salaries

Earnings for Arts Council Directors vary greatly depending on the geographic location, size, prestige and budget of the arts council. Other variables include the experience and responsibilities of the individual.

Salaries for full-time Arts Council Directors can range from $15,000 to $55,000 plus annually. Salaries on the lower end of the scale go to individuals with little experience working in smaller organizations with limited budgets. Those with more experience and working in larger organizations in culturally active cities earn salaries on the higher end of the scale.

Employment Prospects

Employment prospects are fair for Arts Council Directors. While there are arts councils located through the country, individuals may have to relocate to find a position. Culturally active cities offer more opportunities.

It should be mentioned that all arts councils do not employ full-time directors. Some use the services of a volunteer to handle the tasks of the director.

Advancement Prospects

Advancement prospects are limited for Arts Council Directors. In order to climb the career ladder individuals must find a similar position in a more prestigious arts council with a larger budget. This may be difficult.

Some Arts Council Directors advance their careers by becoming booking agents or managers for performers, arenas, halls or theaters.

Education and Training

Educational requirements vary for Arts Council Directors. Some positions require a high school diploma while others require a bachelor's or a master's degree.

Good choices for college majors include arts management, public relations, communications, theater arts, business and liberal arts. Any courses, seminars or workshops in fund raising, grant writing, public relations, business or arts management are also useful.

Experience/Skills/Personality Traits

Arts Council Directors come from different types of backgrounds. Many have had experience in some facet of the performing arts, public relations or marketing. Others have worked in fund raising, or in other not-for-profit organizations. There are some who were promoted to Arts Council Director from an assistant's position.

Most people in this job have a genuine love for the performing arts. They enjoy ballets, orchestras, dancers, chamber music, theatrical productions and operas. They also enjoy being around others who have the same interests.

Arts Council Directors should be very organized and detail-oriented. Individuals must handle many different tasks at the same time. They need to be able to coordinate the activities of both staff members and volunteers.

Verbal and written communications skills are essential. The ability to research and write grants is helpful. Fund-raising skills are a must. The Director should also have the ability to carry out the full spectrum of public relations skills.

A knowledge of the performing arts industry is necessary, as are a variety of business skills, including the ability to negotiate and understand performers' contracts.

Unions/Associations

Arts Council Directors may be members of their specific state's council of the arts or the National Endowment for the Arts. Individuals may also belong to other associations.

Tips for Entry

1. Look for jobs under such heading classifications as "Arts Council," "Performing Arts" and "Executive Director" in the display or classified section of the newspaper. Openings may also be listed in local arts council newsletters.

2. Become a member of your local arts council. Volunteer to work on a number of committees. This work will provide you with experience and help you make contacts.

3. Offer to do the publicity or fund-raising for a local not-for-profit organization. It does not matter if the organization is related to the performing arts or not. If you can do publicity or fund-raising for one organization, you can do it for any type of group.

4. Many arts councils have Internet Web sites; check them for job possibilities.

ADVANCE PERSON

CAREER PROFILE

Duties: Arriving ahead of the performance of a theatrical or performing arts show to prepare for the program; assisting road manager or show coordinator with details prior to performance.

Alternate Title(s):   Advance Agent; Advance Man/Advance Woman.

Salary Range: $22,000 to $50,000+ a year.

Employment Prospects: Fair.

Best Geographical Location(s) for Position: Positions are located in culturally active cities.

Prerequisites:

Education or Training: No formal educational requirement.

Experience: Publicity or promotion experience helpful, but not required.

Special Skills and Personality Traits: Ability to travel alone; organizational skills; dependability; good communication skills.

CAREER LADDER

```
┌─────────────────────────────────────┐
│          Tour Manager,              │
│   Company Tour Coordinator          │
│              or                     │
│       Advance Person for            │
│   More Prestigious Productions      │
└─────────────────────────────────────┘

┌─────────────────────────────────────┐
│          Advance Person             │
└─────────────────────────────────────┘

┌─────────────────────────────────────┐
│  Publicist or Promotional Staff Person │
│              or                     │
│           Entry Level               │
└─────────────────────────────────────┘
```

Position Description

Many theatrical productions, including plays, concerts, ballets, opera, and circuses, travel from city to city. The Advance Person is the individual who goes out on the road from the home city before the rest of the entourage departs to set up before a theatrical or performing arts production takes place. As a rule, the Advance Person leaves a town before the performance and moves on to the next location.

The main function of the Advance Person is to make sure that everything is set up as planned in the city and venue where a performance is scheduled to occur. The individual checks to see that posters and billboards are put up in the area. If they are not, he or she might either put them up personally or hire a crew. The individual also sees that fliers and other promotional material are distributed throughout the area.

The Advance Person is responsible for checking advance ticket sales to determine how they are selling. With smaller events, the Advance Person is responsible for physically bringing the tickets for the event to ticket sellers. Larger concerts, plays and ballets, however, generally use the services of a computerized ticket agency such as Ticketron.

The Advance Person, who is also referred to as the Advance Man or Advance Woman, may be responsible for delivering press passes or press lists issued by the publicist, public relations company or organization sponsoring the event. Other promotional responsibilities may include delivering press packages, photographs and programs to sponsors or promoters in each city.

The Advance Person is responsible for checking out the venue, hall or auditorium where the theatrical event is scheduled to take place. The individual looks into the seating, exits, entrances and loading docks of each hall and reports all information to the tour manager handling the event. The Advance Person is expected to measure mileage and check routes between cities on the tour. He or she might see what options are available for transportation as well as hotels, motels and restaurants in each city. All of this information is relayed back to the tour manager or road coordinator of the show.

The Advance Person is responsible for bringing camera ready advertisements to local newspapers, video advertisements to television stations and copy for radio ads to stations.

In most instances, the Advance Person is expected to visit the local promoter or director of the organization sponsoring the event to go over last minute details which must be taken care of before a show.

In order to be successful as an Advance Person, the individual must be very dependable and responsible. He or she must be able to structure his or her own day in order to get everything accomplished.

The amount of traveling the Advance Person does depends to a great extent on the specific job. Some theatrical Advance People travel from coast to coast while others stay within a 100- or 200-mile radius of the home city.

Salaries

Salaries for Advance People vary depending on the specific job. Salaries may start out at $400 per week and may go up to $1,000 or more. Advance People always receive either a per diem or reimbursement for their traveling expenses.

Individuals are usually paid by the week for the time that they work. For weeks that they are not on the road, they might receive a reduction in salary, no salary or a retainer.

Employment Prospects

Employment prospects for Advance People are fair. They may find work with theater, ballet, concert or opera companies, or they may be employed by circuses, musical acts, management companies or promoters.

Advancement Prospects

Advance People may become road or tour managers or coordinators for any type of performing artist or company.

Other individuals advance their careers by finding more prestigious types of shows to work with.

Education and Training

There is no formal education requirement for this position; however, a valid driver's license is usually required.

Experience/Skills/Personality Traits

Many Advance People obtain their job having no prior experience. Others have worked as publicity or promotional assistants.

The Advance Person must like to travel and not mind traveling alone. He or she must be extremely organized and detail oriented and should be responsible and dependable.

Successful Advance People are personable and articulate.

Unions/Associations

There is no union or trade association specifically geared towards Advance People working in theater or other performing arts.

Tips for Entry

1. Send your resume and a short cover letter to the head offices of theatrical, ballet, symphony and opera companies. You might also send resumes to circuses and touring rock, country and easy listening acts.
2. Advertise your availability in a small display or classified ad in any of the trade magazines.
3. Check ads for this position in the classified or display section of newspapers in larger culturally active cities.
4. Prepare your resume, listing all skills and experience that might interest a potential employer.

DANCE THERAPIST

CAREER PROFILE

Duties: Using dance and movement activities to treat physical, mental and emotional disabilities in patients.

Alternate Title(s): Dance/Movement Therapist.

Salary Range: $18,000 to $65,000+ a year.

Employment Prospects: Excellent.

Best Geographical Location(s) for Position: Positions are located throughout the country.

Prerequisites:

Education or Training: Master's degree required.

Experience: Internship required.

Special Skills and Personality Traits: Dancing and movement skills; researching skills; emotional stability; ability to work with the handicapped and disabled; compassion; patience; empathy.

CAREER LADDER

```
┌─────────────────────────────────────┐
│       Supervisory Position          │
│                or                   │
│  Dance Therapist in Private Practice │
└─────────────────────────────────────┘

┌─────────────────────────────────────┐
│          Dance Therapist            │
└─────────────────────────────────────┘

┌─────────────────────────────────────┐
│             Intern                  │
│               or                    │
│             Dancer                  │
└─────────────────────────────────────┘
```

Position Description

A rewarding way to work in the performing arts is to do so while helping others. Dance Therapists use dance, movement and related activities to treat disabilities in patients. The function of a Dance Therapist is to provide a patient with a means of expression. A patient may be referred to a Dance Therapist for a variety of reasons, including physical, mental or emotional disabilities or illness. Victims of various diseases, accidents or handicaps may also become patients of Dance Therapists.

Dance Therapists are registered with the American Dance Therapy Association (ADTA) and must go through a program of training. There are two levels of Dance Therapists. The first is called DTR (Dance Therapist Registered) for those who have completed the training and education for the basic level of competency in the job. Individuals who complete additional requirements go to the next level called ADTR (Academy of Dance Therapists Registered).

The Dance Therapist's main function is to help restore a patient's health. This is accomplished with the help of other professionals, including doctors, nurses, teachers, physical therapists, music therapists, psychologists and psychiatrists. Together this team determines what course of action to take for a patient's therapy. Dance Therapy, along with other expressive arts therapies, can often provide a breakthrough

with a patient who cannot be reached in any other manner. The Dance Therapist uses various forms of dance and movement to help the patient regain his or her health. The Therapist must have a complete knowledge and understanding of body movement and what it can accomplish.

The responsibilities of the Dance Therapist vary depending on the specific job and the specific patient. He or she must observe, assess and evaluate each patient before developing the best course of treatment.

The Dance Therapist plans dance and other movement activities based on the knowledge and experience gained while training for the job. In some instances, the Dance Therapist works with one patient at a time. In other instances, he or she works with a group of patients. Dance Therapists use dance and movement to accomplish their goals in treatment of the patient. They may teach a variety of forms of dance to a patient or may have the patient move freely and observe his or her movements, facial expressions and other body language. It is important for the Dance Therapist to realize that what works for one patient will not always work with another.

Dance therapy may be used to soothe patients who are angry or irritated. It may also be used to evoke various reactions. Sometimes when a patient uses a great deal of energy moving around, he or she loses inhibitions or gains the ability to talk about a problem. Dance and movement may also make people feel less self-conscious. In some cases, patients are able to express emotions through movement.

Conferences are often held with other members of the professional team as well as with the patient's family to discuss the individual's needs and progress.

This job can be very fulfilling. Seeing a patient with an unhealthy emotional or physical condition change and become healthier through dance and movement is very rewarding.

Salaries

Earnings for Dance Therapists vary greatly depending on a number of factors, including the specific facility an individual is working for, its size, prestige and geographic location. Other factors affecting salary include the individual's experience, responsibilities and educational level.

Dance Therapists earn between $18,000 and $65,000 annually. The average yearly salary is between $35,000 and $45,000.

Employment Prospects

Employment prospects are excellent for Dance Therapists. They can work full or part time in a variety of health-care situations including hospitals, other health-care facilities, psychiatric hospitals, mental health centers, rehabilitation centers, nursing homes, extended care facilities, schools, correctional facilities or independent expressive arts therapy centers. Opportunities are located throughout the country.

Advancement Prospects

Dance Therapists have good advancement prospects. With drive and determination, individuals can move into supervisory positions, including that of director of recreation therapy or expressive arts therapy.

An individual may also advance by locating a similar position at a more prestigious facility, with increased responsibilities and earnings.

Another path many individuals take is to go into private practice. In order to go into private practice or to teach, Dance Therapists may need to fulfill additional requirements.

Education and Training

Dance Therapists must hold a master's degree. The American Dance Therapy Association has approved the programs of a number of colleges throughout the country offering graduate degrees in dance therapy. They also allow alternative education requirements for individuals who do not attend one of the schools participating in approved programs.

Dance Therapists may have undergraduate degrees in any area including liberal arts, dance, psychology or physical education. As most aspiring Dance Therapists are extremely interested in dance, they usually take a large number of classes in that area. Other helpful undergraduate classes include those in kinesiology and dance education.

Experience/Skills/Personality Traits

In order to be registered by the American Dance Therapy Association, the registering agency for this profession, Dance Therapists must fulfill certain requirements. They also need the experience received through internship programs.

Dance Therapists must have the ability to work with ill, handicapped and disabled patients. They must have a great deal of patience as it often takes a long time for a patient to make any progress.

The Dance Therapist must be compassionate, empathetic and emotionally stable. He or she must have training in a variety of forms of dance. The ability to do research is helpful.

Unions/Associations

Dance Therapists may belong to the American Dance Therapy Association (ADTA). This organization offers education, professional support and guidance to their members as well as bringing individuals interested in the field together. It is also the registering agency for Dance Therapists.

Tips for Entry

1. Check the college job placement office for schools offering degrees in dance therapy. These schools often have listings of job openings. Many facilities send employment opportunities to these schools in hopes of locating qualified applicants.

2. Look under heading classifications of "Dance Therapy," "Health Care," "Therapists," "Recreation Therapy" and "Expressive Arts Therapists" in the display or classified section of the newspaper.

3. Contact the American Dance Therapy Association (ADTA) for the requirements for becoming a registered Dance Therapist.

4. Send your resume and a short cover letter to the personnel director of facilities, schools or independent expressive arts therapies centers. Request that they keep your resume on file if there is not a current opening.

5. There are positions for Dance Therapists available through the state and federal government. These civil service positions can be located by contacting your state and federal employment service.

6. Check the Internet for job possibilities. Search the major job and employment sites, and sites related to dance or dance therapy.

MUSIC THERAPIST

CAREER PROFILE

Duties: Using music or musical activities to treat physical, mental or emotional disabilities in patients.

Alternate Title(s): None.

Salary Range: $18,000 to $48,000+ a year.

Employment Prospects: Excellent.

Best Geographical Location(s) for Position: Positions are located throughout the country.

Prerequisites:

Education or Training: Minimum requirement is a bachelor's degree in music therapy; some positions may require master's degree.

Experience: Internship in music therapy usually required; experience working with the handicapped or disabled helpful.

Special Skills and Personality Traits: Ability to play a musical instrument; ability to sing in front of others; emotional stability; ability to work with the handicapped and disabled; compassion; patience; empathy.

CAREER LADDER

```
┌─────────────────────────────────────┐
│  Music Therapist in Larger or More  │
│         Prestigious Facility         │
│                  or                  │
│         Supervisory Position         │
└─────────────────────────────────────┘

┌─────────────────────────────────────┐
│           Music Therapist            │
└─────────────────────────────────────┘

┌─────────────────────────────────────┐
│                Intern                │
│                  or                  │
│               Student                │
└─────────────────────────────────────┘
```

Position Description

One of the more rewarding ways to work in the performing arts is to do so while helping others. Music Therapists use music and musical activities to treat physical, mental or emotional disabilities in patients. They attempt to restore an individual's health, working with a number of other professionals. These professionals include physicians, nurses, teachers, physical therapists, dance therapists, psychologists and psychiatrists.

The Music Therapist will use various forms of music as therapy for individuals who have physical, mental or emotional disabilities or illness. The Therapist can often make a breakthrough in a patient's therapy when all else has failed.

Music Therapists have varied duties depending on the specific job and patient. They may be responsible for choosing pieces of music to be used as background in certain rooms in a facility. Background music may be used to either soothe patients or to evoke various reactions.

Music Therapists who work in a hospital, nursing home or extended-care facility may be responsible for bringing together a group of patients to sing or play instruments for the facility staff and other patients. This type of therapy is used to bring people out of their shells, to build self-confidence and to express memories and emotions when verbal attempts have failed.

The Music Therapist is responsible for planning musical activities for one person at a time or for a group. He or she may teach a group of patients in a nursing home a new song or play a tape of songs that were popular when the patients were younger. This type of therapy often helps to engage a withdrawn patient.

In some cases, Music Therapists work with handicapped children. For example, they may be responsible for teaching a blind child how to play a musical instrument. This activity gives the child a tremendous sense of accomplishment that he or she might not have had before.

Through the use of all these therapies, the Therapist can often accomplish a degree of healing by giving a patient a sense of accomplishment, helping another patient express a long suppressed emotion, or simply making patients feel more secure.

The Therapist works with a patient on a one-to-one basis or in a group, depending on the patient and his or her needs. Conferences are often held with other members of the professional team as well as with the patient's family, where the Therapist discusses the individual's needs and progress.

As in most therapy, Music Therapists realize that progress may be slow, but even the slightest progress can mean a great deal to the patient. The reward some Music Therapists receive when they see a patient acting or feeling better is often as exciting to the Therapist as a recital would be to a performance artist.

The object of music therapy is not to make a patient an accomplished musician or vocalist. It is, rather, through the medium of music, to improve the emotional, mental and physical stability of the patient.

Salaries

Salaries for Music Therapists vary from job to job. Factors affecting salaries include experience, responsibilities and education of the Therapist. Other factors include the specific job and the size, prestige and geographic location of the facility.

Therapists entering the field can expect to earn from $18,000 to $24,000 annually. Those working at larger facilities and who have more experience may command yearly salaries ranging from $24,000 to $38,000. Supervisory positions in the field of music therapy may offer annual earnings of $48,000 and up.

Employment Prospects

Employment prospects for Music Therapists are excellent. There are currently more positions than there are qualified individuals. Music Therapists work in a variety of settings, including hospitals, other health-care facilities, rehabilitation centers, nursing homes, extended-care facilities, schools or independent expressive arts therapy centers. Opportunities are located throughout the country.

Advancement Prospects

Advancement prospects are good for Music Therapists who have the education, drive and determination. Individuals climb the career ladder by locating a similar position in a more prestigious facility with increased responsibilities and earnings.

Another method of career advancement is for the Music Therapist to assume a supervisory or administrative position. One of the drawbacks of this career path for many is that it limits the contact the Therapist has with patients.

The Music Therapist can also climb the career ladder by finding a position in research or by teaching at a university. There are some individuals who advance their careers by going into private practice or consulting.

Education and Training

The minimum educational requirement for a Music Therapist is a bachelor's degree in music therapy. Courses usually include music theory, voice studies, instrument lessons, psychology, sociology and biology in addition to general liberal arts courses. Music Therapists who aspire to work in the public school system must also have a teaching degree.

Many positions require a master's degree. There are a great many colleges throughout the country that offer both an undergraduate and a postgraduate degree program in music therapy.

Music Therapists in most situations must be licensed in order to obtain employment.

Experience/Skills/Personality Traits

Music Therapists obtain experience in a number of ways. In order to be licensed, individuals go through a six-month internship program. Many Music Therapists have also worked at health-care facilities or schools in part-time jobs or in voluntary positions to gain additional experience.

One of the most important personality traits a good Music Therapist must have is the ability to work with the handicapped and disabled. He or she must also have a great deal of patience. As noted previously, it often takes the Music Therapist a long time to see results. The Music Therapist must also be compassionate, empathetic and emotionally stable to be successful.

Music Therapists must have the ability to play a musical instrument. Knowing how to play more than one is a plus as is the ability to sing in front of others. They must be able to teach others to play an instrument or sing. A good knowledge of all forms of music is essential.

Unions/Associations

Music Therapists may belong to the American Association for Music Therapy (AAMT). This organization provides valuable assistance to those in the field. It helps place qualified Music Therapists, does research and acts as liaison for colleges that offer music therapy programs.

Tips for Entry

1. Check with the college placement office for openings for Music Therapists. Many facilities or schools looking for people to fill positions send a list of openings to colleges and universities granting degrees in music therapy.

2. Contact both the National Association for Music Therapy, Inc. (NAMT) and the American Association for Music Therapy (AAMT) for registration and placement services.

3. Many positions for Music Therapists are available through the federal government. These civil service positions can be located through federal and state employment services.

4. Look under heading classifications of "Music Therapist," "Therapist," "Health Care" or "Expressive Arts Therapist" in the classified or display sections of newspapers.

5. Search the major job and employment sites on the Internet for job openings. Also, look for sites related to music or music therapy.

APPENDIXES

APPENDIX I
DEGREE AND NONDEGREE PROGRAMS

A. COLLEGES AND UNIVERSITIES THAT OFFER DEGREES IN DRAMA AND THEATER ARTS

Although a college degree does not guarantee a job in the theatrical field, many people feel it is in their best interest to pursue an education beyond high school to gain knowledge and new skills and to make important contacts. As the theatrical and performing arts industries are competitive, a higher education may give one person a competitive edge.

The following is a list of four-year schools granting degrees in drama and theater arts. They are grouped by state.

More colleges are beginning to grant degrees in this area every year. Check the newest copy of *Lovejoy*'s *College Guide* (found in the reference section of libraries or in guidance or counseling centers) for additional schools giving degrees in this field.

There are also numerous two-year schools that offer study in theater arts, as well as four year-schools that have courses in the theater arts but do not offer a degree in the field.

ALABAMA

Alabama State University
PO Box 271
915 South Jackson Street
Montgomery, AL 36195

Auburn University
Mary E. Martin Hall
Auburn University, AL 36849

Auburn University–Montgomery
PO Box 244023
Montgomery, AL 36124

Birmingham–Southern College
Arkadelphia Road
Birmingham, AL 35254

Huntingdon College
1500 East Fairview Avenue
Montgomery, AL 36194

Jacksonville State University
North Pelham Road
Jacksonville, AL 36265

Samford University
800 Lakeshore Drive
Birmingham, AL 35229

Troy State University
University Avenue
Troy, AL 36082

University of Alabama
Box 870132
Tuscaloosa, AL 35487

University of Alabama–Birmingham
University Station
University Center
Birmingham, AL 35294

University of Montevallo
Montevallo, AL 35115

University of North Alabama
Wesleyan Avenue
Florence, AL 35632

University of South Alabama
307 University Boulevard
Mobile, AL 36688

ALASKA

University of Alaska Anchorage
3211 Providence Drive
Anchorage, AK 99508

University of Alaska Fairbanks
320 Signers' Hall
Fairbanks, AK 99701

ARIZONA

Arizona State University
Tempe, AZ 85287

Grand Canyon College
3300 West Camelback Road
Phoenix, AZ 85017

Northern Arizona University
Box 4084
Flagstaff, AZ 86011

University of Arizona
Tucson, AZ 85721

ARKANSAS

Arkansas State University
PO Box 1630
State University, AR 72467

Harding University
Box 762–Station A
Searcy, AR 72143

Henderson State University
Arkadelphia, AR 71923

Hendrix College
Conway, AR 72023

Quachita Baptist University
410 Quachita Street
Arkadelphia, AR 71998

Southern Arkansas University
SAU Box 1382
Magnolia, AR 71753

University of Arkansas
Administration 222
Fayetteville, AR 72701

University of Arkansas–Little Rock
2801 South University
Little Rock, AR 72204

University of Arkansas–Pine Bluff
1200 University Drive
Pine Bluff, AR 71601

CALIFORNIA

California Baptist College
8432 Magnolia Avenue
Riverside, CA 92504

California Institute of the Arts
24700 McBean Parkway
Valencia, CA 91355

California Lutheran University
60 Olsen Road
Thousand Oaks, CA 91360

California State Polytechnic University–Pomona
3801 West Temple Avenue
Pomona, CA 91768

California State University–Bakersfield
9001 Stockdale Highway
Bakersfield, CA 93311

California State University–Chico
Chico, CA 95929

California State University–Dominguez Hills
Carson, CA 90747

California State University–Fresno
Shaw and Cedar Avenues
Fresno, CA 93740

California State University–Fullerton
Fullerton, CA 92634

California State University–Hayward
Hayward, CA 94542

California State University–Long Beach
1250 Bellflower Boulevard
Long Beach, CA 90840

California State University–Los Angeles
5151 State University Drive
Los Angeles, CA 90032

California State University–Northridge
18111 Nordoff Street
Northridge, CA 91330

California State University–Sacramento
6000 J Street
Sacramento, CA 95819

California State University–San Bernadino
5500 University Parkway
San Bernadino, CA 92407

California State University–Stanislaus
801 West Monte Vista Avenue
Turlock, CA 95380

Chapman College
333 North Glassell Street
Orange, CA 92666

Claremont McKenna College
890 Columbia Avenue
Claremont, CA 91711

College of Notre Dame
1500 Ralston Avenue
Belmont, CA 94002

Concordia College
Irvine, CA 92715

Humboldt State University
Arcata, CA 95521

Loyola Marymount University
Loyola Boulevard at West 80th Street
Los Angeles, CA 90045

Mills College
5000 MacArthur Boulevard
Oakland, CA 94613

New College of California
777 Valencia
San Francisco, CA 94110

Occidental College
1600 Campus Road
Los Angeles, CA 90041

Pepperdine University–Seaver College
24255 Pacific Coast Highway
Malibu, CA 90265

Pitzer College
1050 North Mills Avenue
Claremont, CA 91711

Point Loma Nazarene College
3900 Lomaland Drive
San Diego, CA 92106

Pomona College
333 North College Way
Claremont, CA 91711

San Diego State University
5300 Campanile Drive
San Diego, CA 92182

San Francisco State University
1600 Holloway Avenue
San Francisco, CA 94132

San Jose State University
1 Washington Square
San Jose, CA 95192

Santa Clara University
Santa Clara, CA 95053

Scripps College
1030 Columbia Avenue
Claremont, CA 91711

Sonoma State University
1801 East Cotati Avenue
Rohnert Park, CA 94928

Southern California College
55 Fair Drive
Costa Mesa, CA 92626

St. Mary's College of California
Moraga, CA 94575

University of California–Berkeley
120 Sproul Hall
Berkeley, CA 94720

University of California–Davis
178 Mrak Hall
1 Shields Avenue
Davis, CA 95616

University of California–Irvine
204 Administration Building
Irvine, CA 92697

University of California–Los Angeles
405 Hilgard Avenue
Los Angeles, CA 90024

University of California–Riverside
1100 Administration Building
Riverside, CA 92521

University of California–San Diego
9500 Gilman Drive
La Jolla, CA 92093

University of California–Santa Barbara
Admissions Office
Santa Barbara, CA 93106

University of California–Santa Cruz
Cook House
Santa Cruz, CA 95064

University of La Verne
1950 Third Street
La Verne, CA 91750

University of Southern California
University Park
Los Angeles, CA 90089

University of the Pacific
3601 Pacific Avenue
Stockton, CA 95211

Westmont College
955 La Paz Road
Santa Barbara, CA 93108

Whittier College
13406 East Philadelphia
Whittier, CA 90608

COLORADO

Colorado Christian College
180 South Garrison Street
Lakewood, CO 80226

Colorado College
Colorado Springs, CO 80903

Colorado State University
Administration Annex
Fort Collins, CO 80523

Mesa State College
PO Box 2647
Grand Junction, CO 81502

Naropa Institute
2130 Arapahoe Avenue
Boulder, CO 80302

University of Colorado–Boulder
Campus Box B-7
Boulder, CO 90309

University of Colorado–Denver
Campus Box 167
1200 Larimer
Denver, CO 80204

University of Northern Colorado
Carter Hall 3006
Greeley, CO 80639

University of Southern Colorado
2200 Bonforte Boulevard
Pueblo, CO 81001

Western State College of Colorado
College Heights
Gunnison, CO 81230

CONNECTICUT

Albertus Magnus College
700 Prospect Street
New Haven, CT 06511

Central Connecticut State University
1615 Stanley Street
New Britain, CT 06050

Connecticut College
New London, CT 06320

Sacred Heart University
5151 Park Avenue
Fairfield, CT 06432

Trinity College
300 Summit Street
Hartford, CT 06106

University of Connecticut
Storrs, CT 06269

University of Hartford
200 Bloomfield Avenue
West Hartford, CT 06117

Wesleyan University
North College
Middletown, CT 06457

Western Connecticut State University
181 White Street
Danbury, CT 06810

Yale University
Box 1520A
Yale Station
New Haven, CT 06520

DELAWARE

Delaware State University
1200 North Dupont Highway
Dover, DE 19901

University of Delaware
116 Hullihen Hall
Newark, DE 19716

DISTRICT OF COLUMBIA

American University
4400 Massachusetts Avenue NW
Washington, DC 20016

Catholic University of America
Washington, DC 20064

George Washington University
2121 I Street NW
Washington, DC 20052

Howard University
2400 Sixth Street NW
Washington, DC 20059

University of the District of Columbia
4200 Connecticut Avenue NW
Washington, DC 20008

FLORIDA

Barry University
11300 Northeast Second Avenue
Miami Shores, FL 33161

Eckerd College
4200 54th Avenue South
St. Petersburg, FL 33711

Flagler College
PO Box 1027
St. Augustine, FL 32085

Florida Agriculture and Mechanical University
Tallahassee, FL 32307

Florida Atlantic University
PO Box 3091
Boca Raton, FL 33431

Florida International University
Tamiami Trail
Miami, FL 33199

Florida Southern College
111 Lake Hollingsworth Drive
Lakeland, FL 33801

Florida State University
Tallahassee, FL 32306

Jacksonville University
2800 University Boulevard
Jacksonville, FL 32211

Rollins College
Box 2720
Winter Park, FL 32789

Stetson University
DeLand, FL 32720

University of Central Florida
PO Box 160111
Orlando, FL 32816

University of Florida
302 Little Hall
PO Box 118140
Gainesville, FL 32611

University of Miami
PO Box 248025
Coral Gables, FL 33124

University of South Florida
4202 Fowler Avenue
Tampa, FL 33620

University of Tampa
401 West Kennedy Boulevard
Tampa, FL 33606

University of West Florida
11000 University Parkway
Pensacola, FL 32514

GEORGIA

Agnes Scott College
141 East College Avenue
Decatur, GA 30030

Albany State College
504 College Drive
Albany, GA 31705

Berry College
PO Box 159
Mount Berry Station
Mount Berry, GA 30149

Clark Atlanta University
240 James P. Brawley Drive
Atlanta, GA 30314

Columbus College
Richards Building
Algonquin Drive
Columbus, GA 31993

Emory University
Boisfeuillet Jones Center
Atlanta, GA 30303

Georgia College
Campus Box 499
Milledgeville, GA 31061

Georgia Southern University
Box 8024
Statesboro, GA 30458

Georgia State University
University Plaza
Atlanta, GA 30303

La Grange College
601 Broad Street
La Grange, GA 30240

Mercer University
1400 Coleman Avenue
Macon, GA 31207

Moorehouse College
830 Westview Drive SW
Atlanta, GA 30314

Shorter College
315 Shorter Avenue
Rome, GA 30165

Spelman College
350 Spelman Lane SW
Atlanta, GA 30314

University of Georgia
212 Terrell Hall
Athens, GA 30602

Valdosta State College
1500 North Patterson Street
Valdosta, GA 30698

Wesleyan College
4760 Forsyth Road
Macon, GA 31297

West Georgia College
Carrolton, GA 30118

The Women's College of Brenau University
1 Centennial Circle
Gainesville, GA 30501

HAWAII

University of Hawaii–Manoa
2600 Campus Road
Honolulu, HI 96822

IDAHO

Boise State University
1910 University Drive
Boise, ID 83725

Idaho State University
PO Box 8054
Pocatello, ID 83209

Lewis Clark State College
Eight Avenue and Sixth Street
Lewiston, ID 83501

University of Idaho
141 Administration Building
Moscow, ID 83844

ILLINOIS

Angustana College
639 38th Street
Rock Island, IL 61201

Barat College
700 East Westleigh Road
Lake Forest, IL 60045

Bradley University
1501 West Bradley
Peoria, IL 61525

Columbia College
600 South Michigan
Chicago, IL 60605

Concordia College
7400 Augusta Street
River Forest, IL 60305

DePaul University
25 East Jackson Boulevard
Chicago, IL 60604

Eastern Illinois University
Room 116
Old Main
Charleston, IL 61920

Elmhurst College
190 Prospect Avenue
Elmhurst, IL 60216

Eureka College
College Avenue
Eureka, IL 61530

Greenville College
315 East College Avenue
Greenville, IL 62246

Illinois College
West College Avenue
Jacksonville, IL 62650

Illinois State University
Campus Box 2200
Normal, IL 61761

Illinois Wesleyan University
Bloomington, IL 61702

Judson College
1151 North State Street
Elgin, IL 60120

Knox College
Galesburg, IL 61401

Lewis University
Route 53
Romeoville, IL 60441

Loyola University of Chicago
820 North Michigan Avenue
Chicago, IL 60611

Monmouth College
700 East Broadway
Monmouth, IL 61462

National–Louis University
2840 Sheridan Road
Evanston, IL 60201

North Park College
3225 West Forester Avenue
Chicago, IL 60625

Northeastern Illinois University
5500 North St. Louis Avenue
Chicago, IL 60625

Northern Illinois University
De Kalb, IL 60115

Northwestern University
PO Box 3060
1801 Hinman Avenue
Evanston, IL 60201

Principle College
Elsah, IL 62028

Rockford College
5050 East State Street
Rockford, IL 61109

Roosevelt University
430 South Michigan Avenue
Chicago, IL 60605

Shimer College
PO Box A500
Waukegan, IL 60085

Southern Illinois University–Carbondale
Woody Hall
Carbondale, IL 62901

Southern Illinois University–Edwardsville
Box 1047
Edwardsville, IL 62026

St. Xavier University
3700 West 103rd Street
Chicago, IL 60655

University of Illinois at Chicago
Box 5220
Chicago, IL 60680

University of Illinois at Urbana–Champaign
506 South Wright Street
Urbana, IL 61801

Western Illinois University
900 West Adams Street
Macomb, IL 61455

INDIANA

Anderson University
Anderson, IN 46012

Ball State University
2000 University Avenue
Muncie, IN 47306

Butler University
46th and Sunset Avenue
Indianapolis, IN 46208

Earlham College
National Road West
Richmond, IN 47374

Franklin College
Monroe Street
Franklin, IN 46131

Hanover College
Hanover, IN 47243

Huntington College
2303 College Avenue
Huntington, IN 46750

Indiana State University
Tirey Hall
Terre Haute, IN 47809

Indiana University–Bloomington
Bloomington, IN 47405

Indiana University-Northwest
3400 Broadway
Gary, IN 46408

**Indiana University–Purdue University
at Fort Wayne**
2101 Coliseum Boulevard East
Fort Wayne, IN 46805

Indiana University–South Bend
PO Box 7111
1700 Mishawaka Avenue
South Bend, IN 46634

Marian College
3200 Cold Spring Road
Indianapolis, IN 46222

Purdue University
Schleman Hall
West Lafayette, IN 47907

Purdue University–Calumet
2233 171st Street
Hammond, IN 46323

St. Mary's College
Notre Dame, IN 46556

Taylor University
Reade Avenue
Upland, IN 46989

University of Evansville
1800 Lincoln Avenue
Evansville, IN 47722

University of Indianapolis
1400 East Hanna Avenue
Indianapolis, IN 46227

University of Notre Dame
Notre Dame, IN 46556

University of Southern Indiana
8600 University Boulevard
Evansville, IN 47714

Valparaiso University
Valparaiso, IN 46383

IOWA

Briar Cliff College
3303 Rebecca Street
Sioux City, IA 51104

Buena Vista University
610 West Fourth Street
Storm Lake, IA 50588

Central College
812 University Street
Pella, IA 50219

Clark College
1550 Clarke Drive
Dubuque, IA 52001

Coe College
1220 First Avenue
Cedar Rapids, IA 52402

Cornell College
600 First Street West
Mount Vernon, IA 52314

Dordt College
Sioux Center, IA 51250

Drake University
25th and University Streets
Des Moines, IA 50311

Graceland College
Lamoni, IA 50140

Grand View College
1200 Grandview Avenue
Des Moines, IA 50316

Grinnell College
Grinnell, IA 50112

Iowa State University
100 Alumni Hall
Ames, IA 50011

Luther College
Decorah, IA 52101

Morningside College
1501 Morningside Avenue
Sioux City, IA 51106

Northwestern College
101 College Lane
Orange City, IA 51041

Simpson College
Indianola, IA 50125

St. Ambrose University
518 West Locust Street
Davenport, IA 52803

University of Iowa
108 Calvin Hall
Iowa City, IA 52242

University of Northern Iowa
West 27th Street
Cedar Falls, IA 50614

KANSAS

Baker University
Baldwin City, KS 66006

Benedictine College
North Campus
Atchison, KS 66002

Bethany College
421 North First
Lindsberg, KS 67456

Emproria State University
12th and Commercial Streets
Emporia, KS 66801

Fort Hays State University
600 Park Street
Hays, KS 67601

Friends University
2100 University Avenue
Wichita, KS 67213

Kansas State University
Anderson Hall
Manhattan, KS 66506

Kansas Wesleyan University
100 East Claflin
Salina, KS 67401

McPherson College
1600 East Euclid
McPherson, KS 67460

Ottawa University
1001 South Cedar Street
Ottawa, KS 66067

Pittsburg State University
1701 South Broadway
Pittsburgh, KS 66762

Saint Mary College
4100 South Fourth Street Trafficway
Leavenworth, KS 66048

Southwestern College
100 College Street
Winfield, KS 67156

Sterling College
North Broadway
Sterling, KS 67579

University of Kansas
126 Strong Hall
Lawrence, KS 66045

Washburn University
1700 College Street
Topeka, KS 66621

Witchita State University
1845 Fairmount Street
Wichita, KS 67208

KENTUCKY

Ashbury College
North Lexington Avenue
Wilmore, KY 40390

Bellarmine College
2001 Newburg Road
Louisville, KY 42718

Berea College
CPO 2344
Berea, KY 40404

Campbellsville College
200 West College Street
Campbellsville, KY 42718

Centre College
600 West Walnut Street
Danville, KY 40422

Eastern Kentucky University
Lancaster Avenue
Richmond, KY 40475

Georgetown College
400 East College Street
Gerogetown, KY 40324

Kentucky Wesleyan College
3000 Frederica Street
Ownensboro, KY 42301

Morehead State University
Morehead, KY 40351

Murray State University
Murray, KY 42071

Northern Kentucky University
Nunn Drive
Highland Heights, KY 41076

Thomas More College
Crestview Hills, KY 41017

Transylvania University
300 North Broadway
Lexington, KY 40508

Union College
310 College Street
Barbourville, KY 40506

University of Kentucky
100 Funkhouser Building
Lexington, KY 40506

University of Louisville
Louisville, KY 40292

Western Kentucky University
Potter Hall
1 Big Red Way
Bowling Green, KY 42101

LOUISIANA

Centenary College of Louisiana
2911 Centenary Boulevard
Shreveport, LA 71104

Dillard University
2601 Gentilly Boulevard
New Orleans, LA 70122

Grambling State University
Grambling, LA 71245

**Louisiana State University and
    Agricultural and Mechanical
    College**
110 Thomas Boyd Hall
Baton Rouge, LA 70803

Loyola University
6363 St. Charles Avenue
New Orleans, LA 70118

McNeese State University
Lake Charles, LA 70609

Nicholls State University
PO Box 2004
University Station
Thibodaux, LA 70310

Southern University–Baton Rouge
PO Box 9901–Southern Branch
Baton Rouge, LA 70813

Tulane University
6823 St. Charles Avenue
New Orleans, LA 70118

University of New Orleans
Lakefront
New Orleans, LA 70148

University of Southwestern Louisiana
PO Box 41770
Lafayette, LA 70504

MAINE

Bates College
23 Campus Avenue
Lewiston, ME 04240

Colby College
Waterville, ME 04901

University of Maine at Orono
Chadbourne Hall
Orono, ME 04469

University of Maine at Presque Isle
181 Main Street
Presque Isle, ME 04769

University of Southern Maine
37 College Avenue
Gorham, ME 04038

MARYLAND

Bowie State College
Jericho Park Road
Bowie, MD 20715

Frostburg State University
Frostburg, MD 21532

Goucher College
Dulaney Valley Road
Baltimore, MD 21204

Loyola College
4501 North Charles Street
Baltimore, MD 21210

Morgan State University
Cold Spring Lane and Hillen Road
Baltimore, MD 21239

Mount Saint Mary's College
Emmitsburg, MD 21727

Salisbury State University
Camden Avenue
Salisbury, MD 21801

St. Mary's College of Maryland
St. Mary's City, MD 20686

Towson State University
Towson, MD 21204

**University of Maryland–
    Baltimore County**
Baltimore, MD 21228

University of Maryland–College Park
College Park, MD 20742

Washington College
Chestertown, MD 21620

Western Maryland College
2 College Hall
Westminster, MD 21157

MASSACHUSETTS

Amherst College
Amherst, MA 012167

Boston College
Lyons Hall, Room 106
Chestnut Hill, MA 02167

Boston Conservatory
8 The Fenway
Boston, MA 02215

Boston University
121 Bay State Road
Boston, MA 02215

Bradford College
320 South Main Street
Bradford, MA 01835

Brandeis University
415 South Street
Waltham, MA 02254

Bridgewater State College
Bridgewater, MA 02325

Clark University
950 Main Street
Worcester, MA 01610

College of the Holy Cross
College Street
Worcester, MA 01610

Curry College
1071 Blue Hill Avenue
Milton, MA 02186

Emerson College
100 Beacon Street
Boston, MA 02116

Hampshire College
Amherst, MA 01002

Massachusetts Institute of Technology
77 Massachusetts Avenue
Cambridge, MA 02139

Mount Holyoke College
College Street
Harriet Newhall Center
South Hadley, MA 01075

North Adams State College
Church Street
North Adams, MA 01247

Northeastern University
360 Huntington Avenue
Boston, MA 02115

Salem State College
352 Lafayette Street
Salem, MA 01970

Simon's Rock of Bard College
Great Barrington, MA 01230

Smith College
Northampton, MA 01063

Suffolk University
8 Ashburton Place
Beacon Hill
Boston, MA 02018

Tufts University
Medford, MA 02155

University of Massachusetts–Amherst
University Admissions Center
Amherst, MA 01003

University of Massachusetts–Boston
100 Morrissey Boulevard
Boston, MA 02125

Westfield State College
Western Avenue
Westfield, MA 01085

Williams College
PO Box 487
Williamstown, MA 01267

Worcester State College
486 Chandler Street
Worcester, MA 01602

MICHIGAN

Albion College
Albion, MI 49224

Alma College
Alma, MI 48801

Central Michigan University
100 Warriner Hall
Mount Pleasant, MI 48859

Eastern Michigan University
400 Pierce Hall
Ypsilanti, MI 48197

Grand Valley State University
1 Seidman House
Allendale, MI 49401

Hillsdale College
33 East College Street
Hillsdale, MI 49242

Hope College
Holland, MI 49423

Kalamazoo College
1200 Academy Street
Kalamazoo, MI 49007

Michigan State University
Administration Building
East Lansing, MI 48824

Northern Michigan University
Cohodas Administration Center
Marquette, MI 49855

Saginaw Valley State University
2250 Pierce Road
University Center, MI 48710

Siena Heights College
1247 East Siena Heights Drive
Adrian, MI 49221

University of Detroit
4001 West McNicholls Road
Detroit, MI 48221

University of Michigan–Ann Arbor
515 East Jefferson
Ann Arbor, MI 48109

University of Michigan–Flint
Flint, MI 48502

Wayne State University
Detroit, MI 48202

Western Michigan University
Administration Building
Kalamazoo, MI 49008

MINNESOTA

Augsburg College
2211 Riverside Avenue
Minneapolis, MN 55454

Bemidji State University
Bemidji, MN 56601

Bethel College
3900 Bethel Drive
St. Paul, MN 55112

Carlton College
Northfield, MN 55057

College of St. Benedict
37 South College Avenue
St. Joseph, MN 56374

College of St. Catherine
2004 Randolph Avenue
St. Paul, MN 55105

College of St. Thomas
2115 Summit Avenue
St. Paul, MN 55105

Concordia College
Moorhead, MN 56560

Condordia College
Hamline and Marshall Avenue
St. Paul, MN 55104

Gustavus Adolphus College
St. Peter, MN 56082

Hamline University
St. Paul, MN 55104

Macalester College
1600 Grand Avenue
St. Paul, MN 55105

Mankato State University
Box 55
Mankato, MN 56001

Moorhead State University
1104 Seventh Avenue South
Moorhead, MN 56560

North Central Bible College
910 Elliot Avenue South
Minneapolis, MN 55404

Pillsbury Baptist Bible College
315 South Grove
Owatonna, MN 55060

Southwest State University
Marshall, MN 56258

St. Cloud State University
Seventh Street and
   Fourth Avenue South
St. Cloud, MN 56303

St. John's University
Collegeville, MN 56321

St. Mary's College of Minnesota
700 Terrace Heights
Winona, MN 55987

St. Olaf College
Northfield, MN 55057

University of Minnesota–Duluth
184 Darland Administration Building
Duluth, MN 55812

University of Minnesota–Morris
Behmler Hall
Morris, MN 56267

University of Minnesota–Twin Cities
231 Pillsbury Drive SE
Minneapolis, MN 55455

Winona State University
Winona, MN 55987

MISSISSIPPI

Blue Mountain College
Blue Mountain, MS 38610

Jackson State University
1325 J. R. Lynch Street
Jackson, MS 39217

Millsaps College
1701 North State Street
Jackson, MS 39210

Mississippi College
PO Box 4203
Clinton, MS 39058

Mississippi University for Women
Columbus, MS 39701

University of Mississippi
Lyceum Building
University, MS 38677

University of Southern Mississippi
Box 5011–Southern Station
Hattiesburg, MS 39401

William Carey College
Tuscan Avenue
Hattiesburg, MS 39401

MISSOURI

Avila College
11901 Wornall Road
Kansas City, MO 64145

Central Methodist College
411 Central Methodist Square
Fayette, MO 65248

Central Missouri State University
Warrensburg, MO 64093

College of the Ozarks
Point Lookout, MO 65726

Culver-Stockton College
Canton, MO 63435

Drury College
900 North Benton Avenue
Springfield, MO 65802

Evangel College
1111 North Glenstone
Springfield, MO 65802

Fontbonne College
6800 Wydown Boulevard
St. Louis, MO 63105

Lindenwood College
St. Charles, MO 63301

Missouri Southern State College
Newman and Duquesne Roads
Joplin, MO 64801

Missouri Valley College
500 East College
Marshall, MO 65340

Northeast Missouri State University
McClain Hall
Kirksville, MO 63501

Northwest Missouri State University
Maryville, MO 64468

Rockhurst College
1100 Rockhurst Road
Kansas City, MO 64110

Southwest Baptist University
1601 South Springfield Avenue
Bolivar, MO 65613

Southwest Missouri State University
901 South National
Springfield, MO 65804

Stephens College
Columbia, MO 65215

St. Louis University
221 North Grand Boulevard
St. Louis, MO 63103

University of Missouri–Columbia
130 Jesse Hall
Columbia, MO 65211

University of Missouri–Kansas City
5100 Rockhill Road
Kansas City, MO 64110

Washington University
Campus Box 1089
St. Louis, MO 63130

Webster University
470 East Lockwood
St. Louis, MO 63119

Westminster College
501 Westminster Avenue
Fulton, MO 65251

MONTANA

Carroll College
1601 North Benton Avenue
Helena, MT 59625

Montana State University–Billings
1500 North 30th Street
Billings, MT 59717

Montana State University–Bozeman
Montana Hall
Bozeman, MT 59717

Northern Montana College
Havre, MT 59501

Rocky Mountain College
1511 Poly Drive
Billings, MT 59102

University of Montana
Lodge 101
Missoula, MT 59812

NEBRASKA

Chadron State College
10th and Main Streets
Chadron, NE 69337

Concordia College
800 North Columbia Avenue
Seward, NE 68434

Creighton University
California at 24th Street
Omaha, NE 68178

Doane College
Crete, NE 68333

Hastings College
Seventh and Turner Avenues
Hastings, NE 68901

Midland Lutheran College
720 East Ninth Street
Fremont, NE 68025

Nebraska Wesleyan University
5000 St. Paul Avenue
Lincoln, NE 68504

Peru State College
Peru, NE 68421

University of Nebraska at Kearney
905 West 25th Street
Kearney, NE 68849

University of Nebraska–Lincoln
14th and R Streets
Lincoln, NE 68588

University of Nebraska–Omaha
60th and Dodge Streets
Omaha, NE 68182

Wayne State College
1111 Main Street
Wayne, NE 68787

NEVADA

University of Nevada–Las Vegas
4505 Maryland Parkway
Las Vegas, NV 89154

University of Nevada–Reno
Reno, NV 89557

NEW HAMPSHIRE

Dartmouth College
Hanover, NH 03755

Franklin Pierce College
Rindge, NH 03461

Keene State College
Main Street
Keene, NH 03431

New England College
Henniker, NH 03242

Plymouth State College
Plymouth, NH 03264

University of New Hampshire
Garrison Avenue
Grant House
Durham, NH 03824

NEW JERSEY

**Drew University–College of
    Liberal Arts**
Madison, NJ 07940

Fairleigh Dickinson University
1000 River Road
Teaneck, NJ 07666

Jersey City State College
2039 Kennedy Boulevard
Jersey City, NJ 07305

Kean College of New Jersey
1000 Morris Avenue
Union, NJ 07083

Montclair State College
Valley Road and Normal Avenue
Upper Montclair, NJ 07043

Princeton University
PO Box 430
Princeton, NJ 08544

Ramapo College of New Jersey
505 Ramapo Valley Road
Mahwah, NJ 07430

**The Richard Stockton College of
    New Jersey**
Pomona, NJ 08240

Rider College
2083 Lawrenceville Road
Lawrenceville, NJ 08648

Rowan College of New Jersey
201 Mullica Hill Road
Glassboro, NJ 08028

**Rutgers, The State University of
    New Jersey**
Camden College of Arts and Sciences
406 Penn Street
Camden, NJ 08102

**Rutgers, The State University of
    New Jersey**
Douglass College
PO Box 2101
New Brunswick, NJ 08903

**Rutgers, The State University of
    New Jersey**
Livingston College
PO Box 2101
New Brunswick, NJ 08903

**Rutgers, The State University of
    New Jersey**
Mason Gross School of the Arts
PO Box 2101
New Brunswick, NJ 08903

**Rutgers, The State University of
    New Jersey**
Newark College of Arts and Sciences
249 University Avenue
Newark, NJ 07102

**Rutgers, The State University of
    New Jersey**
Rutgers College
PO Box 2101
New Brunswick, NJ 08903

**Rutgers, The State University of
    New Jersey**
University College–Camden
406 Penn Street
Camden, NJ 08102

**Rutgers, The State University of
    New Jersey**
University College–New Brunswick
14 College Avenue
New Brunswick, NJ 08903

Thomas A. Edison State College
101 West State Street
Trenton, NJ 08625

William Paterson College
300 Pompton Road
Wayne, NJ 07470

NEW MEXICO

College of Santa Fe
St. Michael's Drive
Santa Fe, NM 87501

Eastern New Mexico University
Highway 70
Portales, NM 88130

New Mexico Highlands University
National Avenue
PO Box 13
Las Vegas, NM 87701

New Mexico State University
Box 30001–Department 3A
Las Cruces, NM 88003

University of New Mexico
Albuquerque, NM 87131

NEW YORK

Adelphi University
South Avenue
Garden City, NY 11530

Alfred University
PO Box 765
Alfred, NY 14802

Bard College
Annandale-On-Hudson, NY 12504

Barnard College
Columbia University
3009 Broadway
New York, NY 10027

CUNY–Brooklyn College
Bedford Avenue and Avenue H
Brooklyn, NY 11210

CUNY–City College
Convent Avenue at 138th Street
New York, NY 10031

CUNY–College of Staten Island
715 Ocean Terrace
Staten Island, NY 10301

CUNY–Hunter College
695 Park Avenue
New York, NY 10021

CUNY–Lehman College
Bedford Park Boulevard West
Bronx, NY 10468

CUNY–Queens College
65-30 Kissena Boulevard
Flushing, NY 11367

Colgate University
Hamilton, NY 13346

**Columbia University–
    Columbia College**
212 Hamilton Hall
New York, NY 10027

Cornell University
410 Thurston Avenue
Ithaca, NY 14853

Dowling College
Idle Hour Boulevard
Oakdale, NY 11769

Elmira College
Park Place
Elmira, NY 14901

Hamilton College
198 College Hill Road
Clinton, NY 13323

Hartwick College
Bresee Hall
Oneonta, NY 13820

Hobart and William Smith Colleges
Geneva, NY 14456

Hofstra University
Hempstead, NY 11550

Iona College
715 North Avenue
New Rochelle, NY 10801

Ithaca College
Ithaca, NY 14850

Julliard School
60 Lincoln Center Plaza
New York, NY 10023

**Long Island University–
    C. W. Post Campus**
Northern Boulevard
College Hall
Greenvale, NY 11548

Marymount College
Tarrytown, NY 10591

Marymount Manhattan College
221 East 71st Street
New York, NY 10021

Mount Saint Mary College
330 Powell Avenue
Newburgh, NY 12550

Nazareth College of Rochester
4245 East Avenue
Rochester, NY 14610

New School for Social Research
Eugene Lang College
65 West 11th Street
New York, NY 10011

New York University
22 Washington Square North
New York, NY 10011

Niagara University
Niagara University, NY 14109

Pace University
Pace Plaza
New York, NY 10038

Pace University–Pleasantville–Briarcliff
Bedford Road
Pleasantville, NY 10570

Purchase College, State University of New York
735 Anderson Hill Road
Purchase, NY 10577

Sarah Lawrence College
1 Meadway
Bronxville, NY 10708

Skidmore College
Saratoga Springs, NY 12866

St. Lawrence University
Canton, NY 13617

SUNY–Albany
1400 Washington Avenue
Albany, NY 12222

SUNY–Binghamton
Vestal Parkway East
Binghamton, NY 13901

SUNY–Buffalo
3435 Main Street
Buffalo, NY 14214

SUNY–College at Brockport
Kenyon Street
Brockport, NY 14420

SUNY–College at Buffalo
1300 Elmwood Avenue
Buffalo, NY 14222

SUNY–College at Cortland
Box 2000
Graham Avenue
Cortland, NY 13045

SUNY–College at Fredonia
Fredonia, NY 14063

SUNY–College at Geneseo
Erwin Hall
Geneseo, NY 14454

SUNY–College at New Paltz
New Paltz, NY 12561

SUNY–College at Old Westbury
PO Box 307
Old Westbury, NY 11568

SUNY–College at Oneonta
Oneonta, NY 13820

SUNY–College at Oswego
Oswego, NY 13126

SUNY–College at Plattsburgh
Plattsburgh, NY 12901

SUNY–College at Potsdam
Pierrepont Avenue
Potsdam, NY 13676

SUNY–Stony Brook
Stony Brook, NY 11794

Syracuse University
201 Tolley Administration Building
Syracuse, NY 13244

Vassar College
Raymond Avenue
Poughkeepsie, NY 12601

Wagner College
631 Howard Avenue
Staten Island, NY 10301

Wells College
Main Street
Aurora, NY 13026

NORTH CAROLINA

Appalachian State University
Boone, NC 28608

Campbell University
PO Box 546
Buies Creek, NC 27506

Catawba College
2300 West Innes Street
Salisbury, NC 28144

Davidson College
Davidson, NC 28036

Duke University
2138 Campus Drive
Durham, NC 27706

East Carolina University
Greenville, NC 27834

Elizabeth City State University
Parkview Drive
Elizabeth City, NC 27909

Elon College
Elon College, NC 27244

Fayetteville State University
Murchison Road
Fayetteville, NC 28301

Greensboro College
815 West Market Street
Greensboro, NC 27401

Guildford College
5800 West Friendly Avenue
Greensboro, NC 27410

High Point College
University Station–Montlieu Avenue
High Point, NC 27262

Lenoir-Rhyne College
Box 7227
Hickory, NC 28603

Mars Hill College
124 Cascade Street
Mars Hill, NC 28754

Meredith College
3800 Hillsborough Street
Raleigh, NC 27607

Methodist College
5400 Ramsey Street
Fayetteville, NC 28311

North Carolina Agricultural and Technical State University
1601 East Market Street
Greensboro, NC 27411

North Carolina Central University
PO Box 19717
1902 Fayetteville Street
Durham, NC 27797

North Carolina School of the Arts
PO Box 12189
200 Waughtown Street
Winston-Salem, NC 27127

North Carolina Wesleyan College
College Station
Rocky Mount, NC 27801

Pembroke State University
Pembroke, NC 28372

Pfeiffer College
Misenheimer, NC 28109

Queens College
1900 Selwyn Avenue
Charlotte, NC 28274

Shaw University
118 East South Street
Raleigh, NC 27611

St. Andrew's Presbyterian College
Laurinburg, NC 28352

University of North Carolina–Asheville
1 University Heights
Asheville, NC 28804

University of North Carolina–Chapel Hill
Campus Box 2200
Chapel Hill, NC 27514

University of North Carolina–Charlotte
University City Boulevard
Charlotte, NC 28223

University of North Carolina–Greensboro
1000 Spring Garden Street
Greensboro, NC 27412

University of North Carolina–Wilmington
601 South College Road
Wilmington, NC 28403

Western Carolina University
520 H. F. Robinson Administration
  Building
Cullowhee, NC 28723

NORTH DAKOTA

Dickinson State University
Dickinson, ND 58601

North Dakota State University
124 Ceres Hall
Fargo, ND 58105

University of North Dakota
Grand Forks, ND 58202

OHIO

Antioch College
Yellow Springs, OH 45387

Ashland College
College Avenue
Ashland, OH 44805

Baldwin-Wallace College
275 Eastland Road
Berea, OH 44017

Bowling Green State University
110 McFall Center
Bowling Green, OH 43403

Case Western Reserve University
Tomlinson Hall
Cleveland, OH 44106

Central State University
Bush Row Road
Wilberforce, OH 45384

Cleveland State University
East 24th and Euclid Avenue
Cleveland, OH 44115

College of Wooster
Wooster, OH 44691

Denison University
PO Box H
Granville, OH 43023

Heidelberg College
310 East Market Street
Tiffin, OH 44883

Hiram College
PO Box 96
Hiram, OH 44234

Kent State University
PO Box 5190
Kent, OH 44242

Kenyon College
Gambier, OH 43022

Marietta College
Fifth Street
Marietta, OH 45750

Miami University
Oxford, OH 45056

Mount Union College
1972 Clark Street
Alliance, OH 44601

Muskingum College
New Concord, OH 43762

Oberlin College
Carnegie Building
Oberlin, OH 44074

Ohio Northern University
525 South Main Street
Ada, OH 45810

Ohio State University–Columbia
1800 Cannon Drive–Lincoln Tower
Columbus, OH 43210

Ohio University
120 Chubb Hall
Athens, OH 45701

Ohio Wesleyan University
Delaware, OH 43015

Otterbein College
Waterville, OH 43081

University of Akron
381 East Buchtel Commons
Akron, OH 44325

University of Cincinnati
100 Edwards Center
PO Box 210091
Cincinnati, OH 45221

University of Dayton
300 College Park Avenue
Dayton, OH 45469

University of Findlay
1000 North Main Street
Findlay, OH 45840

University of Toledo
2801 West Bancroft Street
Toledo, OH 43606

Wilmington College of Ohio
Box 1325–Pyle Center
Wilmington, OH 45177

Wittenberg University
PO Box 720
Springfield, OH 45501

Wright State University
Colonel Glenn Highway
Dayton, OH 45435

Youngstown State University
Youngstown, OH 44555

OKLAHOMA

Cameron University
2800 Gore Boulevard
Lawton, OK 73505

Langston University
PO Box 728
Langston, OK 73050

Northwestern Oklahoma State University
709 Oklahoma Boulevard
Alva, OK 73717

Oklahoma Baptist University
500 West University
Shawnee, OK 74801

Oklahoma City University
2501 North Blackwelder
Oklahoma City, OK 73106

Oklahoma State University
103 Whitehurst Hall
Stillwater, OK 74078

Oral Roberts University
7777 South Lewis
Tulsa, OK 74171

Phillips University
100 South University
Enid, OK 73701

Southeastern Oklahoma State University
Box 4118–Station A
Durant, OK 74701

Southwestern Oklahoma State University
Weatherford, OK 73096

University of Central Oklahoma
Edmond, OK 73034

University of Oklahoma–Norman
1000 Asp Avenue
Norman, OK 73019

University of Science and Arts of Oklahoma
17th Street and Grand Avenue
Chickasha, OK 73018

University of Tulsa
600 South College Avenue
Tulsa, OK 74104

OREGON

Condordia College
2811 Northeast Holman
Portland, OR 97211

Eastern Oregon State College
1410 L Avenue
La Grande, OR 97850

Lewis and Clark College
Portland, OR 97219

Linfield College
McMinnville, OR 97128

Pacific University
2043 College Way
Forest Grove, OR 97116

Portland State University
PO Box 751
Portland, OR 97207

Reed College
3203 Southeast Woodstock Boulevard
Portland, OR 97202

Southern Oregon State College
1250 Siskiyou Boulevard
Ashland, OR 97520

University of Oregon
240 Oregon Hall
Eugene, OR 97403

University of Portland
5000 North Willamette Boulevard
Portland, OR 97203

Western Oregon State College
345 Monmouth Avenue
Monmouth, OR 97361

Willamette University
900 State Street
Salem, OR 97301

PENNSYLVANIA

Allegheny College
Meadville, PA 16335

**Allentown College of St. Francis
De Sales**
2755 Station Avenue
Canter Valley, PA 18034

Beaver College
Church and Easton Roads
Glenside, PA 19038

**Bloomsburg University of
Pennsylvania**
Ben Franklin Building
Bloomsburg, PA 17815

Bucknell University
Lewisburg, PA 17837

Cabrini College
King of Prussia Road
Radnor, PA 19087

California University of Pennsylvania
250 Third Street
California, PA 15419

Carnegie Mellon University
5000 Forbes Avenue
Pittsburgh, PA 15213

Cedar Crest College
100 College Drive
Allentown, PA 18104

Chatham College
Woodland Road
Pittsburgh, PA 15232

Cheyney University of Pennsylvania
Cheyney, PA 19319

Clarion University of Pennsylvania
Clarion, PA 16214

Dickinson College
Carlisle, PA 17013

Duquesne University
600 Forbes Avenue
Pittsburgh, PA 15282

**East Stroudsburg University of
Pennsylvania**
East Stroudsburg, PA 18301

Edinboro University of Pennsylvania
Edinboro, PA 16444

Elizabethtown College
One Alpha Drive
Elizabethtown, PA 17604

Franklin and Marshall College
PO Box 3003
Lancaster, PA 17604

Gannon University
University Square
Erie, PA 16541

Gettysburg College
Eisenhower House
Gettysburg, PA 17325

Indiana University of Pennsylvania
Indiana, PA 15705

Juniata College
1700 Moore Street
Huntingdon, PA 16652

King's College
133 North River Street
Wilkes-Barre, PA 18711

Kutztown University
College Hill
Kutztown, PA 19530

Lehigh University
27 Memorial Drive West
Bethlehem, PA 18015

**Lock Haven University of
Pennsylvania**
Lock Haven, PA 17745

Lycoming College
Williamsport, PA 17701

Mansfield University of Pennsylvania
Alumni Hall
Mansfield, PA 16933

Marywood College
2300 Adams Avenue
Scranton, PA 18509

Mercyhurst College
Glenwood Hills
Erie, PA 16546

Messiah College
College Avenue
Grantham, PA 17027

Millersville University of Pennsylvania
PO Box 1002
Millersville, PA 17551

Muhlenberg College
2400 Chew Street
Allentown, PA 18104

Penn State University Park
201 Shields Building
University Park, PA 16802

Point Park College
201 Wood Street
Pittsburgh, PA 15222

Saint Vincent College
Latrobe, PA 15650

Seton Hill College
Greensburg, PA 15601

**Shippensburg University of
Pennsylvania**
Shippensburg, PA 17257

Susquehanna University
514 University Avenue
Selinsgrove, PA 17870

Swarthmore College
500 College Avenue
Swarthmore, PA 19081

Temple University
Philadelphia, PA 19122

University of the Arts
Broad and Pine Streets
Philadelphia, PA 19102

University of Pennsylvania
1 College Hall
Philadelphia, PA 19104

University of Pittsburgh
4200 Fifth Avenue
Pittsburgh, PA 15260

University of Pittsburgh–Johnstown
Johnstown, PA 15904

**West Chester University of
Pennsylvania**
West Chester, PA 19383

Westminister College
New Wilmington, PA 16142

Wilkes University
South River Street–Chase Hall
Wilkes-Barre, PA 18766

RHODE ISLAND

Brown University
45 Prospect Street
Providence, RI 02912

Providence College
River Avenue
Providence, RI 02918

Rhode Island College
Providence, RI 02809

Roger Williams College
Bristol, RI 02809

Salve Regina College
Ochre Point Avenue
Newport, RI 02840

University of Rhode Island
Kingston, RI 02881

SOUTH CAROLINA

Charleston Southern University
PO Box 10087
Charleston, SC 29411

Coastal Carolina University
PO Box 1954
Myrtle Beach, SC 29578

Coker College
College Avenue
Hartsville, SC 29550

College of Charleston
66 George Street
Charleston, SC 29424

Converse College
580 East Main Street
Spartanburg, SC 29301

Francis Marion University
PO Box 100547
Florence, SC 29501

Furman University
3300 Poinsett Highway
Greenville, SC 29613

Lander University
Stanley Avenue
Greenwood, SC 29646

Newberry College
Newberry, SC 29108

Presbyterian College
Broad Street
Clinton, SC 29325

South Carolina State University
Orangeburg, SC 29117

University of South Carolina
Columbia, SC 29208

Winthrop University
Oakland Avenue
Rock Hill, SC 29733

SOUTH DAKOTA

Augustana College
29th and Summit Avenue
Sioux Falls, SD 59197

Black Hills State College
1200 University Street
Spearfish, SD 57783

Dakota Wesleyan University
1200 West University Avenue
Mitchell, SD 57301

Northern State College
Aberdeen, SD 57401

Sioux Falls College
1501 South Prairie Street
Sioux Falls, SD 57105

South Dakota State University
Box 2201–Administration Building
Brookings, SD 57007

University of South Dakota
414 East Clark
Vermillion, SD 57069

TENNESSEE

Austin Peay State University
601 College Street
Clarksville, TN 37040

Belmont College
1900 Belmont Boulevard
Nashville, TN 37203

Bryan College
Box 7000
Dayton, TN 37321

Christian Brothers College
650 East Parkway South
Memphis, TN 38104

East Tennessee State University
Campus Box 24430-A
Johnson City, TN 37614

Fisk University
17th Avenue North
Nashville, TN 37203

Freed-Hardman University
158 East Main Street
Henderson, TN 38340

Lambuth College
Lambuth Boulevard
Jackson, TN 38301

Maryville College
502 East Lamar Alexander Parkway
Maryville, TN 37804

Memphis State University
Memphis, TN 38152

Middle Tennessee State University
Murfreesboro, TN 37132

Rhodes College–Memphis
200 North Parkway
Memphis, TN 38112

Tennessee State University
3500 John Merritt Boulevard
Nashville, TN 37203

Trevecca Nazarene College
333 Murfreesboro Road
Nashville, TN 37210

Tusculum College
Greeneville, TN 37743

Union University
2447 Highway 45 By-Pass
Jackson, TN 38305

University of Tennessee–Chattanooga
McCallie Avenue
129 Hooper Hall
Chattanooga, TN 37402

University of Tennessee–Knoxville
320 Student Services Building
Knoxville, TN 37996

University of Tennessee–Martin
Martin, TN 38238

University of the South
735 University Avenue
Sewanee, TN 37375

Vanderbilt University
2305 West End Avenue
Nashville, TN 37213

TEXAS

Abilene Christian University
Box 6000–ACU Station
Abilene, TX 79699

Angelo State University
PO Box 11009–ASU Station
San Angelo, TX 76909

Baylor University
PO Box 97008
Waco, TX 76798

East Texas Baptist University
1209 North Grove
Marshall, TX 75670

**East Texas State University East
    Texas Station**
Commerce, TX 75428

Hardin-Simmons University
Abilene, TX 79698

Howard Payne University
Howard Payne Station Box 174
Brownwood, TX 76801

Incarnate Word College
4301 Broadway
Austin, TX 78209

Lamar University
PO Box 10009
Beaumont, TX 77710

McMurry College
Box 85–McMurry Station
Abilene, TX 79697

Midwestern State University
3400 Taft Boulevard
Wichita Falls, TX 76308

University of North Texas
Box 13797
Denton, TX 76203

Our Lady of the Lake University of San Antonio
411 Southwest 24th Street
San Antonio, TX 78285

Prairie View A & M University
PO Box 2610
Prairie View, TX 77446

Sam Houston State University
Huntsville, TX 77341

Southern Methodist University
PO Box 296
Dallas, TX 75275

Southwestern University
Georgetown, TX 78626

Southwest Texas State University
429 North Guadalupe
San Marcos, TX 78666

St. Edward's University
3001 South Congress
Austin, TX 78704

Stephen F. Austin State University
1936 North Street
Box 13051–SFA Station
Nacogdoches, TX 75962

Sul Ross State University
PO Box C-1
Alpine, TX 79832

Tarleton State University
Stephenville, TX 76402

Texas A & M University
217 John J. Koldus Building
College Station, TX 77843

Texas A & M University–Kingsville
Campus Box 116
Kingsville, TX 78363

Texas Christian University
2800 South University Drive
Forth Worth, TX 76129

Texas Southern University
3100 Cleburne
Houston, TX 77004

Texas Tech University
PO Box 45005
Lubbock, TX 79409

Texas Wesleyan College
PO Box 50010
3101 East Rosedale
Fort Worth, TX 76105

Texas Woman's University
PO Box 22909–TWU Station
Denton, TX 76204

Trinity University
715 Stadium Drive
San Antonio, TX 78284

University of Dallas
1845 East Northgate Drive
Irving, TX 75062

University of Houston
4800 Calhoun
Houston, TX 77004

University of St. Thomas
3800 Montrose Boulevard
Houston, TX 77006

University of Texas–Arlington
Box 19088–UTA Station
Arlington, TX 76019

University of Texas–Austin
Austin, TX 78712

University of Texas–Dallas
PO Box 830688
Richardson, TX 75083

University of Texas–El Paso
El Paso, TX 79968

University of Texas–Pan American
1201 West University Drive
Edinburg, TX 78539

University of Texas–Tyler
3900 University Boulevard
Tyler, TX 75701

Wayland Baptist University
1900 West Seventh Street
Plainview, TX 79072

West Texas State University
Canyon, TX 79016

UTAH

Brigham Young University
A-153 ASB
Provo, UT 84602

Southern Utah State College
351 West Center
Cedar City, UT 84720

University of Utah
250 Student Services Building
Salt Lake City, UT 84112

Utah State University
Logan, UT 84322

Weber State College
3750 Harrison Boulevard
Ogden, UT 84408

VERMONT

Bennington College
Bennington, VT 05201

Castleton State College
Castleton, VT 05735

Goddard College
Plainfield, VT 05667

Johnson State College
Stowe Road
Johnson, VT 05656

Marlboro College
Marlboro, VT 05344

Middlebury College
The Emma Willard House
Middlebury, VT 05753

University of Vermont
194 South Prospect Street
Burlington, VT 05401

VIRGINIA

Averett College
West Main Street
Danville, VA 24541

Bluefield College
Bluefield, VA 24605

Christopher Newport University
Newport News, VA 23606

College of William and Mary
Williamsburg, VA 23185

Emory and Henry College
Emory, VA 24227

Ferrum College
Ferrum, VA 24088

George Mason University
4400 University Drive
Fairfax, VA 22030

Hampton University
Hampton, VA 23688

Hollins College
PO Box 9657
Roanoke, VA 24020

James Madison University
Harrisonburg, VA 22807

Liberty University
3765 Candlers Mountain Road
Lynchburg, VA 24506

Longwood College
Farmville, VA 23901

Lynchburg College
1501 Lakeside Drive
Lynchburg, VA 24501

Mary Baldwin College
Staunton, VA 24401

Mary Washington College
Fredericksburg, VA 22401

Old Dominion University
Hampton Boulevard
Norfolk, VA 23508

Radford University
Radford, VA 24142

Randolph-Macon College
Ashland, VA 23005

Randolph-Macon Woman's College
Lynchburg, VA 24503

Roanoke College
226 High Street
Salem, VA 24153

Shenandoah College and Conservatory
1460 College Drive
Winchester, VA 22601

Sweet Briar College
Sweet Briar, VA 24595

University of Richmond
Sarah Brunet Hall
Richmond, VA 23173

University of Virginia
Box 9017–University Station
Charlottesville, VA 22906

Virginia Commonwealth University
PO Box 2526-821
West Franklin Street
Richmond, VA 23284

**Virginia Polytechnic Institute and
    State University**
104 Burruss Hall
Blacksburg, VA 24061

Virginia Wesleyan College
Wesleyan Drive
Norfolk-Virginia Beach, VA 23502

Washington and Lee University
Lexington, VA 24450

WASHINGTON

Central Washington University
Mitchell Hall
Ellensburg, WA 98926

Cornish College of the Arts
710 East Roy Street
Seattle, WA 98102

Eastern Washington University
Showalter Hall
Cheney, WA 99004

Evergeen State College
Olympia, WA 98505

Gonzaga University
Spokane, WA 99258

Pacific Lutheran University
Tacoma, WA 98447

Seattle Pacific University
Third Avenue West at West Bertona
Seattle, WA 98119

Seattle University
12th and East Columbia
Seattle, WA 98122

University of Puget Sound
1500 North Warner
Tacoma, WA 98416

University of Washington
Seattle, WA 98195

Western Washington University
Old Main–Room 200
Bellingham, WA 98225

Whitman College
345 Boyer Street
Walla Walla, WA 99362

Whitworth College
Spokane, WA 99251

WEST VIRGINIA

Alderson-Broaddus College
Philippi, WV 26416

Bethany College
Bethany, WV 26032

Concord College
Athens, WV 24712

David and Elkins College
Elkins, WV 26241

Fairmont State College
Locust Avenue Extension
Fairmont, WV 26554

Marshall University
400 Hal Greer Boulevard
Huntington, WV 25705

West Virginia University
PO Box 6009
Morgantown, WV 26506

West Virginia Wesleyan College
59 College Avenue
Buckhannon, WV 26201

WISCONSIN

Beloit College
Beloit, WI 53511

Cardinal Stritch College
6801 North Yates Road
Milwaukee, WI 53217

Carroll College
100 North East Avenue
Waukesha, WI 53186

Edgewood College
855 Woodrow Street
Madison, WI 53711

Lakeland College
PO Box 359
Sheboygan, WI 53082

Lawrence University
Appleton, WI 54912

Marquette University
1217 West Wisconsin Avenue
Milwaukee, WI 53233

Ripon College
PO Box 248
300 Seward Street
Ripon, WI 54971

St. Norbert College
100 Grant Street
De Pere, WI 54115

University of Wisconsin–Eau Claire
Box 4004
Eau Claire, WI 54701

University of Wisconsin–Green Bay
2420 Nicolet Drive
Green Bay, WI 54302

University of Wisconsin–La Crosse
1725 State Street
La Crosse, WI 54601

University of Wisconsin–Madison
750 University Avenue
Madison, WI 53706

University of Wisconsin–Milwaukee
PO Box 749
Milwaukee, WI 53201

University of Wisconsin–Parkside
900 Wood Road
Kenosha, WI 53141

University of Wisconsin–Platteville
1 University Plaza
Platteville, WI 53818

University of Wisconsin–Stevens Point
Stevens Point, WI 54481

University of Wisconsin–Superior
1800 Grand Avenue
Superior, WI 54880

University of Wisconsin–Whitewater
800 West Main Street
Whitewater, WI 53190

Viterbo College
815 South 9th Street
La Crosse, WI 54601

WYOMING

University of Wyoming
Box 3435–University Station
Laramie, WY 82071

B. COLLEGES AND UNIVERSITIES THAT OFFER DEGREES IN ARTS MANAGEMENT AND ADMINISTRATION

The following is a list of four-year schools granting degrees in arts management and administration in the visual and performing arts fields. They are grouped by state.

While possession of a college degree does not guarantee a job, many feel that it is in their best interest to continue their education after high school to gain knowledge and new skills and to make important contacts. A higher education may also provide a competitive edge.

More colleges are beginning to grant degrees in arts management and administration every year. Check the newest copy of *Lovejoy's College Guide* (found in the reference section of libraries or in guidance or counseling centers) for additional schools offering degrees in this field.

ALABAMA

Spring Hill College
4000 Dauphin Street
Mobile, AL 36608

ARIZONA

Northern Arizona University
Box 4084
Flagstaff, AZ 86011

ARKANSAS

University of the Ozarks
415 College Avenue
Clarksville, AR 72830

CALIFORNIA

Point Loma Nazarene College
3900 Lomaland Drive
San Diego, CA 92106

University of the Pacific
3601 Pacific Avenue
Stockton, CA 95211

CONNECTICUT

University of Hartford
200 Bloomfield Avenue
West Hartford, CT 06117

DELAWARE

Delaware State University
1200 North DuPont Highway
Dover, DE 19901

FLORIDA

Barry University
11300 Northeast Second Avenue
Miami Shores, FL 33161

Florida Southern College
111 Lake Hollingsworth Drive
Lakeland, FL 33801

Jacksonville University
2800 University Boulevard
Jacksonville, FL 32211

GEORGIA

Georgia College
Campus Box 499
Milledgeville, GA 31061

Shorter College
315 Shorter Avenue
Rome, GA 30165

Women's College of Brenau University
1 Centennial Circle
Gainesville, GA 30501

IDAHO

Boise State University
1910 University Drive
Boise, ID 83725

ILLINOIS

Columbia College
600 South Michigan
Chicago, IL 60605

DePaul University
25 East Jackson Boulevard
Chicago, IL 60604

Elmhurst College
190 Prospect Avenue
Elmhurst, IL 60216

Lewis University
Route 53
Romeoville, IL 60441

North Park College
3225 West Forester Avenue
Chicago, IL 60625

Roosevelt University
430 South Michigan Avenue
Chicago, IL 60605

Southern Illinois University–Edwardsville
Box 1047
Edwardsville, IL 62026

St. Xavier University
3700 West 103rd Street
Chicago, IL 60655

Trinity Christian College
6601 West College Drive
Palos Heights, IL 60463

INDIANA

Anderson University
Anderson, IN 46012

Butler University
46th and Sunset Avenue
Indianapolis, IN 46208

DePauw University
313 South Locust Street
Greencastle, IN 46135

University of Evansville
1800 Lincoln Avenue
Evansville, IN 47722

Valparaiso University
Valparaiso, IN 46383

IOWA

Drake University
25th and University Streets
Des Moines, IA 50311

KANSAS

Friends University
2100 University Avenue
Wichita, KS 67213

Sterling College
North Broadway
Sterling, KS 67579

KENTUCKY

Eastern Kentucky University
Lancaster Avenue
Richmond, KY 40475

Union College
College Street
Barbourville, KY 40906

University of Kentucky
100 Funkhouser Building
Lexington, KY 40506

LOUISIANA

Southeastern Louisiana University
Box 752–University Station
Hammond, LA 70402

MARYLAND

Goucher College
Dulaney Valley Road
Baltimore, MD 21204

MASSACHUSETTS

Anna Maria College for Men and Women
Sunset Lane
Paxton, MA 01612

Berkline College of Music
1140 Bolyston Street
Boston, MA 02215

Simmons College
300 The Fenway
Boston, MA 02115

University of Massachusetts–Lowell
1 University Avenue
Lowell, MA 01854

Westfield State College
Western Avenue
Westfield, MA 01085

MICHIGAN

Adrian College
110 South Madison Street
Adrian, MI 49221

Madonna College
36600 Schoolcraft Road
Livonia, MI 48150

Wayne State University
Detroit, MI 48202

MISSISSIPPI

William Carey College
Tuscan Avenue
Hattiesburg, MS 39401

MISSOURI

Culver-Stockton College
Canton, MO 63435

Fontbonne College
6800 Wydown Boulevard
St. Louis, MO 63105

NEBRASKA

Bellevue University
1000 Galvin Road South
Bellevue, NE 68005

NEW MEXICO

Eastern New Mexico University
Station 7
Portales, NM 88130

NEW YORK

CUNY–Baruch College
17 Lexington Avenue
New York, NY 10010

CUNY–Brooklyn College
Bedford Avenue and Avenue H
Brooklyn, NY 11210

Ithaca College
Ithaca, NY 14850

Manhattanville College
125 Purchase Street
Purchase, NY 10577

Marymount Manhattan College
221 East 71st Street
New York, NY 10021

Russell Sage College
51 First Street
Troy, NY 12180

SUNY–College at Freedonia
Freedonia, NY 14063

SUNY–College at Oneonta
Oneonta, NY 13820

Wagner College
631 Howard Avenue
Staten Island, NY 10301

NORTH CAROLINA

Bennett College
900 East Washington Street
Greensboro, NC 27401

Catawba College
2100 West Innes Street
Salisbury, NC 28144

Elizabeth City State University
Parkview Drive
Elizabeth City, NC 27909

Methodist College
5400 Ramsey Street
Fayetteville, NC 28311

Pfeiffer College
Misenheimer, NC 28109

Salem College
PO Box 10548
Winston-Salem, NC 27108

Wingate College
Wingate, NC 28174

NORTH DAKOTA

Jamestown College
Jamestown, ND 58401

OHIO

Baldwin-Wallace College
275 Eastland Road
Berea, OH 44017

Capital University
2199 East Main Street
Columbus, OH 43209

Heidelberg College
310 East Market Street
Tiffin, OH 44883

Marietta College
Fifth Street
Marietta, OH 45750

Ursuline College
2550 Lander Road
Pepper Pike, OH 44124

OKLAHOMA

Phillips University
100 South University
Enid, OK 73701

OREGON

Southern Oregon State College
1250 Siskiyou Boulevard
Ashland, OR 97520

PENNSYLVANIA

Cabrini College
King of Prussia Road
Radnor, PA 19087

Geneva College
Beaver Falls, PA 15010

Mansfield University of Pennsylvania
Alumni Hall
Mansfield, PA 16933

Marywood College
2300 Adams Avenue
Scranton, PA 18509

Mercyhurst College
Glenwood Hills
Erie, PA 16546

Saint Vincent College
Latrobe, PA 15650

Seton Hill College
Greensburg, PA 15650

Wilkes College
South River Street–Chase Hall
Wilkes-Barre, PA 18766

SOUTH CAROLINA

Newberry College
Newberry, SC 29108

TENNESSEE

Middle Tennessee State University
Murfreesboro, TN 37132

TEXAS

Abilene Christian University
Box 6000–ACU Station
Abilene, TX 79699

Incarnate Word College
4301 Broadway
San Antonio, TX 78209

West Texas State University
Canyon, TX 79016

VIRGINIA

Radford University
Radford, VA 24142

Randolph-Macon College
Ashland, VA 23005

WASHINGTON

Eastern Washington University
Showalter Hall, Room 117
Cheney, WA 99004

University of Puget Sound
1500 North Warner
Tacoma, WA 98416

Whitworth College
Spokane, WA 99251

WISCONSIN

Viterbo College
815 South Ninth Street
La Crosse, WI 54601

C. COLLEGES, UNIVERSITIES AND SCHOOLS THAT OFFER PROGRAMS IN DANCE

The following is a list of schools that offer programs in dance and some of which grant degrees. This list was provided by the National Association of Schools of Dance (NASD).

Check the newest copy of *Lovejoy's College Guide* (found in the reference sections of libraries or in guidance counseling centers) for additional schools with programs in this field.

ARIZONA

University of Arizona
Tucson, AZ 85721

CALIFORNIA

California Institute of the Arts
24700 McBean Parkway
Valencia, CA 91355

California State University–Fullerton
PO Box 6850
Fullerton, CA 92834

**California State University–
  Long Beach**
1250 Bellflower Boulevard
Long Beach, CA 90840

Loyola Marymount University
7900 Loyola Boulevard
Los Angeles, CA 90045

San Jose State University
1 Washington Square
San Jose, CA 95192

**University of California–
  Santa Barbara**
Santa Barbara, CA 93106

CONNECTICUT

Nutmeg Ballet
21 Water Street
Torrington, CT 06790

School of the Hartford Ballet
Hartford Courant Arts Center
224 Farmington Avenue
Hartford, CT 06105

FLORIDA

Jacksonville University
Jacksonville, FL 32211

Florida State University
Tallahassee, FL 32306

Harid Conservatory
22285 Potomac Road
Boca Raton, FL 33431

New World School of the Arts
300 Northeast Second Avenue
Miami, FL 33132

ILLINOIS

University of Illinois
907 West Nevada
Urbana, IL 61801

INDIANA

Butler University
4600 Sunset Avenue
Indianapolis, IN 46208

KANSAS

Wichita State University
1845 Fairmount
Campus 101
Wichita, KS 67208

MARYLAND

Towson State University
8000 York Road
Towson, MD 21252

MICHIGAN

Hope College
Holland, MI 49423

Western Michigan University
1201 Oliver Street
Kalamazoo, MI 49008

MINNESOTA

University of Minnesota–Twin Cities
172 Pillsbury Drive SE
Norris Hall 106
Minneapolis, MN 55455

Saint Olaf College
1520 Saint Olaf Avenue
Northfield, MN 55057

MISSISSIPPI

University of Southern Mississippi
Box 5052–Southern Station
Hattiesburg, MS 39406

NEW JERSEY

Montclair State College
Upper Montclair, NJ 07043

**Rutgers, The State University of
New Jersey**
Douglas Campus
PO Box 270
New Brunswick, NJ 08903

NEW MEXICO

University of New Mexico
Albuquerque, NM 87131

NEW YORK

Alvin Ailey American Dance Center
211 West 61st Street
New York, NY 10023

**American Ballet Center, Joffrey Ballet
School**
434 Avenue of the Americas
New York, NY 10011

Barnard College
Columbia University
3009 Broadway
New York, NY 10027

Dance Theater of Harlem, Inc.
466 West 152nd Street
New York, NY 10031

**Laban/Bartenieff Institute of
Movement Studies, Inc.**
11 East Fourth Street
New York, NY 10002

**Martha Graham School of
Contemporary Dance, Inc.**
316 East 63rd Street
New York, NY 10021

Merce Cunningham Studio
55 Bethune Street
New York, NY 10014

New York University
35 West Fourth Street
New York, NY 10012

SUNY–College at Brockport
Brockport, NY 14420

OHIO

Ohio State University
1813 North High Street
Columbus, OH 43210

Ohio University
Athens, OH 45701

University of Akron
Akron, OH 44325

**University of Akron
(Preparatory Program)**
Akron, OH 44325

University of Cincinnati
PO Box 2100003
Cincinnati, OH 45221

PENNSYLVANIA

Temple University
Broad and Cecil B. Moore Streets
Philadelphia, PA 19122

SOUTH CAROLINA

Columbia College
1301 Columbia College Drive
Columbia, SC 29203

Winthrop University
701 Oakland Avenue
Rock Hill, SC 29733

TEXAS

Houston Ballet Academy
PO Box 130487
1921 West Bell
Houston, TX 77219

Southern Methodist University
Dallas, TX 75275

University of Texas at Austin
Austin, TX 78212

UTAH

Brigham Young University
294 Richard Building
Provo, UT 84602

WASHINGTON

Pacific Northwest Ballet School
301 Mercer Street
Seattle, WA 98109

WISCONSIN

University of Wisconsin–Stevens Point
Stevens Point, WI 54481

D. COLLEGES AND UNIVERSITIES THAT OFFER DEGREES IN MUSIC THERAPY

The following lists colleges and universities granting degrees in music therapy. Schools are arranged by state.

Check the newest copy of *Lovejoy's College Guide* (found in the reference section of libraries or in guidance or counseling centers) for additional schools offering degrees in this field.

ARIZONA

Arizona State University
PO Box 810112
Tempe, AZ 85287

CALIFORNIA

University of the Pacific
3601 Pacific Avenue
Stockton, CA 95211

COLORADO

Colorado State University
Administration Annex
Fort Collins, CO 80523

DISTRICT OF COLUMBIA

Howard University
2400 Sixth Street NW
Washington, DC 20059

FLORIDA

Florida State University
Tallahassee, FL 32306

University of Miami
PO Box 248025
Coral Gables, FL 33124

GEORGIA

Georgia College
Campus Box 499
Milledgeville, GA 31061

University of Georgia
212 Terrell Hall
Athens, GA 30602

INDIANA

Indiana University–Purdue University at Fort Wayne
2101 Coliseum Boulevard East
Fort Wayne, IN 46805

St. Mary-of-the-Woods College
St. Mary-of-the-Woods, IN 47876

University of Evansville
1800 Lincoln Avenue
Evansville, IN 47722

IOWA

University of Iowa
107 Calvin Hall
Iowa City, IA 52242

Wartburg College
PO Box 1003
222 Ninth Street NW
Waverly, IA 50677

KANSAS

University of Kansas
126 Strong Hall
Lawrence, KS 66045

LOUISIANA

Dillard University
2601 Gentilly Boulevard
New Orleans, LA 70122

Loyola University
6363 St. Charles Avenue
New Orleans, LA 70118

MASSACHUSETTS

Anna Maria College for Men and Women
Sunset Lane
Paxton, MA 01612

MICHIGAN

Eastern Michigan University
214 Pierce Hall
Ypsilanti, MI 48197

Michigan State University
Administration Building
East Lansing, MI 48824

Wayne State University
Detroit, MI 48202

Western Michigan University
Administration Building
Kalamazoo, MI 49008

MINNESOTA

Augsburg College
2211 Riverside Drive
Minneapolis, MN 55454

University of Minnesota–Twin Cities
231 Pillsbury Drive SE
Minneapolis, MN 55455

MISSISSIPPI

William Carey College
Tuscan Avenue
Hattiesburg, MS 39401

MISSOURI

Maryville College–St. Louis
13550 Conway Road
St. Louis, MO 63141

NEW JERSEY

Montclair State College
Valley Road and Normal Avenue
Upper Montclair, NJ 07043

NEW MEXICO

Eastern New Mexico University
Highway 70
Portales, NM 88130

NEW YORK

Molloy College
1000 Hemstead Avenue
Rockville Centre, NY 11570

Nazareth College of Rochester
4245 East Avenue
Rochester, NY 14610

Russell Sage College
51 First Street
Troy, NY 12180

SUNY–College at Fredonia
Fredonia, NY 14063

SUNY–College at New Paltz
75 South Manheim Boulevard
New Paltz, NY 12561

NORTH CAROLINA

East Carolina University
Greenville, NC 27834

Livingstone College
701 West Monroe Street
Salisbury, NC 28144

Queens College
1900 Selwyn Avenue
Charlotte, NC 28274

OHIO

Baldwin-Wallace College
275 Eastland Road
Berea, OH 44017

Cleveland State University
East 24th and Euclid Avenue
Cleveland, OH 44115

College of Mount St. Joseph
5701 Delhi Road
Mount St. Joseph, OH 44051

College of Wooster
Wooster, OH 44691

Ohio University
120 Chubb Hall
Athens, OH 45701

University of Dayton
300 College Park Avenue
Dayton, OH 45469

OKLAHOMA

Phillips University
1000 South University
Enid, OK 73701

Southwestern Oklahoma State University
Weatherford, OK 73096

OREGON

Willamette University
900 State Street
Salem, OR 97301

PENNSYLVANIA

Duquesne University
600 Forbes Avenue
Pittsburgh, PA 15282

Elizabethtown College
1 Alpha Drive
Elizabethtown, PA 17022

Immaculata College
Immaculata, PA 19345

Mansfield University of Pennsylvania
Alumni Hall
Mansfield, PA 16933

Marywood College
2300 Adams Avenue
Scranton, PA 18509

Slippery Rock University of Pennsylvania
Slippery Rock, PA 16057

Temple University
Philadelphia, PA 19122

SOUTH CAROLINA

Charleston Southern University
PO Box 10087
Charleston, SC 29411

TENNESSEE

Tennessee Technological University
Dixie Avenue
Cookeville, TN 38505

TEXAS

Sam Houston State University
Huntsville, TX 77341

Southern Methodist University
PO Box 296
Dallas, TX 75275

Texas Woman's University
PO Box 22909–TWU Station
Denton, TX 76204

West Texas State University
Canyon, TX 79016

UTAH

Utah State University
Logan, UT 84322

VIRGINIA

Radford University
Radford, VA 24142

Shenandoah University
1460 University Drive
Winchester, VA 22601

WEST VIRGINIA

Shepherd College
Shepherdstown, WV 25443

WISCONSIN

Alverno College
3401 South 39th Street
Milwaukee, WI 53215

University of Wisconsin–Eau Claire
Eau Claire, WI 54701

University of Wisconsin–Milwaukee
PO Box 749
Milwaukee, WI 53201

University of Wisconsin–Oshkosh
135 Depsey Hall
Oshkosh, WI 54901

E. COLLEGES AND UNIVERSITIES THAT OFFER DEGREES IN DANCE THERAPY

The following colleges and universities grant graduate degrees in dance therapy. All schools listed are approved by the American Dance Therapy Association. Graduates from approved programs meet professional requirements necessary for membership in DTR (Dance Therapy Registry). This list is provided by the American Dance Therapy Association.

CALIFORNIA

University of California–Los Angeles
124 Dance Building
Box 951608
Los Angeles, CA 90095

COLORADO

Naropa Institute
2130 Arapahoe Avenue
Boulder, CO 80302

ILLINOIS

Columbia College–Chicago
600 South Michigan
Chicago, IL 60605

NEW HAMPSHIRE

Antioch/New England Graduate School
40 Avon Street
Keene, NH 03431

PENNSYLVANIA

Hahnemann University
Mail Stop 905
230 North Broad Street
Philadelphia, PA 19102

APPENDIX II
WORKSHOPS, SEMINARS AND SYMPOSIUMS

The following is a list of workshops, seminars, courses and symposiums, and the general subject matter covered in each. You may want to contact associations related to your area of interest for additional information on programs not listed here.

This list is offered to help you find programs of interest. The author does not endorse one program over another and is not responsible for subject content.

Actors Studio (AS)
432 West 44th Street
New York, NY 10036
212-757-0870
AS offers workshops of interest to professional actors, directors and playwrights.

Alliance of Resident Theatres/New York (A.R.T./New York)
131 Varick Street
New York, NY 10013
212-989-5257
A.R.T./New York offers seminars, roundtables and workshops for members in a variety of areas.

American Association of Community Theatre (AACT)
47123 Enchanted Oaks
College Station, TX 77845
409-774-0611
AACT sponsors workshops to promote excellence in community theater.

American Conservatory Theater Foundation (ACTF)
30 Grant Avenue
San Francisco, CA 94108
415-749-2200
ACTF sponsors a variety of programs, workshops and courses for those interested in acting.

The American Mime Theatre (TAMT)
61 Fourth Avenue
New York, NY 10003
212-777-1710
TAMT offers courses, classes and workshops in the art of mime.

American Place Theatre (APT)
111 West 46th Street
New York, NY 10036
212-840-2960
APT offers a large number of workshops each year to those interested in learning more about developing and presenting plays.

American Society of Composers and Publishers (ASCAP)
1 Lincoln Plaza
New York, NY 10023
212-595-3050
ASCAP offers a variety of workshops for songwriters.

American Society of Music Arrangers and Composers (ASMAC)
PO Box 11
Hollywood, CA 90078
213-658-5997
ASMAC conducts workshops about new techniques in music.

American Symphony Orchestra League (ASOL)
777 14th Street, NW
Washington, DC 20005
202-628-0900
ASOL offers regional workshops, seminars and symposiums in every phase of orchestra business and craft, including orchestra management, marketing, fundraising and conducting. ASOL also holds an annual conference that presents many informative programs.

American Theatre Critics Association (ATCA)
The Tennessean
2200 Hemingway Drive
Nashville, TN 37215
615-665-0595
ATCA conducts mentor critic programs.

Bilingual Foundation of the Arts (BFA)
421 North Avenue 19
Los Angeles, CA 90031
213-225-4044
BFA sponsors training programs for theater technicians and actors.

Black Theatre Network
PO Box 11502
Fisher Building Station
Detroit, MI 48211
313-577-7906
The Black Theatre Network organizes workshops for those interested in developing black theater.

Broadcast Music, Inc. (BMI)
320 West 57th Street
New York, NY 10019
212-586-2000
BMI conducts seminars throughout the country on various aspects of the music business.

Career Opportunities Seminars and Speakers
PO Box 711
Monticello, NY 12701
914-794-7312
Career Opportunities Seminars and Speakers offers seminars and workshops throughout the country on a broad variety of career and career-oriented subjects.

Center for Dance Medicine (CDM)
41 East 42nd Street
New York, NY 10017
212-661-2716
CDM offers preventive medicine seminars and workshops to dancers so as to avoid dance-related injuries.

Dance Theater Workshop (DTW)
219 West 19th Street
New York, NY 10011
212-691-6500
DTW conducts a number of different seminars in a variety of dance- and theater-related subjects, including one on economic survival.

Dramatists Guild (DG)
234 West 44th Street
New York, NY 10036
212-398-9366

DG sponsors symposia and other educational programs in a variety of areas of interest to playwrights, lyricists and composers.

Eugene O'Neill Memorial Theater Center (EOMTC)
305 Great Neck Road
Waterford, CT 06385
203-443-5378

This group sponsors a number of seminars of interest to those involved in the theatrical industry.

Glitter, Glamour & Gold™ Seminars
PO Box 711
Monticello, NY 12701
914-794-7312

These seminars are offered throughout the United States for people who want to break into the music and entertainment industry. Various topics are covered for performers as well as those who aspire to work in the business end of the industry.

Independent Music Association (IMA)
c/o Don Kulak
317 Skyline Lake Drive
Ringwood, NJ 07345
201-831-1317

IMA sponsors a number of educational programs for those involved in the independent record and music industry.

International Dance-Exercise Association (IDEA)
6190 Cornerstone Street East
San Diego, CA 92121
619-535-8979

IDEA offers workshops for continuing education credits for professionals, studio and club owners, and trainers.

International Theatrical Arts Association (ITAA)
3900 Lemmon
Dallas, TX 75219
214-528-6112

ITAA conducts educational seminars for its members regarding booking entertainers into live music venues.

Making It In Theater™ Seminars and Speakers
PO Box 711
Monticello, NY 12701
914-794-7312

These workshops and seminars on subjects related to careers in theater and the performing arts can be found throughout the United States.

National Academy of Songwriters (NAS)
6381 Hollywood Boulevard
Hollywood, CA 90028
213-463-7178

NAS holds frequent workshops in a variety of areas of interest to songwriters.

National Association of Dramatic and Speech Arts (NADSA)
208 Cherokee Drive
Blacksburg, VA 24060
703-552-6862

NADSA offers educational programs for those interested in educational, community, children's and professional theater.

National Critics Institute (NCI)
c/o Ernest Schier
Eugene O'Neill Theater Center
234 West 44th Street
New York, NY 10036
212-695-3752

NCI holds workshops in both writing and theater crafts.

National Music Publishers Association (NMPA)
711 Third Avenue
New York, NY 10017
212-370-5330

The NMPA holds periodic forums for people involved in music publishing. Forums are put together by the Los Angeles and Nashville chapters, as well as by the New York chapter.

National Theatre Workshop of the Handicapped (NTWH)
354 Broome Street, Loft 5-F
New York, NY 10013
212-941-9511

NTWH offers workshops that provide training in the theater arts to physically challenged adults interested in preparing for professional acting careers.

New Dramatists (ND)
424 West 44th Street
New York, NY 10036
212-757-6960

The ND conducts classes in playwriting on a regular basis.

Non-Traditional Casting Project (NTCP)
1560 Broadway
Suite 1600
New York, NY 10036
212-730-4750

NTCP sponsors forums in a variety of areas for artists interested in learning more about increasing employment for artists of color, women and those with disabilities.

Opera America
777 14th Street NW, Suite 520
Washington, DC 20005
202-347-9262

Opera America conducts seminars and workshops in various opera-related subject areas.

Public Relations Society of America (PRSA)
33 Irving Place
New York, NY 10003
212-995-2230

PRSA offers a multitude of seminars and workshops in public relations and publicity.

Shelly Field
Public Relations Office
PO Box 711
Monticello, NY 12701
914-794-7312

Shelly Field offers seminars, workshops and speeches throughout the United States to corporations, educational institutions, businesses and private groups. Subject matter includes motivation, empowerment and career and career-oriented subjects, including the entertainment, sports and music industries.

Society for the Preservation of Variety Arts (SPVA)
c/o Milt Larsen
7001 Franklin Avenue
Hollywood, CA 90028
213-851-3443

SPVA conducts seminars and classes in comedy and variety entertainment.

Songwriters Guild of America (SGA)
1500 Harbor Boulevard
Weehawken, NJ 07087
201-686-6820

The SGA offers workshops in both the business of and the craft of songwriting. These are held throughout the year.

Theater Communications Group (TCG)
355 Lexington Avenue
New York, NY 10017
212-697-5230

TCG conducts workshops and seminars in a variety of areas relating to theater.

APPENDIX III
INTERNSHIPS IN THEATER AND THE PERFORMING ARTS

The following is a list of agencies and associations offering internships in theater and the performing arts. Many associations, schools, nonprofit organizations, arts councils, theatrical groups and dance companies throughout the country offer programs of this type. This is not a complete listing but will serve as a starting point.

Keep in mind that some internships are paid positions, while others are not. However, many of these programs offer course credits toward a college degree.

Write or call to inquire about eligibility requirements and application procedures for internships.

The Alliance of Resident Theatres/New York (A.R.T./New York)
131 Varick Street, Room 904
New York, NY 10013
212-989-5257
A.R.T./New York offers internship positions in theater and arts management and production.

American Symphony Orchestra League
777 14th Street NW
Washington, DC 20005
202-628-0099
The American Symphony Orchestra League offers intern programs in orchestra management.

Berkshire Theatre Festival
Main Street
Stockbridge, MA 01262
413-298-5536
The Berkshire Theatre Festival offers internships in everything from acting to the business of theater.

Center Stage
700 North Calvert Street
Baltimore, MD 21202
410-685-3200
Center Stage has internship programs in production, costuming, business and administration.

Cincinnati Playhouse in the Park
Box 6537
Cincinnati, OH 45206
513-345-2242
This group offers internship programs in acting, directing, playwriting and production.

Circle in the Square Theatre
1633 Broadway
New York, NY 10019
Circle in the Square Theatre has intern programs in a range of theater disciplines.

Cleveland Playhouse
8500 Euclid Avenue
Cleveland, OH 44106
216-795-7010
The Cleveland Playhouse offers intern programs in administrative, artistic and technical fields of theater.

College Light Opera Company
Robert Haslun
162 South Cedar Street
Oberlin, OH 44024
216-774-8485
The College Light Opera Company has programs in a variety of summer stock theater specialties.

Dallas Theater Center
3636 Turtle Creek Boulevard
Dallas, TX 75219
214-526-8210
The Dallas Theater Center has intern programs in theater production, arts administration and management and technical fields.

Drama League
165 West 46th Street
New York, NY 10036
The Drama League offers a variety of internships in theater production, marketing development, business and administration.

The Guthrie Theater
725 Vineland Place
Minneapolis, MN 55403
612-347-1100
The Guthrie Theater offers internships in a variety of theater disciplines.

Indiana Repertory Theatre
140 West Washington
Indianapolis, IN 46204
317-635-5277
The Indiana Repertory Theatre has intern programs in technical production and artistic and administrative areas.

John F. Kennedy Center for the Performing Arts
2700 F Street NW
Washington, DC 20566
202-416-8800
The National Institute for Music Theater (NIMT) at the Kennedy Center offers internships in a variety of areas to individuals interested in working in musical theater. These include administration, production management, stage direction, design and music.

Julliard School Stage Department
144 West 66th Street
New York, NY 10023
212-799-5000
Julliard offers intern programs in a range of theater and the performing arts disciplines.

Lincoln Center for the Performing Arts
70 Lincoln Center Place
New York, NY 10023
212-875-5100
Lincoln Center for the Performing Arts offers internships in theater administration.

L.A. Theatre Center
514 South Spring Street
Los Angeles, CA 90013
213-627-6500
The L.A. Theater Center has internship programs in the technical aspects of theater as well as theater management.

Maine State Music Theatre
14 Main Street
Brunswick, ME 04011
207-725-8769
The Maine State Music Theatre offers programs for performers, theater technicians, stage managers and other fields of theater.

New Dramatists
424 West 44th Street
New York, NY 10036
New Dramatists offers programs in a variety of areas of theater.

Pearl Theatre Company, Inc.
80 St. Mark's Place
New York, NY 10003
212-505-3401
The Pearl Theatre Company offers intern programs in stage management, costume design and theater administration.

The Roundabout Theatre Company
1530 Broadway
New York, NY 10036
212-719-9393
The Roundabout Theatre Company has internships available in marketing, fund-raising, business management and production.

San Jose Repertory Company
Box 2399
San Jose, CA 95109
408-291-2281
The San Jose Repertory has intern programs in production, artistic management and marketing.

Stagewest
Springfield Theatre Arts Association
1 Columbus Center
Springfield, MA 01103
413-781-4470
Stagewest has internships in various aspects of theater including acting, producing and administration.

Steppenwolf Theatre Company
1650 North Halsted Street
Chicago, IL 60614
312-335-1888
The Steppenwolf Theatre Company offers internships in stage management, front house management, public relations and technical production.

Theatre Communications Group
355 Lexington Avenue
New York, NY 10017
212-697-5230
The Theatre Communications Group has internships available in arts administration, management services and publications, artist services and literary services.

Theatre Development Fund/The Costume Collection
1501 Broadway
New York, NY 10036
212-221-0885
The Theatre Development Fund offers internships in costuming.

Thirteenth Street Playhouse
50 West 13th Street
New York, NY 10011
212-675-6677
The Thirteenth Street Playhouse offers a variety of internships in various aspects of theater.

Walnut Street Theatre
Ninth and Walnut Streets
Philadelphia, PA 19107
215-574-3550
The Walnut Street Theatre offers internships in acting, marketing, stage management and various aspects of production.

APPENDIX IV
TRADE ASSOCIATIONS AND UNIONS

The following is a list of associations and unions discussed in this book, as well as other associations that might be useful to you. Names, addresses and phone numbers are included so that you can contact any of these organizations for information about membership, career guidance, scholarships or internships, and where the branch office nearest you is located.

Academy of Country Music (ACM)
6255 Sunset Boulevard
Suite 923
Hollywood, CA 90028
213-462-2351

Academy of Television Arts and Sciences (ATAS)
5220 Lankershim Boulevard
North Hollywood, CA 91601
818-754-2800

Acoustical Society of America (ASA)
500 Sunnyside Boulevard
Woodbury, NY 11797
516-576-2360

Actors' Equity Association (AEA)
165 West 46th Street
New York, NY 10036
212-869-8530

Actors Studio (AS)
423 West 44th Street
New York, NY 10036
212-757-0870

Alliance of Resident Theatres/New York (A.R.T./New York)
131 Varick Street, Room 904
New York, NY 10013
212-989-5257

American Alliance for Theatre and Education (AATE)
Theatre Department
Box 873411
Tempe, AZ 85287
602-965-6064

American Association for Music Therapy (AAMT)
PO Box 80012
Valley Forge, PA 19484
610-265-4006

American Association of Community Theatre (AACT)
4712 Enchanted Oaks
College Station, TX 77845
409-774-0611

American Association of Laban Movement Analysts (AALMA)
c/o Laban/Bartenieff Institute for Movement Studies
11 East Fourth Street
New York, NY 10003
212-477-4299

American Ballet Competition (ABC)
Box 328
Philadelphia, PA 19105
215-829-9800

American Bandmasters Association (ABA)
110 Wyanoke Drive
San Antonio, TX 78209
210-829-5555

American Center for Stanislavski Theatre Art (ACSTA)
485 Park Avenue
New York, NY 10022
212-755-5120

American Choral Directors Association (ACDA)
PO Box 6310
Lawton, OK 73506
405-355-8161

American Choral Foundation (ACF)
c/o Chorus America
2111 Sansom Street
Philadelphia, PA 19103
215-563-2430

American College Dance Festival Association (ACDFA)
201 Wood Street
Pittsburgh, PA 15222
412-392-3496

American Composers Alliance
170 West 74th Street
New York, NY 10023
212-362-8900

American Conservatory Theatre Foundation (ACTF)
30 Grant Avenue
San Francisco, CA 94108
415-749-2200

American Dance Guild (ADC)
31 West 21st Street
New York, NY 10010
212-627-3790

American Dance Therapy Association (ADTA)
2000 Century Plaza, Suite 108
Columbia, MD 21044
410-997-4040

American Federation of Musicians (AFM)
1501 Broadway, Suite 600
New York, NY 10036
212-869-1330

American Federation of Teachers (AFT)
555 New Jersey Avenue NW
Washington, DC 20001
202-879-4400

American Federation of Television and Radio Artists (AFTRA)
260 Madison Avenue
New York, NY 10016
212-532-0800

American Guild of Music (AGM)
6652 Sarden Court
Downers Grove, IL 60516
708-769-6154

American Guild of Musical Artists (AGMA)
1727 Broadway
New York, NY 10019
212-265-3687

American Guild of Organists (AGO)
475 Riverside Drive, Suite 1260
New York, NY 10115
212-870-2310

American Guild of Variety Artists (AGVA)
184 Fifth Avenue
New York, NY 10010
212-675-1003

American Harp Society (AHS)
6331 Quebec Drive
Hollywood, CA 90068
213-463-0716

American Israel Opera Foundation (AIOF)
200 Madison Avenue
New York, NY 10016
212-686-1128

American Library Association (ALA)
185 Madison Avenue
New York, NY 10016
212-679-3930

American Lithuanian Musicians Alliance (ALMA)
c/o Anthony P. Giedratis
73210 South California Avenue
Chicago, IL 60629
312-737-2421

The American Mime Theatre (TAMT)
61 Fourth Avenue
New York, NY 10003
212-777-1710

American Musical Instrument Society (AMIS)
1664 Corbin Avenue
Tarzana, CA 92356
817-776-9446

American Music Center (AMC)
30 West 26th Street, Suite 1001
New York, NY 10010
212-366-5260

American Music Conference (AMC)
5140 Avenida Encinas
Carlsbad, CA 92804
619-431-9124

American Music Festival Association (AMFA)
2430 West Broadway
Anaheim, CA 92804
714-826-1375

American Musicological Society (AMS)
201 South 34th Street
University of Pennsylvania
Philadelphia, PA 19104
215-898-8698

American Music Scholarship Association (AMSA)
1030 Carew Tower
Cincinnati, OH 45202
513-421-5342

American Place Theatre (APT)
111 West 46th Street
New York, NY 10036
212-840-2960

American Society for Jewish Music (ASJM)
170 West 74th Street
New York, NY 10023
212-874-4456

American Society for Theatre Research (ASTR)
Theatre Department
Fine Arts Center
Kingston, RI 02881
401-792-2706

American Society of Composers and Publishers (ASCAP)
1 Lincoln Plaza
New York, NY 10023
212-595-3050

American Society of Journalists and Authors, Inc. (ASJA)
1501 Broadway
New York, NY 10036
212-997-0947

American Society of Music Arrangers and Composers (ASMAC)
PO Box 11
Hollywood, CA 90078
213-658-5997

American Society of Music Copyists (ASMC)
Box 2557
New York, NY 10108
212-222-3742

American Symphony Orchestra League (ASOL)
777 14th Street NW
Washington, DC 20005
202-628-0099

American Theatre Arts For Youth (ATAFY)
1429 Walnut Street
Philadelphia, PA 19102
215-563-3501

American Theatre Critics Association (ATCA)
The Tennessean
2200 Hemingway Drive
Nashville, TN 37215
615-665-0595

American Theatre Organ Society (ATOS)
PO Box 130463
Houston, TX 77219
713-523-8214

American Viola Society (AVS)
c/o Allan de Veritch
24883 Sage Crest Road
Newhalf, CA 91321
805-255-0693

American Women in Radio and Television (AWRT)
1650 Tysons Boulevard
McLean, VA 22102
703-506-3290

Americas Boychoir Federation (ABF)
12 South Third Street
Connellsville, PA 15425
412-628-8000

Art Resources in Collaboration (ARC)
131 West 24th Street
New York, NY 10011
212-206-6492

Associated Actors and Artists of America (AAAA)
165 West 46th Street
New York, NY 10036
212-869-0358

Associated Councils for the Arts
1 East 53rd Street
New York, NY 10022
212-223-2787

Association for Theatre in Higher Education (ATHE)
PO Box 15282
Evansville, IN 47716
812-474-0549

Association of Theatrical Press Agents and Managers, AFL-CIO (ATPAM)
165 West 46th Street
New York, NY 10036
212-719-3666

Audience Development Committee (AUDELCO)
PO Box 30–Manhattanville Station
New York, NY 10027
212-368-6906

Authors Guild (AG)
330 West 42th Street
New York, NY 10036
212-563-5904

Ballet Theatre Foundation (BTF)
890 Broadway
New York, NY 10003
212-477-3030

Big Band Academy of America (BBAA)
6565 West Sunset Boulevard, Suite 516
Hollywood, CA 90028
213-463-4825

Bilingual Foundation of the Arts (BFA)
421 North Avenue 19
Los Angeles, CA 90031
213-225-4044

Black Theatre Network
PO Box 11502
Fisher Building Station
Detroit, MI 48211
313-577-7906

Broadcast Music, Inc. (BMI)
320 West 57th Street
New York, NY 10019
212-586-2000

Burlesque Historical Society (BHS)
c/o Exotic World
29053 Wild Road
Helendale, CA 92342
619-243-5261

Caledonian Foundation (CF)
PO Box 564
Laurinsburg, NC 28352
910-377-5236

Callerlab–International Association of Square Dance Callers
829 Third Avenue SE, Suite 285
Rochester, MN 55904
507-288-5121

Catholic Actors Guild of America (CAG)
1501 Broadway, Suite 518
New York, NY 10036
212-398-1868

Cecchetti Council of America (CCA)
PO Box 74
Manchester, MI 48158
313-428-7782

Center for Dance Medicine (CDM)
41 East 42nd Street
New York, NY 10017
212-661-8401

Chamber Music America (CMA)
548 Eighth Avenue
New York, NY 10018
212-244-2772

Chinese Musical and Theatrical Association (CMTA)
24 Pell Street
New York, NY 10013
212-385-3531

Choreographers Guild (CG)
256 South Robertson
Beverly Hills, CA 90211
310-275-2533

Choreographers Theatre (CT)
94 Chambers Street
New York, NY 10007
212-227-9067

Choristers Guild
2834 West Kingsley Drive
Garland, TX 75041
214-271-1521

Chorus America: Association of Professional Vocal Ensembles (CA APVE)
2111 Sansom Street
Philadelphia, PA 19103
215-563-2430

College Music Society
202 West Spruce
Missoula, MT 59802
406-721-9616

Composers Theatre (CT)
94 Chambers Street
New York, NY 10007
212-227-9067

Conference of Personal Managers
210 East 51st Street
New York, NY 10022
212-421-2670

Congress on Research in Dance (CORD)
Department of Dance
Brockport, NY 14420
716-395-2590

Costume Designers Guild (CDG)
13949 Ventura Boulevard
Sherman Oaks, CA 91423
818-905-1557

Country Dance and Song Society of America (CDSSA)
17 New South Street
Northampton, MA 01060
413-584-9913

Country Music Association (CMA)
1 Music Circle South
Nashville, TN 37203
615-244-2840

Creative Music Foundation (CMF)
PO Box 671
Woodstock, NY 12498
914-679-8847

Cultural Exchange Society of America (CESA)
1410 York Avenue, Suite 2D
New York, NY 10021
212-628-6315

Dance Critics Association (DCA)
PO Box 1882–Old Chelsea Station
New York, NY 10011
212-243-3584

Dance Educators of America (DEA)
PO Box 509
Oceanside, NY 11572
516-766-6615

Dance Films Association (DFA)
31 West 21st Street
New York, NY 10010
212-727-0764

Dance Masters of America (DMA)
PO Box 438
Independence, MO 64051

Dance Notation Bureau (DNB)
31 West 21st Street
New York, NY 10010
212-807-7899

Dance Theater Workshop (DTW)
219 West 19th Street
New York, NY 10011
212-691-6500

Dance/U.S.A.
1156 15th Street NW, Suite 820
Washington, DC 20005
202-833-1717

Directors Guild of America (DGA)
7920 Sunset Boulevard
Hollywood, CA 90046
310-289-2000

Drama Desk (DD)
c/o Alvin Klein
722 Broadway
New York, NY 10003
212-674-4436

Dramatists Guild (DG)
234 West 44th Street
New York, NY 10036
212-398-9366

The Drama Tree (DT)
158 West 15th Street
New York, NY 10011
212-620-0855

Episcopal Actor's Guild of America (EAGA)
1 East 29th Street
New York, NY 10016
212-685-2927

Ethnic Cultural Preservation Council (ECPC)
6500 South Pulaski Road
Chicago, IL 60629
312-582-5143

Eugene O'Neill Memorial Theater Center (EOMTC)
305 Great Neck Road
Waterford, CT 06385
203-443-5378

Exotic Dancers League of America (EDLA)
29053 Wild Road
Helendale, CA 92342
619-243-5261

Ford's Theatre Society (FTS)
511 10th Street NW
Washington, DC 20004
202-638-2941

Friars Club (FC)
57 East 55th Street
New York, NY 10022
212-751-7272

Friends of the Tange (FT)
99-40 64th Road
Rego Park, NY 11374
718-275-9560

Gospel Music Association (GMA)
1205 Division Street
Nashville, TN 37203
615-242-0303

Gospel Music Workshop of America (GMWA)
3908 West Warren Street
Detroit, MI 49208
313-898-2340

Graphic Artists Guild (GAG)
11 West 20th Street
New York, NY 10011
212-463-7730

Hebrew Actors Union (HAU)
31 East Seventh Street
New York, NY 10003
212-674-1923

Hospital Audiences (HAI)
220 West 42nd Street
New York, NY 10036
212-575-7676

Independent Music Association (IMA)
c/o Don Kulak
317 Skyline Lake Drive
Ringwood, NJ 07345
201-831-1317

Institute for Advanced Studies in the Theatre Arts (IASTA)
250 West 56th Street, No. 729
New York, NY 10017
212-581-3133

Institute of Outdoor Drama (IOD)
3240 Nations Bank Plaza
Chapel Hill, NC 27599
919-962-1328

Institute of the American Musical (IAM)
121 North Detroit Street
Los Angeles, CA 90036
213-934-1221

International Alliance of Theatrical Stage Employees and Moving Picture Machine Operators of the United States and Canada (IATSE)
1515 Broadway, Suite 601
New York, NY 10036
212-730-1770

International Association of Auditorium Managers (IAAM)
4425 West Airport Freeway, Suite 590
Irving, TX 75062
214-255-8020

International Brotherhood of Electrical Workers (IBEW)
1125 15th Street NW
Washington, DC 20005
202-833-7000

International Conference of Symphony and Opera Musicians (ICSOM)
6607 Waterman
St. Louis, MO 63130
314-863-0633

International Council of Kinetography Laban (ICKL)
554 South Sixth Street
Columbus, OH 43206
614-469-9984

International Dance Alliance (IDA)
c/o Renee Renouf
1120 Broderick Street
San Francisco, CA 94115
415-922-0560

International Dance-Exercise Association (IDEA)
6190 Cornerstone Street East
San Diego, CA 92121
619-535-8979

International Society for Contemporary Music (ISCM, also known as League-ISCM)
c/o American Music Center
30 West 26th Street, Suite 1001
New York, NY 10019
212-366-5260

International Society of Dramatists (ISD)
1638 Euclid Avenue
Miami, FL 33139
305-538-3111

International Theatre Institute of the United States (ITI/US)
220 West 42nd Street, Suite 1710
New York, NY 10036
212-944-1490

International Theatrical Arts Society (ITAA)
3900 Lemmon
Dallas, TX 75219
214-528-6112

Italian Actors Union (IAU)
1 World Trade Center, Suite 2565
New York, NY 10048
212-488-7573

Kentucky Callers Association (KCA)
c/o Al Eisert
2914 Hunsinger Lane
Louisville, KY 40220
502-491-4567

Laban/Bartenieff Institute of Movement Studies (LIMS)
11 East Fourth Street
New York, NY 10003
212-477-4299

League of American Theatres and Producers (LAPT)
226 West 47th Street
New York, NY 10036
212-764-1122

League of Historic American Theatres (LHAT)
1511 K Street NW, Suite 923
Washington, DC 20005
202-783-6966

League of Off-Broadway Theatres and Producers (LOBTP)
130 West 42nd Street, Suite 1300
New York, NY 10036
212-730-7130

League Of Resident Theaters (LORT)
Glick & Weintraub, PC
1501 Broadway, Suite 2401
New York, NY 10036
212-944-1501

Legacy
1100 Revere Drive
Oconomowoc, WI 53066
414-567-3454

Lloyd Shaw Foundation (LSF)
2924 Hickory Court
Manhattan, KS 66502
913-539-6306

Masquers
11110 Victory Boulevard
North Hollywood, CA 91606
213-856-4554

Meet The Composer (MTC)
2112 Broadway, Suite 505
New York, NY 10023
212-787-3601

Metropolitan Opera Association (MOA)
Lincoln Center
New York, NY 10023
212-799-3100

Metropolitan Opera Guild (MOG)
70 Lincoln Center Plaza
New York, NY 10023
212-769-7000

Music Critics Association (MCA)
7 Pine Court
Westfield, NJ 07090
908-233-8468

Music Educators National Conference (MENC)
1806 Robert Fulton Drive
Reston, VA 22091
703-860-4000

**Music Publishers Association of the
United States (MPA)**
711 Third Avenue
New York, NY 10017
212-370-5330

**Music Teachers National Association
(MTNA)**
441 Vine Street, Suite 505
Cincinnati, OH 45202
513-421-1420

**Nashville Entertainment Association
(NEA)**
PO Box 121948
Nashville, TN 37212
615-327-4308

**Nashville Songwriters Association,
International (NSAI)**
15 Music Square West
Nashville, TN 37203
615-256-3354

**National Academy of Popular Music
(NAPM)**
600 Madison Avenue
New York, NY 10022
212-319-1444

**National Academy of Recording Arts
and Sciences (NARAS)**
3402 Pico Boulevard
Santa Monica, CA 90405
310-392-3777

**National Academy of Songwriters
(NAS)**
6381 Hollywood Boulevard, Suite 780
Hollywood, CA 90028
213-463-7178

**National Academy of Television Arts
and Sciences (NATAS)**
111 West 57th Street
New York, NY 10019
212-586-8424

**National Association of Broadcast
Employees and Technicians
(NABET)**
501 Third Street NW
Washington, DC 20001
202-434-1254

**National Association of Broadcasters
(NAB)**
1771 N Street NW
Washington, DC 20036
202-429-5300

**National Association of Composers,
U.S.A. (NACUSA)**
Box 49652–Barington Station
Los Angeles, CA 90049
310-541-8213

**National Association of Dramatic and
Speech Arts (NADSA)**
208 Cherokee Drive
Blacksburg, VA 24060
703-552-6862

**National Association of Performing
Arts Managers and Agents
(NAPAMA)**
137 East 30th Street, Suite 38
New York, NY 10016
212-683-0801

**National Association of Schools of
Dance (NASD)**
11250 Roger Bacon Drive, No. 21
Reston, VA 22090
703-437-0700

**National Association of Schools of
Music (NASM)**
11250 Roger Bacon Drive, No. 21
Reston, VA 22090
703-437-0700

**National Association of Schools of
Theatre (NAST)**
11250 Roger Bacon Drive, No. 21
Reston, VA 22090
703-437-0700

**National Clogging and Hoedown
Council (NCHC)**
PO Box 5068
Hendersonville, NC 28793
904-222-5064

**National Corporate Fund for Dance
(NCFD)**
309 West 49th Street
New York, NY 10019
212-237-7638

**National Corporate Theatre Fund
(NCTF)**
321 Avenue of the Americas
New York, NY 10013
212-387-5115

National Critics Institute (NCI)
c/o Ernest Schier
Eugene O'Neill Theater Center
234 West 44th Street
New York, NY 10036
212-695-3752

National Dance Association (NDA)
1900 Association Drive
Reston, VA 22091
703-476-3436

**National Dance Council of America
(NDCA)**
PO Box 2432
Vienna, VA 22183
703-281-1581

**National Dance-Exercise Instructor's
Training Association (NDEITA)**
1503 South Washington Avenue
Minneapolis, MN 55454
612-340-1306

National Dance Institute (NDI)
594 Broadway, Room 805
New York, NY 10012
212-226-0083

**National Federation of Music Clubs
(NFMC)**
1336 North Delaware Street
Indianapolis, IN 46202
317-638-4003

**National Federation of Press Women
(NFPW)**
Box 99
Blue Springs, MO 64015
816-229-1666

**National Hairdressers and
Cosmetologists Association (NHCA)**
3510 Olive Street
St. Louis, MO 63103
314-534-7980

**National Movement Theatre
Association (NMTA)**
c/o Pontine Movement Theatre
Portsmouth, NH 03802
603-436-6660

**National Music Publishers Association
(NMPA)**
711 Third Avenue
New York, NY 10017
212-370-5330

National Opera Association (NOA)
School of Music
Northwestern University
711 Elgin Road
Evanston, IL 60208
708-467-2422

**National Orchestral Association
(NOA)**
245 Park Avenue
New York, NY 10167
212-272-7995

National Performance Network (NPN)
Dance Theater Workshop
219 West 19th Street
New York, NY 10011
212-645-6200

**National Playwrights Conference
(NPC)**
234 West 44th Street, Suite 901
New York, NY 10036
212-382-2790

National Press Club (NPC)
National Press Building
529 14th Street NW
Washington, DC 20045
202-662-7500

National Press Photographers Association (NPPA)
3200 Croasdaile Drive, Suite 306
Durham, NC 27705
919-383-7246

National Square Dance Convention (NSDC)
2936 Bella Vista
Midwest City, OK 73110
405-732-0566

National Symphony Orchestra Association (NSOA)
John F. Kennedy Center for the
Performing Arts
Washington, DC 20566
202-416-8100

National Theatre Conference (NTC)
c/o Barry Witham
University of Washington
School of Drama
DX-20
Seattle, WA 98195
206-543-5140

National Theatre Institute (NTI)
305 Great Neck Road
Waterford, CT 06385
203-443-5378

National Theatre of the Deaf (NTD)
PO Box 659
Chester, CT 06412
203-526-4971

National Theatre Workshop of the Handicapped (NTWH)
354 Broome Street, Loft 5-F
New York, NY 10013
212-941-9511

New Dramatists (ND)
424 West 44th Street
New York, NY 10036
212-757-6960

New England Theatre Conference (NETC)
Northeastern University
Department of Theatre
360 Huntington Avenue
Boston, MA 02115
617-424-9275

New York Drama Critics Circle (NYDCC)
c/o Michael Kuchwara
Associated Press
50 Rockefeller Plaza
New York, NY 10020
212-621-1841

Northwest Drama Conference (NWDC)
c/o Bruce Brockman
University of Idaho
Department of Theatre Arts
Moscow, ID 83434
208-885-6465

Opera America
777 14th Street NW, Suite 520
Washington, DC 20005
202-347-9262

Organization of Professional Acting Coaches and Teachers (OPACT)
3968 Eureka Drive
Studio City, CA 91604
213-877-4988

Outer Critics Circle (OCC)
101 West 57th Street
New York, NY 10019
212-765-8557

Paper Bag Players (PBP)
50 Riverside Drive
New York, NY 10024
212-362-0432

The Players
16 Gramercy Park
New York, NY 10003
212-475-6116

Producers Group (PG)
c/o Didia Productions
165 West 46th Street
New York, NY 10036
212-354-5040

Professional Dance Teachers Association (PDTA)
PO Box 91
Waldwick, NJ 07463
201-447-0355

Public Relations Society of America (PRSA)
33 Irving Place
New York, NY 10003
212-995-2230

Public Relations Student Society of America (PRSSA)
33 Irving Place
New York, NY 10003
212-460-1474

Radio Television News Directors Association (RTNDA)
1000 Connecticut Avenue NW
Suite 615
Washington, DC 20036
202-659-6510

Recording Industry Association of America (RIAA)
1020 19th Street NW, Suite 200
Washington, DC 20036
202-775-0101

Recording Institute of America (RIA)
15 Columbus Circle
New York, NY 10023
212-582-0400

Roundalab
8917 Alliston Hollow Way
Gaithersburg, MD 20879
301-670-9214

Royal Academy of Dancing
15 Franklin Place
Rutherford, NJ 07070
201-438-4400

Screen Actors Guild (SAG)
5757 Wilshire Boulevard
Los Angeles, CA 90036
213-549-6400

Screen Composers of America (SCA)
2451 Nichols Canyon
Los Angeles, CA 90046
213-876-6040

Screen Extras Guild (SEG)
3253 North Knoll Drive
Los Angeles, CA 90068
213-851-4301

SESAC, Inc.
PO Box 296–Old Chelsea Station
New York, NY 10013
212-899-2605

Society for the Preservation of Variety Arts (SPVA)
c/o Milt Larsen
7001 Franklin Avenue
Hollywood, CA 90028
213-851-3443

Society of American Fight Directors (SAFD)
University of Houston
School of Theatre
Houston, TX 77204
713-743-2915

Society of Dance History Scholars (SDHS)
Ohio State University
Department of Dance
1813 North High Street
Columbus, OH 43210
614-292-7977

Society of Stage Directors and Choreographers (SSDC)
1501 Broadway, 31st Floor
New York, NY 10036
212-391-1070

Songwriters and Lyricists Club (SLC)
c/o Robert Makinson
PO Box 023304
Brooklyn, NY 11202
718-855-5057

Songwriters Guild of America (SGA)
1500 Harbor Boulevard
Weehawken, NJ 07087
201-686-6820

Special Libraries Association (SLA)
1700 18th Street NW
Washington, DC 20009
202-234-4700

Theatre Authority (TA)
16 East 42nd Street, Suite 202
New York, NY 10017
212-682-4215

Theatre Committee for Eugene O'Neill (TCEO)
c/o Eugene O'Neill Theater Center
234 West 44th Street
New York, NY 10036
212-695-3752

Theatre Communications Group (TCG)
355 Lexington Avenue
New York, NY 10017
212-697-5230

Theatre Development Fund (TDF)
1501 Broadway
New York, NY 10036
212-221-0885

Theatre Guild (TG)
226 West 47th Street
New York, NY 10036
212-869-5470

Theatre Historical Society (THS)
York Theatre Building
152 North York Road, Suite 200
Elmhurst, IL 60126
708-782-1800

Theatre in Education (TE)
PO Box 357
Old Lyme, CT 06371
203-434-2480

United Scenic Artists (USA)
16 West 61st Street
New York, NY 10023
212-581-0300

United Square Dancers of America (USDA)
8913 Seaton Drive
Huntsville, AL 35802
205-881-6044

United States Amateur Ballroom Dancers Association (USABDA)
PO Box 128
New Freedom, PA 17349
717-235-6656

United States Ballroom Branch of the Imperial Society of Teachers of Dancing
c/o Lorraine Hahn
68 Centennial Road
Warminster, PA 18974
215-491-9696

United States Institute for Theatre Technology (USITT)
10 West 19th Street, Suite 54
New York, NY 10011
212-924-9088

University Resident Theatre Association (URTA)
1560 Broadway, Suite 903
New York, NY 10036
212-221-1130

Up With People (UWP)
1 International Court
Broomfield, CO 80021
303-460-7100

Women In Communications, Inc. (WIC)
3717 Columbia Pike, No. 310
Arlington, VA 22204
703-528-4200

World Congress of Teachers of Dancing (WCTD)
c/o U.S. National Institute of Dance
38 South Arlington Avenue
PO Box 245
East Orange, NJ 07019
201-673-9225

Writers Guild of America East (WGA)
555 West 57th Street
New York, NY 10019
212-767-7800

Writers Guild of America West (WGA)
8955 Beverly Boulevard
West Hollywood, CA 90048
310-550-1000

Yiddish Theatrical Alliance (YTA)
31 East Seventh Street
New York, NY 10003
212-674-3437

Young Concert Artists (YCA)
250 West 57th Street
New York, NY 10019
212-307-6655

APPENDIX V
BROADWAY THEATERS

The following is a listing of Equity-affiliated theaters in New York City. They are located in Manhattan's theater district and specialize in lavish, commercial productions. Names, addresses and box office phone numbers are included for each. Many theaters are represented by a common organization and share a phone number, which is also used for ticket sales. When you call, simply explain what kind of information you need, and the operator will route you to the correct party. Use this list to obtain general information and to locate internships and job opportunities.

Belasco Theatre
111 West 44th Street
New York, NY 10036
212-239-6200

Booth Theatre
222 West 45th Street
New York, NY 10036
212-239-6200

Broadhurst Theatre
235 West 44th Street
New York, NY 10036
212-239-6200

Broadway Theatre
235 West 44th Street
New York, NY 10036
212-239-6200

Ethel Barrymore Theatre
243 West 47th Street
New York, NY 10036
212-239-6200

Eugene O'Neill Theatre
230 West 49th Street
New York, NY 10019
212-239-6200

Ford Center for the Performing Arts
213 West 42nd Street
New York, NY 10036
212-996-1100

Gershwin Theatre
222 West 51st Street
New York, NY 10019
212-586-6510

Helen Hayes Theatre
240 West 44th Street
New York, NY 10036
212-944-9450

Imperial Theatre
249 West 45th Street
New York, NY 10036
212-239-6200

John Golden Theatre
252 West 45th Street
New York, NY 10036
212-239-6200

Longacre Theater
220 West 48th Street
New York, NY 10034
212-239-6200

Lunt-Fontanne Theatre
205 West 46th Street
New York, NY 10036
212-575-9200

Marquis Theatre
1535 Broadway
New York, NY 10019
212-382-0100

Martin Beck Theatre
302 West 45th Street
New York, NY 10036
212-239-6200

Minskoff Theatre
200 West 45th Street
New York, NY 10036
212-869-0550

Music Box Theatre
239 West 45th Street
New York, NY 10036
212-239-6200

Nederlander Theater
208 West 41st Street
New York, NY 10036
212-921-8000

Neil Simon Theatre
250 West 52nd Street
New York, NY 10019
212-757-8646

New Amsterdam Theatre
214 West 42nd Street
New York, NY 10036
212-282-2900

Palace Theatre
1564 Broadway
New York, NY 10019
212-730-8200

Plymouth Theatre
236 West 45th Street
New York, NY 10036
212-239-6200

Royale Theatre
242 West 45th Street
New York, NY 10036
212-239-6200

Shubert Theatre
225 West 44th Street
New York, NY 10036
212-239-6200

St. James Theatre
246 West 44th Street
New York, NY 10036
212-239-6200

Vivian Beaumont Theatre
150 West 65th Street
New York, NY 10023
212-787-6868

Virginia Theatre
245 West 52nd Street
New York, NY 10019
212-239-6200

Walter Kerr Theater
219 West 48th Street
New York, NY 10034
212-239-6200

Winter Garden Theatre
1634 Broadway
New York, NY 10019
212-239-6200

APPENDIX VI
OFF BROADWAY THEATERS

The following is a listing of off Broadway theaters in New York City provided by Actors' Equity Association. They specialize in productions less commercial than those on Broadway and often encourage serious drama. Names, addresses and box office phone numbers are included. Use this list to obtain general information and to locate internships and job possibilities.

Actor's Playhouse
100 Seventh Avenue
New York, NY 10014
212-741-1215

Astor Place Theatre
434 Lafayette Street
New York, NY 10003
212-254-4370

Cherry Lane Theatre
38 Commerce Street
New York, NY 10014
212-989-2020

Circle in the Square Theatre
159 Bleecker Street
New York, NY 10012
212-581-3270

Douglas Fairbanks Theatre
432 West 42nd Street
New York, NY 10036
212-239-4321

John Houseman Theatre Center
450 West 42nd Street
New York, NY 10036
212-967-7079

Joyce Theatre
175 Eighth Avenue
New York, NY 10011
212-691-9740

Kaufman Theatre
534 West 42nd Street
New York, NY 10036
212-563-1684

La Mama, Etc.
74A East Fourth Street
New York, NY 10003
212-254-6468

Lucille Lortel
121 Christopher Street
New York, NY 10014
212-924-8782

Manhattan Theatre Club at City Center
131 West 55th Street
New York, NY 10019
212-645-5590

Minetta Lane
18 Minetta Lane
New York, NY 10012
212-420-8000

New York Shakespeare Festival
425 Lafayette Street
New York, NY 10003
212-598-7100

Orpheum Theatre
126 Second Avenue
New York, NY 10003
212-477-3932

Players Theatre
115 MacDougal Street
New York, NY 10012
212-254-8138

Playhouse 91
316 East 91st Street
New York, NY 10128
212-831-2001

Playhouse on Vandam
15 Vandam Street
New York, NY 10013
212-691-1555

Playwrights Horizons
416 West 42nd Street
New York, NY 10036
212-564-1235

Promenade Theatre
2162 Broadway
New York, NY 10024
212-580-3777

Provincetown Theatre
133 MacDougal Street
New York, NY 10012
212-477-5048

St. Peter's Church
619 Lexington Avenue
New York, NY 10022
212-935-2200

Sullivan Street Playhouse
181 Sullivan Street
New York, NY 10012
212-674-3838

Theatre East
211 East 60th Street
New York, NY 10022
212-838-9090

Theatre Four
424 West 55th Street
New York, NY 10019
212-246-8545

Union Square Theatre
100 East 17th Street
New York, NY 10003
212-982-5800

Westside Theatre
407 West 43rd Street
New York, NY 10036
212-315-2244

APPENDIX VII
OFF-OFF BROADWAY THEATERS

The following is a listing of off-off Broadway theaters in New York City provided by Actors' Equity Association. They tend to be venues for serious theater and provide an alternative to the commercial tradition of Broadway. Names, addresses and box office phone numbers are included for each. Use this list to obtain general information and to locate internships and job possibilities.

Altered Stages
212 West 29th Street
New York, NY 10023
212-465-0575

American Theatre of Actors
Beckman Theater
Sargeant Theater
314 West 54th Street
New York, NY 10019
212-581-3044

Art and Work Ensemble Theatre
870 Avenue of the Americas
New York, NY 10001
212-213-0231

Art for Living Center
466 Grand Street
New York, NY 10022
212-598-0400

Baca Theatre
111 Willoughby Street
Brooklyn, NY 11201
718-596-2222

Castillo Cultural Center
7 East 20th Street, 10th Floor
New York, NY 10003
212-427-9013

Claremont Community Center
489 East 169th Street
Bronx, NY 10456
212-588-1000

Courtyard Theatre
39 Grove Street
New York, NY 10014
212-741-9317

Clark Studio Theatre
70 Lincoln Center Plaza
New York, NY 10023
212-642-1025

Danse Mirage Theatre
513 Mercer Street
New York, NY 10012
212-226-5767

Duo Theatre
62 East Fourth Street
New York, NY 10003
212-598-4320

The Family Repertory Theatre
9 Second Avenue
New York, NY 10003
212-477-2522

45th Street Theatre
354 West 45th Street
New York, NY 10036
212-582-7862

Frank Silvera Workshop
317 West 125th Street
New York, NY 10027
212-662-8463

Gallery Players
199 14th Street
Brooklyn, NY 11215
718-832-0617

Gene Frankel Theatre
24 Bond Street
New York, NY 10014
212-777-1710

Good Shepherd Church Theatre
152 West 66th Street
New York, NY 10023
212-877-0685

Grace and St. Paul's Church
123 West 71st Street
New York, NY 10023
212-877-5810

Hamlet of Bank Street
155 West Bank Street
New York, NY 10009
212-674-7806

Harold Clurman Theatre
412 West 42nd Street
New York, NY 10036
212-736-7932

Hartley House Theatre
413 West 46th Street
New York, NY 10036
212-315-2052

Here
145 Avenue of the Americas
New York, NY 10013
212-431-7434

Intar Theatre II
420 West 42nd Street
New York, NY 10036
212-664-8561

Jan Hus Theatre
351 East 74th Street
New York, NY 10021
212-288-6743

Judith Anderson Theatre
422 West 42nd Street
New York, NY 10036
212-921-9341

Kittredge Club
109 East 39th Street
New York, NY 10016
212-687-0868

Kraine Club Gallery
85 East Fourth Street
New York, NY 10003

Louis Abrons Arts Center
466 Grand Street
New York, NY 10002
212-598-0400

Mazur Theatre
555 East 90th Street
New York, NY 10128
212-831-4372

Mint Theatre Company
311 West 43rd Street
New York, NY 10036
212-245-3084

Morse Theatre Center
121 West 91st Street
New York, NY 10024
212-873-1650

The Nat Horne Theatre
442 West 42nd Street
New York, NY 10036
212-736-7128

The New Theatre
62 East Fourth Street
New York, NY 10003
212-674-9066

Noho Playhouse
3 Bond Street
New York, NY 10012
212-677-1409

Ohio Theatre
66 Wooster Street
New York, NY 10013
212-226-9044

Our Lady of the Scapula
339 East 28th Street
New York, NY 10016
212-532-2232

Pelican Studio
750 Eighth Avenue
New York, NY 10036
212-730-2030

The Performing Garage
33 Wooster Street
New York, NY 10013
212-966-3651

Perry Street Theatre
31 Perry Street
New York, NY 10011
212-255-7190

Pfizer Center
219 East 42nd Street
New York, NY 10017
212-573-4443

Pride Theatre Ensemble
1501 Broadway, Suite 1401
New York, NY 10036
212-229-PRIDE

The Producers Club
358 West 44th Street
New York, NY 10036
212-246-9069

Raft Theatre
432 West 42nd Street
New York, NY 10036
212-947-8389

Rapp Theatre Company
220 East Fourth Street
New York, NY 10003
212-529-5921

Richard Allen Center
550 West 155th Street
New York, NY 10032
212-281-2220

Samuel Beckett Theatre
410 West 42nd Street
New York, NY 10036
212-659-5429

Sanford Meisner Theatre
164 11th Avenue
New York, NY 10011
212-206-1764

Shandol Theatre
137 West 22nd Street
New York, NY 10011
212-243-9504

Stage Arts Theatre
120 West 28th Street
New York, NY 10001
212-316-9037

Staret Theatre
331 West 43rd Street, Sixth FLoor
New York, NY 10036
212-246-5877

St. Michael's Church
225 West 99th Street
New York, NY 10025
212-222-2700

Ten Ten Players Theatre
1010 Park Avenue
New York, NY 10028
212-879-7669

Theatre 133
133 West 22nd Street
New York, NY 10011
212-627-8411

Theatre on 3
10 West 18th Street
New York, NY 10011
212-255-2282

Theatre Row Theatre
426 West 42nd Street
New York, NY 10036
212-695-5429

Theatre 22
54 West 22nd Street
New York, NY 10025
212-243-2805

Third Step Theatre Company
308 West 103rd Street
New York, NY 10025
212-865-1094

Thirteenth Street Playhouse
50 West 13th Street
New York, NY 10011
212-675-6677

T. Schreiber Studio
83 East Fourth Street
New York, NY 10003
212-420-1249

Washington Square Church
135 West Fourth Street
New York, NY 10014
212-777-2528

Westbeth Theatre
151 Bank Street
New York, NY 10014
212-691-2272

William Redfield Theatre
354 West 45th Street
New York, NY 10036
212-582-7862

Women's Interart Annex
552 West 53rd Street
New York, NY 10019
212-246-1050

The Writers Theatre
145 West 46th Street
New York, NY 10036
212-869-9770

APPENDIX VIII
DINNER THEATERS

The following list of dinner theaters around the country is provided by Actors' Equity Association. Dinner theaters are restaurants in which a play is performed following a meal. Names, addresses and phone numbers are included. Use the listing to obtain general information and to locate internships and job possibilities.

CALIFORNIA

Lawrence Welk Village Theatre
8975 Lawrence Welk Drive
Escondido, CA 92026
619-749-3000

COLORADO

Country Dinner Playhouse
6875 South Clinton
Engelwood, CO 80110
303-790-9311

FLORIDA

Alhambra Dinner Theatre
12000 Beach Boulevard
Jacksonville, FL 32216
904-641-1212

Golden Apple Dinner Theatre
25 North Pineapple Avenue
Sarasota, FL 33577
941-366-2646

Mark II Dinner Theatre
3376 Edgewater Drive
Orlando, FL 32804
407-422-3191

The Royal Palm Dinner Theatre
303 South East Mizner Boulevard
Royal Palm Plaza
Boca Raton, FL 33432
561-392-3755

ILLINOIS

Marriott's Lincolnshire Theatre
101 Half Day Road
Lincolnshire, IL 60015
847-643-0204

Drury Lane Oakbrook Theatre
100 Drury Lane
Oakbrook Terrace, IL 60181
312-538-3800

Drury Lane South
2500 West Drury Lane
Evergreen Park, IL 60642
312-799-4000

INDIANA

Beef 'n' Boards Dinner Theatre
9301 North Michigan
Indianapolis, IN 46268
317-872-9664

MINNESOTA

Chanhassen Dinner Theatre
501 West 78th Street
Chanhassen, MN 55317
612-934-1500

Fireside Dinner Theatre
51 West 78th Street
Chanhassen, MN 55317
612-934-1500

MISSOURI

The American Heartland Theatre
2450 Grand Avenue, Suite 314
Kansas City, MO 64108
816-842-9999

NEW YORK

Lake George Dinner Theatre
PO Box 266
Lake George, NY 12845
518-668-1258

Westchester Broadway Theatre
1 Broadway Plaza
Elmsford, NY 10523
914-592-2222

OHIO

Carousel Dinner Theatre
PO Box 7530
Akron, OH 44306
330-724-9855

APPENDIX IX
RESIDENT THEATERS

The following information, provided by Actor's Equity Association, lists Equity-affiliated resident theaters throughout the United States. These theaters operate under the LORT (League of Resident Theaters) contract. Names, addresses and phone numbers are included for each. Use this listing to obtain general information and to locate internships and job possibilities.

ALABAMA

Alabama Shakespeare Festival
1 Festival Drive
Montgomery, AL 36117
334-271-5300

ARIZONA

Arizona Theatre Company
PO Box 1631
Tucson, AZ 85702
602-884-8210

CALIFORNIA

American Conservatory Theatre
30 Grant Avenue
San Francisco, CA 94108
415-834-3200

Berkeley Repertory Theatre
2025 Addison Street
Berkeley, CA 94704
510-841-6108

California Shakespeare Festival
2531 Ninth Street
Berkeley, CA 94701
510-204-8901

Geffen Playhouse
10886 Le Conte
Los Angeles, CA 90024
310-208-6500

La Jolla Playhouse
PO Box 12039
La Jolla, CA 92037
619-534-6760

L.A. Theatre Center
514 South Spring Street
Los Angeles, CA 90013
213-627-6500

Mark Taper Forum
Los Angeles Music Center
135 North Grand Avenue
Los Angeles, CA 90012
213-972-7384

Old Globe Theatre
PO Box 2171
San Diego, CA 92112
619-231-1941

Pasadena Playhouse
39 South El Molino
Pasadena, CA 91101
818-792-8672

San Jose Repertory Company
Box 2399
San Jose, CA 95109
408-291-2281

South Coast Repertory Theatre
Box 2197
Costa Mesa, CA 92628
714-957-2602

COLORADO

Denver Center Theatre Company
1050 13th Street
Denver, CO 80204
870-893-4100

CONNECTICUT

Eugene O'Neill Memorial Theatre Center
National Playwrights Conference
305 Great Neck Road
Waterford, CT 06385
203-443-5378

Goodspeed Opera House
East Haddam, CT 06423
860-873-8664

Hartford Stage Company
50 Church Street
Hartford, CT 06103
860-525-5601

Long Wharf Theatre
222 Sargent Drive
New Haven, CT 06522
203-787-4284

Yale Repertory Theatre
Box 1903A–Yale Station
New Haven, CT 06520
203-432-1515

DELAWARE

Delaware Theatre Company
200 Water Street
Wilmington, DE 19801
302-594-1104

DISTRICT OF COLUMBIA

Arena Stage
Sixth and Main Avenue SW
Washington, DC 20024
202-554-9066

Shakespeare Theatre
301 East Capitol Street SE
Washington, DC 20003
202-547-3230

FLORIDA

Asolo Theatre Company
5555 North Tamiami Trail
Sarasota, FL 34242
941-351-9010

Caldwell Theatre Company
PO Box 277
Boca Raton, FL 33432
561-241-7432

Coconut Grove Playhouse
3500 Main Highway
Miami, FL 33133
305-442-2662

GEORGIA

Alliance Theatre Company
1280 Peachtree Street NE
Atlanta, GA 30309
404-733-4650

ILLINOIS

Goodman Theatre Company
200 South Columbus Drive
Chicago, IL 60603
312-443-3811

The Northlight Theatre, Inc.
North Shore Center for Performing Arts
   in Skokie
9501 North Skokie Boulevard
Skokie, IL 60076
847-679-9501

INDIANA

Indiana Repertory Theatre
140 West Washington Street
Indianapolis, IN 46204
317-635-5277

KENTUCKY

Actors Theatre of Louisville
316-320 West Main Street
Louisville, KY 40202
502-584-1265

MAINE

Portland Stage Company
PO Box 1458
Portland, ME 04104
207-774-1043

MARYLAND

Center Stage
700 North Calvert Street
Baltimore, MD 21202
410-685-3200

MASSACHUSETTS

**American Repertory Theatre
   Company**
Loeb Drama Center
64 Brattle Street
Cambridge, MA 02138
617-495-2668

Berkshire Theatre Festival
Main Street
Stockbridge, MA 01262
413-298-5536

The Huntington Theatre Company
Boston University Theatre
264 Huntington Avenue
Boston, MA 02115
617-266-7900

Merrimack Regional Theatre
50 East Merrimack Street
Lowell, MA 01852
508-454-6324

Stagewest
Springfield Theatre Arts Association
1 Columbus Center
Springfield, MA 01103
413-781-4470

MICHIGAN

Meadow Brook Theatre
Oakland University
Rochester, MI 48309
810-370-3310

MINNESOTA

The Guthrie Theater
725 Vineland Place
Minneapolis, MN 55403
612-347-1100

MISSOURI

Missouri Repertory Theatre
4949 Cherry Street
Kansas City, MO 64110
816-235-1451

The Repertory Theatre of St. Louis
PO Box 191730
130 Edgar Road
St. Louis, MO 63119
314-968-7340

NEW JERSEY

Crossroads Theatre Company
7 Livingston Street
New Brunswick, NJ 08901
908-249-5581

George Street Playhouse
9 Livingston Avenue
New Brunswick, NJ 08901
908-846-2895

McCarter Theatre Company, Inc.
91 University Place
Princeton, NJ 08540
609-683-9100

NEW MEXICO

Santa Fe Stages
105 East Marcy Street, Suite 107
Santa Fe, NM 87501
505-982-6680

NEW YORK

Acting Company
420 West 42nd Street, Third Floor
New York, NY 10036
212-564-3510

Bay Street Theatre
PO Box 810
Sag Harbor, NY 11963
516-725-0818

Capital Repertory Company
111 North Pearl Street
Albany, NY 12207
518-462-4531

Geva Theatre
75 Woodbury Boulevard
Rochester, NY 14605
716-232-1366

Lincoln Center Theatre Company
150 West 65th Street
New York, NY 10023
212-362-7600

Long Island Stage
Box 9001
Rockville Centre, NY 11571
516-867-3090

National Actors Theatre
Niko Associates
234 West 44th Street, Suite 902
New York, NY 10036
212-382-3410

New York Shakespeare Festival
Joseph Papp Public Theatre
425 Lafayette Street
New York, NY 10003
212-539-8500

Pearl Theatre Company, Inc.
80 Saint Marks Place
New York, NY 10003
212-505-3401

The Roundabout Theatre Company
1530 Broadway
New York, NY 10036
212-719-9393

Studio Arena Theatre
710 Main Street
Buffalo, NY 14202
716-856-8025

Syracuse Stage
John D. Archbold Theatre
820 East Genesee Street
Syracuse, NY 13210
315-443-4008

Theatre for a New Audience
154 Christopher Street, Suite 3D
New York, NY 10014
212-229-2819

NORTH CAROLINA

Playmakers Repertory Company
206 Graham Memorial 052A
Chapel Hill, NC 27514
919-962-1122

OHIO

Cincinnati Playhouse in the Park
PO Box 6537
Cincinnati, OH 45206
513-345-2242

Cleveland Playhouse
8500 Euclid Avenue
Cleveland, OH 44106
216-795-7010

Great Lakes Theatre Festival
1501 Euclid Avenue, Suite 250
Cleveland, OH 44115
216-241-5490

OREGON

Oregon Shakespeare Company
PO Box 159
Ashland, OR 97520
503-482-2111

Portland Center Stage
Portland Center for the Performing Arts
PO Box 9008
1111 Southwest Broadway
Portland, OR 97205
503-248-6309

PENNSYLVANIA

**The People's Light and Theatre
Company**
39 Congestoga Road
Malvern, PA 19355
610-647-1900

Philadelphia Theatre Company
The Belgravia
1811 Chestnut Street, Suite 300
Philadelphia, PA 19103
215-568-1920

Pittsburgh Public Theatre
Allegheny Square
Pittsburgh, PA 15212
412-323-8200

The Walnut Street Theatre
Ninth and Walnut Streets
Philadelphia, PA 19107
215-574-3550

Wilma Theatre
Broad and Spruce Streets
Philadelphia, PA 19107
215-893-9456

RHODE ISLAND

Trinity Repertory Company
201 Washington Street
Providence, RI 02903
401-521-1100

TENNESSEE

Clarence Brown Theatre
PO Box 8450 Knoxville, TN 37996
423-974-3447

Tennessee Repertory Theatre
427 Chestnut Street
Nashville, TN 37203
615-244-4878

TEXAS

Alley Theatre
615 Texas Avenue
Houston, TX 77002
713-228-9341

Dallas Theatre Center
3636 Turtle Creek Boulevard
Dallas, TX 75219
214-526-8210

UTAH

Pioneer Theatre Company
University of Utah
Salt Lake City, UT 84112
801-581-6356

VIRGINIA

Barter Theatre
Box 867
Abingdon, VA 24210
540-628-2281

Theatre Virginia
2800 Grove Avenue
Richmond, VA 23221
804-353-6100

Virginia Stage Company
PO Box 3770
254 Granby Street
Norfolk, VA 23514
757-627-6988

WASHINGTON

A Contemporary Theatre
Box 19400
100 West Roy Street
Seattle, WA 98119
206-285-3220

Intiman Theatre Company
PO Box 19760
Seattle, WA 98109
206-269-1901

Seattle Repertory Theatre
Bagley Wright Theatre
155 Mercer Street
Seattle, WA 98109
206-443-2210

WISCONSIN

**Milwaukee Repertory Theatre
Company**
108 East Wells Street
Milwaukee, WI 53202
414-224-1761

APPENDIX X
STOCK THEATERS

The following information, provided by Actors' Equity Association, lists selected Equity-affiliated stock theaters throughout the country. Names, addresses and phone numbers are included for each, as well as distinction between resident and non-resident theaters. (Resident theater hires actors for the season; non-resident, for the performance.) Use this listing to obtain general information and to locate internships and job possibilities.

CALIFORNIA

La Mirada Civic Theatre
  (non-resident dramatic stock &
  indoor musical stock)
14900 La Mirada Boulevard
La Mirada, CA 90637
714-994-6310

Sacramento Music Circus
  (resident musical)
1510 J Street, No. 100
Sacramento, CA 95811
916-446-5880

CONNECTICUT

Westport Country Playhouse
  (non-resident dramatic stock &
  indoor musical stock)
25 Powers Court
PO Box 629
Westport, CT 06880
203-227-5137

FLORIDA

Parker Playhouse (non-resident
  dramatic stock & indoor musical
  stock)
707 Northeast Eighth Street
Ft. Lauderdale, FL 33304
407-833-0705

Royal Poinciana Playhouse
  (non-resident dramatic stock &
  indoor musical stock)
PO Box 231
Palm Beach, FL 33480
407-833-0705

GEORGIA

Theatre of the Stars (musical stock
  unit attractions)
PO Box 11748
Atlanta, GA 30342
404-252-8960

MAINE

Maine State Music Theatre
  (resident dramatic stock)
14 Main Street, No. 109
Brunswick, ME 04011
207-725-8769

Ogunquit Playhouse (non-resident
  dramatic stock & indoor musical
  stock)
Route 1
Ogunquit, ME 03907
207-646-2402

MARYLAND

Olney Theatre (non-resident dramatic
  stock & indoor musical stock)
PO Box 550
Route 108
Olney, MD 20832
301-924-2654

MASSACHUSETTS

The Cape Playhouse (non-resident
  dramatic stock & indoor musical
  stock)
Box 2001
Route 6A
Dennis, MA 02638
508-385-3838

North Shore Music Theatre
  (non-resident dramatic stock &
  indoor musical stock)
PO Box 62
Route 128
Beverly, MA 01915
508-922-8220

Williamstown Theatre Festival
  (resident dramatic stock)
Adams Memorial Theatre
1000 Main Street
Box 517
Williamstown, MA 01267
413-597-3377

MICHIGAN

Barn Theatre
  (resident dramatic stock)
13351 West M-96
Augusta, MI 49012
616-731-4545

Cherry County Playhouse
  (non-resident dramatic stock &
  indoor musical stock)
Fruenthal Theatre
411 West Western
Muskegon, MI 49440
616-722-8888

Michigan Ensemble Theatre
  (non-resident dramatic stock &
  indoor musical stock)
3055 Cass Road
Traverse City, MI 49684
616-929-7260

MINNESOTA

Old Log Theatre
  (resident dramatic stock)
PO Box 250
Excelsior, MN 55331
612-474-5951

MISSOURI

K.C. Starlight Association
  (musical stock unit attractions)
4600 Starlight Drive
Kansas City, MO 64105
816-333-9481

St. Louis Municipal Opera Theatre
  (musical stock unit attractions)
Opera Theatre
Forest Park
St. Louis, MO 63112
314-361-1900

NEW HAMPSHIRE

The Barnstormers
  (resident dramatic stock)
Box 102
Tamworth, NH 03886
603-323-8500

Hampton Playhouse
(resident dramatic stock)
357 Winnacunnett Road
Hampton, NH 03842
603-926-3073

Peterborough Players
(resident dramatic stock)
PO Box 118
Off Middle Hancock Road
Peterborough, NH 03458
603-924-7585

NEW JERSEY

Paper Mill Playhouse (non-resident
dramatic stock & indoor musical
stock)
Brookside Drive
Milburn, NJ 14092
201-379-3636

NORTH CAROLINA

Flat Rock Playhouse
(resident dramatic stock)
PO Box 310
Flat Rock, NC 28731
704-693-0731

OHIO

Blue Jack (outdoor dramatic stock)
First Frontier, Inc.
PO Box 312
Xenia, OH 45385
513-376-4358

Tecumseh (outdoor dramatic stock)
The Scioto Society, Inc.
PO Box 73
Chillicothe, OH 45601
614-775-4100

OKLAHOMA

Discoveryland
(outdoor dramatic stock)
2502 East 71st Street
Tulsa, OK 74316
918-496-0190

PENNSYLVANIA

Civic Light Opera (resident musical)
The Benedum
719 Liberty Avenue
Pittsburgh, PA 15222
412-281-3973

Mountain Playhouse
(resident dramatic stock)
PO Box 205
Jennerstown, PA 15547
814-629-9201

Totem Pole Playhouse
(resident dramatic stock)
9555 Golf Course Road
Caledonia State Park
Fayetteville, PA 17222
717-352-2164

TEXAS

Casa Mañana Theatre (non-resident
dramatic stock & indoor musical
stock)
3101 West Lancaster
Ft. Worth, TX 76107
817-332-9319

Dallas Summer Musicals (musical
stock unit attractions)
PO Box 710336
Dallas, TX 75371
214-421-0662

UTAH

Utah Heritage Arts Foundation
(outdoor dramatic stock)
PO Box 1996
St. George, UT
801-674-0012

VERMONT

St. Michael's Playhouse
(resident dramatic stock)
Winooski Park
Colchester, VT 05439
802-654-2449

WISCONSIN

Peninsula Players
(resident dramatic stock)
4351 West Peninsula Players Road
Fishcreek, WI 54212
414-868-3288

APPENDIX XI
U.S. ORCHESTRAS

The following lists selected orchestras of various sizes located throughout the United States. Names, addresses and phone numbers are included for each. Use this listing to obtain general information, locate internships and inquire about auditions and job possibilities.

ALABAMA

Huntsville Symphony Orchestra
PO Box 2400
Huntsville, AL 35804
205-539-4818

Montgomery Symphony
301 North Hull Street
Montgomery, AL 38104
334-240-4004

Tuscaloosa Symphony Orchestra
PO Box 1
Tuscaloosa, AL 35402
205-752-5515

ALASKA

Fairbanks Symphony Orchestra
PO Box 82104
Fairbanks, AK 99708
907-479-3407

Juneau Symphony
PO Box 21236
Juneau, AK 98802
907-586-4676

ARIZONA

**Flagstaff Festival of the Arts
    Symphony**
PO Box 1607 Flagstaff, AZ 86002
602-774-7750

Flagstaff Symphony Orchestra
PO Box 122
Flagstaff, AZ 86002
602-774-5107

Phoenix Symphony
455 North Third Street, No. 390
Phoenix, AZ 85004
602-495-1117

Scottsdale Symphony Orchestra
PO Box 664
Scottsdale, AZ 85552
602-945-8071

Tucson Philharmonic Youth Orchestra
PO Box 41662
Tucson, AZ 85717
520-326-2793

Tucson Symphony Orchestra
443 South Stone Avenue
Tucson, AZ 85701
520-792-9155

ARKANSAS

North Arkansas Symphony Orchestra
229 North School
PO Box 1243
Fayetteville, AR 72702
501-521-4166

South Arkansas Symphony
315 East Oak, Suite 206
El Dorado, AR 71730
501-862-0521

CALIFORNIA

American Youth Symphony
343 Church Lane
Los Angeles, CA 90049
310-476-2825

Beach Cities Symphony Orchestra
PO Box 248
Redondo Beach, CA 90277
310-379-9275

Berkeley Symphony Orchestra
2322 Shattuck Avenue
Berkeley, CA 94704
510-841-2800

Beverly Hills Symphony
PO Box 5429
Beverly Hills, CA 90210
310-276-8385

Camellia Orchestra
PO Box 19786
Sacramento, CA 95819
916-441-5188

Chapman Symphony Orchestra
Champan University
Orange, CA 92666
714-997-6774

CSUN Youth Orchestra
CSUN Music Building, Room 149
18111 Nordoff Street
Northridge, CA 91330
818-677-3074

Diablo Symphony Orchestra
PO Box 2222
Walnut Creek, CA 94595
415-935-7764

Fremont Symphony Orchestra
PO Box 104
Fremont, CA 94537
510-794-1652

Fresno Philharmonic Orchestra
2610 West Shaw Avenue, Suite 103
Fresno, CA 93711
209-261-0600

Glendale Symphony
401 North Brand Boulevard, Suite 520
Glendale, CA 91203
818-500-8720

Heartland Symphony Orchestra
PO Box 241
Brainerd, CA 56401
800-826-1997

Hollywood Bowl Orchestra
c/o Columbia Artists Management, Inc.
165 West 57th Street
New York, NY 10019
212-841-9500

Imperial Valley Symphony
PO Box 713
El Centro, CA 922242
619-352-8791

**Livermore Amador Symphony
    Orchestra**
PO Box 1049
Livermore, CA 94551
510-447-8789

Long Beach Symphony Orchestra
555 East Ocean Boulevard, Suite 106
Long Beach, CA 90802
562-436-3203

Los Angeles Philharmonic Orchestra
c/o Columbia Artists Management Inc.
165 West 57th Street
New York, NY 10019
212-841-9500

Los Angeles Pops Orchestra
2 North Lake Avenue, No. 800
Pasedena, CA 91101
818-577-1130

Los Angeles Solo Repertory Orchestra
7242 Louise Avenue
Van Nuys, CA 91406
818-342-8400

Marin Symphony Orchestra
4340 Redwood Highway, Suite 409
San Rafael, CA 94903
415-479-8100

Marin Symphony Youth Orchestra
4340 Redwood Highway, Suite 409
San Rafael, CA 94903
415-479-8100

**Monterey County Symphony
    Orchestra**
PO Box 3965
Carmel, CA 92921
408-624-8511

Napa Valley Symphony Association
2407 California Boulevard
Napa, CA 94558
707-226-3046

Nova Vista Symphony
PO Box 60312
Sunnyvale, CA 94088
408-245-3116

Orange County Junior Orchestra
PO Box 18692
Anaheim Hills, CA 92817
714-692-0909

Orange County Symphony
12866 Main Street, Suite 106
Garden Grove, CA 92540
714-534-1103

Pacific Symphony Orchestra
131 East Dyer Road, Suite 200
Santa Ana, CA 92705
714-755-5788

Palisades Symphony Orchestra
1081 Palisair Place
Pacific Palisades, CA 90272
213-454-8040

Paradise Symphony Orchestra
6626 Skyway
Paradise, CA 95969
916-877-6211

Pasadena Symphony
150 South Los Robles Avenue
Pasadena, CA 91101
818-793-7172

Pasadena Youth Symphony
51 West Dayton Street, No. 100
Pasadena, CA 91105
818-584-0011

Peninsula Symphony Orchestra
PO Box 2602
Palos Verdes Peninsula, CA 00274
213-544-0320

**Peninsula Symphony Orchestra of
    Northern California**
1650 South Amphlett Boulevard
Suite 112
San Mateo, CA 94402
415-574-0244

Pomona College Symphony Orchestra
Pomona College
Claremont, CA 91711
909-621-8155

Sacramento Symphony Association
660 J Street, Suite 400
Sacramento, CA 95814
916-449-6490

San Bernardino Chamber Orchestra
5500 University Parkway
San Bernardino, CA 92407
714-887-7454

San Diego Symphony Orchestra
12145 Seventh Avenue
San Diego, CA 92101
619-233-4200

San Diego Youth Symphony
PO Box 2150
San Diego, CA 92112
619-233-3232

San Francisco Symphony
c/o Columbia Artists Management Inc.
165 West 57th Street
New York, NY 10019
212-841-9500

**San Francisco Symphony Youth
    Orchestra**
Davies Symphony Hall
201 Van Ness Avenue
San Francisco, CA 94102
415-552-8000

San Jose Symphony Orchestra
495 Almaden Boulevard
San Jose, CA 95110
408-287-7383

San Luis Obispo Symphony
Symphony House
214 East Victoria
Santa Barbara, CA 93101
805-955-6596

**Santa Cruz County Symphony
    Association, Inc.**
200 Seventh Avenue, Suite 225
Santa Cruz, CA 95062
408-462-0553

Santa Monica Symphony Orchestra
PO Box 2101
Santa Monica, CA 90408
310-841-4152

Shasta Symphony Orchestra
PO Box 496006
11555 North Old Oregan Trail Road
Redding, CA 96049
916-225-4761

Sonoma County Junior Symphony
PO Box 9261
Santa Rosa, CA 954045
707-546-8742

Stockton Symphony Association
37 West Yokuts, C-4
Stockton, CA 95207
209-951-0196

Ventura County Symphony
PO Box 1088
Ventura, CA 93002
805-643-8646

Women's Philharmonic
44 Page Street, Suite 604D
San Francisco, CA 94102
415-427-0123

Young People's Symphony Orchestra
PO Box 7010
Berkeley, CA 94707
510-849-9776

COLORADO

Arapahoe Philharmonic
4301 South Broadway, Suite 203
Englewood, CO 80110
303-781-1892

Breckenridge Music Festival
PO Box 6336
Breckenridge, CO 80424
303-453-4420

Denver Young Artists Orchestra
1415 Larimer Street, No. 300
Denver, CO 80202
303-571-1935

Fort Collins Symphony Orchestra
PO Box 1963
Fort Collins, CO 80522
970-482-4823

Grand Junction Symphony Orchestra
130 North Fourth Street, Suite 100
PO Box 3039
Grand Junction, CO 81502
303-243-6787

Greeley Philharmonic Orchestra
PO Box 1535
Greeley, CO 80632
303-356-6406

Longmont Symphony Orchestra
PO Box 74
519 Main Street
Longmont, CO 80502
303-772-5796

CONNECTICUT

Connecticut Philharmonic Orchestra
165 West Putnam Avenue
Greenwich, CT 06830 704-258-0989

Eastern Connecticut Symphony
26 Meridian Street
New London, CT 06320
860-443-2876

Greater Bridgeport Symphony Orchestra
446 University Avenue
Bridgeport, CT 06604
203-576-0263

Hartford Symphony Orchestra
228 Farmington Avenue
Hartford, CT 06105
860-246-8742

Haritt Symphony Orchestra
University of Hartford
200 Bloomfield Avenue
West Hartford, CT 06117
203-243-4948

New Britain Symphony Society
PO Box 1253
New Britain, CT 06050
203-826-6344

New Haven Symphony
70 Audobon Street
New Haven, CT 06510
203-865-0831

Norwalk Symphony Orchestra
83 East Avenue
Norwalk, CT 06856
203-866-2455

Norwalk Youth Symphony
PO Box 73
Norwalk, CT 06856
203-866-4100

Orchestra New England
1124 Campbell Avenue
PO Box 1845
West Haven, CT 06516
203-934-8863

Philharmonia Orchestra of Yale
PO Box 208426
New Haven, CT 06520
203-432-4158

Ridgefield Symphony Orchestra
PO Box 613
Ridgefield, CT 06877
203-438-3889

Stamford Symphony Orchestra
400 Main Street
Stamford, CT 06901
203-325-1407

Waterbury Symphony Orchestra
PO Box 1762
Waterbury, CT 06721
203-574-4283

DISTRICT OF COLUMBIA

D.C. Youth Orchestra
PO Box 56198
Brightwood Station
Washington, DC 20011
202-723-1612

Georgetown Symphony Orchestra
Box 2284–Hoya Station
Washington, DC 20057
703-866-7106

National Symphony Orchestra
John F. Kennedy Center
Washington, DC 20566
202-785-8100

FLORIDA

Boca Pops
100 Northeast First Avenue
Boca Raton, FL 33432
407-393-7677

Brevard Symphony Orchestra
PO Box 36195
Melbourne, FL 32936
407-242-2024

Florida Orchestra
c/o Siegel Artists Management
1416 Hinman Avenue, Suite 6
Everston, IL 60201
847-475-4424

Florida Philharmonic Orchestra
1430 North Federal Highway
Ford Lauderdale, FL 33304
305-561-2997

Florida Symphonic Pops, Inc.
100 Northeast First Avenue
Boca Raton, FL 33432
407-393-7677

Florida West Coast Symphony Orchestra
709 North Tamiami Trail
Sarasota, FL 34236
941-953-3059

Greater Miami Youth Symphony
PO Box 431125
Miami, FL 33143
305-263-8699

Greater Palm Beach Symphony
235 Sunrise Avenue
Palm Beach, FL 33480
561-655-2657

Greater Pensacola Symphony Orchestra
321 South Palafox Street
PO Box 1705
Pensacola, FL 32598
904-435-2533

Imperial Symphony Orchestra
217 South Tennessee Avenue
PO Box 2623
Lakeland, FL 33806
813-688-3743

Jacksonville Symphony Orchestra
33 South Hogan Street, Suite 400
Jacksonville, FL 32202
904-354-5479

Miami Chamber Symphony
5690 Kendall Drive
Miami, FL 33156
305-858-3500

The New World Symphony
541 Lincoln Road
Miami Beach, FL 33139
305-673-3330

Southwest Florida Symphony Orchestra
8695 College Parkway
Fort Myers, FL 33919
813-433-3040

GEORGIA

Albany Symphony Orchestra
PO Box 70065
Albany, GA 31708
912-430-6799

Atlanta Community Symphony Orchestra
PO Box 15455
Atlanta, GA 30333
404-872-9670

Atlanta Pops Orchestra
PO Box 723172
Atlanta, GA 30339
404-435-1222

Atlanta Symphony Orchestra
1293 Peachtree Street NE, Suite 300
Atlanta, GA 30309
404-733-4800

Augusta Symphony Orchestra
PO Box 579
Augusta, GA 30903
706-826-4705

Columbus Symphony Orchestra
PO Box 5361
Columbus, GA 31906
614-224-5281

Dekalb Symphony Orchestra
PO Box 1313
Tucker, GA 30085
404-299-4341

Macon Symphony Orchestra
PO Box 5700
Macon, GA 31208
912-474-5700

Savannah Symphony
225 Abercorn Street
PO Box 9505 Savannah, GA 31412
912-236-9536

HAWAII

Honolulu Symphony Orchestra
677 Ala Moana Boulevard
Honolulu, HI 96813
808-524-0815

IDAHO

Idaho Falls Symphony Society, Inc.
545 Shoup Avenue, Suite 101
Idaho Falls, ID 83402
208-529-1080

Idaho State Civic Symphony
PO Box 8099
48 Tulane
Pocatello, ID 83209
208-236-3479

ILLINOIS

Alton Symphony Orchestra
1198 McPherson Avenue
PO Box 1055
Alton, IL 60202
618-465-7048

Augusta College Symphony Orchestra
Office of Cultural Events
Augusta College
Rock Island, IL 61201
309-794-7307

Central Illinois Youth Symphony
PO Box 3736
Peoria, IL 61612
309-822-8290

Champaign-Urbana Symphony
701 Devonshire Drive
Champaign, IL 61820
217-351-9139

Chicago Bar Association Symphony Orchestra
734 North LaSalle, Suite 10234
Chicago, IL 60610
517-265-3607

Chicago Chamber Orchestra
332 South Michigan Avenue
Chicago, IL 60604
312-922-5570

Chicago Philharmonia
5528 South Hyde Park Boulevard
Chicago, IL 60637
773-493-1915

Chicago Sinfonietta
c/o Joanne Rile Artists Management
Noble Plaza
801 Old Yolk Road
Jenkintown, PA 19046
215-885-6400

Chicago String Ensemble
3524 West Belmont
Chicago, IL 60618
312-332-0567

Civic Orchestra of Chicago
220 South Michigan Avenue
Chicago, IL 60604
312-294-3420

Classical Symphony Orchestra/Protege Philharmonic
Chicago Music Mart at DePaul Center
333 South State Street
Chicago, IL 60604
312-341-1521

Eglin Symphony Orchestra
20 DuPage Court
Elgin, IL 60120
847-888-4000

Fox Valley Symphony
5 East Galena Boulevard
Aurora, IL 60506
708-896-1133

Grant Park Symphony Orchestra
425 East McFetridge Drive
Chicago, IL 60605
312-742-7638

Illinois Philharmonic Orchestra
210 Illinois Street
Park Forest, IL 60466
708-481-7774

Illinois Symphony Orchestra
PO Box 5191
Springfield, IL 62705
217-522-2838

Knox-Galesburg Symphony
Box 31–Knox Cottage
Galesburg, IL 61401
309-343-0122

Millikin Decautur Symphony Orchestra
School of Music
Millikin University
1184 West Main Street
Decatur, IL 62522
217-424-3374

Music Center Symphony Orchestra
Music Center of the North Shore
300 Green Bay Road
Winnetka, IL 60093
847-446-3822

New Philharmonic
College of DuPage
Glen Ellyn, IL 60137
708-858-2800

Quincy Symphony Orchestra
428 Main Street, Suite 270
Quincy, IL 62301
217-222-2856

Rockford Symphony Orchestra
Riverfront Museum Park
711 North Main Street
Rockford, IL 61103
815965-0642

INDIANA

Anderson Symphony Orchestra
PO Box 741
Anderson, IN 46015
317-641-4545

Bloomington Symphony Orchestra
PO Box 1823
Bloomington, IN 47402
812-331-2320

Carmel Symphony Orchestra
PO Box 761
Carmel, IN 46032
317-844-9717

Elkhart Country Symphony Orchestra
PO Box 144
Elkhart, IN 46515
219-293-1087

Evansville Philharmonic Orchestra
PO Box 84
Evansville, IN 47701
812-425-5050

Fort Wayne Philharmonic
2340 Fairfield Avenue
Fort Wayne, IN 46807
219-744-1700

Indianapolis Symphony Orchestra
45 Monument Circle
Indianapolis, IN 46204
317-262-1100

Kokomo Symphony Orchestra
PO Box 6115
2601 South Webster
Kokomo, IN 46904
317-455-1659

Lafayette Symphony
PO Box 52
Lafayette, IN 47902
765-742-6463

Marion Philharmonic Orchestra
PO Box 272
Marion, IN 46952
765-662-2667

Richmond Symphony Orchestra
PO Box 982
Richmond, IN 47374
765-966-5181

South Bend Symphony Orchestra
120 West LaSalle Street, Suite 404
South Bend, IN 46601
219-232-6343

Terre Haute Symphony Orchestra
25 North Sixth Street
PO Box 957
Terre Haute, IN 47808
812-234-6060

IOWA

Cedar Rapids Youth Symphony
205 Second Street SE
Cedar Rapids, IA 52401
319-366-8206

Clinton Symphony Orchestra
PO Box 116
Clinton, IA 52733
319-243-2049

Des Moines Community Orchestra
7754 Northwest 54th Avenue
Johnston, IA 50131
515-276-2270

Dubuque Symphony Orchestra
1072 Locust
PO Box 881
Dubuque, IA 52004
319-557-1677

Quad City Symphony Orchestra
PO Box 1144
Davenport, IA 52805
319-322-0931

**Quad City Youth Symphony
Orchestra**
PO Box 1144
Davenport, IA 52805
319-322-0931

Sioux City Symphony Orchestra
PO Box 754
Sioux City, IA 51101
712-277-2111

Southeast Iowa Symphony Orchestra
601 North Main Street
Mount Pleasant, IA 52641
319-385-6352

**Waterloo–Cedar Falls Symphony
Orchestra**
225 Commercial Street
PO Box 864
Waterloo, IA 50704
319-235-6331

KANSAS

Emporia Symphony Orchestra
Division of Music
2300 Commercial
Emporia, KS 65801
316-3421-5431

Hays Symphony Orchestra
Fort Hays State University
Department of Music
600 Park Street
Hays, KS 67601
913-628-4280

Hutchinson Symphony
PO Box 1241
Hutchinson, KS 67504
316-663-8000

Salina Symphony
PO Box 792
Salina, KS 67402
913-823-8309

Salina Youth Symphony
PO Box 792
Salina, KS 67402
913-823-8309

Wichita Symphony
225 West Douglas
Wichita, KS 67202
316-267-5259

Wichita Youth Orchestra
225 West Douglas
Wichita, KS 67202
316-267-5259

Youth Symphony of Kansas City
7301 Mission Road, Suite 143
Prairie Village, KS 66208
913-622-6810

KENTUCKY

Louisville Orchestra
611 West Main Street
Louisville, KY 40202
502-587-8681

Owensboro Symphony Orchestra
122 East 18th Street
Owensboro, KY 42303
502-683-0740

**Owensboro Youth and Cadet
Orchestra**
122 East 18th Street
Owensboro, KY 42303
502-683-0740

Paducah Symphony Orchestra
PO Box 1763
Paducah, KY 42002
502-444-0065

LOUISIANA

Lake Charles Symphony Orchestra
PO Box 3102
Lake Charles, LA 70602
318-433-1611

Shreveport Symphony Orchestra
PO Box 205
Shreveport, LA 71162
318-222-7496

MAINE

Portland Symphony
100 Fore Street
Portland, ME 04101
207-773-8191

MARYLAND

Annapolis Symphony Orchestra
801 Chase Street
Annapolis, MD 21401
410-269-1132

Baltimore Symphony Orchestra
1212 Cathedral Street
Baltimore, MD 21201
410-783-8100

Gettysburg Symphony Orchestra
4707 Renwick Avenue
Baltimore, MD 21206
410-485-4011

Hopkins Symphony Orchestra
3400 North Charles Street
Baltimore, MD 21218
410-516-6542

Maryland Symphony Orchestra
12 Rochester Place
Hagerstown, MD 21740
301-797-4000

**Maryland Youth Symphony
Orchestra**
PO Box 27
Glenwood, MD 21738
410-489-7268

**Montgomery County Youth
Orchestras**
PO Box 30036
Bethesda, MD 20824
301-654-2018

Peabody Symphony Orchestra
1 East Mount Vernon Place
Baltimore, MD 21202
301-659-8142

MASSACHUSETTS

Berkshire Symphony
Berhard Music Center
Williams College
Willamstown, MA 01267
413-597-2127

Boston Baroque
c/o Joanne Rile Artists Management
Noble Plaza
801 Old York Road
Jenkintown, PA 19046
215-885-6400

Boston Pops Orchestra
Symphony Hall
Boston, MA 02115
617-266-1492

Boston Symphony Orchestra
Symphony Hall
301 Massachusetts Avenue
Boston, MA 02115
617-266-1492

Brockton Symphony Orchestra
PO Box 143
Brockton, MA 02403
508-596-3841

Cape Ann Symphony
PO Box 1343
Gloucester, MA 01930
617-281-0543

Concord Orchestra
PO Box 381
Concord, MA 01742
508-369-4967

**Greater Boston Youth Symphony
  Orchestras**
855 Commonwealth Avenue
Boston, MA 02215
617-353-3348

Handel and Haydn Society
300 Massachussetts Avenue
Boston, MA 02115
617-262-1815

New Bedford Symphony Orchestra
PO Box 2053
New Bedford, MA 02741
508-999-6276

New England Philharmonic
1972 Massachussetts Avenue
Newton, MA 02168
617-965-2555

Pioneer Valley Symphony
PO Box 268
Greenfield, MA 01302
413-256-6950

Plymouth Philharmonic Orchestra
130R Court Street
PO Box 3174
Plymouth, MA 02361
508-746-8008

Springfield Symphony Orchestra
75 Market Place
Springfield, MA 01103
413-733-0636

Thayer Symphony Orchestra
PO Box 271
South Lancaster, MA 01561
508-368-0656

MICHIGAN

Adrian Symphony Orchestra
110 South Madison
Adrian, MI 49221
517-264-3121

Allen Park Symphony
PO Box 145
Allen Park, MI 48101
313-381-1111

**Alma Symphony Orchestra Alma
  College**
Alma, MI 48801
517-463-7167

Battle Creek Symphony Orchestra
PO Box 1319
Battle Creek, MI 49016
616-962-2518

**Birmingham-Bloomfield Symphony
  Orchestra**
1592 Buckingham
Birmingham, MI 48009
810-645-8850

Cadillac Area Symphony Orchestra
PO Box 2063
Dearborn, MI 48123
313-565-2424

Detroit Symphony Orchestra
Orchestra Hall
3711 Woodward Avenue
Detroit, MI 48201
313-833-3362

Grand Rapids Symphony
169 Louis Campau Promenade NW
No. 1
Grand Rapids, MI 49503
616-454-9451

Greater Lansing Symphony
230 North Washington Square
Suite 100
Wharton Center for Performing Arts
Lansing, MI 49833
517-487-5001

Jackson Symphony Orchestra
215 West Michigan Avenue
Jackson, MI 49201
517-782-3221

Kalamazoo Symphony
426 South Park Street
Kalamazoo, MI 49007
616-349-7759

Keweensaw Symphony Orchestra
Walker Arts-Humanities Center
Michigan Technical University
Houghton, MI 49931
906-487-2207

Metropolitan Youth Symphony
PO Box 244
Southfield, MI 48037
810-649-0045

Michigan Youth Symphony
University of Michigan
School of Music
1100 Baits Drive
Ann Arbor, MI 48109
313-763-1279

Midland Symphony Orchestra
1801 West Saint Andrews
Midland, MI 48640
517-631-4234

Northwood Orchestra
Northwood University
3225 Cook Road
Midland, MI 48640
517-837-4364

Pontiac-Oakland Symphony Orchestra
17 South Saginaw Street, 3rd Floor
Pontiac, MI 48343
248-334-6024

Saginaw Bay Orchestra
PO Box 415
Saginaw, MI 48606
517-755-6471

Saginaw Symphony Youth Orchestra
PO Box 415
Saginaw, MI 48606
517-755-6471

**Southwest Michigan Symphony
  Orchestra**
615 Broad Street
St. Joseph, MI 49085
616-893-4334

Warren Symphony–The Michigan Orchestra
4504 East 9 Mile Road
Warren, MI 48091
810-754-2950

West Shore Symphony Orchestra
425 Western Avenue, Suite 409
Muskegon, MI 49440
616-726-3231

West Shore Youth Symphony
425 Western Avenue, Suite 409
Muskegon, MI 49440
616-726-3231

MINNESOTA

Civic Orchestra of Minneapolis
624 Morgan Avenue South
Minneapolis, MN 55405
612-690-3648

Duluth-Superior Symphony Orchestra
506 West Michigan Street
Duluth, MN 55802
218-727-7429

Greater Twin Cities' Youth Symphonies
430 Oak Grove
Minneapolis, MN 55403
612-870-7611

Itasca Symphony Orchestra
Box 140
Grand Rapids, MN 55744
3218-327-1651

Lakewood Symphony Orchestra
Lakewood Community College
3401 Century Avenue
White Bear Lake, MN 55110
612-779-3214

Mankato Area Youth Symphony Orchestra
Box 4311
Mankato, MN 56002
507-345-5995

Mankato Symphony Orchestra
Box 645
120 South Broad Street
Mankato, MN 56002
507-625-8880

Minnesota Orchestra
1111 Nicollet Mall
Minneapolis, MN 55403
612-371-5600

Minnesota Sinfonia
1820 Stevens Avenue South, Suite E
Minneapolis, MN 55043
612-871-1701

Minnetonka Symphony Orchestra
1001 Highway 7
Minneapolis, MN 55343
612-935-4615

St. Cloud Symphony Orchestra
PO Box 234
St. Cloud, MN 56032
320-259-4044

MISSISSIPPI

Jackson Symphony Youth Orchestra
PO Box 2052
201 East Pascagoula
Jackson, MS 39225
601-960-1565

Meridian Symphony Orchestra
PO Box 2171
Meridian, MS 39302
601-693-2224

Mississippi Symphony Orchestra
PO Box 2052
201 East Pascagoula
Jackson, MS 39335
601-960-1565

MISSOURI

Brentwood Symphony Orchestra
1024 Orchard Lakes Drive
St. Louis, MO 62146
314-991-4905

Independence Symphony Orchestra
PO Box 3184
Independence, MO 64055
816-356-2588

Liberty Symphony Orchestra
PO Box 30
Liberty, MO 64068
816-781-7700

Missouri Symphony Society
203 South Ninth Street
PO Box 1121
Columbia, MO 65205
314-875-0600

Northland Symphony Orchestra
PO Box 12255
Kansas City, MO 64152
816-741-4221

Springfield Symphony Orchestra
1536 East Division
Springfield, MO 65803
417-864-6683

St. Louis Philharmonic Orchestra
PO Box 3858
St. Louis, MO 63122
314-421-3600

St. Louis Symphony Orchestra
718 North Grand Boulevard
St. Louis, MO 63103
314-533-2500

MONTANA

Billings Symphony Orchestra
401 North 31st Street
Box 7055
Billings, MT 59103
406-252-3610

Bozeman Symphony Orchestra and Symphonic Choir
PO Box 1174
Bozeman, MT 597771
406-585-9774

Great Falls Symphony Association
PO Box 1078
Civic Center Building
Great Falls, MT 59403
406-453-4102

Missoula Symphony Orchestra
131 South Higgins
PO Box 8301
Missoula, MT 59807
406-721-3194

NEBRASKA

Lincoln Symphony Orchestra
1200 N Street
Lincoln, NE 68508
402-474-5610

Nebraska Chamber Orchestra
NBC Center, Suite 749
Lincoln, NE 68508
402-477-0366

NEVADA

Las Vegas Civic Symphony
Reed Whipple Center
821 Las Vegas Boulevard North
Las Vegas, NV 89101
702-229-6211

Reno Philharmonic Association
300 South Wells Avenue, Suite 5
Reno, NV 89502
702-825-5905

NEW HAMPSHIRE

Nashua Symphony Orchestra
PO Box 324
Nashua, NH 03061
603-880-7538

New Hampshire Philharmonic Orchestra
83 Hanover Street
Manchester, NH 03101
603-647-6476

New Hampshire Symphony Orchestra
PO Box 1298
Manchester, NH 03105
603-669-3559

NEW JERSEY

Bergen Philharmonic Orchestra
PO Box 174
Teaneck, NJ 07666

Bridgeton Symphony
PO Box 872
Bridgeton, NJ 08302
609-451-4380

Garden State Philharmonic Intermediate Orchestra
34 East Water Street
Toms River, NJ 08753
908-349-6277

Garden State Philharmonic Prep Orchestra
34 East Water Street
Toms River, NJ 08753
908-349-6277

Garden State Philharmonic Symphony Orchestra
34 East Water Street
Toms River, NJ 08753
908-349-6277

Garden State Philharmonic Youth Orchestra
34 East Water Street
Toms River, NJ 08753
908-349-6277

Greater Princeton Youth Orchestra
1141 Stuart Road
Princeton, NJ 08540
609-683-0777

Masterwork Orchestra
Masterwork Music and Art Foundation
Morristown, NJ 07962
201-887-1732

New Jersey Symphony Orchestra
2 Central Avenue
Newark, NJ 07102
201-624-3713

Plainfield Symphony Orchestra
PO Box 5093
Plainfield, NJ 07061
908-561-5140

Westfield Symphony Orchestra
PO Box 491
Westfield, NJ 07091
908-232-9400

NEW MEXICO

New Mexico Symphony Orchestra
PO Box 769
Albuquerque, NM 87103
505-843-7657

Santa Fe Pro Musica
PO Box 2091
320 Gasisteo, Suite 502
Santa Fe, NM 87504
505-988-4640

Santa Fe Symphony
1050 Old Pecos Trail
PO Box 9692
Santa Fe, NM 87504
505-983-3530

NEW YORK

American Composers Orchestra
1775 Broadway, Suite 525
New York, NY 10019
212-977-8495

BC Pops
1 Marine Midland Plaza
West Tower
Binghamton, NY 13901
607-724-0007

Binghamton Symphony and Choral Society
31 Front Street
Binghamton, NY 13905
607-722-6717

Brockport Symphony Orchestra
PO Box 344
Brockport, NY 14420
716-637-2115

Bronx Arts Ensemble Orchestra
Van Cortlandt Park
Bronx, NY 10471
718-601-7399

Brooklyn Philharmonic Orchestra
Brooklyn Academy of Music
30 Lafayette Avenue
Brooklyn, NY 11217
718-636-4137

Buffalo Philharmonic Orchestra
71 Symphony Circle
Buffalo, NY 14201
716-885-0331

Catskill Symphony Orchestra
PO Box 14
Oneonta, NY 13820
607-436-2670

Chautauqua Symphony Orchestra
Chautauqua Institution
PO Box 28
Chautauqua, NY 14722
716-357-6200

Clarion Music Society
123 West Third Street
New York, NY 10012
212-477-3663

Classic Orchestra
Box 82
Briarcliff Manor, NY 10510
914-762-8878

Columbia University Orchestra
Department of Music
618 Dodge Hall
New York, NY 10027
212-854-5409

East Philharmonia
Eastman School of Music
26 Gibbs Street
Rochester, NY 14604
716-274-1110

Empire State Pops–Symphony and Chamber Orchestras
Empire State Concert Productions
130 Garth Road, Suite 123
Scarsdale, NY 10583
914-723-2694

Freeway Philharmonic
58 West 58th Street
New York, NY 10019
212-753-0450

Glens Falls Symphony Orchestra
PO Box 2036
Glens Falls, NY 12801
518-793-1348

Hudson Valley Philharmonic
129 North Water Street
PO Box 191
Poughkeepsie, NY 12602
914-454-1222

Little Orchestra Society of New York
220 West 42nd Street
New York, NY 10036
212-704-2100

Long Island Philharmonic Orchestra
1 Huntington Quandrangle
Melville, NY 11747
516-293-2223

Met Orchestra
c/o Columbia Artists Management
165 West 57th Street
New York, NY 10019
212-841-9500

Mostly Mozart Festival Orchestra
c/o Columbia Artists Management
165 West 57th Street
New York, NY 10019
212-841-9500

Nassau Symphony
185 California Avenue
Uniondale, NY 11553
516-481-3196

New York Orchestra of Westchester
111 North Central Avenue, No. 425
Hartsdale, NY 10530
914-682-3707

New York Chamber Symphony
Tisch Center for the Arts
1395 Lexington Avenue
New York, NY 10128
212-415-5740

New York Philharmonic
c/o Columbia Artists Management
165 West 57th Street
New York, NY 10019
212-841-9500

New York Youth Symphony
850 Seventh Avenue, Suite 505
New York, NY 10019
212-581-5933

Onondaga Civic Symphony Orchestra
301 Pleasant Avenue
North Syracuse, NY 13212
315-458-6981

Opera Orchestra of New York
239 West 72nd Street, Suite 2A
New York, NY 10023
212-799-1982

Orchard Park Symphony
33 Sherburn Drive
Hamburg, NY 14075
716-649-6155

Orchestra of St. Luke's
130 West 42nd Street, Suite 804
New York, NY 10036
212-840-7470

Philharmonia Virtuosi
145 Palisade Street
Dobbs Ferry, NY 110522
914-693-5595

Queens Festival Orchestra
2502 Navy Place
Bellmore, NY 11710
516-785-2532

Riverside Symphony
258 Riverside Drive, No. 7C
New York, NY 10025
212-864-4197

Rochester Philharmonic
108 East Avenue
Rochester, NY 14604
716-454-2620

Rochester Philharmonic Youth Orchestra
108 East Avenue
Rochester, NY 14604
716-454-2620

Schenectady Symphony
111 South Church Street
Schenectady, NY 12305
518-372-2500

Staten Island Symphony
Wagner College
631 Howard Avenue
Staten Island, NY 10301
716-390-3426

Symphony for United Nations (SUN)
170 West End Avenue
New York, NY 10023
212-873-2872

Syracuse Symphony Orchestra
Civic Center
411 Montgomery Street
Syracuse, NY 13202
315-424-8222

Syracuse Symphony Youth Orchestra
Civic Center
411 Montgomery Street
Syracuse, NY 13202
315-424-8222

NORTH CAROLINA

Ashville Symphony Orchestra
PO Box 2852
Ashville, NC 28802
704-254-7046

Brevard Chamber Orchestra
PO Box 1547
Brevard, NC 28712
704-884-4979

Brevard Music Center
PO Box 592
Brevard, NC 28712
704-884-2011

Charlotte Symphony Orchestra
North Carolina Blumenthal Performing
    Arts Center
211 North College Street
Charlotte, NC 28202
704-332-0468

Charlotte Youth Symphony Orchestra
North Carolina Blumenthal Performing
    Arts Center
211 North College Street
Charlotte, NC 28202
704-332-0468

Eastern Philharmonic Orchestra
PO Box 220026
Greensboro, NC 27420
919-333-7450

Fayetteville Symphony Orchestra Association
PO Box 53234
Fayetteville, NC 28305
910-433-4690

Greensboro Symphony Orchestra
200 North Davie Street, Suite 328
Greensboro, NC 27420
910-333-7490

Hendersonville Symphony Orchestra
PO Box 1811
Hendersonville, NC 28793
704-697-5884

Salisbury Symphony Orchestra
PO Box 4264
Salisbury, NC 28145
704-637-4314

Western Piedmont Symphony
243 Third Avenue NE
Hickory, NC 28601
704-324-8603

Winston-Salem/Piedmont Triad Symphony
610 Coliseum Drive
Winston-Salem, NC 27106
919-725-1035

NORTH DAKOTA

Bismarck Mandan Symphony Orchestra
PO Box 2031
Bismarck, ND 58502
701-258-8345

Fargo-Moorhead Symphony Orchestra
PO Box 1753
Fargo, ND 58107
218-233-8397

Minot Symphony Orchestra
PO Box 461
Minot, ND 58702
701-839-8844

OHIO

Akron Symphony Orchestra
17 North Broadway
Akron, OH 44308
330-535-8131

Ashland Symphony Orchestra
PO Box 13
Ashland, OH 44805
419-289-5115

Cincinnati Pops Orchestra
c/o TRM Management Inc.
625 South Lazelle Street
Columbus, OH 432006
614-444-0039

Cincinnati Symphony Orchestra
1241 Elm Street
Cincinnati, OH 45210
513-621-2132

Cleveland Orchestra
11001 Euclid Avenue
Cleveland, OH 44106
216-231-7300

Cleveland Philharmonic Orchestra
PO Box 16251
Cleveland, OH 44116
216-341-7474

Columbus Symphony Orchestra
55 East State Street
Columbus, OH 43215
614-228-9600

Hamilton-Fairfield Symphony
101 South Monument Avenue
Hamilton, OH 45011
513-474-1584

Lakeland Civic Orchestra
Lakeland Community College
7700 Clocktower Drive
Kiriland, OH 44094
216-953-7090

Lakeside Summer Symphony
236 Walnut Avenue
Lakeside, OH 43440
419-798-4461

Lima Symphony Orchestra
67 Town Square
PO Box 1651
Lima, OH 45802
419-222-5701

Mansfield Symphony Youth Orchestra
142 Park Avenue West
Mansfield, OH 44902
419-524-5927

Richland Performing Arts Associates
138 Park Avenue West
Mansfield, OH 44902
419-524-5927

Shaker Symphony Orchestra
2843 Edgehill Road
Cleveland Heights, OH 44118
216-321-3704

Southeastern Ohio Symphony Orchestra
PO Box 42
New Concord, OH 43752
614-826-8197

Springfield Symphony Orchestra
PO Box 1374
Springfield, OH 45501
937-325-8100

Toledo Symphony Orchestra
2 Maritime Plaza
Toledo, OH 43604
419-241-1272

Tuscarwas Philharmonic
PO Box 406
New Philadelphia, OH 44663
216-477-6153

Westerville Civic Symphony
PO Box 478
Westerville, OH 43081
614-895-1102

Youngstown Symphony Orchestra
260 Federal Plaza West
Youngstown, OH 44503
330-744-4269

OKLAHOMA

Bartlesville Symphony Orchestra
PO Box 263
Bartlesville, OK 74005
918-337-2787

Enid-Phillips Symphony Orchestra
301 West Maine, Suite 15
Enid, OK 73701
405-237-9646

Lawton Philharmonic Orchestra
PO Box 1473
Lawton, OK 73502
405-340-8805

Oklahoma City Philharmonic Orchestra
428 West California Avenue
Oklahoma City, OK 734102
405-232-7575

Ponca City Orchestra
2413 Canterbury
Ponca City, OK 74604
405-762-8539

Tulsa Philharmonic
2901 South Harvard
Tulsa, OK 74114
918-747-7473

OREGON

Eugene Symphony Association
45 West Broadway, Suite 201
Eugene, OR 97401
541-687-9487

Grande Ronde Symphony Orchestra
PO Box 824
La Grande, OR 97850
503-636-8141

PENNSYLVANIA

Allentown Symphony
Symphony Hall
23 North Sixth Street
Allentown, PA 18101
610-432-6715

Altoona Symphony Orchestra
PO Box 483
Altoona, PA 16603
814-943-2500

Ambler Symphony Orchestra
PO Box 221
Ambler, PA 19002
215-483-3304

Bucknell University Symphony Orchestra
Bucknell University
Lewisburg, PA 17837
717-524-1216

Erie Philharmonic
100 State Street
Erie, PA 16501
814-455-1375

European Women's Orchestra
c/o Marilyn Gilbert Artists Management
516 East Wadsworth Avenue
Philadelphia, PA 19119
215-242-4620

Johnstown Symphony Orchestra
227 Franklin Street
Johnstown, PA 15901
814-535-6738

Kennett Symphony Orchestra
110 East State Street
PO Box 72
Kennett Square, PA 19348
215-444-6363

Lansdowne Symphony Orchestra
PO Box 184
Lansdowne, PA 19050
610-289-3719

McKeesport Symphony Orchestra
PO Box 354
McKeesport, PA 15134
412-672-1168

Nittany Valley Symphony
PO Box 1375
State College, PA 16804
814-231-8224

North Penn Symphony Orchestra
PO Box 694
Lansdale, PA 195446
215-393-8532

Northeastern Pennsylvania Philharmonic
PO Box 71
Avoca, PA 18641
717-457-8301

Orchestra of the Pennsylvania Ballet
1101 South Broad Street
Philadelphia, PA 19147
215-551-7000

Pennsylvania Sinfonia Orchestra
1424 Linden Street
Allentown, PA 18102
215-434-7811

Philadelphia Orchestra
1420 Locust Street
Philadelphia, PA 19102
215-893-1900

Philadelphia Youth Orchestra
PO Box 41810
Philadelphia, PA 19101
215-563-7308

Pittsburgh Symphony Orchestra
600 Penn Avenue
Pittsburgh, PA 15222
412-392-4900

Reading Symphony Orchestra
147 North Fifth Street
Reading, PA 19601
610-373-7557

Schuylkill Symphony Orchestra
PO Box 1310
Pottsville, PA 17901
717-622-0360

West Chester University Symphony
West Chester University
West Chester, PA 19383
610-436-2628

Williamsport Symphony Orchestra
360 Market Street
Willamsport, PA 17701
717-322-0227

York Symphony Orchestra
1732 Crescent Road
York, PA 17403
717-846-4188

York Youth Symphony
1732 Crescent Road
York, PA 17403
717-846-4188

RHODE ISLAND

Brown University Orchestra
Brown University
Box 1924
Providence, RI 02912
401-863-3234

Rhode Island Philharmonic Orchestra
222 Richmond Street, Suite 112
Providence, RI 02903
401-831-3123

Rhode Island Philharmonic Youth Orchestra
222 Richmond Street, Suite 112
Providence, RI 02903
401-831-3123

SOUTH CAROLINA

Carolina Youth Symphony
PO Box 6401
Greenville, SC 29606
864-232-3963

Charleston Symphony Orchestra
14 George Street
Charleston, SC 29401
803-723-7528

Greenville Symphony Orchestra
PO Box 10002
Greenville, SC 29603
864-232-0344

South Carolina Philharmonic Orchestra
1237 Gadsden Street
Columbia, SC 29201
803-771-7937

SOUTH DAKOTA

Black Hills Symphony Orchestra
PO Box 2246
Rapid City, SD 57709
605-348-4676

South Dakota Symphony
300 North Dakota Avenue
Sioux Falls, SD 57104
605-335-7933

TENNESSEE

Chattanooga Symphony and Opera Association
630 Chestnut Street
Chattanooga, TN 37402
615-267-8583

Jackson Symphony Orchestra
PO Box 3429
Jackson, TN 38303
901-427-6440

Johnson City Symphony
PO Box 533
Johnson City, TN 37605
615-926-8742

Kingsport Symphony Orchestra
Kingsport Renaissance Center
1200 East Center Street
Box 13
Kingsport, TN 37660
423-392-8423

Knoxville Symphony Orchestra
708 Gay Street
Knoxville, TN 37902
615-523-1178

Memphis Symphony Orchestra
3100 Walnut Grove Road
Memphis, TN 38111
901-324-3627

Memphis Youth Symphony Orchestra
3100 Walnut Grove Road
Memphis, TN 38111
901-324-3627

Nashville Symphony Orchestra
209 10th Avenue South, Suite 448
Cummins Station
Nashville, TN 37203
615-255-5656

Oak Ridge Symphony Orchestra
PO Box 4271
Oak Ridge, TN 37831
615-483-5569

TEXAS

Abilene Philharmonic
402 Cypress, Suite 130
Abilene, TX 79601
915-677-6710

Amarillo Symphony Orchestra
PO Box 2552
Amarillo, TX 79105
806-376-8782

Austin Symphony Orchestra
1101 Red River
Austin, TX 78701
512-476-6064

Clear Lake Symphony
PO Box 89055582
Houston, TX 77289
713-639-0702

Corpus Christi Symphony Orchestra
PO Box 495
Corpus Christi, TX 78403
512-882-2717

Dallas Symphony Orchestra
2301 Flora, Suite 300
Dallas, TX 75201
214-871-4000

East Texas Symphony Orchestra
PO Box 6323
911 South Broadway
Tyler, TX 75711
903-592-1427

El Paso Symphony Orchestra
PO Box 180
El Paso, TX 79942
915-532-3776

Fort Worth Symphony
4401 Trail Lake Drive
Fort Worth, TX 76109
817-921-2676

Houston Symphony Orchestra
615 Louisiana Street
Houston, TX 77002
713-224-4240

Houston Youth Symphony and Ballet
PO Box 56104
Houston, TX 77256
713-621-2411

Lubbock Symphony Orchestra
Northwest Center
1721 Broadway
Lubbock, TX 79401
806-762-1688

Midland-Odessa Symphony and
Chorale
PO Box 60658
Midland, TX 79711
915-563-0921

Sam Houston State University
Symphony Orchestra
Sam Houston State University
PO Box 2208
Huntsville, TX 77341
409-294-3808

San Angelo Symphony Orchestra
PO Box 5922
San Angelo, TX 76902
915-658-5877

Symphony North
PO Box 73591
Houston, TX 77273
713-867-3465

Symphony of Southeast Texas
2626 Calder
Beaumont, TX 77702
409-835-7100

Waco Symphony Orchestra
PO Box 1201
600 Austin Avenue, Suite 22
Waco, TX 76703

Wichita Falls Symphony
4500 Seymour Highway, Suite 104
Wichita Falls, TX 76309
817-692-2255

UTAH

Rocky Mountain Symphony
Eccles Community Art Center
2580 Jefferson Avenue
Ogden, UT 84401
801-479-3790

Utah Symphony Orchestra
123 West South Temple
Salt Lake City, UT 84101
801-533-5626

VERMONT

Vermont Symphony Orchestra
2 Church Street
Burlington, VT 05401
802-864-5741

VIRGINIA

Alexandria Symphony Orchestra
PO Box 1035
Alexandria, VA 22313
703-548-0045

Amadaus Orchestra
PO Box 543
Great Falls, VA 22066
703-759-5334

Arlington Symphony
933 North Globe Road
Arlington, VA 22203
703-528-1817

Fairfax Symphony Orchestra
PO Box 1300
Annandale, VA 22003
703-642-7200

Richmond Symphony Orchestra
300 West Franklin Street
Richmond, VA 23220
804-788-4717

Roanoke Symphony Orchestra
541 Luck Avenue SW
Roanoke, VA 24016
540-343-6221

Virginia Beach Symphony Orchestra
PO Box 2544
Virginia Beach, VA 23450
757-671-8611

The Virginia Symphony Orchestra
PO Box 26
Norfolk, VA 23501
804-623-8590

WASHINGTON

Bellevue Philharmonic Orchestra
PO Box 1582
924 Bellvue Way NE
Bellevue, WA 98009
206-455-4171

Bremerton Symphony Orchestra
535B Sixth Street
PO Box 996
Bremerton, WA 98337
206-373-1722

Cascade Symphony Orchestra
PO Box 550
Edmonds, WA 98020
206-778-4688

Everett Symphony Orchestra
Everett Center for the Arts
2733 Colby
Everett, WA 90201
206-259-0380

Mid-Columbia Symphony Orchestra
PO Box 65
Richland, WA 99352
509-735-7356

Port Angeles Symphony Orchestra
PO Box 2148
Port Angeles, WA 98362
206-457-5579

Seattle Symphony
305 Harrison Street
Seattle, WA 98109
206-443-4740

Seattle Youth Symphony Orchestra
11065 Fifth NE
Seattle, WA 98125
206-362-2300

Tacoma Symphony Orchestra
PO Box 19
Tacoma, WA 98401
206-272-7264

Tacoma Youth Symphony Association
901 Broadway Plaza
Tacoma, WA 98402
206-627-2792

Washington Idaho Symphony
115 Northwest State Street
Pullman, WA 99163
509-332-3408

Yakima Symphony Orchestra
PO Box 307
Yakima, WA 98907
509-248-1414

WEST VIRGINIA

West Virginia Symphony
1210 Virginia Street East
PO Box 2292
Charleston, WV 25328
304-342-0151

West Virginia Symphony Youth
Orchestra
1210 Virginia Street East
PO Box 2292
Charleston, WV 25328
304-342-0151

Wheeling Symphony Society
Hawley Building, Suite 307
Wheeling, WV 26003
304-232-6191

WISCONSIN

Beloit Janesville Symphony Orchestra
PO Box 185
Beloit, WI 53512
608-363-2554

Central Wisconsin Symphony Orchestra
PO Box 65
Stevens Point, WI 54481
715-345-2976

Fox Valley Symphony
1477 Kenwood Center
Menasha, WI 54952
414-729-5468

Green Bay Symphony Orchestra
PO Box 222
Green Bay, WI 54305
414-435-3465

Kenosha Symphony Orchestra
4917 68th Street
Kenosha, WI 53142
414-654-9080

Madison Symphony
211 North Caroll Street
Madison, WI 53703
608-257-3734

Marshfield-Wood County Symphony Orchestra
2000 West Fifth Street
Marshfield, WI 5449
715-389-6542

Milwaukee Symphony Orchestra
330 East Kilbourn Avenue, Suite 900
Milwaukee, WI 53202
414-291-6010

Milwaukee Youth Symphony Orchestra
929 North Water Street
Milwaukee, WI 53202
414-272-8540

Oshkosh Symphony Orchestra
PO Box 522
Oshkosh, WI 54902
414-233-7510

Racine Symphony Orchestra
800 Center Street, 13B
PO Box 1751
Racine, WI 53401
414-636-9285

Waukesha Symphony Orchestra
PO Box 531
Waukesha, WI 53187
414-547-1858

Wisconsin Chamber Orchestra
22 North Caroll, Suite 104
Madison, WI 53701
608-257-0638

WYOMING

Cheyenne Symphony Orchestra
PO Box 851
Cheyenne, WY 82003
307-778-8561

Wyoming Symphony Orchestra
Box 667
Casper, WY 82602
307-266-1478

APPENDIX XII
CANADIAN ORCHESTRAS

The following lists selected orchestras of various sizes located throughout Canada. Names, addresses and phone numbers are included for each. Use this listing to obtain general information, locate internships and inquire about auditions and job possibilities. Orchestras are listed alphabetically by province.

ALBERTA

Calgary Philharmonic Orchestra
205 Eight Avenue SE
Calgary, AB T2G 0K9 Canada
403-294-7420

Lethbridge Symphony Association
Yates Memorial Center
PO Box 1101
Lethbridge, AB T1J 4A2 Canada
403-328-6808

BRITISH COLUMBIA

Okanagan Symphony Orchestra
PO Box 1120
Kelowna, BC V1Y 7P8 Canada
604-763-7544

Prince George Symphony Orchestra
2880 15th Avenue
Prince George, BC V2M 1T1 Canada
604-562-0800

Vancouver Symphony Orchestra
601 Smithe Street
Vancouver, BC V6B 5G1 Canada
604-684-9100

Victoria Symphony
846 Broughton Street
Victoria, BC V8W 1E4 Canada
250-385-7767

MANITOBA

Winnepeg Symphony Orchestra
101–555 Main Street
Winnipeg, MB R3B 1C3 Canada
204-949-3950

ONTARIO

Brantford Symphony Orchestra
PO Box 101
Brantford, ON N3T 5M3 Canada
519-759-8781

Georgian Bay Symphony
PO Box 133
Owen Sound, ON N4K 5P1 Canada
519-371-4065

Hamilton Philharmonic Society
25 Main Street West
Hamilton, ON L8P 1H1 Canada
905-526-8800

Kingston Symphony
PO Box 1616
Kingston, ON K7L 5C8 Canada
613-546-9729

Kitchener-Waterloo Symphony
101 Queen Street North
Kitchener, ON N2H 6 P7 Canada
519-745-4711

Niagara Symphony Orchestra
PO Box 401
St. Catharines, ON L2R 6V9 Canada
416-687-4993

Orchestra London Canada
520 Wellingston Street
London, ON N6A 3P9 Canada
519-679-8558

Thunder Bay Symphony Orchestra
PO Box 24036
45 Beverly Street
Thunder Bay, ON P7A 7A9 Canada
807-345-4331

Windsor Symphony
174-198 Pitt Street West
Windsor, ON N9A 5L4 Canada
519-973-1238

York Symphony Orchestra
Box 355
Richmond Hill, ON L4C 4Y6 Canada
416-881-2886

SASKATCHEWAN

Saskatchewan Symphony Orchestra
703-601 Spadina Crescent East
Saskatchewan, SK S7K 3G8 Canada
306-665-6414

APPENDIX XIII
BALLET COMPANIES

The following is a listing of selected ballet companies throughout the United States. Names, addresses and phone numbers are included for each. Use this listing to obtain general information, locate internships, and inquire about auditions and job possibilities.

ALABAMA

Alabama Ballet/Ballet South
PO Box 370005
Birmingham, AL 35237
205-252-2475

Alabama Dance Theater
1018 Madison Avenue
Montgomery, AL 36104
334-241-2590

Montgomery Ballet
69009 East Shirley Lane
Montgomery, AL 36117
334-409-0522

Montgomery Performing Arts Company
1062 Woodley Road
Montgomery, AL 36106
205-264-4886

ALASKA

Alaska Dance Theatre
2602 Gambell Street
Anchorage, AK 99503
907-277-9591

ARIZONA

Ballet Arizona
3645 East Indian School Road
Phoenix, AZ 85018
602-381-0184

Yuma Ballet Theatre
PO Box 1275
Yuma, AZ 85366
520-341-1925

ARKANSAS

Ballet Arkansas
PO Box 7574
Little Rock, AR 72217
501-654-9509

CALIFORNIA

Ballet Pacifica
1824 Kaiser Avenue
Irvine, CA 92614
714-851-9330

Ballet Theatre San Jose
753 North Ninth Street
San Jose, CA 95112
408-293-5665

Berkeley Ballet Theater
2640 College Avenue
Berkeley, CA 94704
510-843-4687

Berkeley City Ballet
1800 Dwight Way
Berkeley, CA 94703
510-841-8913

California Ballet Company
8276 Ronson Road
San Diego, CA 92111
619-560-5676

California's Riverside Ballet
3480 Lemon Street
Riverside, CA 92501
909-787-7850

Central California Ballet
1752 West Bullad
Fresno, CA 93711
209-222-3129

Dance Peninsula
3607 West 244th Street
Torrance, CA 90505
310-719-9729

The Francisco Martinez Dance Theatre
6723 Matilija Avenue
Van Nuys, CA 91405
818-988-2192

Fresno Ballet
1432 Fulton
Fresno, CA 93721
209-233-2623

Lines Contemporary Ballet
San Francisco Dance Center
50 Oak Street
San Francisco, CA 94102
415-863-3040

Los Angeles Chamber Ballet
503 North Norton Avenue
Los Angeles, CA 90004
310-453-4952

Los Angeles Classical Ballet
1122 East Wardow Road
Long Beach, CA 90807
310-424-8489

Mendocino Ballet
209 South State
Ukiah, CA 95482
707-463-2290

Oakland Ballet
Alice Arts Center
1428 Alice Street
Oakland, CA 94612
510-452-9288

Pasadena Dance Theatre
PO Box 93455
Pasadena, CA 91109
818-683-3459

Sacramento Ballet
1631 K Street
Sacramento, CA 95814
916-552-5800

San Francisco Ballet
455 Franklin Street
San Francisco, CA 94102
415-861-5600

San Jose/Cleveland Ballet
PO Box 1666
San Jose, CA 95109
408-288-2820

Santa Clara Ballet Company
3086 El Camino Real
Santa Clara, CA 95051
408-247-9178

Santa Cruz Ballet Theatre
2800 South Rodeo Gulch Road
Soquel, CA 95073
408-479-1600

Theatre Ballet of San Francisco
Golden Gate Theater Building
25 Taylor Street
San Francisco, CA 94102
415-567-0988

COLORADO

Aspen Ballet Company
750 Meadowood Drive
Aspen, CO 81611
970-925-7175

Ballet Arts Theatre
816 Acoma Street
Denver, CO 80204
303-825-7570

Colorado Ballet
1278 Lincoln Street
Denver, CO 80203
303-861-7174

Pueblo Ballet
1038 Claremont Avenue
Pueblo, CO 81004
719-543-7382

CONNECTICUT

Connecticut Ballet
20 Acosta Street
Stamford, CT 06902
203-964-1211

Hartford Ballet
224 Farmington Avenue
Hartford, CT 06105
203-525-9396

Nutmeg Ballet Company
21 Water Street
Torrington, CT 06790
203-482-4413

DELAWARE

Delaware Regional Ballet Company
177 Old Camden Road
Camden, DE 19934
302-674-1020

DISTRICT OF COLUMBIA

Capitol Ballet Company
1200 Delafield Place NW
Washington, DC 20011
202-723-2210

Washington Ballet
3515 Wisconsin Avenue NW
Washington, DC 20016
202-362-3606

FLORIDA

Ballet Classique, Inc.
6735 First Avenue South
St. Petersburg, FL 33707
813-343-4122

Ballet Concerto Company of Miami
4180 Southwest 74 Court
Miami, FL 33155
305-266-0050

Ballet Florida
500 Fern Street
West Palm Beach, FL 33401
407-659-1212

Ballet Spectacular
59 Northwest 25th Avenue
Miami, FL 33125
305-642-8000

Dance Arts Guild of Tallahassee
PO Box 933
Tallahassee, FL 32302
904-224-4413

Florida Ballet
123 East Forsyth Street
PO Box 4903
Jacksonville, FL 32202
904-353-7518

Florida Ballet Theatre, Inc.
3021 West Waters
Tampa, FL 33614
813-933-9321

Fort Lauderdale Ballet Classique
508 Northeast 43rd Street
Oakland Park, FL 33334
305-537-4195

Miami Ballet
5818 Southwest 73rd Street
South Miami, FL 33143
305-667-5543

Miami City Ballet
905 Lincoln Road
Miami Beach, FL 33139
305-532-4880

Northwest Florida Ballet
101 Chicago Avenue
Fort Walton Beach, FL 32549
904-664-7787

Sarasota Ballet of Florida
PO Box 49094
Sarasota, FL 34230
813-359-0771

Southern Ballet Theatre
976 Orange Avenue
Orlando, FL 32804
407-426-1734

Tallahassee Civic Ballet
3213 Del Rio Terrace
Tallahassee, FL 32312
904-385-6684

GEORGIA

Atlanta Ballet
1400 West Peachtree Street NW
Atlanta, GA 30309
404-873-5811

Augusta Ballet Company
PO Box 3828
Augusta, GA 30904
706-826-4721

Festival Ballet Company
2266 Lake Harbin Road
Morrow, GA 30260
404-366-3494

Gainesville Ballet
PO Box 663
Gainesville, GA 30501
404-534-6382

HAWAII

Hawaii State Ballet
1418 Kapiolani Boulevard
Honolulu, HI 96814
808-947-2755

ILLINOIS

Ballet Chicago
185 North Wabash Avenue
Chicago, IL 60601
312-251-8840

Ballet Entre Nous
1237 Ridgwood Drive
Highland Park, IL 60035
847-432-1510

Joffrey Ballet of Chicago
70 East Lake Street
Suite 1300
Chicago, IL 60601
312-739-0120

Le Ballet Petit Dance Ensemble
4630 North Francisco Street
Chicago, IL 60625
312-463-3385

Peoria Ballet Company
416 Hamilton
Peoria, IL 61602
309-673-3680

U.S.A. Ballet
3808 North Ashland Avenue
Chicago, IL 60613
312-989-9191

INDIANA

Anderson Young Ballet Theatre
20 Dillon
PO Box 631
Anderson, IN 40016

Ballet Internationale
502 North Capitol Avenue
Indianapolis, IN 46204
317-637-8979

Butler Ballet
Butler University–Jordan College of
    Fine Arts
4600 Sunset Avenue
Indianapolis, IN 46208
317-940-9346

Evansville Dance Theatre
233 Plaza East
Evansville, IN 47715
812-473-8937

Fort Wayne Ballet, Inc.
324 Penn Avenue
Fort Wayne, IN 46805
219-484-9646

IOWA

Ballet Iowa
2501 Vine Street
West Des Moines, IA 50265
515-222-0698

Gateway Contemporary Ballet
233 Fifth Avenue South
PO Box 1183
Clinton, IA 52733
319-242-1002

KANSAS

Metropolitan Ballet of Wichita
939 South Parklane
Wichita, KS 67218
316-687-5880

KENTUCKY

Lexington Ballet
Arts Place
161 North Mill Street
Lexington, KY 40507
606-233-3925

The Louisville Ballet
315 East Main Street
Louisville, KY 40202
502-583-3150

LOUISIANA

Baton Rouge Ballet Theatre
PO Box 82288
Baton Rouge, LA 70884
504-766-8379

Delta Festival Ballet of New Orleans
3850 North Causeway Boulevard
Metarie, LA 70002
504-836-7165

Lake Charles Civic Ballet Company
922 Kirby Street
Lake Charles, LA 70601
318-423-1125

Louisiana Dance Theatre
4801 Line Avenue, No. 18
Shreveport, LA 71106
318-861-3006

Shreveport Metropolitan Ballet
6040 Fairfield Avenue
Shreveport, LA 71106
318-865-2947

MARYLAND

Ballet Theatre of Annapolis
Maryland Hall for the Creative Arts
PO Box 3311
Annapolis, MD 21403
410-283-8289

Metropolitan Ballet Theatre, Inc.
10076 Darnestown Road
Rockville, MD 20850
301-762-1757

Montgomery Ballet Company
9209 Gaither Road
Gaithersburg, MD 20877
301-831-3534

MASSACHUSETTS

The Amherst Ballet Theatre Company
29 Strong Street
Amherst, MA 01002
413-549-1555

Boston Ballet
19 Clarendon Street
Boston, MA 02116
617-695-6950

Chambers Ballet Company
81 North Main Street
PO Box 445
Randolph, MA 02368
617-986-2787

National Youth Ballet of Walnut Hill
12 Highland Street
Natick, MA 017860
508-653-4312

MICHIGAN

Ann Arbor Civic Ballet
548 Church Street
Ann Arbor, MI 48104
313-662-2942

Floyd Contemporary Civic Ballet
939 North Main Street
Royal Oak, MI 48067
810-641-9063

Grand Rapids Civic Ballet Company
233 East Fulton Street
Grand Rapids, MI 49503
616-454-4771

Kalamazoo Ballet Company
326 West Kalamazoo Avenue
Kalamazoo, MI 49007
616-343-3027

Michigan Ballet Theatre
6841 North Rochester Boulevard
Rochester, MI 48306
313-652-3117

MINNESOTA

Minnesota Ballet
c/o The Depot
506 West Michigan Street
Deluth, MN 55802
218-733-7538

MISSISSIPPI

Ballet Mississippi
Mississippi Arts Center
PO Box 1787
Jackson, MS 39215
601-960-1560

Mississippi Youth Ballet
PO Box 1787
Jackson, MS 39205
601-960-1560

MISSOURI

Alexandria Ballet Company
68 Four Seasons Center
Chesterfield, MO 63017
314-469-6222

Gateway Ballet of St. Louis
10674 St. Charles Rock Road
St. Ann, MO 63074
314-423-1600

State Ballet of Missouri
706 West 42nd Street
Kansas City, MO 64113
816-931-2232

St. Louis Ballet
PO Box 2101
St. Louis, MO 63043
314-567-4299

NEBRASKA

Ballet Omaha
2665 Farnam Street
Omaha, NE 68132
402-346-7394

NEVADA

Ballet Colbert
4225 Spencer
Las Vegas, NV 89919
702-893-9782

Nevada Dance Theatre
1555 East Flamingo Road
Las Vegas, NV 89119
702-732-3888

Nevada Festival Ballet
1790 West Fourth Street
Reno, NV 89503
702-785-7915

Theatre Ballet of Las Vegas
3265 East Patrick Lane
Las Vegas, NV 89102
702-458-7577

NEW HAMPSHIRE

Ballet New England
PO Box 4501
Portsmouth, NH 03802
603-430-9309

St. Paul's School Ballet Company
Concord, NH 03301
603-225-3341

NEW JERSEY

American Repertory Ballet Company
80 Albany Street
New Brunswick, NJ 08901
908-249-1254

Garden State Ballet
45 Academy Street
Newark, NJ 07102
201-623-0267

Irine Fokine Ballet Company
33 Chestnut Street
Ridgewood, NJ 07450
201-652-9653

National Ballet of New Jersey, Inc.
5113 Church Road
Mount Laurel, NJ 080544
609-235-5342

New Jersey Ballet Company
15 Microlab Road
Livingston, NJ 07039
201-597-9600

New Jersey Dance Theater
202 Maplewood Avenue
Maplewood, NJ 07040
201-762-3033

Shore Ballet Company
PO Box 8191
Red Bank, NJ 07701
908-842-8404

NEW MEXICO

Ballet Theatre International
223 North Guadalupe, Suite 195
Santa Fe, NM 87501
505-672-9808

NEW YORK

American Ballet Theatre
890 Broadway
New York, NY 10003
212-477-3030

Ballet Manhattan
61 West 62nd Street, No. 17M
New York, NY 10023
212-315-4478

Ballet Tech
890 Broadway
New York, NY 10003
212-777-7710

Dance Theatre of Harlem
466 West 152nd Street
New York, NY 10031
212-690-2800

Dance Theatre of Long Island
12 South Washington Street
Port Washington, NY 11050
516-944-3859

Ithaca Ballet
105 Sheldon Road
Ithaca, NY 14850
607-257-6066

Mid-Hudson Ballet Company
2206 Route 9
Fishkill, NY 12524
914-897-2667

New American Ballet Ensemble
250 West 88th Street, No. 405
New York, NY 10024
212-877-3306

New Amsterdam Ballet
290 Riverside Drive
New York, NY 10025
212-678-0320

New York City Ballet
New York State Theatre
20 Lincoln Center
New York, NY 10023
212-870-5500

New York Theatre Ballet
30 East 31st Street
New York, NY 10016
212-679-0401

NORTH CAROLINA

Concert Dancers of Raleigh
PO Box 30543
Raleigh, NC 27612
919-782-0622

Greensboro Ballet
200 North Davie Street
Greensboro, NC 27401
919-333-7480

North Carolina Dance Theatre
8900 North College Street
Charlotte, NC 28206
704-372-0101

OHIO

Ballet Met
322 Mt. Vernon Avenue
Columbus, OH 43215
614-229-4860

Canton Ballet Company
Cultural Center for the Arts
1001 Market Avenue North
Canton, OH 44702
330-455-7220

Cincinnati Ballet
1555 Central Parkway
Cincinnati, OH 45214
513-621-5219

Dayton Ballet
140 North Main Street
Dayton, OH 45202
937-449-5060

Ohio Ballet
354 East Market Street
Akron, OH 44325
330-972-7902

Toledo Ballet
PO Box 8872
Toledo, OH 43623
419-471-0049

OKLAHOMA

Ballet Oklahoma
7421 North Classen
Oklahoma City, OK 73116
405-843-9898

Bartlesville Civic Ballet
PO Box 921
Bartlesville, OK 74005
918-336-4746

Oklahoma Festival Ballet
University of Oklahoma
Department of Dance
563 Elm Avenue
Norman, OK 73019
405-325-4021

Tulsa Ballet Theatre
4512 South Peoria
Tulsa, OK 74105
918-749-6030

Western Oklahoma Ballet Theatre
512 Frisco
PO Box 1602
Clinton, OK 73601
405-323-5954

OREGON

Eugene Ballet Company
PO Box 11200
Eugene, OR 97400
503-485-3992

Medford Civic Ballet
9 Hawthorne Street
Medford, OR 97504
503-772-1362

Oregon Ballet Theatre
1120 Southwest 10th Avenue
Portland, OR 97205
503-227-0977

PENNSYLVANIA

Allegheny Ballet Company
PO Box A369
Altoona, PA 16603
814-943-6081

Ballet Guild of Lehigh Valley/Lehigh Valley Ballet Company
556 Main Street
Bethlehem, PA 18018
610-855-0353

Ballet Petrov
39 Dilworth Street
Pittsburgh, PA 15211
412-765-2236

Bucks County Dance Company
1761 Bustleton Pike
Feasterville, PA 19047
215-355-2333

Harrisburg Ballet
PO Box 61635
Harrisburg, PA 17106
717-558-1540

Pennsylvania Ballet
1101 South Broad Street
Philadelphia, PA 19147
215-551-7000

Pittsburgh Ballet Theatre
2900 Liberty Avenue
Pittsburgh, PA 15201
412-281-0360

RHODE ISLAND

American Ballet
1254 Round Top Road
Harrisville, RI 02830
401-568-0864

Festival Ballet of Rhode Island
5 Hennessey Avenue
North Providence, RI 02911
401-353-1129

Island Moving Company
3 Charles Street
Newport, RI 02840
401-847-4470

State Ballet of Rhode Island
Brae Crest School of Ballet
52 Sherman Avenue
Lincoln, RI 02865
401-334-2560

SOUTH CAROLINA

Charleston Ballet Theatre
477 King Street
Charleston, SC 29403
803-723-7334

Columbia City Ballet
PO Box 11898
Columbia, SC 29211
803-799-7605

Greenville Ballet
9 La Grand Boulevard
Greenville, SC 29607
864-233-5321

Robert Ivey Ballet
1910 Savannah Highway
Charleston, SC 29047
803-556-1343

TENNESSEE

Appalachian Ballet Company
215 West Broadway
Maryville, TN 37801
615-982-8463

Ballet Memphis
4569 Summer Avenue
Memphis, TN 38122
901-763-0139

Ballet Tennessee
3202 Kelly's Ferry Road
Chattanooga, TN 37419
423-821-2055

Knoxville Metropolitan Dance Theatre
201 Sherway Road
Knoxville, TN 37922
615-691-2671

Nashville Ballet
2976 Sidco Drive
Nashville, TN 37204
615-244-7233

Nashville Contemporary Ballet Company
PO Box 50580
Nashville, TN 37005
615-352-8078

Oak Ridge Civic Ballet Association
PO Box 6185
Oak Ridge, TN 37831
615-483-7469

TEXAS

Allegro Ballet of Houston
1570 Dairy Ashford
Houston, TX 77077
281-496-4670

Ballet Austin
3002 Guadalupe Street
Austin, TX 78705
512-476-9051

Corpus Christi Ballet
5610 Everhart Road
Corpus Christi, TX 78411
512-991-9521

Dallas Metropolitan Ballet
6815 Hillcrest Avenue
Dallas, TX 75205
214-361-0278

El Paso Ballet
PO Box 68335
El Paso, TX 79968
915-533-2200

Fort Worth Ballet
6845 Greek Oaks Road
Fort Worth, TX 76116
817-763-0207

Houston Ballet
1921 West Bell
Houston, TX 77219
713-523-6300

Lone Star Ballet
PO Box 1133
Amarillo, TX 79105
806-372-2463

San Antonio Ballet Company
2800 Northeast Loop 410
San Antonio, TX 78218
210-590-0210

Wichita Falls Ballet Theatre
1717 Grant Street
Wichita Falls, TX 76309
817-322-5538

UTAH

Ballet West
Capitol Theatre
50 West 200 South
Salt Lake City, UT 84101
801-364-4343

Utah Regional Ballet
Box 321
American Fork, UT 84003
801-756-8091

VIRGINIA

Bristol Ballet Company
628 Cumberland Street
Bristol, VA 24201
540-466-6051

Concert Ballet of Virginia
Box 25501
Richmond, VA 22360
804-780-1279

Petersburg Ballet
44 Goodwich Avenue
Petersburg, VA 23805
804-733-9998

Richmond Ballet
614 North Lombardy Street
Richmond, VA 23220
804-359-0906

Virginia Ballet Theatre
134 West Olney Road
Norfolk, VA 23510
804-622-4822

VERMONT

Vermont Ballet Theatre
Box 5069
Burlington, VT 05402
802-862-6466

WASHINGTON

Olympic Ballet Theatre
Anderson Cultural Center
700 Main Street
Edmonds, WA 98020
206-774-7570

Pacific Northwest Ballet
301 Mercer Street
Seattle, WA 98109
206-441-9411

Peninsula Dance Theatre
515 Chester Avenue
Bremerton, WA 98337
360-377-6214

Spokane Ballet Company
820 West Sprague
Spokane, WA 99204
509-747-0360

Tocoma Performing Dance Company
2315 Sixth Avenue
Tacoma, WA 98403
206-627-8272

WEST VIRGINIA

Charleston Ballet
822 Virginia Street East
Charleston, WV 25301
304-342-6541

Mid Ohio Valley Ballet
1311 Ann Street
PO Box 4204
Parkersburg, WV 261044
304-422-5538

Parkersburg Civic Ballet Company
PO Box 4204
Parkersburg, WV 26104
304-428-2010

WISCONSIN

Milwaukee Ballet
504 West National Avenue
Milwaukee, WI 53204
414-643-7677

APPENDIX XIV
U.S. OPERA COMPANIES

The following is a list of selected opera companies throughout the United States. Names, addresses and phone numbers are included for each. Use this listing to obtain general information, locate internships and inquire about auditions and job possibilities. Companies are listed alphabetically by state.

ALABAMA

Birmingham Civic Opera
Box 76230
Birmingham, AL 35253
205-322-6737

Mobile Opera
PO Box 66633
Mobile, AL 36660
205-460-2900

ALASKA

Anchorage Opera
1507 Spar Avenue
Anchorage, AK 99501
907-279-2557

ARIZONA

Arizona Opera Company
3501 North Mountain Avenue
Tucson, AZ 85719
520-293-4336

CALIFORNIA

Fullerton Civic Light Opera
218 West Commonwealth
Fullerton, CA 92632
714-526-3832

Hidden Valley Opera Ensemble
PO Box 116
Carmel Valley, CA 93294
408-659-3115

Long Beach Opera
PO Box 14895
Long Beach, CA 90803
213-596-5556

Los Angeles Music Center Opera
135 North Grand Avenue
Los Angeles, CA 90012
213-972-7219

The Music Center of Los Angeles
135 North Grand Avenue
Los Angeles, CA 90012
213-972-7479

Opera A La Carte
PO Box 39606A
Los Angeles, CA 90039
818-791-0844

Opera Pacific
9 Executive Circle, Suite 190
Irvine, CA 92714
714-546-7372

Opera San Jose
2149 Paragon Way
San Jose, CA 95131
408-283-4888

Pocket Opera
44 Page Street, Suite 406A
San Francisco, CA 94102
415-575-1100

Sacramento Opera
PO Box 161027
Sacramento, CA 95816
916-442-4224

San Diego Civic Light Opera Association
PO Box 3519
San Diego, CA 92103
619-544-7800

San Diego Opera
PO Box 988
San Diego, CA 92112
619-232-7636

San Francisco Opera
War Memorial Opera House
301 Van Ness Avenue
San Francisco, CA 94102
415-861-4008

San Francisco Opera Center
War Memorial Opera House
301 Van Ness Avenue
San Francisco, CA 94102
415-565-6491

West Coast Opera Theatre
PO Box 166
Palm Desert, CA 92261
619-779-0061

Western Opera Theater
War Memorial Opera House
201 Van Ness Avenue
San Francisco, CA 94102
415-565-3329

COLORADO

Central City Opera House
621 17th Street, Suite 1601
Denver, CO 80293
303-292-6500

Colorado Opera Festival
PO Box 1484
Colorado Springs, CO 80901
719-473-0073

Opera Colorado
695 South Colorado Boulevard, Suite 20
Denver, CO 80333
303-778-1500

CONNECTICUT

Connecticut Opera
226 Farmington Avenue
Hartford, CT 06105
203-527-0713

DELAWARE

Opera Delaware
4 South Poplar Street
Wilmington, DE 19801
302-658-8063

DISTRICT OF COLUMBIA

Summer Opera Theatre Company
620 Michigan Avenue NE
Washington, DC 20064
202-526-1669

Washington Opera
Kennedy Center for the Performing Arts
Washington, DC 20566
202-416-7890

FLORIDA

Florida Grand Opera
1200 Coral Way
Miami, FL 33145
305-854-1643

The Opera Guild, Inc.
(Affiliate of the Florida Grand Opera)
Ft. Lauderdale, FL 33312
954-728-9700

Orlando Opera Company
1111 North Orange Avenue
Orlando, FL 32801
407-426-1717

Piccolo Opera Company
24 Del Rio Boulevard
Boca Raton, FL 33432
800-282-3161

Sarasota Opera Association
61 North Pineapple Avenue
Sarasota, FL 34236
941-366-8450

GEORGIA

Augusta Opera
PO Box 3865–Hill Station
Augusta, GA 30904
706-826-4710

HAWAII

Hawaii Opera Theatre
987 Waimanu Street
Honolulu, HI 96814
808-596-0379

ILLINOIS

Chicago Opera Theater
20 East Jackson Boulevard
Chicago, IL 60604
312-663-0555

DuPage Opera Theatre
College of DuPage
Glen Ellyn, IL 60137
630-942-4229

Light Opera Works
927 Noyes
Evanston, IL 60201
847-869-7930

Lyric Opera of Chicago
20 North Wacker Drive
Chicago, IL 60606
312-332-2244

INDIANA

Whitewater Opera Company
1118 East Main Street
Richmond, IN 47274
317-962-7106

IOWA

Des Moines Metro Opera
106 West Boston
Indianola, IA 50125
515-961-6221

KENTUCKY

Kentucky Opera
Kentucky Opera Building
101 South Eighth Street
Louisville, KY 40202
502-584-4500

LOUISIANA

New Orleans Opera Association
333 St. Charles Avenue, Suite 907
New Orleans, LA 70130
504-529-2278

Shreveport Opera
212 Texas Street, Suite 101
Shreveport, LA 71101
318-227-9503

MARYLAND

Annapolis Opera
PO Box 24
Annapolis, MD 21404
410-267-8135

Children's Opera Theater
3203 Pickwick Lane
Chevy Chase, MD 20815
301-656-2442

MASSACHUSETTS

Boston Lyric Opera
45 Franklin Street
Boston, MA 02110
617-542-4912

College Light Opera
Drawer F
Falmouth, MA 02541
508-548-2211

MICHIGAN

Michigan Opera Theater
6519 Second Avenue
Detroit, MI 48202
313-874-7850

Opera Grand Rapids
Waters Building
161 Ottawa NW, Suite 207
Grand Rapids, MI 49503
616-451-2741

Opera Lenawee
Cornelius House
110 South Madison Street
Adrian, MI 49221
517-264-3121

MISSISSIPPI

Gulf Coast Opera
PO Box 7067
Gulfport, MS 39501
601-432-5956

Mississippi Opera Association
Box 1551
Jackson, MS 39205
601-960-1528

MISSOURI

Opera Theatre of St. Louis
PO Box 191910
St. Louis, MO 63119
314-961-0171

MONTANA

InterMountain Opera Association
PO Box 37
Bozeman, MT 59771
406-587-2889

NEBRASKA

Opera Omaha
1613 Farnham Street, Suite 200
Omaha, NE 68102
402-346-4398

NEVADA

Nevada Opera
PO Box 3256
Reno, NV 89505
702-786-4046

NEW HAMPSHIRE

Monadnock Music
PO Box 255
Peterborough, NH 03458
603924-7610

NEW JERSEY

Metro Lyric Opera
40 Ocean Avenue
Box 35
Allenhurst, NJ 07711
908-531-2378

New Jersey State Opera
1020 Broad Street
Newark, NJ 07102
201-623-5757

Queens Opera Association, Inc.
PO Box 1574
Sayreville, NJ 08872
908-390-9473

NEW MEXICO

Santa Fe Opera
PO Box 2408
Santa Fe, NM 87504
505-986-5950

NEW YORK

Amas Musical Theatre, Inc.
1 East 104th Street
New York, NY 10029
212-369-8000

Amato Opera Theatre
319 Bowery
New York, NY 10003
212-228-8200

Ambassadors of Opera and Concerts Worldwide
240 Central Park South, Suite 16M
New York, NY 10019
718-236-7779

American Opera Projects, Inc.
463 Broome Street
New York, NY 10013 212-431-8102

Bronx Opera Company
5 Minerva Place
Bronx, NY 10468
212-385-4209

Chautauquia Opera Company
PO Box 28
Chautauquia, NY 14722
716-357-9014

Concert Royal
235 West 102nd Street, Suite 3D
New York, NY 10025
212-662-8829

Downtown Opera Players
Downtown Art Company
327 East 12th Street
New York, NY 10003
212-732-1201

Glimerglass Opera
Box 191
Route 80 at Allen Lake Road
Cooperstown, NY 13326
607-547-5704

Ithaca Opera Association
109 East Seneca Street
Ithaca, NY 114850
607-272-0168

La Gran Scena Opera Company
c/o Columbia Artists Management, Inc.
165 West 57th Street
New York, Ny 10019
212-841-9500

Lake George Opera Festival
PO Box 2172
28 Sheeman Avenue
Glens Falls, NY 12801
518-793-3858

Light Opera of Manhattan
Playhouse 91
316 East 91st Street
New York, NY 10128
212-831-2000

L'Opera Français de New York
515 West 111th Street, Suite 3F
New York, NY 10025
212-678-0548

Metropolitan Opera
Lincoln Center
New York, NY 10023
212-799-3100

National Music Theater Conference
O'Neill Theater Center
234 West 44th Street, Suite 901
New York, NY 10036
212-382-2790

New York City Opera
c/o Columbia Artists Management, Inc.
165 West 57th Street
New York, NY 10019
212-841-9500

New York Gilbert and Sullivan Players
251 West 91st Street
New York, NY 10024
212-769-1000

Opera Ebony/New York
2109 Broadway, No. 1418
New York, NY 10023
212-877-2110

Opera Northeast, Inc.
PO Box 6700
New York, NY 10128
212-472-2168

Opera Orchestra of New York
239 West 72nd Street, Suite 2R
New York, NY 10023
212-799-1982

Syracuse Opera Company
PO Box 1223
Syracuse, NY 13201
315-475-5915

Touring Concert Opera Company
228 East 80th Street
New York, NY 10021
212-9-988-2542

Tri-Cities Opera
215 Clinton Street
Binghamton, NY 13905
607-729-3444

NORTH CAROLINA

Opera Carolina
345 North College Street, No. 409
Charlotte, NC 28202
704-332-7177

Piedmont Opera Theatre, Inc.
7990 North Point Boulevard, Suite 109
Winston-Salem, NC 27106
910-759-2277

NORTH DAKOTA

Fargo-Moorhead Civic Opera Company
806 Northern Pacific Avenue
Fargo, ND 58102
701-239-4558

OHIO

Cincinnati Opera Association
1241 Elm Street
Cincinnati, OH 45210
513-621-1919

Cleveland Opera
1422 Euclid Avenue, Suite 1052
Cleveland, OH 44115
216-575-0903

Dayton Opera Association
125 East First Street
Dayton, OH 45202
937-228-0662

Lyric Opera Cleveland
PO Box 606198
11300 Juniper Road
Cleveland, OH 44106
216-231-2484

Opera/Columbus
177 Naghten Street
Columbus, OH 43215
614-461-8101

Toledo Opera
1700 North Reynolds Road
Toledo, OH 43615
491-531-5511

OKLAHOMA

Cimarron Circuit Opera
555 South University
PO Box 1085
Norman, OK 73070
405-364-8962

Tulsa Opera
1610 South Boulder Avenue
Tulsa, OK 74119
918-582-4035

OREGON

Eugene Opera
PO Box 11200
Eugene, OR 97440
503-485-3985

Portland Opera Company
1516 Southwest Morrison
Portland, OR 97205
503-241-1407

PENNSYLVANIA

Pennsylvania Opera Theater
1217 Sansom Street
Philadelphia, PA 19107
215-440-9797

Pittsburgh Civic Light Opera
719 Liberty Avenue
Pittsburgh, PA 15222
412-281-3973

Pittsburgh Opera
711 Penn Avenue
Pittsburgh, PA 15222
412-281-0912

SOUTH CAROLINA

Spoleto Festival U.S.A.
PO Box 157
Charleston, SC 29402
803-722-2764

TENNESSEE

**Chattanooga Symphony and Opera
Association**
630 Chestnut Street
Chattanooga, TN 37402
615-267-8583

Knoxville Opera
PO Box 16
Knoxville, TN 37901
423-524-0795

TEXAS

Fort Worth Opera
3505 West Lancaster
Fort Worth, TX 76107
817-731-0833

Houston Grand Opera
Wortham Theater Center
510 Preston Street, Suite 500
Houston, TX 77002
713-546-0200

UTAH

Utah Opera Company
50 West 200 South
Salt Lake City, UT 84101
801-323-6868

VIRGINIA

**Martinsville-Henry County Festival
of Opera**
Box 406
South College Street
Martinsville, VA 24112
703-632-5861

Opera Theatre of Northern Virginia
2700 South Lang Street
Arlington, VA 22206
703-549-5039

Wolf Trap Opera Company
1624 Trap Road
Vienna, VA 22182
703-255-1924

WASHINGTON

Seattle Opera Company
PO Box 9248
Seattle, WA 98109
206-443-4700

WISCONSIN

Madison Opera
333 Glenway Street
Madison, WI 53705
608-238-8085

APPENDIX XV
CANADIAN OPERA COMPANIES

The following is a list of selected opera companies in Canada. Names, addresses and phone numbers are included for each. Use this listing to obtain general information, locate internships and inquire about auditions and job possibilities. Companies are listed alphabetically by province.

ALBERTA

Edmonton Opera Association
10232-112th Street, No. 320
Edmonton, AB T5K 1M4 Canada
403-424-4040

BRITISH COLUMBIA

Pacific Opera Victoria
1316B Government Street
Victoria, BC V8W 1Y8 Canada
250-385-0222

MANITOBA

Manitoba Opera Association
393 Portage Avenue
Box 31027
Winnepeg, MB R3B 3K9 Canada
204-942-7479

ONTARIO

Canadian Opera Company
227 Front Street East
Toronto, ON M5A 1EB Canada
416-363-6671

Opera Hamilton
100 King Street West, Suite 200
Hamilton, ON L8P 1A2 Canada
905-527-7627

QUEBEC

L'Opéra de Montréal
260 Boulevard de Maisonneuve Ouest
Montreal, QC AH2X 1Y9 Canada
514-985-2222

APPENDIX XVI
ARTS COUNCILS AND AGENCIES

The following is a list of federal, state and regional arts councils and agencies. Names, addresses and phone numbers are included for each. Use this list to obtain general industry information, find out about state and federal programs and locate internships, fellowships and grants.

FEDERAL

Americans for the Arts
1000 Vermont Avenue NW
Washington, DC 20005
202-371-2830

National Assembly of State Arts Agencies
1029 Vermont Avenue NW
Second Floor
Washington, DC 20005
202-347-6352

National Endowment for the Arts
1100 Pennsylvania Avenue NW
Washington, DC 20506
202-682-5400

REGIONAL

Arts Midwest
Hennepin Center for the Arts
528 Hennepin Avenue, Suite 310
Minneapolis, MN 55403
612-341-0755

Consortium for Pacific Arts and Cultures
2141C Atherton Road
Honolulu, HI 96822
808-946-7381

Mid-America Arts Alliance
912 Baltimore Avenue, Suite 700
Kansas City, MO 64105
816-421-1388

Mid Atlantic Arts Foundation
22 Light Street, No. 330
Baltimore, MD 21202
410-539-6656

New England Foundation for the Arts
330 Congress Street, Sixth Floor
Boston, MA 02210
617-951-0010

Southern Arts Federation
181 Fourteenth Street NE, Suite 400
Atlanta, GA 30309
404-874-7244

Western States Arts Federation
1543 Champa Street, Suite 220
Denver, CO 80202
303-629-1166

STATE

Alabama State Council on the Arts
1 Dexter Avenue
Montgomery, AL 36130
334-242-4076

Alaska State Council on the Arts
411 West Fourth Avenue, Suite 1E
Anchorage, AK 99501
907-269-6610

Arizona Commission on the Arts
417 West Roosevelt
Phoenix, AZ 85003
602-255-5882

Arkansas Arts Council
1500 Tower Building
323 Center Street
Little Rock, AR 72201
501-324-9766

California Arts Council
1300 I Street, No. 930
Sacramento, CA 95814
916-322-6555

Colorado Council on the Arts
750 Pennsylvania Street
Denver, CO 80203
303-894-2617

Connecticut Commission on the Arts
755 Main Street
Gold Building
Hartford, CT 06103
860-566-4770

Delaware Division of the Arts State Office Building
820 North French Street
Wilmington, DE 19801
302-577-3540

District of Columbia Commission on the Arts and Humanities
410 Eighth Street NW
Washington, DC 20004
202-724-5613

(Florida) Division of Cultural Affairs
Florida Department of State
The Capitol
Tallahassee, FL 32399
850-487-2980

Georgia Council for the Arts
530 Means Street NW, Suite 115
Atlanta, GA 30318
404-651-7920

(Hawaii) State Foundation on Culture and the Arts
44 Merchant Street
Honolulu, HI 96813
808-586-0300

Idaho Commission on the Arts
PO Box 83720
Boise, ID 83720
208-334-2119

Illinois Arts Council
State of Illinois Center
100 West Randolph, Suite 10-500
Chicago, IL 60601
312-814-6750

Indiana Arts Commission
402 West Washington Street, Room 072
Indianapolis, IN 46204
317-232-1268

Iowa Arts Council
600 East Locust
State Capitol Complex
Des Moines, IA 50319
515-281-4451

Kansas Arts Commission
Jayhawk Tower
700 Jackson, Suite 1004
Topeka, KS 66603
913-296-3335

Kentucky Arts Council
31 Fountain Place
Frankfort, KY 40601
502-564-3757

Louisiana Division of the Arts
1051 North Third Street
PO Box 44247
Baton Rouge, LA 70804
225-342-8180

Maine Arts Commission
55 Capitol Street
State House Station 25
Augusta, ME 04333
207-287-2724

Maryland State Arts Council
601 North Howard Street, First Floor
Baltimore, MD 21201
410-333-8232

Massachusetts Cultural Council
120 Boylston Street
Boston, MA 02116
617-727-3668

**Michigan Council for Arts and
Cultural Affairs**
1200 Sixth Street
Executive Plaza
Detroit, MI 48226

Minnesota State Arts Board
Park Square Court
400 Sibley Street, Suite 200
St. Paul, MN 55101
612-215-1600

Mississippi Arts Commission
239 North Lamar Street, Second Floor
Jackson, MS 39201
601-359-6030

Missouri State Council on the Arts
Wainwright Office Complex
111 North Seventh Street, Suite 105
St. Louis, MO 63101
314-340-6845

Montana Arts Council
316 North Park Avenue, Room 252
Helena, MT 59620
406-444-6430

Nebraska Arts Council
The Joslyn Castle Carriage House
3838 Davenport Street
Omaha, NE 68131
402-595-2122

Nevada State Council on the Arts
Capitol Complex
602 North Curry Street
Carson City, NV 89710
702-687-6680

**New Hampshire State Council on the
Arts**
40 North Main Street
Concord, NH 03301
603-271-2789

New Jersey State Council on the Arts
20 West State Street
Trenton, NJ 08625-0306
609-292-6130

New Mexico Arts Division
228 East Palace Avenue
Santa Fe, NM 87501
505-827-6490

New York State Council on the Arts
915 Broadway
New York, NY 10010
212-387-7000

North Carolina Arts Council
Department of Cultural Resources
Raleigh, NC 27601
919-733-2821

North Dakota Council on the Arts
418 East Broadway Avenue, Suite 70
Bismarck, ND 58501
701-328-3954

Ohio Arts Council
727 East Main Street
Columbus, OH 43205
614-466-2613

Oklahoma Arts Council
PO Box 52001-2001
Oklahoma City, OK 73152
405-521-2931

Oregon Arts Commission
775 Summer Street NE
Salem, OR 97310
503-986-0082

**Pennsylvania Council on the Arts,
Commonwealth of**
Finance Building
Room 216A
Harrisburg, PA 17120
717-787-6883

Rhode Island State Council on the Arts
95 Cedar Street, Suite 103
Providence, RI 02903
401-277-3880

South Carolina Arts Commission
1800 Gervais Street
Columbia, SC 29201
803-734-8696

South Dakota Arts Council
Office of Arts
800 Governors Drive
Pierre, SD 57501-2294
605-773-3131

Tennessee Arts Commission
Citizens Plaza
401 Charlotte Avenue
Nashville, TN 37243-0780
615-741-1701

Texas Commission on the Arts
PO Box 13406
Capitol Station
Austin, TX 78711
512-463-5535

Utah Arts Council
617 East South Temple Street
Salt Lake City, UT 84102
801-533-5895

Vermont Arts Council
136 State Street
Montpelier, VT 05633-6001
802-828-3291

Virginia Commission for the Arts
223 Governor Street
Richmond, VA 23219
804-225-3132

Virgin Islands Council on the Arts
41-42 Norre Gade
PO Box 103
St. Thomas, VI 00802
809-774-5984

Washington State Arts Commission
234 East Eighth Avenue
PO Box 42675
Olympia, WA 98504
360-753-3860

**West Virginia Division of Culture and
History**
Arts and Humanities Section
1900 Kanawha Boulevard East
Capitol Complex
Charleston, WV 25305
304-558-0220

Wisconsin Arts Board
101 East Wilson Street
Madison, WI 53702
608-266-0190

Wyoming Arts Council
2320 Capitol Avenue
Cheyenne, WY 82002
307-777-7742

APPENDIX XVII
BIBLIOGRAPHY

A. BOOKS

There are thousands of books written on all aspects of theater and the performing arts. The books listed below are separated into general categories. The subject matter in many of the books overlaps into other categories.

These books can be found in bookstores or libraries. If your local library does not have one you want to read, you can ask your librarian to order it for you through the inter-library loan system.

This list is meant as a starting point. For other books that might interest you, look in the performing arts section of bookstores and libraries. You can also check *Books In Print* (found in the reference section of libraries) for other books on the subject.

ACTING AND DIRECTING

Bartlow, Arthur. *The Director's Voice: Twenty-One Interviews.* New York: Theatre Communications Group, 1988.

Basting, Anne D. *The Stages of Age: Performing Age in Contemporary American Culture.* Ann Arbor: University of Michigan Press, 1998.

Epstein, Helen. *Joe Papp: An American Life.* New York: Da Capo Press, 1996.

Gaines, Ann G. *Women in Entertainment and Performing Arts.* Broomall, Penn.: Chelsea House, 1998.

Grandstaff, Russell J. *Acting and Directing.* Lincolnwood, Ill.: National Textbook Company, 1989.

Greenspon, Jaq. *Acting (VGM Career Portraits).* Lincolnwood, Ill.: VGM Career Horizons, 1996.

Lee, Josephine. *Performing Asian America: Race and Ethnicity on the Contemporary Stage.* Philadelphia: Temple University Press, 1998.

Perry, John. *Encyclopedia of Acting Techniques.* Cincinnati: F & W Publications, 1997.

Stevens, Jon. *Actors Turned Directors: On Eliciting the Best Performance from an Actor and Other Secrets of Successful Directing.* Beverly Hills: Silman-James Press, 1997.

Taylor, Don. *Directing Plays.* New York: Theatre Arts Books, 1997.

BALLET

Lee, Sandra. *At the Ballet: Onstage, Backstage.* New York: Universe Publishing, 1998.

Medova, Marie-Laure. *Ballet for Beginners.* New York: Sterling Publishing, 1997.

Nagrin, Daniel. *The Six Questions: Acting Techniques for Dance Performance.* Pittsburgh: University of Pittsburgh Press, 1997.

CLASSICAL MUSICIANS AND ORCHESTRAS

American Symphony Orchestra League. *Policies and Procedures of Orchestra Administration: A Survey and Study by the American Symphony Orchestra League.* Washington, D.C.: American Symphony Orchestra League, 1992.

Christlieb, Don. *Recollections of a First Chair Bassoonist: 52 Years in the Hollywood Studio Orchestras.* Sherman Oaks, Calif.: Chritlieb Products, 1996.

Craven, Robert R. *Symphony Orchestras of the World.* Westport, Conn.: Greenwood Publishing Group, 1987.

Handy, D. Antoinette. *Black Women in American Bands and Orchestras.* Latham, Md.: Scarecrow Press, 1998.

Kornblut, Jane S. *The Gold Book, 1996–97: A Sourcebook of Successful and Creative Orchestra Fundraising, Education, Ticket Sales, and Service Projects.* Washington, D.C.: American Symphony Orchestra League, 1997.

Myers, Margaret. *Blowing Her Own Trumpet: European Ladies' Orchestras and Other Women Musicians in Sweden, 1870–1950.* Philadelphia: Coronet Books, 1993.

Oppenheim, Lois. *Making Music in Looking Glass Land: A Guide to Survival and Business Skills for the Classical Musician.* New York: Concert Artists Guild, 1993.

COMEDY

Double, Oliver. *Stand-Up: On Being a Comedian.* Portsmouth, N.H.: Heinemann, 1997.

EDUCATION

Peterson's Staff. *Professional Degree Programs in the Visual and Performing Arts.* Princeton, N.J.: Peterson, 1998.

INTERNATIONAL

Schneider, Thereseedt. *Musical America, 1998: International Directory of the Performing Arts.* Hightstown, N.J.: Primedia Information, 1997.

MAKING A LIVING IN MUSIC

Baker, Bob. *Making Money Right Now in the Music Business.* San Diego: Rockpress Publishing, 1995.

Buttwinick, Marty. *How to Make a Living as a Musician: So You Never Have to Have a Day Job Again.* Glendale, Calif.: Sonato Publishing, 1994.

Cosola, Mary. *Independent Working Musician: A Complete Guide to Do-It-Yourself Success in the Music Industry.* Overland Park, Kans.: Intertec Publishing Corporation, 1998.

Field, Shelly. *Career Opportunities in the Music Industry.* 3d ed. New York: Facts On File, 1995.

Livingston, Robert A. *Music Business Inside Out.* LaPlace, Ill.: G L G L C Music, 1997.

Newsam, Barbara. *Making Money Teaching Music.* Cincinnati: F & W Publications, 1995.

Olsen, Eric. *This Business of Networking in the Music Industry.* New York: Watson-Guptill Publications, 1997.

Passman, Donald S. *All You Need to Know About the Music Business.* New York: Simon & Schuster, 1997.

Steinberg, Irwin. *Understanding the Music Business: A Comprehensive View.* New York: IHS Corporation, 1997.

Stephan, Garree. *How to Make Money Writing, Performing and Teaching Music: For All Musicians.* Jenison, Mich.: Stephan Publications, 1998.

MUSIC AND THEATER CRITICISM

Hornby, Richard. *Mad About Theatre.* New York: Applause Theatre Book Publishers, 1996.

Stefanova-Peteva, Kalina. *Who Calls the Shots on the New York Stages?* Newark, N.J.: Gordon and Breach, 1993.

Wingell, Richard. *Writing About Music.* Paramus, N.J.: Prentice Hall, 1996.

Wolter, Jugen C. *The Dawning of American Drama: American Dramatic Criticism, 1746–1915.* Westport, Conn.: Greenwood Publishing Group, 1993.

MUSIC PUBLISHING AND LAW

Hurst, Walter E. *How to Be a Music Publisher.* Los Angeles: Borden Publishing Company, 1981.

———. *How to Manage Talent.* Hollywood: Seven Arts Press, 1985.

———. *The Music Industry Book: Protect Yourself Before You Lose Your Rights and Royal Ties.* Hollywood: Seven Arts Press, 1981.

McPherson, Brian. *Get It in Writing: A Musicians Guide to Music Law.* Milwaukee: Hal Leonard Corporation, 1996.

Schulenberg, Richard. *Legal Aspects of the Music Industry.* New York: Watson-Guptill Publications, 1998.

Singer, Dana. *Stage Writers Handbook: A Complete Business Guide for Playwrights, Composers, Lyricists and Librettists.* New York: Theatre Communications Group, 1997.

Whitsett, Tim. *Music Publishing: The Real Road to Music Business Success.* Emeryville, Calif.: Cardinal Business Media, Music & Entertainment, 1997.

MUSIC THERAPY

Andrews, Ted. *Music Therapy for Non-Musicians.* Cedar Grove, Tenn.: Life Magic Enterprises, 1997.

Bruscia, Kenneth E. *Defining Music Therapy.* Lower Village Gilsum, N.H.: Barcelona Publishing, 1989.

Clair, Alicia Ann. *Therapeutic Uses of Music with Older Adults.* Baltimore: Health Professions Press, 1996.

Gardner, Kay. *Sounding the Inner Landscape: Music as Medicine.* Boston: Element, 1997.

Holland, John. *The Nature of Music: For the Performing Musician.* Lexington, Mass.: American Sound Press, 1990.

Lingerman, Hal A. *The Healing Energies of Music.* Wheaton, Ill.: Quest Books, 1995.

OPERA

Bourne, Joyce. *Who's Who in Opera: A Guide to Opera Characters.* New York: Oxford University Press, 1998.

Camner, James. *Opera Stars, 1970s–1990s: 200 Photographs by Winnie Klotz.* London: Dover Publications, 1998.

Janssen, Johannes. *Opera.* Haupauge, N.Y.: Barron's Educational Series, 1998.

Lee, M. Owen. *A Season of Opera: From Orpheus to Ariadne.* Buffalo: University of Toronto Press, 1998.

Martin, George. *Twentieth Century Opera: A Guide.* New York: Limelight Editions, 1998.

PLAYWRIGHTING

Catron, Louis E. *The Elements of Playwriting.* New York: Macmillan, 1994.

Hatcher, Jeffrey. *The Art and Craft of Playwriting.* Cincinnati: F & W Publications, 1996.

Partnow, Elaine, and Hyatt, Lesley. *Female Dramatists: Profiles of Women Playwrights from the Middle Ages to the Present Day.* New York: Facts On File, 1998.

Seger, Linda. *Creating Unforgettable Characters.* New York: Henry Holt, 1990.

Sweet, Jeff. *The Dramatist's Toolkit: The Craft of the Working Playwright.* Portsmouth, N.H.: Heinemann, 1993.

PUBLICITY

DeFrancesco, John. *The Common Sense Guide to Publicity: Practical Advice on How to Use the Power of Publicity.* Chicago: DeFrancesco/Goodfriend Public Relations, 1996.

Kingdon, Lorraine B. *Take the Mystery Out of Media: Make Your Publicity Newsworthy.* Tucson, Ariz.: Communication Skills Institute, 1994.

Pettigrew, Jim. *The Billboard Book of Music Publicity.* New York: Watson-Guptill Publications, 1997.

Smith, Jeanette. *The New Publicity Kit.* New York: John Wiley & Sons, 1995.

Yale, David R. *Publicity and Media Relations Checklist: 59 Proven Checklists to Save Time, with Attention, and Maximize Exposure with Every Public Relations and Publicity Contact.* Lincolnwood, Ill.: N T C Contemporary Publishing, 1995.

SONGWRITING

Braheny, John. *The Craft and Business of Songwriting.* Cincinnati: Writers Digest, 1995.

Davis, Dee. *Looking for Number 1: Portraits and Passions of Nashville Songwriters.* Nashville, Tenn.: Eggman Publishing, 1994.

Davis, Sheila. *The Craft of Lyric Writing.* Cincinnati: F & W Publications, 1985.

———. *The Songwriter's Idea Book: 40 Strategies to Excite Your Imagination, Help You Design Distinctive Songs, and Keep Your Creative Flow.* Cincinnati: Writers Digest, 1996.

Gorow, Ron. *Hearing and Writing Music: Practical Training for Today's Musician.* Studio City, Calif.: September Publishing, 1998.

Horton, Tara, ed. *1999 Songwriter's Market.* Cincinnati: F & W Publications, 1998.

Jordan, Barbara L. *Songwriters Playground: Innovative Exercises in Creative Songwriting.* Boston: Creative Music Marketing, 1993.

Josefs, Jai. *Writing Music for Hit Songs: Including Songs from the '90s.* New York: Macmillan, 1996.

Makinson, R. B. *Songwriters and Lyricists Handbook.* Brooklyn: R. B. Makinson, 1996.

Stewart, Johnill. *Write from the Heart.* Buckingham, Va.: Crow Press, 1991.

Stone, Cliffie. *Everything You Always Wanted to Know About Songwriting But Didn't Know Who to Ask.* North Hollywood: Showdown Enterprises, 1992.

Tucker, Susan. *The Soul of a Writer: Intimate Interviews with Successful Songwriters.* Nashville, Tenn.: Journey Publishing Company, 1996.

Webb, Jimmy. *Tunesmith: Inside the Act of Songwriting.* New York: Hyperion, 1998.

STAGECRAFT AND DESIGN

Cunningham, Glen. *Stage Lighting Revealed: A Design and Execution Handbook.* Cincinnati: F & W Publications, 1993.

Dearing, Shirley; Middleton, Pat; and Zapel, Arthur L. *Elegantly Frugal Costumes!: The Poor Man's Do-It-Yourself Costume Maker's Guide.* Colorado Springs, Colo.: Meriwether Publishing, 1992.

Glerum, Jay O. *Stage Rigging Handbook.* Carbondale, Southern Illinois University Press, 1997.

Ionazzi, Daniel A. *The Stagecraft Handbook.* Cincinnati: F & W Publications, 1996.

———. *The Stage Management Handbook.* Cincinnati: F & W Publications, 1992.

James, Thurston. *The Prop Builder's Molding and Casting Handbook.* Cincinnati: F & W Publications, 1990.

Kidd, Mary T. *Stage Costume Step-By-Step.* Cincinnati: F & W Publications, 1996.

Oddey, Alison. *Devising Theatre: A Practical and Theoretical Handbook.* New York: Routledge, 1996.

Reid, Francis. *The Stage Lighting Handbook.* London: A & C Black, 1996.

Swinfield, Rosemarie. *Period Make-Up for the Stage: Step by Step.* Cincinnati: F & W Publications, 1997.

Walne, Graham, and Aveline, Joe. *Effects for the Theatre.* New York: Drama Publishers, 1995.

B. PERIODICALS

Magazines, newspapers, membership bulletins and newsletters are an essential tool for keeping yourself informed and current on topics related to your field of interest. They are also an important source of information about job opportunities.

This is a list of some of the most important trade periodicals and should serve as a starting point. Check your local library and newspaper/magazine stores with a broad selection for other periodicals of interest.

CHAMBER MUSIC

Chamber Music
Chamber Music America
305 Seventh Avenue
New York, NY 10001

CIRCUS AND MAGIC

Circus Magazine
6 West 18th Street
New York, NY 10011

Magic
7380 South Eastern Avenue
Suite 124-179
Las Vegas, NV 89123

CLASSICAL MUSIC

BBC Music Magazine
80 Wood Lane
London, England W12 OTT

CRITICS AND REVIEWS

Entertainment Weekly
Time, Inc.
1675 Broadway
New York, NY 10019

Rolling Stone
1290 Avenue of the Americas
New York, NY 10104

Victory Music Review
PO Box 7515
Bonney Lake, WA 98390

DANCE AND CHOREOGRAPHY

Attitude: The Dancers Magazine
1040 Park Plaza
Brooklyn, NY 11213

Ballet News
The Metropolitan Opera Guild, Inc.
70 Lincoln Center Plaza
New York, NY 10023

Ballet Review
46 Morton Street
New York, NY 10014

Dance Chronicle
270 Madison Avenue
New York, NY 10016

Dance Ink
145 Central Park West
New York, NY 10023

Dance Magazine
33 West 60th Street
New York, NY 10023

Dance View
PO Box 34435
Martin Luther King Station
Washington, DC 20043

Dancing Through Life
PO Box 15087
Washington, DC 20003

Studies in Dance History
PO Box 380
Pennington, NJ 08534

DANCE THERAPY

American Journal of Dance Therapy
233 Spring Street
New York, NY 10013

HALLS, ARENAS, CLUBS AND OTHER VENUES

Amusement Business
Billboard Publications, Inc.
PO Box 24970
Nashville, TN 37202

Music Clubs Magazine
1336 North Delaware Street
Indianapolis, IN 46202

MUSICIANS

American Organist
American Guild of Organists
475 Riverside Drive, No. 1260
New York, NY 10115

Down Beat
180 West Park Avenue
Elmhurst, IL 60126

Guitar Player Magazine
Miller Freeman, Inc.
411 Borel Avenue, Suite 100
San Mateo, CA 94402

Guitar Review
40 West 25th Street
New York, NY 10010

Hit Parader
210 Route 4 East, Suite 401
Paramus, NJ 07652

How to Play Guitar
Miller Freeman, Inc.
411 Borel Avenue, Suite 100
San Mateo, CA 94402

International Musician
American Federation of Musicians
1501 Broadway
New York, NY 10036

Jam Magazine
PO Box 151720
Altamonte Springs, FL 32715

Modern Drummer
12 Old Bridge Road
Cedar Grove, NJ 07009

Musician
Billboard Publications
1515 Broadway
New York, NY 10036

Music Trades Magazine
80 West Street
Englewood, NJ 07631

Strings
PO Box 767
San Anselmo, CA 94979

OPERA

Opera Journal
National Opera Association
Northwestern University
  School of Music
711 Elgin Road
Evanston, IL 60208

Opera News
Metropolitan Opera Guild
70 Lincoln Center Plaza
New York, NY 10023

ORCHESTRAS

Symphony Magazine
1156 15th Street NW
Washington, DC 20005

PERFORMING ARTS—GENERAL

Afterimages
PO Box 743
Falls Church, VA 22040

Arts Management
110 Riverside Drive
New York, NY 10024

BCA News
Business Committee for the Arts, Inc.
1775 Broadway, Suite 510
New York, NY 10019

Directory of Theatre Facilities in Colleges and Universities: U.S. and Canada
CMS Publications, Inc.
PO Box 8208
Missoula, MT 59807

IEG Sponsorship Report
IEG, Inc.
640 North LaSalle, Suite 600
Chicago, IL 60610

Inside Arts
Association of Performing Arts Presenters
1112 16th Street NW, Suite 400
Washington, DC 20036

International Arts Manager
Arts Publishing International, Ltd.
4 Assam Street
London, England E1 7QS

Journal of Arts Management Law and Society
1319 18th Street NW
Washington, DC 20036

Lively Foundation International Newsletter
2565 Washington Street
San Francisco, CA 94115

Performing Arts Performing Arts Network
10350 Santa Monica Boulevard
Los Angeles, CA 90025

Performing Arts Journal
The John Hopkins University Press
PO Box 260–Village Station
New York, NY 10014

The Source
594 Broadway, Suite 510
New York, NY 10012

PUBLIC RELATIONS, PUBLICITY AND PROMOTION—GENERAL

Contacts
CAP Communications Associates
35-20 Broadway
Astoria, NY 11106

PR Aids' Party Line
35 Sutton Place
New York, NY 10022

Public Relations Journal
PRSA
33 Irving Place
New York, NY 10003

TALENT AND WRITING

American Songwriter
121 17th Avenue South
Nashville, TN 37203

ASCAP in Action
1 Lincoln Plaza
New York, NY 10023

BMI: The Many Worlds of Music
320 West 57th Street
New York, NY 10019

Down Beat
180 West Park Avenue
Elmhurst, IL 60126

Songwriters Market
1507 Dana Avenue
Cincinnati, OH 45207

TEACHING

American Music Teacher
441 Vine Street, Suite 505
Cincinnati, OH 45202

Dance Teacher Now
PO Box 18869
Raleigh, NC 27619

Music Educators Journal
Music Educators National Conference
806 Robert Fulton Drive
Reston, VA 22091

Teaching Music
Journal of Research in Music Education
Music Educators National Conference
806 Robert Fulton Drive
Reston, VA 22091

THEATER

American Theater
355 Lexington Avenue
New York, NY 10017

Callboard
657 Mission Street, No. 402
San Francisco, CA 94105

The Drama Review
MIT Press Journals
5 Cambridge Center
Cambridge, MA 03242

Dramatics Magazine
3368 Central Parkway
Cincinnati, OH 45225

Dramatists Guild Quarterly
234 West 44th Street
New York, NY 10036

Dramatists Sourcebook
Theatre Communications Sourcebooks
355 Lexington Avenue
New York, NY 10017

Institute of Outdoor Drama Newsletter
3240 Nations Bank Plaza
Chapel Hill, NC 27599

New York On Stage
1501 Broadway, Room 2110
New York, NY 10036

Theater Magazine
222 York Street
New Haven, CT 06520

Theatre Directory
Theatre Communications Group
355 Lexington Avenue
New York, NY 10017

Theatrical Index
Price Berkley
888 Eighth Avenue
New York, NY 10019

THEATER—BUSINESS AND ADMINISTRATION

Box Office Magazine
RLD Publishing Company
6640 Sunset Boulevard
Hollywood, CA 20028

THEATER—PRODUCTION

DGA News
Directors Guild of America
7920 Sunset Boulevard
Los Angeles, CA 90036

Lighting Dimensions
32 West 18th Street
New York, NY 10011

Stage Directions
3101 Poplarwood Court, Suite 310
Raleigh, NC 27604

Stages
Curtains, Inc.
301 West 45th Street
New York, NY 10036

Theatre Crafts International
32 West 18th Street
New York, NY 10011

Theatre Design and Technology
10 West 19th Street, Suite 5A
New York, NY 10011

TOURING

Performance Magazine
2929 Cullen
Fort Worth, TX 76107

TRADES

Backstage
1515 Broadway
New York, NY 10036

Back Stage West
BPI Communications
5055 Wilshire Boulevard
Los Angeles, CA 90036

Billboard
Billboard Publications
1515 Broadway
New York, NY 10036

Cashbox
51 East Eighth Street
New York, NY 10003

Daily Variety
5700 Wilshire Boulevard, Suite 120
Los Angeles, CA 90036

Hollywood Reporter
5055 Wilshire Boulevard
Los Angeles, CA 90036

Show Business News
244 Madison Avenue
New York, NY 10016

Variety
249 West 17th Street
New York, NY 10011

APPENDIX XVIII
GLOSSARY

The following is a list of abbreviations, acronyms and industry jargon that will prove helpful to individuals interested in theater and the performing arts. Entries are listed alphabetically.

AAAA	Associated Actors and Artists of America
AAMT	American Association for Music Therapy
AATE	American Alliance for Theatre and Education
ACA	American Composers Alliance
ACDA	American Choral Directors Association
ACDFA	American College Dance Festival Association
ACF	American Choral Foundation
ACFA	Associated Councils for the Arts
ACM	Academy of Country Music
ACSTA	American Center for Stanislavski Theatre Art
ACTF	American Conservatory Theatre Foundation
ADF	American Dance Festival
ADG	American Dance Guild
ADTA	American Dance Therapy Association
ADTR	Academy of Dance Therapists Registered
Advance	A prepayment of monies against future royalties or fees
AE	Account Executive
AEA	Actors' Equity Association
Affiliate	A broadcast station that belongs to a network; for example, WABC in New York and KABC in Los Angeles are both affiliates of the ABC network
AFM	American Federation of Musicians
AFT	American Federation of Teachers
AFTRA	American Federation of Television and Radio Artists
Agent	The person who represents actors and actresses to help them obtain jobs
AGMA	American Guild of Musical Artists
AGO	American Guild of Organists
AGVA	American Guild of Variety Artists
AIOF	American Israel Opera Foundation
AMA	American Marketing Association
AMC	American Music Center
AMC	American Music Conference
AMFA	American Music Festival Association
AMIS	American Musical Instrument Society
AMS	American Musicological Society
AMSA	American Music Scholarship Association
Angel	A person who gives money or backs a theatrical production
ANTA	American National Theatre and Academy
APT	American Place Theatre
Apprentice	A person just beginning to learn a skill
Arbitron Ratings	A television and radio rating service that indicates what percentage of people are viewing or listening to a particular show or station. Commercial rates are often based on these ratings
ARC	Art Resources in Collaboration
Arrangement	The adaptation of a song for a performance or a recording
A.R.T./NY	Alliance of Resident Theatres/New York
AS	Actors Studio
ASA	Acoustical Society of America
ASCAP	American Society of Composers and Publishers
ASJA	American Society of Journalists and Authors, Inc.
ASMA	American Society of Music Arrangers
ASOL	American Symphony Orchestra League
Assignment	The transfer of rights from a songwriter to publisher
ASTR	American Society for Theatre Research
ATAFY	American Theatre Arts for Youth
ATAS	Academy of Television Arts and Sciences
ATCA	American Theatre Critics Association
ATHE	Association for Theatre in Higher Education

ATOS	American Theatre Organ Society
ATPAM	Association of Theatrical Press Agents and Managers, AFL-CIO
AUDELCO	Audience Development Committee
AVS	American Viola Society
AWRT	American Women in Radio and Television
AWTF	American Writers Theatre Foundation
B & W Glossy	Used by publicists, press agents and public relations people when putting together press kits. It is an 8 x 10 glossy photograph of their client that can be used for reproduction purposes in newspapers or magazines
BBAA	Big Band Academy of America
BFA	Bilingual Foundation of the Arts
Bio	A biography of a client put together by press agents, publicists or public relations people
Billing	The position, size and/or order of an actress's or actor's name on a marquee, in advertisements and in programs
Blocking	The on-stage movements suggested by the director for actors or actresses in a theatrical production
BMI	Broadcast Music, Inc.
Book	A collection of samples done by someone in either the art or writing field to show prospective employers an applicant's potential. Also known as a portfolio
Booking Agent	Business representative responsible for seeking and securing venues for performers and entertainers
BTF	Ballet Theatre Foundation
CA:APVE	Chorus America: Association of Professional Vocal Ensembles
CAG	Catholic Actors Guild of America
CAG	Concert Artists Guild
Camera-ready	The condition of everything in an ad being ready for a printer to produce a print of the advertising. Nothing has to be retouched
Campaign	A series of advertisements used to promote and advertise a product or group of products
Casting	Choosing and hiring the actors and actresses to star in a theatrical production, television show or movie
Catalog	The collection of songs to which a music publisher owns the rights
CCA	Cecchetti Council of America

CDSSA	Country Dance and Song Society of America
CESA	Cultural Exchange Society of America
CG	Choreographers Guild
Charts	Lists of current hits, found in the trade magazines
Circulation	The number of copies of a newspaper or magazine that are distributed
CMA	Chamber Music America
CMA	Country Music Association
CMS	College Music Society
CNDW	Coalition for National Dance Week
Commission	A percentage of artist's fee paid to agents and managers for representing the artist's interests
Contractor	The person who hires session musicians for a recording session
Copyright	A legal protection granted to an author or composer for the exclusive rights to his or her work
Costumes	Clothing and accessories worn by actors and actresses to help them look the part that they are playing
Copywriter	The person who develops the words used in advertisements, brochures, marketing and promotional pieces
CORD	Congress on Research in Dance
CORST	Council of Resident Summer Theatres
COS	Central Opera Service
CPM	Conference of Personal Managers
CSA	Casting Society of America
CT	Choreographers Theatre
CT	Composers Theatre
DCA	Dance Critics Association
DD	Drama Desk
DEA	Dance Educators of America
Demo	Demonstration tape, CD or videotape used for selling a tune, act, group or the like
DFA	Dance Films Association
DG	Dramatists Guild
DGA	Directors Guild of America
DMF	Dance Magazine Foundation
DNB	Dance Notation Bureau
Dressing the House	A method of selling tickets in a box office that makes a theater look fuller than it really is
Dress Rehearsal	The rehearsal in a theatrical production in which everything, including costumes, makeup, lighting, sound and special effects are tried out just as if the

	play was actually going on in front of an audience
DT	The Drama Tree
DTW	Dance Theater Workshop
EAGA	Episcopal Actor's Guild of America
ECPC	Ethnic Cultural Preservation Council
EDLA	Exotic Dancers League of America
EOMTC	Eugene O'Neill Memorial Theater Center
Equity	Actors' Equity Association
FC	Friars Club
FCC	Federal Communications Commission
FED	Foundation for Ethnic Dance
FFD	Fund for Dance
FTS	Ford's Theatre Society
GAG	Graphic Artists Guild
Gig	A job for musicians
GMA	Gospel Music Association
GMWA	Gospel Music Workshop of America
HAI	Hospital Audiences
HAU	Hebrew Actors Union
HCC	Hollywood Comedy Club
Hype	Extensive publicity used to promote people, products or events. Hype is not always true
IAAM	International Association of Auditorium Managers
IAM	Institute of the American Musical
IASTA	Institute for Advanced Studies in the Theatre Arts
IASTE	International Alliance of Theatrical Stage Employees and Moving Picture Machine Operators of the U.S. and Canada
IAU	Italian Actors Union
IBEW	International Brotherhood of Electrical Workers
ICSOM	International Conference of Symphony and Opera Musicians
IDEA	International Dance-Exercise Association
IOD	Institute of Outdoor Drama
IPRA	International Public Relations Association
ITI/US	International Theatre Institute of the United States
ITS	Italian Thespian Society
Jingle	The music in a commercial advertisement
KCA	Kentucky Callers Association

LAPT	League of American Theatres and Producers
LHAT	League of Historic American Theatres
Librettist	A person who writes librettos
Libretto	The book in an opera
LIMS	Laban/Bartenieff Institute of Movement Studies
Literary Agent	The person who tries to sell a playwright's work
LOBTP	League of Off Broadway Theatres and Producers
Local	The local affiliation in a particular geographic area of a national or international union
LOPTTP	League of Professional Theatre Training Programs
LORT	League of Resident Theaters
LOS	Little Orchestra Society
LSF	Lloyd Shaw Foundation
Lyrics	The words of a song
Matinee	An afternoon performance of a theatrical production
MENC	Music Educators National Conference
MOA	Metropolitan Opera Association
MOG	Metropolitan Opera Guild
MTC	Meet the Composer
MTNA	Music Teachers National Association
NAB	National Association of Broadcasters
NABET	National Association of Broadcast Employees and Technicians
NADSA	National Association of Dramatic and Speech Arts
NAPM	National Academy of Popular Music
NARAS	National Academy of Recording Arts and Sciences
NAS	National Academy of Songwriters
NASD	National Association of Schools of Dance
NASM	National Association of Schools of Music
NAST	National Association of Schools of Theatre
NATAS	National Academy of Television Arts and Sciences
NCHC	National Clogging and Hoedown Council
NCTF	National Corporate Theatre Fund
ND	New Dramatists
NDA	National Dance Association
NDCA	National Dance Council of America

NDEITA	National Dance-Exercise Instructor's Training Association
NDI	National Dance Institute
NEA	Nashville Entertainment Association
Neilsen Ratings	A television rating service
NETC	New England Theatre Conference
Network	A group of television or radio stations affiliated and interconnected for simultaneous broadcast of the same programming
NFMC	National Federation of Music Clubs
NFPW	National Federation of Press Women
NMPA	National Music Publishers Association
NOA	National Opera Association
NOA	National Orchestral Association
Non-Resident Theater	Theater for which actors are hired on a per-performance basis
Not-for-Profit Theaters and Companies	Theaters, orchestras, ballet and opera companies that are set up to provide a community service and do not make a profit for any one person or company. These organizations are usually sustained by donations, grants and other fund-raising efforts
Notices	Reviews for a production
NPC	National Playwrights Conference
NPC	National Press Club
NPN	National Performance Network
NPPA	National Press Photographers Association
NSAI	Nashville Songwriters Association, International
NSDC	National Square Dance Convention
NSOA	National Symphony Orchestra Association
NTC	National Theatre Conference
NTD	National Theatre of the Deaf
NTWH	National Theatre Workshop of the Handicapped
NWDC	Northwest Drama Conference
NYDCC	New York Drama Critics Circle
OA	Opera America
OCC	Outer Critics Circle
OPACT	Organization of Professional Acting Coaches and Teachers
Opening Night	The night a performance formally opens to the public
Option	An agreement between a producer and a playwright that gives the producer the exclusive right to produce the play within a certain amount of time

PBP	Paper Bag Players
PD	Public Domain or Program Director
PDTA	Professional Dance Teachers Association
PFA	Pianists Foundation of America
PG	Producers Group
Playwright	The person who writes the script for a play
Portfolio	A collection of sample pieces done by someone in the creative field (either a writer or artist) that is put together into a book so that prospective employers can get an idea of their potential
PR	Public Relations
Press Kit	A promotional kit containing publicity, photographs and other materials used by publicists, press agents and public relations people to help publicize a client
Preview	A performance of a production that is given before the actual opening of a show
Promo	Promotion
PRSA	Public Relations Society of America
Public Domain	Songs or other works that have no copyright or whose copyright has expired
PRSSA	Public Relations Student Society of America
RAD	Royal Academy of Dancing, United States Branch
Resident Theater	Seasonal theater for which a group of actors is hired to perform during the entire season and is assigned set roles
RIAA	Recording Industry Association of America
Royalties	Monies paid periodically for the sales of records, sheet music and other copyrighted material
Royalty Statement	An itemized accounting of earnings for songwriters or recording artists
RTNDA	Radio Television News Directors Association
SAFD	Society of American Fight Directors
SAG	Screen Actors Guild
SCA	Screen Composers of America
Scale	The minimum wages that can be paid to a union member
Script	A theatrical production's story written in a special way so that the character's names are either next to or above their lines. It may also include stage directions

SDG	Sacred Dance Guild
SDHS	Society of Dance History Scholars
SEG	Screen Extras Guild
SLC	Songwriters and Lyricists Club
SSDC	Society of Stage Directors and Choreographers
Stage Presence	The way an actor or actress stands and moves while on stage
Standby or Stand-In	An actor or actress who must be vailable to go on for a scheduled actor or actress in a production. They must usually call in at a specified amount of time before curtain time to see if they are needed for that night's performance
STC	Southwestern Theatre Conference
STT	Save the Theatres
TA	Theatre Authority
TAMT	The American Mime Theatre
TCEO	Theatre Committee for Eugene O'Neill
TCG	Theatre Communications Group
TDF	Theatre Development Fund
TE	Theatre in Education
TG	Theatre Guild
THS	Theatre Historical Society
TJMS	Traditional Japanese Music Society of the City University of New York
Tony Awards	Annual awards given to those in the theater for excellence in various categories
Tour	A series of concerts, usually in different geographical locations
Trades	Newspapers and magazines that are geared to a specific industry—in this case, the theater and performing arts
Understudy	An actor or actress who substitutes for another actor or actress when he or she is not able to act in a performance
Union Card	A card that is used to identify members of specific unions
URTA	University Resident Theatre Association
USA	United Scenic Artists
USABDA	United States Amateur Ballroom Dancers Association
USDA	United Square Dancers of America
USITT	United States Institute for Theatre Technology
UWP	Up With People
Venue	A hall, auditorium, theater, arena or club where theatrical productions or concerts are presented
WGA	Writers Guild of America
WIC	Women in Communications, Inc.
YCA	Young Concerts Artists
YTA	Yiddish Theatrical Alliance

INDEX